Manhattan Review®

Test Prep & Admissions Consulting

Turbocharge Your GRE:
Reading Comprehension Guide

part of the 3rd Edition Series

April 20th, 2016

- ☐ *Complete & Challenging Training Sets: 23 Passages; 250+ questions*
- ☐ *Never-seen-before Dedicated "Understanding the Passage" section*
- ☐ *Never-seen-before Visually-appetizing "Reading Through Creating Impressions"*
- ☐ *Concept illustration through graphic aids and info-graphic strip*
- ☐ *13 proven RC Strategies*
- ☐ *Ample "Reasoning-based" RC questions*
- ☐ *Highlighting key differences between confusing ASP question types: Strengthen & Weaken, Strengthen & Inference*
- ☐ *Comprehensive Solutions: Three tier explanation*

D0073690

www.manhattanreview.com

Copyright and Terms of Use

Copyright and Trademark

All materials herein (including names, terms, trademarks, designs, images, and graphics) are the property of Manhattan Review, except where otherwise noted. Except as permitted herein, no such material may be copied, reproduced, displayed or transmitted or otherwise used without the prior written permission of Manhattan Review. You are permitted to use material herein for your personal, noncommercial use, provided that you do not combine such material into a combination, collection, or compilation of material. If you have any questions regarding the use of the material, please contact Manhattan Review at info@manhattanreview.com.

This material may make reference to countries and persons. The use of such references is for hypothetical and demonstrative purposes only.

Terms of Use

By using this material, you acknowledge and agree to the terms of use contained herein.

No Warranties

This material is provided without warranty, either express or implied, including the implied warranties of merchantability, of fitness for a particular purpose and noninfringement. Manhattan Review does not warrant or make any representations regarding the use, accuracy or results of the use of this material. This material may make reference to other source materials. Manhattan Review is not responsible in any respect for the content of such other source materials, and disclaims all warranties and liabilities with respect to the other source materials.

Limitation on Liability

Manhattan Review shall not be responsible under any circumstances for any direct, indirect, special, punitive, or consequential damages ("Damages") that may arise from the use of this material. In addition, Manhattan Review does not guarantee the accuracy or completeness of its course materials, which are provided "as is" with no warranty, express or implied. Manhattan Review assumes no liability for any Damages from errors or omissions in the material, whether arising in contract, tort or otherwise.

GRE is a registered trademark of the Educational Testing Services.
ETS does not endorse, nor is it affiliated in any way with, the owner of this product or any content herein.

10-Digit International Standard Book Number: (ISBN: 1-62926-082-7)
13-Digit International Standard Book Number: (ISBN: 978-1-62926-082-2)

Last updated on April 20th, 2016.

Manhattan Review, 275 Madison Avenue, Suite 1429, New York, NY 10016.
Phone: +1 (212) 316-2000. E-Mail: info@manhattanreview.com. Web: www.manhattanreview.com

About the Turbocharge your GRE Series

The Turbocharge Your GRE Series consists of 13 guides that cover everything you need to know for a great score on the GRE. Widely respected among GRE educators worldwide, Manhattan Review's GRE prep books offer the most professional GRE instruction available anywhere. Now in its updated 3rd edition, the full series is carefully designed to provide GRE test-takers with exhaustive GRE preparation for optimal test scores. Manhattan Review's GRE prep books teach you how to prepare for each of the different GRE testing areas with a thorough instructional methodology that is rigorous yet accessible and enjoyable. You'll learn everything necessary about each test section in order to receive your best possible GRE scores. The full series covers GRE verbal, quantitative, and writing concepts from the most basic through the most advanced levels, and is therefore a great study resource for all stages of GRE preparation. Students who work through all books in the series significantly improve their knowledge of GRE subject matter and learn the most strategic approaches to taking and vanquishing the GRE.

- ☐ **GRE Math Essentials Guide (ISBN: 978-1-62926-073-0)**
- ☐ **GRE Number Properties Guide (ISBN: 978-1-62926-074-7)**
- ☐ **GRE Arithmetic Guide (ISBN: 978-1-62926-075-4)**
- ☐ **GRE Algebra Guide (ISBN: 978-1-62926-076-1)**
- ☐ **GRE Geometry Guide (ISBN: 978-1-62926-077-8)**
- ☐ **GRE Word Problems Guide (ISBN: 978-1-62926-078-5)**
- ☐ **GRE Combinatorics & Probability Guide (ISBN: 978-1-62926-079-2)**
- ☐ **GRE Sets, Statistics & Data Interpretation Guide (ISBN: 978-1-62926-080-8)**
- ☐ **GRE Quantitative Question Bank (ISBN: 978-1-62926-081-5)**
- ■ **GRE Reading Comprehension Guide (ISBN: 978-1-62926-082-2)**
- ☐ **GRE Sentence Equivalence & Text Completion Guide (ISBN: 978-1-62926-083-9)**
- ☐ **GRE Analytical Writing Guide (ISBN: 978-1-62926-084-6)**
- ☐ **GRE Vocabulary Builder (ISBN: 978-1-62926-085-3)**

About the Company

Manhattan Review's origin can be traced directly back to an Ivy League MBA classroom in 1999. While teaching advanced quantitative subjects to MBAs at Columbia Business School in New York City, Professor Dr. Joern Meissner developed a reputation for explaining complicated concepts in an understandable way. Prof. Meissner's students challenged him to assist their friends, who were frustrated with conventional test preparation options. In response, Prof. Meissner created original lectures that focused on presenting standardized test content in a simplified and intelligible manner, a method vastly different from the voluminous memorization and so-called tricks commonly offered by others. The new methodology immediately proved highly popular with students, inspiring the birth of Manhattan Review.

Since its founding, Manhattan Review has grown into a multi-national educational services firm, focusing on preparation for the major undergraduate and graduate admissions tests, college admissions consulting, and application advisory services, with thousands of highly satisfied students all over the world. Our GRE material is continuously expanded and updated by the Manhattan Review team, an enthusiastic group of master GRE professionals and senior academics. Our team ensures that Manhattan Review offers the most time-efficient and cost-effective preparation available for the GRE. Please visit www.ManhattanReview.com for further details.

About the Founder

Professor Dr. Joern Meissner has more than 25 years of teaching experience at the graduate and undergraduate levels. He is the founder of Manhattan Review, a worldwide leader in test prep services, and he created the original lectures for its first test preparation classes. Prof. Meissner is a graduate of Columbia Business School in New York City, where he received a PhD in Management Science. He has since served on the faculties of prestigious business schools in the United Kingdom and Germany. He is a recognized authority in the areas of supply chain management, logistics, and pricing strategy. Prof. Meissner thoroughly enjoys his research, but he believes that grasping an idea is only half of the fun. Conveying knowledge to others is even more fulfilling. This philosophy was crucial to the establishment of Manhattan Review, and remains its most cherished principle.

The Advantages of Using Manhattan Review

▶ **Time efficiency and cost effectiveness.**

  – For most people, the most limiting factor of test preparation is time.

  – It takes significantly more teaching experience to prepare a student in less time.

  – Our test preparation approach is tailored for busy professionals. We will teach you what you need to know in the least amount of time.

▶ **Our high-quality and dedicated instructors are committed to helping every student reach her/his goals.**

International Phone Numbers and Official Manhattan Review Websites

Manhattan Headquarters	+1-212-316-2000	www.manhattanreview.com
USA & Canada	+1-800-246-4600	www.manhattanreview.com
Argentina	+1-212-316-2000	www.review.com.ar
Australia	+61-3-9001-6618	www.manhattanreview.com
Austria	+43-720-115-549	www.review.at
Belgium	+32-2-808-5163	www.manhattanreview.be
Brazil	+1-212-316-2000	www.manhattanreview.com.br
Chile	+1-212-316-2000	www.manhattanreview.cl
China	+86-20-2910-1913	www.manhattanreview.cn
Czech Republic	+1-212-316-2000	www.review.cz
France	+33-1-8488-4204	www.review.fr
Germany	+49-89-3803-8856	www.review.de
Greece	+1-212-316-2000	www.review.com.gr
Hong Kong	+852-5808-2704	www.review.hk
Hungary	+1-212-316-2000	www.review.co.hu
India	+1-212-316-2000	www.review.in
Indonesia	+1-212-316-2000	www.manhattanreview.id
Ireland	+1-212-316-2000	www.gmat.ie
Italy	+39-06-9338-7617	www.manhattanreview.it
Japan	+81-3-4589-5125	www.manhattanreview.jp
Malaysia	+1-212-316-2000	www.review.my
Mexico	+1-212-316-2000	www.manhattanreview.mx
Netherlands	+31-20-808-4399	www.manhattanreview.nl
New Zealand	+1-212-316-2000	www.review.co.nz
Philippines	+1-212-316-2000	www.review.ph
Poland	+1-212-316-2000	www.review.pl
Portugal	+1-212-316-2000	www.review.pt
Qatar	+1-212-316-2000	www.review.qa
Russia	+1-212-316-2000	www.manhattanreview.ru
Singapore	+65-3158-2571	www.gmat.sg
South Africa	+1-212-316-2000	www.manhattanreview.co.za
South Korea	+1-212-316-2000	www.manhattanreview.kr
Sweden	+1-212-316-2000	www.gmat.se
Spain	+34-911-876-504	www.review.es
Switzerland	+41-435-080-991	www.review.ch
Taiwan	+1-212-316-2000	www.gmat.tw
Thailand	+66-6-0003-5529	www.manhattanreview.com
Turkey	+1-212-316-2000	www.review.com.tr
United Arab Emirates	+1-212-316-2000	www.manhattanreview.ae
United Kingdom	+44-20-7060-9800	www.manhattanreview.co.uk
Rest of World	+1-212-316-2000	www.manhattanreview.com

Contents

Chapter 1

Welcome

Dear Students,

At Manhattan Review, we constantly strive to provide the best educational content for preparation of standardized tests, putting arduous efforts to make things better and better. This continuous evolution is very important for an examination like the GRE, which too evolves constantly. Sadly, a GRE aspirant is confused with too many options in the market. The challenge is how to choose a book or a tutor that prepares you to reach your goal. Without saying that we are the best, we leave it for you to judge.

This book differs in many aspects from standard books available in the market. Unlike a book from any other prep company, this book discusses as many as 13 Strategies in detail on how to approach GRE-Reading Comprehension passages. We have discusses more than 23 GRE-like passages and approximately 200 questions. Each passage is explained in a never-seen-before dedicated section—Understanding the Passages. It would be a treat to read a passage with never-seen-before Visually-appetizing images to illustrate the concept of "Reading Through Creating Impressions". While discussing options, we explained each option keeping in mind why the correct option is right and why incorrect options are wrong. You will find sufficient number of questions on one of the rare categories—Application or Reasoning based questions.

The book discusses as many as nine Argument Structure Passage (ASP) question types. There are over 100 questions for ASP alone. Another distinctive feature of the book is that each ASP question is explained in a three tier structure—understanding the argument construction; predicting the qualifying answer beforehand; and, explaining each option with an emphasis on why the correct answer is right and the incorrect answers are wrong.

Additionally, GRE aspirants find that a few ASP question types are usually confused with other question types such as Find the Assumption with Strengthen the Argument, and Inference with Strengthen the Argument. This book highlights the key differences between such pairs of confusing question types, and presents their salient features in a tabular form to help students understand their nuances.

Every ASP question type's core concept is also illustrated through a info-graphic strip and other graphic aids to make its gist memorable and easy to relate to. With use of graphics and user-friendly layout, the book is easy to read and grasp concepts.

In a nut shell, Manhattan Review's GRE-Reading Comprehension book is holistic and comprehensive in all respects; it is created so because we listen to what students need. Should you have any questions about the content, please feel free to write to us at *info@manhattanreview.com*.

Happy Learning!

Dr. Joern Meissner
and Manhattan Review team

Chapter 2

Introduction to Reading Comprehension

 Reading Comprehension (RC) is one of the two parts in the Verbal Reasoning section of the GRE. You are given a passage to read, and answer questions about the content, comprehension and structure of the passage. Apart from regular RC passages, there are a few short passages—Argument Structure Passages (ASP), these are similar to the Critical Reasoning arguments of the GMAT. Reading Comprehension questions are intermingled with Sentence Equivalence and Text Completion questions in the Verbal Reasoning section.

You must have seen Reading Comprehension passages from your school days or in other standardized tests, but the GRE passages are relatively dull, and are not like the ones meant for pleasure reading. The GRE seeks to measure your ability to sift through mostly convoluted and unfamiliar topics, generally culled from theses or research papers of a variety of topics, as any graduate student would be expected to do. . The questions test your ability to understand, analyze, and apply the information and concepts.

Although it may look like the easiest part of the Verbal Reasoning section, the time constraints make this aspect very challenging. The topics of the passages mostly do not amuse you as they may came from Natural Science (Astronomy, Physics, Biology etc.), Social Science (Philosophy, History etc.), Business-related content(Business History, Marketing, Economic Theory etc.), and other topics too. The passages presented to you are written in the GRE style; they will look tasteless. Even a passage on your favorite topic may not be an easy ride for you. This calls for applying an approach to solve RC questions. The book will deal with such an approach in detail.

The revised GRE will have two scored, and may have one un-scored Verbal Reasoning sections; however you will not be informed which section is un-scored.

On average, Verbal reasoning section asks approx. 20 questions, and approx. 9-10 questions would be based on RC. You can expect to see at about 5 passages per section. Each passage will ask you 1-4 questions. The passages come in two forms: Long passages and short passages. Long passages are 400-450 words long with 3-5 paragraphs, while short passages are about 150 words long with 1-2 paragraphs. Of these passages, at least two will be short passages and at least one will be a long passage per section.

One of the shortest versions of passages is Argument Structure Passages (ASPs). Though GRE categorizes them a part of RC, they are significantly different from typical RC passages. As stated earlier that these are similar to Critical Reasoning arguments of the GMAT. These argument would be about 25-75 words and there would always be just one question. You can expect to see at least one ASP question per section. The strategy to solve ASP questions is significantly different from that of a typical RC question, calling for more involved critical reasoning skills.

The passage and the questions will be presented through a split-screen. On the left-hand side of the screen, the passage will appear. There may be a vertical scroll bar in the middle of the screen. Be sure that you check it. If there's a scroll bar and you miss it, you will miss out on a chunk of the passage and answer questions incorrectly. The question will appear on the right-hand side of the screen. Once you submit the answer to the question, the next question will appear; however, the passage will remain on the left side of the screen. You can move to the next question, without answering it or come back to the previous question in the section; previewing all the questions can be helpful as before reading the passage you sure what types of General questions (We will talk about General questions in details in the next chapter) and what details are needed to answer questions, but you must not start attempting questions before a complete Active Reading (We will talk about it later in the chapter) of the passage.

There are broadly four categories of questions asked in Reading Comprehension, excluding Argument Structure Passages (ASP). However, few question types may have two to three subdivisions within them. We will discuss these in the next chapter.

One, **General** questions–these questions may ask you to suggest a title of the passage, or state the central idea, or identify the author's primary purpose in writing a part of a sentence or a paragraph. Another variant may be to understand the tone and style of writing used by the author.

Two, **Detail** questions–these questions ask you to understand a specific detail from the passage, or cite a fact used in the passage.

Third, **Inference** questions– these questions ask you to understand the implied meaning of the information presented by the author, or identify the intended meaning of a word or a phrase used figuratively in the passage.

Fourth, **Reasoning** questions–This is minor question category. These questions are similar to assumption, strengthen and weaken question types in Argument Structure Passages (ASP).

Argument Structure Passages (ASP) questions are followed by a question stem. The question stem, followed by the argument, determines which type of reasoning-based RC question ASP belongs to. Each question type requires different type of strategy to solve, hence it very important to identify the question type.

We classified different question types based on the family of question types they belong. GRE-ASP question types can be classified into three families.

(1) **Assumption based family:** Finding the Assumption is at the core of solving these questions. Four question types belong to this classification—Find the Assumption, Strengthen the Argument, Weaken the Argument, and Evaluate the Argument.

(2) **Structure based family:** Understanding the structure of the argument is the key to solving these questions. Three question types belong to this classification—Boldface/Role Play questions and Parallel Reasoning.

(3) **Evidence based family:** Understanding the inference or the evidence from the argument is the key to solving these questions. Two question types belong to this classification—Inference questions, Draw the Conclusion/Complete the Argument and Resolve the Paradox/Explain the discrepancy.

2.1   Reading Strategies

 Whether you love or hate the topic of the passage, you cannot ignore it. The best approach for eating that bitter gourd is to sugar-coat it with your emotions by pretending that you care for the subject and find it very interesting to educate yourself. You can even fake that you like the topic. In fact, you will frequently observe that GMAT passages do add a lot of value to your knowledge bank.

If your mind-set is to wonder why at all you should be bothered to know about the respiratory system of sea-snakes, keep in mind that later in your career you may be asked by your boss to summarize a report on the anatomy of terrestrial animals to understand the environmental impact of some business project. This GMAT RC passage could actually serve you quite well someday.

At least one passage presented to you may be of some interest, but other passages may be on unfamiliar topics. If your background is bio-sciences, you will find the passage on the respiratory system of sea-snakes interesting; on the contrary, the passage on Freudian theory may bore you. If you feel bored, don't just go through the rest of the passage in a hurry; instead, move your eyes away from the computer-screen and look elsewhere, and after a while start again from where you left off. When confronted with a hard CR question, you may choose to give it a blind shot and move on; unfortunately, you cannot afford to give a bitter gourd passage the same treatment because there may be 3-4 questions based on it, and getting all of them wrong comes with a heavy penalty.

Read the first paragraph very cautiously; it sets the purpose and the topic of the passage. Once you understand the topic of the passage, you should gain momentum. There are two extreme approaches for reading the passage: one, read slowly and understand each word, and two, read too fast without comprehending the meaning of the passage. Both approaches have their demerits.

The Slow Approach will put a lot of pressure on you, as you are likely to blindly guess on 2-3 questions due to time constraints and possibly then panic and start committing mistakes.

The Fast Approach will not help you either, as for each question you will have to reread the passage to identify the location where the relevant details are found, and will likely end up reading the passage at least 3 times without a guarantee that the questions attempted are correct. Most GMAT RC questions are not necessarily based on a particular paragraph or a piece of information; they may require you to pool information from 2-3 places in the passage. Even the main point question, which is usually perceived as the one that can be answered with the reading of the first and the last paragraph, can go wrong. GMAT test-makers design the options in such a way that if you miss even one detail, you will get caught in their trap. So, the optimum approach is to read efficiently and effectively.

If you get a convoluted sentence, you should at least look for the main nouns and verbs, just to get a sense of the action going on. Ask yourself: who's doing what, or who's saying what about what? This will gives you the broad idea without too much detail.

At the end of the book, you will find a list of commonly-used words with their meanings to improve your understanding in the Reading Comprehension section.

An effective reader will read efficiently while paying attention to the message, but will side-line intricate details for the time being. This person will keep in mind that this specific detail is parked in this paragraph, and, if needed, will look it up there. Such a reader is basically a big picture reader who reads actively. The key is not to overanalyze the passage as you read it, but to get a general idea of the flow and main point of every paragraph, mentally making a map as you go along.

If you are not a native speaker of English or are not fond of reading, you may improve your reading comprehension by reading from the New York Times, the Wall Street Journal, American Scientist, Popular Science, The Economist, and other competent magazines that contain GMAT-like content. After this, you can even frequent sites that contain research journals to enable you to read complex and verbose data- based passages. You may also read certain novels to improve reading speed.

(2) Keep summarizing

 GMAT passages are deliberately drafted with the use of clever language, and made convoluted to make the gist hard to grasp. Often-times the data is hidden in the passage. Due to the sentence structure and style of writing, you will have to take some sort of notes to understand the nuances of the message because simply keeping the message in mind will not help.

Note-taking style is very subjective. Remember that these notes are only for you, and will be needed for just the space of a few minutes.

There are two distinct advantages to note-making. One, it helps you paraphrase the main point because the central message of the passage comprises all the paragraphs of the passage, and not only the first or only the first and last. Two, it helps you know exactly where to look for details when needed. There may be circumstances when specific detail for a particular question lie in two paragraphs, but notes will guide you to look at those particular paragraphs to find the necessary information for that question.

You can summarize at appropriate intervals. If you are comfortable with the content, you can summarize after each paragraph; however, if you find that the content is quite heavy, you may be better off summarizing after every 2-3 sentences.

Below we present to you a passage from medical science. Read the passage first, and then follow the techniques suggested by us. You will find that there is a marked difference in your understanding of the content.

The following passage will teach you three things; one, how to read by creating impressions; two, how to retain the information from the passage; and three, how to take notes.

Passage – Cancer of the colon

Doctors are working on a new non-invasive technique that allows them to 'fly' through the colon and pick out malignancies. Admittedly the first results have been good enough for the team behind the technique to predict that it will become a universal screening system for one of the world's biggest killers. Thus doctors say it will detect more cancers and polyps than do conventional techniques.

One of the predicaments with cancer of the colon is that it is difficult to detect it with great certainty with many of the current tests. If it can be detected at an early stage, treatment is much more effective. The options currently available to doctors include faecal blood testing, barium enema, and colonoscopy. Unfortunately none of these is optimal in terms of performance, safety, or patient acceptance, so Dr David Ahlquist, an oncologist at the Mayo Clinic in Minnesota, has been working on virtual-reality technology.

Blood testing is the most widely used at present, but it is probably the most imprecise. More than half of cancers are likely to be missed in a single test. So far, based on the results of research on 70 patients, doctors have found that despite initial programming glitches, the virtual-reality technology is far more accurate.

2.2 Reading through creating impressions

Sentence	Impression	Inference/Meaning
Doctors are working on a new non-invasive technique that allows them to 'fly' through the colon and pick out malignancies.		I understand that doctors are working on a new technique that does not involve incision. [because of the use of the word "non-invasive"] The rest I could not get—*fly*, and *colon*. **Gist**: Docs wkg. on non-invasive tech. on any disease (malignancies).
Admittedly the first results have been good enough for the team behind the technique to predict that		**Gist**: Non-invasive tech. ⇒ Decent success in predicting something.
it will become a universal screening system for one of the world's biggest killers.		I am sure that 'universal screening system' is used for non-invasive technique. [because of the use of "it" used for the "non-invasive technique"] It means that this technique will overcome the biggest disease (killers). **Gist**: Non-invasive tech. may detect the dreaded disease, and be accepted by all.

Thus doctors say it will detect more cancers and polyps than do conventional techniques.		Now I know what disease is being talked about - it's CANCER. Well, I do not know what polyps are. I guess it must be related to cancer. The statement seems to be the main point; I must keep this in mind. **Gist**: 1. # of cancer cases > conv. tech. 2. Non-invasive tech. seems better than conv. tech.

Gist of paragraph 1: It says that doctors are working on a non-invasive technique to detect cancer of the colon. It is better than the conventional technique and mostly accepted.

Paragraph 1 notes: P1: Docs wkg. on non-inv. tech.; success in predict'g; may detect disease; accepted; # of cancer > conv. tech.; better.

One of the **predicaments** with cancer of the colon is that it is difficult to detect it with great certainty with many of the current tests.	Cancer of Colon	Oh, now I get that 'colon' is a part of the body. The statement states the limitation of conventional techniques. I am becoming more sure now that the previous statement must be the MAIN POINT. I must be wary that the test maker may make a specific question on 'cancer of the colon'. **Gist**: Current tests: Detection of cancer of the colon ⇒ difficult
If it can be detected at an early stage, treatment is much more effective.	*Early detection ⇒ Effective*	They are talking about 3 tests: Hmm...Early detection is the key to treating 'cancer of the colon'.

The options currently available to doctors include faecal blood testing, barium enema, and colonoscopy.	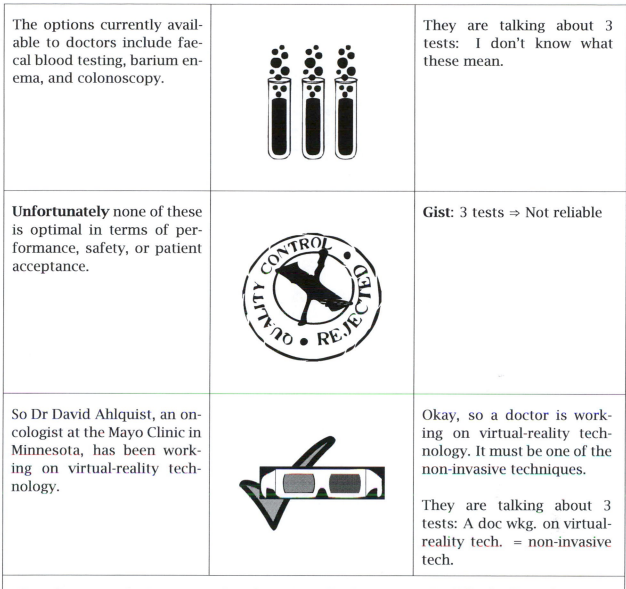	They are talking about 3 tests: I don't know what these mean.
Unfortunately none of these is optimal in terms of performance, safety, or patient acceptance.		**Gist**: 3 tests ⇒ Not reliable
So Dr David Ahlquist, an oncologist at the Mayo Clinic in Minnesota, has been working on virtual-reality technology.		Okay, so a doctor is working on virtual-reality technology. It must be one of the non-invasive techniques. They are talking about 3 tests: A doc wkg. on virtual-reality tech. = non-invasive tech.

Gist of paragraph 2: It says that detection of colon cancer is difficult through current unreliable tests. One of the doctors is working on a virtual-reality technique, a kind of non-invasive technique.

Paragraph 2 notes: P2: Current tests: Detection of colon cancer ⇒ diff.; Early detection == key; 3 tests ⇒ unreliable; A doc wkg. on virtual-reality tech. = non-inv. tech..

Blood testing is the most widely used at present, **but** it is probably the most imprecise.		I think this fact is already stated in the II paragraph. I think the purpose may be to emphasize. **Gist**: Blood test ⇒ Not reliable
More than half of cancers are likely to be missed in a single test.	*(50% – 100%) ⇒ Undetected*	Yes. I was right. They again emphasized the problem with the blood test technique. **Gist**: Blood test ⇒ Not reliable & deceiving
So far based on the results of research on 70 patients, doctors have found that **despite** initial programming glitches, the virtual-reality technology is far more accurate.	Paragraph 1 summary / **Main Point** / Paragraph 2 summary / Paragraph 3 summary	Okay. So there are two points: one, virtual-reality technology is far more accurate than conventional techniques, and two, virtual-reality technology did face some programming challenges. **Gist**: Virtual-reality tech. (non-invasive tech.) is BETTER than conv. tech.. It had few programming challenges.

Gist of paragraph 3: It says that Blood test may give wrong results, and is unreliable. Virtual-reality technique gives better results than the conventional technique does.

Paragraph 3 notes: P3: Bld test ⇒ deceiving; VR tech. » conv. tech.; had challenges.

Paragraph summary

P1: Docs wkg. on non-inv. tech.; success in predict'g; may detect disease; accepted; # of cancer > conv. tech.; better.

P2: Current tests: Detection of colon cancer ⇒ diff.; Early detection = key; 3 tests ⇒ unreliable; A doc wkg. on virtual-reality tech. = non-inv. tech.

P3: Bld test ⇒ deceiving; VR tech. » conv. tech.; had challenges.

(3) **Keep a tab on transition keywords**

 Often the sentences used in the passages are long-winded, and with the use of modifiers, it becomes difficult to grasp the meaning of the sentences. However, with the use of transition words, you can keep a tab on the flow and the direction of the message communicated in the passage.

Transition words such as *however, moreover, furthermore, but, therefore*, and many others tell a lot about the next sentence in relation to the previous sentence. See the following illustration to learn more about them.

Role of furthermore/moreover

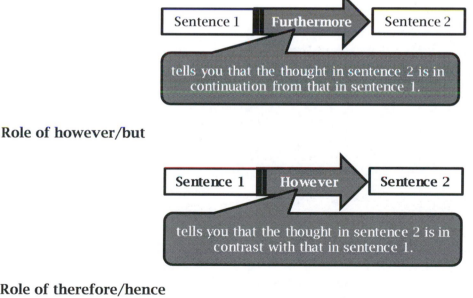

Role of however/but

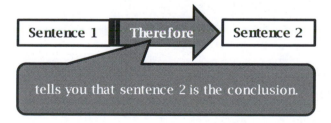

Role of therefore/hence

Role of If then

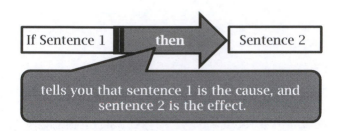

The following table of signaling, or trigger, words may help you understand the tone, style, and the meaning of the passage.

Continuation of thoughts	Opposing thought	Conclusion
Moreover	However	Therefore
Furthermore	But	Hence
In addition	Despite	So
Secondly	In spite of	Implies
Similarly	On the contrary	As a result
Also	Nevertheless	Thus
Too	Conversely	In short
For example	Instead	Inferred
Since	Yet	Consequently
Because	Rather than	In other words
Evidently	Still	
For instance	Surprisingly	
Illustrated by	While	
And	Although	
An analogy	Though	
Analogous	On the other hand	
Considering similar experiences	Even if	
	Actually	
	Notwithstanding	

Let us reexamine the passage we read before, and identify the role of the transition words.

Doctors are working on a new non-invasive technique that allows them to 'fly' through the colon and pick out malignancies. **Admittedly** th̶e̶ behind the tech̶ screening syste̶

> **Admittedly** shows that the next sentence is in continuation of thought from the previous sentence.

Thus d̶ conventi̶

> **Thus** shows that it is a conclusion from the doctors.

One of the predicaments with cancer of the colon is that it is difficult to detect it with great certainty with many of the current tests. **If** it can be detected at an early stage, treatment is much more effecti̶ l blood testing̶

> **If** shows the cause and effect relationship between the detection and the effectiveness of the treatment.

Unfortunately none of these is optimal in terms of performance, safety or pa̶t̶ient acceptance. **So** Dr David Ahlquist, an oncologist at the Mayo ̶ nnology.

> **Unfortunately** shows the opposing thought.

> **So** shows subsequent action as a result of previous thought.

Blood testing is the ̶ it is probably the most imprecise. Mor̶ be missed in a single test. **So far** ba̶ patients, doctors has found that **despite** initial programming glitches, the virtual-reality technology i̶ more accurate.

> **So far** shows the situation and circumstances up to now.

> **despite** shows the opposing thought.

(4) Skim the details and cut the crap

The passage may contain some technical terms which you may not know; however there is no need to know their exact meaning – only the purpose they serve in the passage is important. You should be able to tell what is being said about those technical terms. You should skim the details and cut the crap.

Let us refer to the second paragraph of the passage.

The options currently available to doctors include faecal blood testing, barium enema and colonoscopy. Unfortunately none of these is optimal in terms of performance, safety or patient acceptance. So Dr David Ahlquist, an oncologist at the Mayo Clinic in Minnesota has been working on virtual-reality technology.

We find that there is no need to go into the details of currently available tests–*faecal blood testing, barium enema, and colonoscopy.* At the reading stage it is sufficient to know that there are three tests, what role they play, what the opinion is about the tests, and where in the passage these tests were mentioned. You must have observed that in the paragraph summary and during the exercise of understanding the passage, we did not care much about the meanings of the words 'fly' and 'polyps'. The GMAT test makers write the passages knowing that you may not know all the material. There is no need to know it. The message is: skim the details.

Similarly, it is not important to know what the name is of the doctor researching virtual-reality technology, or what the name of his clinic is. You may refer to the doctor as Doc. The message is: cut the crap. If the need arises to get a detail for a question, you can always go back to the specified location to fetch it.

(5) **Abbreviate difficult technical terms**

You may come across many difficult technical terms in the passages that give you a headache. However, there is a way not to see them again. Since you cannot avoid them, it is better that you make them look pretty. For example, if you have trouble pronouncing the name of the doctor, abbreviate the name of the doctor with Dr AH. There may be a passage in which there is a reference of two or more doctors, so it makes it important to know their names, but by abbreviating, you can retain the information without getting bogged down by heavy words.

You must have observed that we combined the three scary-looking tests–faecal blood testing, barium enema, and colonoscopy as '3 tests'. If we need to refer them, we can still make them look pleasing by abbreviating them as 3 tests–FB, BE, and colon test.

(6) **Infer the meaning of unfamiliar words**

A passage may contain certain words which you do not know. We advise that you develop decent vocabulary, and that can only be developed through diversified reading of GMAT-like content. However, you can also start with non-GMAT-like content and then switch to GMAT-like content.

That said, you may still be caught off guard by unfamiliar words. The good news is that every test taker comes across such words. Keep in mind, however, that you can infer their meaning through the context in which they are used.

Let us view the first two paragraphs of the passage again.

Doctors are working on a new non-invasive technique that allows them to 'fly' through the colon and pick out **malignancies**. Admittedly the first results have been good enough for the team behind the technique to predict that it will become a universal screening system for one of the world's biggest killers. Thus doctors say it will detect more cancers and polyps than do conventional techniques.

*One of the **predicaments** with cancer of the colon is that it is difficult to detect it with great cer-*

*tainty with many of the current tests. If it can be detected at an early stage, treatment is much more effective. The options currently available to doctors include faecal blood testing, barium enema and colonoscopy. Unfortunately none of these is optimal in terms of performance, safety or patient acceptance. So Dr David Ahlquist, an **oncologist** at the Mayo Clinic in Minnesota has been working on virtual-reality technology.*

Let us infer the meaning of these three words from the context of the passage.

Malignancies: Well, it is difficult to infer the meaning of unknown words if they are used in the first sentence of the passage because we do not have any reference to bank on. With regards to the word—**malignancies**, the supporting phrase - 'fly' through the colon and pick out **malignancies** - cannot help, as 'fly' and 'colon' themselves are unfamiliar and seem to be technical terms. All we can so far infer is that doctors are able to catch **malignancies** with the use of a non-invasive technique, so **malignancies** must be something of a negative aspect if doctors fly and catch them with effort.

Let us look at the next sentence– *Admittedly the first results have been good enough for the team behind the technique to predict that **it** will become a universal screening system for one of the world's biggest killers.*

It refers to the non-invasive technique. Our inference is going in the right direction; **malignancies** must be something negative. It may even refer to **world's biggest killers**. The next sentence helps to narrow down the meaning, so we can assume that **malignancies** means **a kind of cancer (disease)**.

The dictionary meaning of **malignancies** is **menaces, enmities, a cancerous growth-tumour**. So, we were correct in inferring the meaning of the unknown word from the context.

Let us examine another word - **predicaments**

It is used in the sentence – *One of the **predicaments** with cancer of the colon is that it is difficult to detect it with great certainty with many of the current tests.* It can be inferred that **predicaments** may be an aspect or a challenge with respect to cancer of the colon because the clause – it is difficult to detect it with great certainty – hints that it is something negative.

The dictionary meaning of **predicaments** is **difficulties**. Again, we were exactly right in inferring the meaning.

Let us take a look at another word– **oncologist.**

It is used in the sentence – *So Dr David Ahlquist, an **oncologist** at the Mayo Clinic in Minnesota, has been working on virtual-reality technology.*

It is probably quite easy for you to infer the contextual meaning of **oncologist**. Even if you infer it as a **specialist**, it is fine. **oncologist** means **cancer specialist**.

2.3 Active Reading

In the above passage, we saw how we can read a passage and extract its gist by **"creating impressions"** in our minds as we read. Now, let us focus a bit on reading closely. The GMAT test makers are very clever in making scary, dense, and boring passages. They will load the passage with technical and almost indecipherable data. However, they can ask questions only on verbal data, because this is the verbal section! Hence, we must learn to read smartly to gather the right data and impressions as we read the passage. While reading the passage sentence by sentence, don't be in a hurry to understand every word. Learn to pick out the main words in a sentence (usually the nouns and the verbs). Skip technical words and read only their initials so that your flow of thought is maintained. Pay extra attention to words of contrast and comparison, because that's where data is hidden. From most of the sentences, you will end up actually reading only fifty percent of the words, but you will understand fully the intent of the author. From a cluster of words in a sentence, pick out the main words (enough to form a sensible statement) and read only those. Initially, you may find that picking the words takes time. That is okay. Take your time to pick the words, then read the sentence made by your picked words. Repeat with the next sentence. Note-making is recommended. Slowly, you will learn to pick words faster and "fly" through the passage while understanding everything.

Go over the passage again. Try to pick words and make a statement.

We will discuss all questions types in Reading Comprehension in the next chapter.

Chapter 3

Question Types

 We discussed in the introduction that there are broadly four categories of questions asked in Reading Comprehension, excluding Argument Structure Passages (ASP). We discuss these in detail now.

3.1 RC Question Types

3.1.1 General

These question types can be further divided into three sub-question types. These questions can be answered after reading the passage and referring to your notes. So in way they save your time. Some test prep companies also call it **Universal** or **Global** question type. You will certainly face one General question in the GRE per passage. There may be 4-5 questions based on this question types out of the total RC questions.

3.1.1.1 Main Point

Main Point questions ask you to suggest a title of the passage, or state the main purpose of writing the passage. Some test prep companies also call it **Purpose** question type.

3.1.1.2 Function

Function questions identify the role or the function of a word or a phrase or a sentence or a paragraph, it can also be called main point of the paragraph. This type of question asks about the logical structure of a passage. Some test prep companies also call it **Organization** or **Why** question type.

3.1.1.3 Tone

Tone questions ask you to understand the tone and style of writing used by the author.

3.1.2 Detail

These questions ask you to fetch a specific detail from the passage, or cite a fact used in the passage. You have to look up for the information or data with the help of keywords in the questions. These questions usually demand that you to go back to the relevant portion of the passage and fetch the data or information to answer the question. Some test prep companies also call it **Specific** question type. There may be 3-4 questions based on this question types out of the total RC questions.

3.1.3 Inference

These questions ask you to understand the implied meaning of the information presented by the author, or identify the intended meaning of a word or a phrase used figuratively in the passage. There may be 2-3 questions based on this question types out of the total RC questions. Inference questions are common with ASPs, however the strategy to deal with them is different from those in typical RC passages.

3.1.3.1 Specific Inference

This type of questions asks about details from the passage. The correct answer is often a paraphrase of something directly stated in the passage. It can also ask about the use of a particular word or phrase.

3.1.3.2 Application

This is a slightly more specific type of inference question, where you're asked to choose an answer which mimics a process or exemplifies a situation described in the passage. It can also be called a **Parallel reasoning** question type.

3.1.4 Reasoning

This is a **minor** question category. These questions are similar to assumption, strengthen and weaken question types in logic-based RCs/ASP. Like ASP questions, you may be asked to pinpoint an underlying assumption, strengthen or weaken a claim made by the author in the passage. There may be at the most one question based on this question types out of the total RC questions.

3.2   Strategies to solve questions

 We know that there are two types of passages in the GRE-RC—short passages, and long passages. You must understand the time allocation for each passage while attempting the questions.

3.2.1   Short passage

A short passage will usually come up with two questions, so you have approximately $2 * 1\frac{1}{2} = 3$ minutes to answer two questions; this includes the time taken to read the passage. Ideally, you should take $1\frac{1}{2}$ minutes to read the passage and takes notes, and on average 45 seconds to answer each question. General category of question may take quite less than 45 seconds, whereas a question from Specific Detail/Inference may take more than 45 seconds. After good practice, you will be attuned to this time constraints.

3.2.2   Long passage

A long passage will usually come up with four questions, so you have approximately $4 * 1\frac{1}{2} = 6$ minutes to answer four questions including the time taken to read the passage. Ideally, you should take 2-3 minutes to read the passage and takes notes, and on average 45 seconds to answer each question.

As soon as the passage appears, the first question also shows up on the right side of the split screen. We recommend that you read the question and then start reading the passage; however, you must not waste time in reading the options. Though on the revised GRE, you can preview all the questions, we do not recommend that you read all the questions before reading the passage, it will eat up your lot of time; however it is a good idea to get to know how many questions are associated with the passage. If there is a question from General question category (Main Point or Tone question) among all the questions, you must read the passages with the intent to extract the Main Point or infer the Tone of the passage.

> **Strategy 1:**
> *Preview all the questions; read the first question, but do not read the options.*

As stated earlier that is a good idea to get to know whether there is a question from General question category (Main Point or Tone question) among all the questions. If there is one, you must read the passages with a purpose. Even if the passage did not ask the main point question, extracting main point and understanding the tone of the passage will help you understand the scope of the passage better.

The approach to drive the main point is discussed in detail in the subsequent section.

3.2.3   Strategies to solve General question

3.2.3.1   Main Point question

 GRE RC passages are complete in itself to communicate a thought; the content in paragraph supports and develops main idea or central point.

Let us see the characteristics of the main point.

(1) It is a one line statement that expresses the intent of the entire passage.

(2) It is broad in scope; it covers the entire passage and is not restricted to an example(s) or paragraph(s) in the passage.

(3) It is precise in scope; it usually does not contain any particular detail discussed in the passage.

Typical question stems of a main point question are as follows.

· The primary purpose of the passage is

· The main idea of the passage is

· Which of the following best describes the organization of the passage?

· The passage as a whole can best be characterized as which of the following?

We will discuss how to derive the main point of a RC passage with the help of paragraph summaries.

We have already seen in couple of examples in the previous chapter about the paragraph summary. It is a one line statement that summarizes the paragraph. The main point of a passage is a summary of paragraph summaries. It represents all the paragraphs.

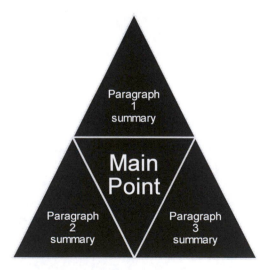

Let us see this in action. We bring to you summaries of three paragraphs of the passage **Cancer of Colon** we discussed in the first chapter.

Paragraph summary

P1: Docs wkg. on non-inv. tech.; success'l in predict'g; may detect disease; accepted; # of cancer > conv. tech.; Better.

P2: Current tests: Detection of colon cancer ⇒ diff.; Early detection == key; 3 tests ⇒ unreliable; A doc wkg. on virtual-reality tech. = non-inv. tech..

P3: Bld test ⇒ Deceiver; VR tech. » conv. tech.; had challenges.

Gist of paragraph 1: It says that doctors are working on non-invasive technique to detect cancer of colon. It is better than the conventional technique and mostly accepted.

Gist of paragraph 2: It says that detection of colon cancer is difficult through current unreliable tests. One of the doctors is working on virtual-reality technique, a kind of non-invasive technique.

Gist of paragraph 3: It says that Blood test may give wrong results, and is unreliable. Virtual-reality technique gives better results than the conventional technique.

The first paragraph introduces the new technique to detect colon cancer, and this technique is better than conventional ones. The second paragraph discusses that detecting colon cancer is difficult currently but the new technique, non-invasive, might turn out better. So, the second paragraph continues the first paragraph by detailing the differences between the better, new technique and unreliable, conventional techniques. The third paragraph finishes this thought by providing specific details about how the most commonly used conventional method fails. It is hoped that the new technique (now called virtual-reality technique) will do better.

Main point: New hopes with non-invasive technique that is being researched, and despair with conventional technique for detection of cancer of colon.

Strategy 2:
Write the Main Point of the passage immediately after finishing the reading of the passage.

Strategy 3:
Make sure that main points of each paragraph are represented in the Main Point of the passage.

Strategy 4:
Be wary of extreme words like most, all, always, never, etc., in the options.

Let us see the main point question with some options from **Cancer of Colon** passage. You can refer to the passage given in first chapter—Introduction.

Question 1 — General, Main Point

(A) The work involved in detecting colon cancer.

(B) The difficulties involved in detecting cancer — the biggest killer.

(C) Virtual reality cancer testing techniques for colon cancer.

(D) Existing technique problems and new technique possibilities.

(E) Colon cancer detection techniques and problems.

Solution

Based on the above deductions, we can analyze the options one by one.

(A) This option is **incorrect** because the passage is not discussing "work" required to detect colon cancer, but rather concerned with successful detection of colon cancer, the lack of success of conventional techniques and hope of success with the new, non-invasive technique.

(B) This option is **incorrect** because this option is too general. The passage is not discussing "cancer" in general. The scope of the passage is only "colon cancer".

(C) This option is **incorrect** because while the passage is discussing the new, non-invasive technique (virtual reality technique), it's not discussing only that. The passage also mentions the lack of success of conventional techniques.

(D) This option is **correct** because it clearly outlines all the main issues discussed in the passage - the lack of success of conventional techniques and hope of success with the new, non-invasive technique.

(E) This option is **incorrect** because while this option is close, it's too general. The passage does discuss colon cancer detection techniques. However, the passage distinguishes between conventional and new, innovative techniques, but this option does not convey that. Also, this option implies that all techniques of colon cancer detection have problems, but the passage conveys that the conventional techniques are problematic but the new one is possibly going to solve the problems.

The correct answer is D.

3.2.3.2 Function questions

 Organization or Function questions ask you why the author wrote a particular paragraph or a sentence or even a word. The answer to these questions depends on the context of the passage or the issue in hand. The answer to the question will lie around the word or the sentence; you will have to look up at the previous sentence or the succeeding sentence to get the information. In 'Why' question you have to think broadly and ask what role the word or the sentence used in the context plays.

These are akin to Bold Face/Role Play questions in ASP in which you identify the role each portion plays. The same is applicable to the function questions.

Typical question stems of a Function question are as follows.

- The author mentioned < something > in third paragraph in order to...

- One of the functions of the second paragraph is to...

- The highlighted word in the first paragraph is used by the author in order to...

- The discussion of < something > is meant to...

> **Strategy 5:**
> *Apply the strategy you apply in Boldface question types in ASP questions.*

Let us look at some examples.

Let us see another question from Cancer of Colon passage. You can refer to the passage given in first chapter—Introduction.

Question 2 — General, Function

What purpose does the second paragraph serve with respect to the passage on the whole?

(A) It explains why the new technique will be more successful than the conventional one

(B) It provides the main point of the passage

(C) It presents one of the main reasons for development of the innovative technique

(D) It describes alternatives available for the virtual reality technique

(E) It provides explanations why conventional techniques are problematic

Solution

The above question asks us to find the purpose of the second paragraph with respect to the whole passage. This is a function question from the general category. We have to figure out what function the second paragraph serves in the bigger scheme of things.

The first paragraph introduces the new technique under development.

The second paragraph contains information about the conventional techniques. However, at the end of second paragraph lies the reason behind mentioning the given information — "Unfortunately none of these is optimal in terms of performance, safety or patient acceptance. So Dr David Ahlquist, an oncologist at the Mayo Clinic in Minnesota has been working on virtual-reality technology." Thus the given information is serving the purpose of explaining why Dr

David has been working on virtual-reality technique.

The third and final paragraph explains why hopes are pinned on this new technique.

The purpose of the passage is to present the hopes with the new technique and despair with the conventional techniques.

Thus the second paragraph provides an excellent basis for the development of the new technique.

Let's analyze the options one by one.

(A)   This option is **incorrect** because the second paragraph does not state that the new technique will be more successful, but the third paragraph does so.

(B)   This option is **incorrect** because discussing only the conventional techniques is not the main point of the passage. The main point is "Colon cancer detection techniques and problems". The second paragraph discusses only the conventional techniques in general.

(C)   This option is **correct** because the last line (So far....accurate) of the second paragraph does provide this clue. The details of the conventional technique are given to explain why the need for a new technique exists. This is the paragraph's purpose in the passage — to explain why the new technique in under development.

(D)   This option is **incorrect** because it is factually incorrect. The whole passage does not present any alternatives to virtual-reality technique.

(E)   This option is **incorrect** because while the paragraph provides information about conventional techniques and their problematic nature, that is not the purpose of the paragraph. It does not provide explanations. The purpose of the paragraph is to explain why Dr David is developing the virtual-reality technique. [This is substantiated by the "So" sentence]. This option is tricky because it contains an answer for "what is presented in the second paragraph?" but this option does not answer "why is the second paragraph present in the passage?"

The correct answer is C.

Let us look at another example.

3.2.3.3   Tone questions

 The tone of a passage is the author's emotion or feeling, associated with his content. The style is the particular way the author uses the language to articulate the content. Most style or tone questions will include the words 'attitude,' 'tone,' 'style,' 'feeling,' etc. The most important things you should do while reading a Reading Comprehension passage is to understand the author's tone. Some information in the passage will come from the author's attitude and writing style.

The way modulation plays an important role in speech, tone plays a role in understanding the intent of the words written by the author. Adjectives and adverbs used by the author to express his emotions form the tone and style because they are openly expressive.

The GRE passages can be categorized into three broad types of tones:

Explanatory, Analytical, and Opinionated.

Explanatory: It can also be considered **Descriptive** tone. The author does not offer any opinion, recommendation or analysis of the issue at hand.

Analytical: It is the tone when the author wants to analyze a situation or topic or problem. The tone will not necessarily be explicit, but it will contain some subjective paragraphs or sentences or phrases with the usage of suggestive adjectives and adverbs.

Opinionated: A tone can be characterized as opinionated if the author clearly expresses his feelings and emotions while presenting his views or evaluating a theory.

Let us see a paragraph written with **neutral** tone.

Morton and Jackson Company registered 2.58% growth rate in the third and the fourth quarters. During the same period, the industry clocked 10.28% growth rate. The management and the CEO are figuring out what caused the growth rate.

You may have observed that the paragraph is written to convey the information about performance of Morton and Jackson Company in the third and the fourth quarters. It neither explains the cause, nor analyses the cause nor offers any opinion.

Let us see the same paragraph written with **opinionated** tone.

It is ironic that Morton and Jackson Company registered dismal growth rate in the third and the fourth quarters despite the industry having touched unduly high double-digit growth rate. It is matter of grave concern that in spite of much acclaimed performance in the first and the second quarters, the company is going downhill.

The passage is presented to you again highlighted with suggestive adjectives and adverbs. These will help you sense the emotions and feeling associated with them.

*It is **ironic** that Morton and Jackson Company registered **dismal** growth rate in the third and the fourth quarters despite the industry not having touched unduly high double-digit growth rate. It is matter of **grave concern** that in spite of much **acclaimed** performance in the first and the second quarters, the company is going **downhill**.*

Let us see the same paragraph written with **analytical** tone.

The Morton and Jackson Company registered 2.58% growth rate in the third and the fourth quarters; however, the industry clocked 10.28% during the same period. There are contradicting theories flying in the company to understand the dip of 7.7% points in the growth rate; on one hand the management blames inefficient operations alluding that the onus lies on the CEO, on the other hand the CEO accuses the workers' union of 'Go-Slow' method of strike. It cannot be decided without acquiring some information about both sides of the story.

The passage is presented to you again highlighted with suggestive adjectives, adverbs, and phrases. These will help you sense the implied intent of the author.

*The Morton and Jackson Company registered 2.58% growth rate in the third and the fourth quarters however the industry clocked 10.28% during the same period. There are contradicting theories flying in the company to **understand the dip of 7.7% points** in the growth rate; on one hand the management blames **inefficient operations alluding that the onus lies on the CEO**, on the other hand the **CEO accuses the workers' union of 'Go-Slow' method of strike**. It cannot be decided without acquiring some information about both sides of the story.*

Let us see the same paragraph written with **explanatory** tone.

The Morton and Jackson Company's 2.58% growth rate in the third and the fourth quarters despite the industry's 10.28% growth rate during the same period is understandable. The management's wish to make the CEO accountable for the low growth rate is natural because the responsibility of efficient operations lies with the CEO. The CEO wishes to make the workers' union accountable for the low growth rate since the responsibility of efficient operations lies with the union.

The passage is presented to you again highlighted with the relevant sentences. Reading the passage you will sense that the author's intent is to explain the causes.

*The Morton and Jackson Company's 2.58% growth rate in the third and the fourth quarters despite the industry's 10.28% growth rate during the same period is understandable. The management's wish to make the CEO accountable for the low growth rate is natural **because** the responsibility of efficient operations lies with the CEO. The CEO wishes to make the workers' union accountable for the low growth rate **since** the responsibility of efficient operations lies with the union.*

At the end of the book, you will find a comprehensive glossary of tones used in the Reading Comprehension passage.

Typical question stems of a Tone question are as follows.

- The tone of the passage can be best described as...

> **Strategy 6:**
> *Write one or two words in short hand describing the tone of the passage immediately after finishing the reading of the passage.*

> **Strategy 7:**
> *Don't be swayed by couple of suggestive adjectives or adverbs; judge the tone for the context as a whole.*

Let us look at an example.

Let us see another question from **Cancer of Colon** passage. You can refer to the passage given in first chapter—Introduction.

Question 3 — Tone

According to the passage, the tone of the author towards the conventional techniques mentioned in the passage can be best described as

(A) Qualified approval

(B) Cautious optimism

(C) Ruthless criticism

(D) Half-hearted acceptance

(E) Despair and lack of trust

Solution

The question asks us to ascertain the tone of the author towards the conventional techniques. This is a tone question from the general category.

The author is clearly not analytical or explanatory, but is opinionated as evidenced by use of words like "unfortunately", "admittedly", etc. The author is not neutral or positive towards the conventional techniques. He bears negative tones towards the conventional methods and uses the word "unfortunately" for those techniques. However, he does not criticize the techniques but merely presents the fact that the tests are imprecise and unreliable.

Let's go over the options one by one.

(A) This option is **incorrect** because the author does not approve but disapproves of the conventional techniques.

(B) This option is **incorrect** because the author expresses optimism about the new technique and not about the conventional ones.

(C) This option is **incorrect** because the author does not ruthlessly (viciously and cruelly) criticize the techniques, but points out that they're not useful and are inaccurate.

(D) This option is **incorrect** because the author does not accept the techniques but rather disapproves of them.

(E) This option is **correct** because the author does despair with the lack of success of the conventional techniques and does not trust them because he calls them imprecise and unreliable.

The correct answer is E.

3.2.4   Strategies to solve Detail question

As the name suggests Detail questions ask about the details in the passage. Your task is to fetch a detail asked in the question from the relevant portion of the passage. It is likely that the words or the phrases used in the question do not match with that of the portion of the passage; however, having understood the meaning from the question, look out for the detail in the passage. Mostly the correct answer would be a restatement of the part of passage.

Frequently test makers make options that are true according to the passage and seem attractive, but they may not be relevant to the question asked. Your task is to find the details not only true w.r.t. the passage, but also relevant to the question.

Sometimes the information you need is cleverly hidden by the author. It may be possible that the correct option is a rephrasing the specific detail, but is written in convoluted manner such that you do not realize that it is written as the same what you want.

Typical question stems of a Detail question are as follows.

 · According to the passage, the author suggests which of the following to...

 · According to the passage, the reason of <detail> is due to...

 · The author quotes all the following as a <danger to the mankind> EXCEPT...

> **Strategy 8:**
> *Test makers cleverly hide the information, unearth it.*

> **Strategy 9:**
> *Any true detail is not the answer; the details must be true as well as relevant.*

Let us look at some examples.

Let us see another question from **Cancer of Colon** passage. You can refer to the passage given in first chapter—Introduction.

Question 4 — Detail

According to the passage, the author would most likely agree with which of the following as an advantage of virtual-reality testing over conventional methods?

(A)   It is completely reliable and yields precise results.

(B)   It has been adopted as the standard test throughout the world.

(C)   It can detect cancerous growth at an earlier stage than can conventional testing.

(D)   Results are obtained much faster than conventional tests.

(E)   Surgical invasion is not required to obtain results.

Solution

The question is to find some detail about virtual-reality testing that the author will agree as an advantage over conventional methods.

Let's go over the options one by one.

(A) This option is **incorrect** because while the author says that the conventional methods are unreliable, he does not necessarily say that the virtual reality technique is completely reliable. In fact, he calls the technique "far more accurate" but not "completely accurate".

(B) This option is **incorrect** because the technique is still being tested and could not have been adopted all over the world.

(C) This option is **incorrect** because we cannot infer whether it can detect cancerous growth at an earlier stage than can conventional testing. All we can say is that the new technique is more accurate.

(D) This option is **incorrect** because we cannot infer whether it detects cancer faster than conventional testing. All we can say is that the new technique is more accurate.

(E) This option is **correct** because this can be inferred from the passage. The author mentions that the technique is "non-invasive".

The correct answer is E.

3.2.5   Strategies to solve Inference question

 These questions are identical to the inference questions asked in critical reasoning. Inference questions ask you to draw the inference from a word, or a phrase, or sentence used in the context. You have to understand the implied meaning unstated by the author, but it **must be true** according to the passage.

These questions pose a challenge as the required information may be found at several places in the passage, and you have to club them together to make a must be true inference.

Detail questions and Inference questions are logically the same as both ask for the must be true detail from the passage, but Inference questions go beyond what is written in the passage, they ask you to infer or imply what is not written, yet they are true according to the passage.

The key is not to infer something that is true in real-life, but necessarily true as per the passage. Be confined to the boundary of the passage.

Typical question stems of Inference question are as follows.

· The author would most likely agree with which of the following...

· It can be inferred from the passage that...

· The passage suggests that <something> may cause <something> if...

> **Strategy 10:**
> *Beware of Real-world true trap; be confined to the scope of the passage.*

> **Strategy 11:**
> *Infer least, and justify all the relevant information; do not satisfy yourself with 'Could be true', strive for 'Must be true'.*

> **Strategy 12:**
> *Beware of boundary line words (Extreme words); be skeptical.*

Let us look at some examples.

Let us see another question from **Cancer of Colon** passage. You can refer to the passage given in first chapter—Introduction.

Question 5 — Specific Inference

According to the passage, which of the following can be inferred?

(A) The screening technique can be used for other types of cancers with the same precision and accuracy.

(B) This technique will make curing colon cancer a relatively simple task.

(C) More than half of cancers go undetected.

(D) There are only three alternatives to virtual reality screening.

(E) Detection is only one of the problems in treatment of colon cancer.

Solution

The question is to find the correct inference. This is a specific inference question from the Inference category.

Let's go over the options one by one.

(A) This option is **incorrect** because we cannot say that the technique will work with the same precision and accuracy for other cancers.

(B) This option is **incorrect** because the technique is meant only for detection and not for curing colon cancer. After detection, there may be other complications in the treatment.

(C) This option is **incorrect** because it is too extreme. We cannot say how many cancers go undetected. All we know is that colon cancer is one of the biggest killers and that detecting it early is one of the problems. However, we don't know all the problems or the other cancer types and their detection facts.

(D) This option is **incorrect** because the passage states that "currently" three alternatives are available, implying that there have been more alternatives in the past and can be in the future.

(E) This option is **correct** because the first line of the second paragraph (One of the predicaments ... current tests) affirms this fact. The detection of colon cancer is one of the problems. Treatment can have other complications too.

The correct answer is E.

Let us look at another example.

3.2.6   Strategies to solve Reasoning based question

 As said that they are the minor types, you will seldom see but one question based on reasoning. You may be asked to identify the underlying assumption while making the conclusion by the author, or which piece of information can make the conclusion strong or weak. These questions are identical to Assumption, Strengthen, and Weaken question types in Critical Reasoning.

Typical question stems of Inference question are as follows.

· Which of the following, if true, would help conclude <something>?

· Which of the following, if true, would undermine the conclusion <something>?

· Which of the following was implied while concluding <something>?

> **Strategy 13:**
> *Treat as if you are attempting a critical reasoning question; apply the strategies used in CR.*

Let us look at an example.

Let us see another question from **Cancer of Colon** passage. You can refer to the passage given in first chapter—Introduction.

Question 6 — Reasoning

Which of the following, if true, would most weaken the implications of the last sentence of the passage keeping it in perspective of the passage?

(A)   Programming glitches, if unresolved, can influence the results of the program.

(B)   Patients are not always enthusiastic about virtual reality programs, especially in cases of serious illnesses.

(C)   Setting up virtual-reality scanners will be quite expensive, even if it's only a one-time cost.

(D)   Colon cancers are fast becoming the biggest "killers" in USA, beaten only by diabetes.

(E)   Blood testing can detect colon cancers usually when the cancer has been around for one and a half years.

Solution

The question is to weaken the last line of the passage. So, this is a reasoning question. The last line is "So far based on the results research on 70 patients, doctors have found that despite initial programming glitches, the virtual-reality technology is far more accurate." The last sentence discusses that the virtual reality technique is far more accurate but some programming glitches need to be worked out. This is based on results obtained from 70 patients. Any information that weakens the conclusion that this technique is more accurate will be the answer.

Let's go over the options one by one.

(A)   This option is **correct** because if this is true, then the programming glitches might have influenced the results and the accuracy results might not be necessarily true.

(B)   This option is **incorrect** because patients' enthusiasm will not affect the technique's accuracy or results.

(C)   This option is **incorrect** because cost is not mentioned as an issue at all in the passage and thus this is out of scope.

(D)   This option is **incorrect** because this does not weaken or strengthen the last sentence. It is a simple fact.

(E)   This option is **incorrect** because we know that blood tests are imprecise and don't yield accurate results. From what point of time they detect is irrelevant to the virtual reality technique.

The correct answer is A.

Now, we should be well-versed in passage reading, question types and their strategies.

Let us try the same on practice questions that follow in the next chapter.

Chapter 4

Practice Questions

4.1 Passage 1 (Whistleblower laws)

Whistleblower laws, as the moniker might imply, are pieces of legislation existing at the federal and state level intended to encourage employees to bring a stop to corruption and mismanagement. On the typical assembly line, a person may physically pull or blow a whistle to halt production in order to correct a faulty production process.

5

Likewise, the federal government has passed legislation to provide incentives, as well as protection, to government employees who witness co-workers, and, now more than ever, managers, who are behaving in ways that can be construed as an abuse of their position, or as an outright violation of the law.

10

Increasingly, the term whistleblower has come to be associated with somebody who informs on a group of trusting co-workers. However, it is exactly this type of connotation that whistleblower laws seek to remove from the mind of the public. Government bureaucracy and state-financed corporations can at times appear to operate above the law, outlasting administrations,
15 evading the discipline of elective review, and oiling their machinery while largely hiding from the public eye. Therefore, it is especially important to make it possible for courageous employees who find themselves entangled in a business or department with its own agenda in mind to be able to speak out on behalf of the larger interests of voters, to whom these entities are responsible. Since an employee who decides to report illegal or unreasonable behavior to
20 the authorities regularly finds himself to be the subject of intense scrutiny, or even fabricated accusations, if he continues to stay at his place of employment, it is necessary to make the act of bringing unethical performance to light appealing enough to outweigh the disincentives posed by angry co-workers, punitive bosses, and a national culture that can frown on disloyalty, even if it is for all the right reasons. In line with this reasoning, whistleblower laws often
25 provide the employee with a percentage of the money considered 'saved' by his honesty. Moreover, a settlement or court award reached as a result of the disclosure of these problematic issues is often paid to the successful whistleblower to compensate for the risk he has assumed.

From another perspective, the employee is simultaneously given protection against undue dis
30 missal and other retaliatory measures that a corporation or department might privately take against the plaintiff after official investigations are underway. These incentives were meant to make whistleblower laws both a progressive reform and effective legislation, so much so that the lucrative prospects of being a whistleblower have not only brought many reluctant employees forward, but also have encouraged some to go into the business of poaching through
35 phonebooks for dubious employers with an eye towards reporting them to government investigators and collecting their prize once a decision is reached.

1. Whistleblower laws have been put in place to achieve which of the following? Indicate all that apply.

   A to encourage employees to report corruption in the workplace

   B to penalize corrupt practitioners

   C to protect employees from the negative consequences of reporting malfeasance

2. Select a sentence in the passes that illustrate that the lawmakers were concerned that the legislation aimed at reforming bureaucracy would be ineffective without financial inducements.

3. In the passage, the effectiveness of whistleblower laws is demonstrated by

    (A) the number of corporations with federal contracts who have adopted the cost plus system

    (B) the high prosecution rate of managers who abuse their power and embezzle money

    (C) the inclusion of practical measures to make the legislation realistic

    (D) the willingness of most people to consider whistleblowers as patriots

    (E) the eagerness of a few employees to become deliberate investigators of corrupt corporations

4. It can be inferred from the passage that lawmakers viewed a need for so many practical incentives to be part of whistleblower legislation because

    (A) there have been laws passed but they have not had the full expected reach

    (B) federal employees make decisions out of self-interest more readily than out of a sense of purpose

    (C) corrupt bureaucracies result in a culture of corruption among all employees

    (D) federal bureaucracies are large and unwieldy

    (E) the federal government may be able to change a bureaucracy's leaders but not all of its employees

5. In the line 15, the phrase 'oiling their machinery' is probably a metaphor for:

    (A) Refusing to obey federal mandates

    (B) Writing laws

    (C) Proposing laws

    (D) Pitting state governments against federal governments

    (E) Running the day to day operations of an organization

6. The attitude of the author towards whistleblower legislation can be described as:

    (A) Suspicious but relenting

    (B) Supportive and objective

    (C) Agreeable but nonplussed

    (D) Implacable but journalistic

    (E) Prohibitive and histrionic

7. In the line 31, the word 'plaintiff' most nearly means

    (A) applicant
    (B) pretender
    (C) claimant
    (D) dissenter
    (E) perpetrator

4.2   Passage 2 (The WTO and sustainable development)

(From a text published in 1999)

Environmental concern and development are inextricably linked. Experience demonstrates that environmental standards and cleaner production are compatible with and supportive of economic growth. Healthy people and ecosystems are more productive. This link between economic growth and environmental improvement is enshrined, together with the commitment
5 to development, in the World Trade Organization's Preamble, which includes sustainable development as a basic objective of the trading system. In endorsing this concept, despite some reservations, WTO members unanimously recognized that trade and the economic growth WTO helps to create must be fostered in the context of sustainable development which integrates economic, social and environmental policies. Economic growth, sustainable development, and
10 opportunity for citizens are fundamental goals of every society. And the record of the past five decades clearly shows how the trading system has helped us reach some of these goals.

Since 1960, the WTO has negotiated a 90% drop in tariffs, and non-tariff barriers to trade have also been dramatically reduced. Moreover, market access for agriculture and services will be
15 further expanded upon conclusion of the next Uruguay Round. Thus, since 1960 trade has grown fifteen-fold; world economic production has quadrupled; and world per capita income has more than doubled. However, has the World Trade Organization done enough to promote sustainable development and protect the environment? The answer is yet to be presented by WTO. In reference to the concept of sustainable development, the Brundtland Commission Re-
20 port of 1987 stated "we must meet the needs of the present without compromising the ability of future generations to meet their own needs." Have any laws been made to make sustainable development mandatory? Taking into account state practice, treaty law, international case law and relevant legal literature, sustainable development is not yet a norm of international law. Currently it reflects a policy goal of the international community. This method of taking
25 a concept so important only as a precautionary guideline has brought the WTO's intentions regarding sustainable development into question.

1. Which of the following titles would be most appropriate for this passage?

   (A) The Work of the WTO

   (B) WTO Measures to Protect the Environment

   (C) Healthy trade and ecosystems

   (D) The WTO and the Environment

   (E) The Link between Trade and the sustainable development

2. According to the passage, under what conditions did the WTO endorse the link between the environment and sustainable development?

   (A) By recognizing that development is the fundamental goal of every society

   (B) By committing the WTO itself to environmental improvement

   (C) By declaring that trade must be based on sustainable development

   (D) By refuting the concept of temporary development as a basis for trade

   (E) By understanding healthy ecosystems

3. Why does the author present the question "… has the World Trade Organization done enough … environment?" in the second paragraph (line 17)?

    (A) To question the WTO on its actions taken so far to assess them

    (B) To suggest that the WTO hasn't done enough towards sustainable development

    (C) To imply that sustainable development is an impossible goal to attain for the WTO

    (D) To create doubts in the readers' minds about the usefulness of the WTO

    (E) To introduce doubts about the WTO's actions since its inception

4. According to the information presented in the passage, with which of the following would the writer of the passage most likely agree? Indicate all that apply.

    A It isn't necessary to compromise on the economic goals to achieve sustainable growth.

    B The WTO is not more motivated by the desire for expanding trade than towards environmental concern.

    C The WTO is not instrumental in protecting the global environment.

5. Select the sentence that illustrates more reductions in tariffs and trading obstacles will take place.

4.3   Passage 3 (Climate change due to volcanic eruptions)

(From a text published in 1999)

Previous studies on understanding the potential of Icelandic volcanic eruptions in modifying the environment have concentrated on the degree of induced climate change but the complex interaction of the processes which control the atmospheric circulation patterns of the earth were imperfectly understood and even with advanced equipment have proved difficult
5 to model.

Documentary evidence suggests that during the Laki fissure eruption, in 1783, severe acid damage to crops occurred in northern Europe and acid pulses killed fish in Scotland. Although an induced climatic change was probably the primary mechanism responsible, the degree to
10 which atmospheric circulation responds to volcanic forcing is uncertain so it is unsatisfactory to suggest that stress in the paleo-environmental record, associated with a volcanic eruption, has inevitably occurred in response to volcanic forcing of climate. The only volcanic eruptions which possess the theoretical ability to bring about climate change are those which emit substantial volumes of volatile gases. "Climate change theories" require that these be injected into
15 the stratosphere and remain in the troposphere. They must inevitably settle and be deposited on the surrounding sea and land rather than distant ecosystems. Despite plenty of excavations, such sedimentary evidence still eludes researchers around the Laki central fissure.

1. The author is primarily concerned with

   (A)   explaining the way volcanic eruptions work.

   (B)   discussing various theories concerning volcanoes and climate change.

   (C)   providing evidence that explains climate change in Europe with volcanic eruption.

   (D)   refuting the suggestion that climate change occurred due to volcanic eruption.

   (E)   rejecting a controversial hypothesis about the climate change phenomena in Europe.

2. According to the passage, which of the following can be concluded about previous studies of volcanic eruptions?

   (A)   The findings were refuted by research results done eventually in Europe.

   (B)   The paleo-environmental record suggested positively that volcanoes were responsible.

   (C)   The findings were invalidated by accepted climate change theories.

   (D)   The findings are difficult to support with evidence and can't be conclusively determined.

   (E)   Volcanic eruptions are likely to have brought about environmental changes.

3. Which of the following is best supported by the passage with regard to the volcanic eruptions in 1783?

    (A) The emissions forced climate change by raising the temperature of the atmosphere.

    (B) Volcanic emissions were injected into the stratosphere and then the troposphere.

    (C) The volcanic emissions were not substantial enough to form a stratosphere layer.

    (D) It modified the climate of Northern Europe.

    (E) Attempts to link it with climate change have not been substantiated yet.

4. According to the passage, what evidence, if provided, would suggest that Icelandic volcanic activity has been a force for environmental change, proving the author incorrect? Indicate all that apply.

    A   Volcanic emissions deposited on sea and land around Northern Europe.

    B   Induced climatic fluctuation documented in Northern and Western Europe.

    C   18th century environmental records of Europe and its changes.

5. In the given passage, what is the purpose of the first paragraph with respect to the second paragraph?

    (A) To explain the various theories concerning induced climate change by volcanic eruptions.

    (B) To lay the groundwork for the implication that volcanic eruptions lack the environmental stress to induce climate change.

    (C) To explain how Laki fissure eruptions could have affected crops and fish in Northern Europe.

    (D) To prove that volcanic eruptions cannot bring about climate change because they lack environmental pressure.

    (E) To explain how volcanic eruptions can bring about climate change in specific cases.

4.4 Passage 4 (Stock options in CEO pay)

(From a text published in 1999)

Defenders of runaway CEO pay argue that market forces are at work determining executive compensation levels and CEOs are rewarded for increasing their company's stock prices. But are America's CEOs entitled to such lucrative pay deals based on their performance? In 1998, the business press exploded with stories of pay for mediocrity: When it comes to executive
5 pay, stock option grants appear to have the Midas touch. As the stock market has broken record after record, they have become an increasingly popular form of executive compensation.

According to compensation analysts, stock options make up two-thirds of a CEOs pay, up from
10 one-third in the 1960s. Instead of having to beat their competitors, CEOs with stock option-fueled compensation packages are graded on a curve: the rising stock market. As stock prices increase generally, even mediocre CEOs can realize large gains from their options. Analysts estimate that only a quarter of option grants awarded to CEOs contain any sort of link to performance, such as premium-priced or indexed stock options. But executive equity incentive
15 plans can hurt shareholders. A recent research studied the largest U.S. companies by adjusting for the value of their executive's stock options. The study found that 11 firms went from profit to loss, and 13 had their profits halved. In addition, the study found that the average potential dilution of shareholder value from stock options is 9.2 percent for S&P 500 companies.

1. The primary purpose of the passage is

   (A) to explain CEOs stock-option-fueled compensation packages.

   (B) to criticize the excessive wages of corporate CEOs.

   (C) to demonstrate the lack of parity among CEO compensation packages.

   (D) to argue against non-performance-rated bonuses and point out the repercussions.

   (E) to prove that paying CEOs through stock-options is doing more bad than good.

2. Select the sentence in the first paragraph that unequivocally demonstrates the absurdity of share option compensation packages.

3. According to the passage, which of the following illustrate(s) that the author denounces CEOs stock-option compensation plans? Indicate all that apply.

   A They have unduly become an increasingly awarded form of compensation package.

   B Their value is not directly determined by company performance.

   C They undermine the value of shares.

4. According to the passage, keeping in view the CEOs stock option compensation packages, with which of the following would the author agree?

   (A) Currently companies consider their stocks' performances more than their actual performances.

(B) The number of stock option compensation packages has risen two thirds over the last few decades.

(C) CEOs stock option compensation packages should consist of premium-priced or indexed stock options only.

(D) CEOs stock option compensation packages are unduly awarded to CEOs despite companies performing well in the market.

(E) CEOs stock option compensation packages enhance only stock market figures, especially in the case of the compensation packages of mediocre CEOs.

5. Which of the following would best categorize the author's attitude towards stock-option-based CEO pay, as given in the passage?

   (A) Restrained criticism

   (B) Conditional approval

   (C) Unconditional disgust

   (D) Absolute intolerance

   (E) Unjustified disapproval

6. According to the passage, which of the following can be inferred?

   (A) Potential dilution of shareholder value stemming from CEOs compensation was less in the 1960s.

   (B) Shareholders did not get hurt by companies in the 1960s.

   (C) CEOs and top executives were not mediocre in the 1960s.

   (D) Companies will accrue more profits if CEOs are paid according to performance.

   (E) A CEO's pay should be linked to the company's performance in the stock market.

4.5   Passage 5 (Rising health care costs & medical malpractice)

In 1990, a Harvard Medical Practice study came to the conclusion that 95,000 deaths a year in the United States are attributable to medical malpractice. Not surprisingly, an additional 700,000 individuals are subject to injury as a result of medical malpractice. These numbers can jar even the most dispassionate observer. A jumbo jet would have to crash every day for
5 a year to reproduce these casualties. Despite the multitudes of people who die or suffer as a result of medical malpractice, fewer than 2,100 doctors a year are disciplined in connection with a malpractice claim. Of those health care providers that do come under scrutiny and censure, the lion's share of them are subject to sanctions on the premises of substance abuse or fraud, rather than malpractice. These facts resurface at a time when federal legislators are
10 considering measures to limit the monetary amount a patient can claim as compensation for damages incurred as a result of medical malpractice.

It is the hope of lawmakers in capping jury awards to plaintiffs that it may be possible to reverse the tide of rising health care costs. Since those costs are ultimately imposed on pa-
15 tients in the form of insurance premiums, the reigning logic dictates that limits on awards will save the patient money, and bring the cost of high quality healthcare within the reach of more Americans. However, the soundness of this approach is called into question when we consider that a Congressional Budget Office report found that only one percent of national health care costs results from the expense of malpractice insurance premiums being passed on to the
20 patient. However, accidents, misdiagnosis and conflicting prescriptions cost the nation nearly sixty billion dollars a year.

Even with these losses imposed on patients and on taxpayers yearly, less than half a percent of all civil cases in state courts sought to charge doctors with medical malpractice. The 2000
25 plus doctors who are disciplined each year amount to hardly one percent of all acting health care providers. Thus the amount of money going back into the hands of victims is a relatively inconsequential contribution to the overall cost of health care in America when compared to the cost of making good the harm of malpractice. Rising health care costs may more pre-dictably be driven back by improving the way in which the health care industry polices itself
30 and removing unreliable doctors from practice.

1. The main theme of this passage can be summarized as:

   (A) Widespread policing is the answer to cutting health care costs.

   (B) Health care costs are the result of too few of the guilty being held accountable.

   (C) The source of high health care costs is difficult to localize.

   (D) Rising health care costs have more to do with the behavior of doctors than with the behavior of patients.

   (E) Traditional government approaches to the health care issue have been disappoint-ing.

2. The main purpose of comparing the number of malpractice victims to the number of jumbo jet accident casualties is

   (A) to exemplify how a dispassionate observer could be caught off guard

(B)   to show that even if we do not consider the several hundred thousand injured, the number of people who die from malpractice every year is absurdly high

(C)   to compare the gravity of airline accidents to the seriousness of medical malpractice

(D)   to note the disparity between airline safety regulations and health care oversight

(E)   to point out the similarity between the number of people killed in air crashes and the number killed through medical malpractice

3.   The main concern voiced over the penalties levied on rogue practitioners is

   (A)   penalties are given out for the wrong reasons

   (B)   penalties given out are not severe enough

   (C)   penalties are given out to only a few

   (D)   penalties are given out to the wrong offenders

   (E)   penalties given out are not levied with enough charges to be a threat

4.   The implication of the Congressional Budget Office report is that

   (A)   awards from malpractice claims are not a substantial source of health care costs

   (B)   placing a limit on malpractice claims will significantly reduce the cost of health care to the end user

   (C)   malpractice insurance premiums are not as high as they could be

   (D)   congressional research is polarized and thus often contradictory

   (E)   insurance companies only charge what is fair based on the size of claims and the number of claimants

5.   The author of this passage would most likely agree with the following argument(s). Indicate all that apply.

   A   Insurance companies will try to inflate their rate of return on premiums

   B   The cost of health care is inflated by the availability of expensive treatments

   C   The cost of health care is increased by the negligence of doctors

6.   Select a sentence in paragraph I that illustrates the fact that Congress is operating under a false premise to limit the compensation a patient can get for damages attributed to medical malpractice.

7.   The conclusion that greater policing of doctors will reduce the incidence of malpractice and drive down costs assumes that

   (A)   most doctors are not up to their responsibilities

   (B)   many more doctors are guilty of substance abuse and fraud than the portion accused

(C) policing will encourage doctors to improve their performance

(D) doctors will never protect one another from investigation on the grounds that they believe they are best equipped to make decisions for the patients

(E) there is unchecked corruption among doctors

8. The notion of reducing jury awards places the blame for high health care costs most directly on:

(A) Patients

(B) Medical malpractice

(C) Controlling doctors

(D) The inability of the justice system to work with the health care system

(E) Lawsuits

9. Which of the following is the **MOST INAPPROPRIATE** in describing the author's tone of the passage?

(A) Distraught

(B) Apathetic

(C) Infuriated

(D) Dire

(E) Disparaging

4.6 Passage 6 (Sales force automation)

(From a text published in 1998)

Companies continue to miss the mark in their quest for Sales Force Automation (SFA), over-looking the most critical success factor–the user. In technology deployment, the implementation team assumes the intended users only have a baseline level of computer discipline but
35 frequently mistake the lack of technology use as low literacy on computers. This leads them to adopt unsuitable training techniques. In reality, today's sales department are mostly made up of users who have been exposed to computers but who have never had to use them consistently and struggle to grasp how much strategic value SFA will have. An SFA project's success hinges on creating a situation where both sales representatives and managers can reap the
40 benefits of the SFA tools but all too often they haven't relied on technology as a strategic tool to meet objectives.

Their compensation and job performance are very quantifiable, based on how well they do against a set of revenue targets so inevitably they tend to define SFA in terms of its usefulness
45 handling the transactions they normally work on. The SFA market has done a good job of selling the benefits of SFA tools to drive sales performance but, having convinced companies to purchase systems, there is intense pressure to achieve a strong return on investment. To ensure a successful SFA implementation, companies need to set realistic expectations and consider issues that are unique when deploying the system.

1. The main purpose of the author in discussing the various aspects of SFA is to

   (A) explain how difficult it is to get any return on investment from SFA
   (B) discuss the various advantages and disadvantages of SFA
   (C) point out how companies are missing out on getting maximum benefit from SFA
   (D) criticize the SFA market for not having trained the users well enough in SFA
   (E) present the idea that SFA is only useful practically in keeping transactional entries

2. According to the passage, traditional training approaches are inappropriate for SFA projects because

   (A) the number of SFA users is too low and the users are too inexperienced
   (B) user management teams lack experience to properly define transactional goals
   (C) these attempt to correct a perceived technology ignorance among SFA users
   (D) these fail to improve computer literacy, a missing component among users
   (E) these are not capable of helping companies accurately define transactional goals as needed

3. Select the sentence in the passes that illustrates the author's implication regarding SFA in recommending that SFA be used optimally.

4. According to the passage, the effective implementation of SFA projects depends on which of the following? Indicate all that apply.

A   Training users for more than baseline functions of SFA.

B   The sales teams could not fully comprehend the extent to which they can utilize SFA.

C   Raising the literacy level of SFA trainers.

5. The author would most likely agree with which of the following actions of a company as being crucial to a positive outcome for SFA projects?

(A) Properly training the training staff

(B) Defining SFA applications in terms of the nature of transactions and goals

(C) Factoring in organizational characteristics to accordingly set attainable goals

(D) Intensifying the pressure on managers to achieve a return on SFA investments

(E) Linking use of sales performance with SFA to ensure return on investment

4.7   Passage 7 (Rising European Union and the U.S.)

The size of the European Union market is exponentially larger than it was in the 1950's, when European integration was first proposed. While today the European Union is the only region with the economic might to challenge the United States for meaningful influence over international trade policies, the United States is noncommittal on E.U. proposals calling for the
5   alignment of labor regulations, the opening of consumer forums and the offer of an audience to environmental groups. As the constituencies calling for these developments have been relegated to peripheral positions in the dialogue over trans-Atlantic economic unification, those with an interest in these groups see a trend towards liberalizing the rules for corporate advantage in the economic co-ordination that has sprung up between the United States and Europe.
10 Much of the current communication between the United States and the European Union is focused on establishing an agreement that codifies the rules of trans-Atlantic trade and that acknowledges the extent of trade conducted between the U.S. and Europe, greater in bulk than between any other pair of regions in the world, without disregarding the efforts European producers must make to satisfy interest groups and regulations.
15

The heated dialogue between the United States and the European Union on this issue has come hard on the heels of the joining of the U.S., Mexico and Canada in the North American Free Trade Agreement: NAFTA. This agreement seeks to standardize industrial and labor regulations between the United States and its neighbors so that tariffs can be reduced, international
20 transport encouraged, and corporate investment diversified. While bringing standards of production into alignment is a goal that ought to raise the quality of production and the level of cooperation across the continent, it also creates an opportunity to establish a standard contra to European expectations of international regulation. As a solution, the E.U. has proposed TAFTA, the Trans-Atlantic Free Trade Agreement, but the United States has repeatedly
25 hesitated at the proposal, seeking to protect its dominance in the Western Hemisphere. This dominance is secured by its ability to protect its factories and corporations from sources of comparable European production and demanding practices of review and concessions popular in Europe as a nod to social consensus.

30 These issues have resulted in the plethora of interest groups with a voice in the matter simultaneously accusing the U.S of brinkmanship, protectionism, callous deregulation, third world exploitation and anti-competitive practices. The route to economic expansion is a prominent issue in both the U.S. and the European Union, and some with a say in the matter repeat these protests as a screen for their own plans to tip the balance of economic advantage towards their
35 own region at the expense of all other involved parties in the process of exploring for parity.

1. The intent of the author in noting the size of the European Union in the first sentence of the passage is to

   (A)   demonstrate the difference between the past E.U. and the present E.U.

   (B)   clarify the number of parties in trans-Atlantic trade

   (C)   establish the importance of one of the leading parties in world markets

   (D)   show that the E.U. cannot be exploited for U.S. self-interest

   (E)   demonstrate why the United States is non-committal about cooperation

2. Which of the following words best substitutes for the term 'heated dialogue' in the line 16?

    (A) impasse

    (B) dispute

    (C) shuttle diplomacy

    (D) brinkmanship

    (E) banter

3. The main concern of the European Union regarding NAFTA is that

    (A) North America will have a higher standard of living than Europe

    (B) North America will improve its standard of living at the expense of Europe

    (C) North America will adopt production standards that are incompatible with Europe's

    (D) North America will flood Europe with cheap, low quality goods

    (E) North America will promote the exploitation of labor

4. It can be inferred from the passage that less stringent production and environmental standards than those of North America are unfavorable to the European Union because

    (A) they unfairly lower the quality of life in Europe

    (B) they reduce the amount of cheap labor entering Europe from the third world

    (C) they damage the European environment

    (D) they encourage European workers to move to the United States

    (E) they make it easy for already dominant North American industries to do trade

5. Select a sentence in the passage that accuses the US of deregulation driven by an uncaring attitude.

6. It can be inferred from the passage that the author believes the range of accusations against the United States made by groups on the periphery of trade talks is

    (A) credible but lacking influence

    (B) credible but irrelevant

    (C) biased

    (D) well-balanced

    (E) incredible but accurate

7. The non-committal attitude of the United States to pursue trade relations with Europe Union is demonstrated by which of the following? Indicate all that apply.

    A The U.S., unwillingness to engage in any new agreements

    B The U.S., seeking keen interest in NAFTA

    C The U.S., decision not to turn down TAFTA while avoiding any commitment to it

4.8 Passage 8 (In-fighting Indian princes and the rise of the British)

For 17th century Europeans, the history of Eastern monarchies, like everything else in Asia, was stereotyped and invariable. According to accounts of Indian events, history unfolded itself with the predictable rituals of heavy-handed folklore. Typically, the founder of a dynasty, a brave soldier, is a desperate intriguer, and expels from the throne the feeble and degenerate
5 scions of a more ancient house. His son may inherit some of the talent of the father, but in two or three generations luxury and indolence do their work, and the feeble inheritors of a great name are dethroned by some new adventurer, destined to bequeath a like misfortune to his degenerate descendants. Thus rebellion and deposition were the correctives of despotism, and therefore, a recurrence, at fixed intervals, of able and vigorous princes through the medium
10 of periodical anarchy and civil war, occurred. It was this perception of history that allowed Britain's rulers to lay claim to the governance of the subcontinent. The British claimed to be interested in avoiding these periods of bloodshed. This claim justified British policy, as well as dictated how they thought about gaining the favor of India's local monarchies.

15 British armies and British administrators were able to insinuate rule over India by setting up native princes in positions of power. Their methods took advantage of existing "doctrines of lapse," and made use of what was already the declared law in cases of heredity. By intervening on behalf of one prince or another, both of whom may have been equally suited to claim the right to the throne in cases in which the rights to leadership lapsed, they put themselves in a
20 position to support a leader they selected, and to maintain his power as long as it was in their interests. In this way the princes became practically obliged to cooperate with the British. The result was two generations of petty despots, insulated from the consequences of misrule by British bayonets. The despots spent their lives in listless debauchery, broken by paroxysms of cruelty and oppression.

1. It can be inferred from the passage that Britain could easily impose a proxy rule on the Indian subcontinent because of

   (A) a language in common with that of the Indians

   (B) a lack of corruption within the British administration

   (C) the deployment of well-trained British soldiers

   (D) superior weaponry

   (E) the use of pre-existing laws of leadership lapses

2. The author of the passage would be likely to agree with which statement(s). Indicate all that apply.

   [A] British intervention in India was a positive influence on India

   [B] The system of rule in India before the British arrived had no faults

   [C] India would have been better off to carry out its cycle of lapse and renewal without British influence

3. The attitude of the author towards the reported cycle of rule can best be described as:

   (A) Disparaging
   (B) Despairing
   (C) Skeptical
   (D) Matter of fact
   (E) Approving

4. The damage caused by British rule to the subcontinent was brought about by

   (A) the refusal of the people to be ruled
   (B) the inability of the people to choose their leader
   (C) the inability of the people to resist oppression
   (D) the demoralization of the Indian identity
   (E) the exploitative nature of the relationship between Britain and the princes

5. One judgment about the British offered by this passage might be that

   (A) they never pretended to undertake socially responsible activity
   (B) they were interested exclusively in exploiting India's resources
   (C) they got involved in governing colonies which they knew were beyond their powers of governance
   (D) they had a benign influence on India
   (E) they sought practical opportunity when their self-interest matched local rulers' objectives

6. The "doctrines of lapse" which positioned princes against one another for regional thrones gave Britain a foothold in India by

   (A) allowing them to exchange a little influence at a critical time for significant influence later.
   (B) offering an opportunity to take over the leadership role in these areas while no one was in charge.
   (C) letting the British act as arbitrators in discussions between the dueling princes.
   (D) positioning the British as an impartial party in Indian politics.
   (E) ensuring there were no local candidates for leadership.

7. From the passage, the attitude of Britain towards Indian politics can be described as:

   (A) Conflicted
   (B) Hypocritical
   (C) Opportunistic
   (D) Fair
   (E) Unbiased

8. Replacement of the word *despotism* highlighted in the first paragraph with which of the following words would result in the LEAST change in meaning in the passage?

  (A)   stubborn

  (B)   tyranny

  (C)   democracy

  (D)   debauchery

  (E)   aristocracy

4.9   Passage 9 (The Belgian economy: from devastation to restoration)

For 200 years until World War I, French-speaking Wallonia was a technically advanced, industrial region, while Dutch-speaking Flanders was predominantly agricultural. This disparity began to fade during the interwar period. When Belgium emerged from World War II with its industrial infrastructure relatively undamaged, the stage was set for a period of rapid de-
5 velopment, particularly in Flanders. The older, traditional industries of Wallonia, particularly steelmaking, began to lose their competitive edge during this period, but the general growth of world prosperity masked this deterioration until the 1973 and 1979 oil price shocks and resultant shifts in international demand sent the economy into a period of prolonged recession.

10 In the 1980s and 1990s, the economic center of the country continued to shift northwards to Flanders. The early 1980s saw the country facing a difficult period of structural adjustment caused by declining demand for its traditional products, deteriorating economic performance, and neglected structural reform. Consequently, the 1980-82 recession shook Belgium to its core–unemployment rose, social welfare costs increased, personal debt soared, the govern-
15 ment deficit climbed to 13% of GDP, and the national debt, although mostly held domestically, mushroomed. Against this grim backdrop, in 1982, Prime Minister Martens' center-right coalition government formulated an economic recovery program to promote export-led growth by enhancing the competitiveness of Belgium's export industries through an 8.5% devaluation. Economic growth rose from 2% in 1984 to a peak of 4% in 1989. In May 1990, the govern-
20 ment linked the franc to the German Mark, primarily through closely tracking German interest rates. Consequently, as German interest rates rose after 1990, Belgian rates increased and contributed to a decline in the economic growth rate.

Although Belgium is a wealthy country, it overspent income and under-collected taxes for
25 years. The Belgian government reacted to the 1973 and 1979 oil price hikes with poor macroeconomic policies: it transferred workers made redundant in the private sector to the public sector and subsidized ailing industries–coal, steel, textiles, glass, and shipbuilding–in order to prop up the economy. As a result, cumulative government debt reached 121% of GNP by the end of the 1980s *(versus a cumulative U.S. federal public debt/GNP ratio of 31.2% in 1990)*.
30 However, thanks to Belgium's high personal savings rate, the Belgian Government managed to finance the deficit mainly from domestic savings. This minimized the deleterious effects on the overall economy.

1.   An appropriate title for this passage might be:

   (A)   The rise of Flanders to domestic leadership

   (B)   Managing the challenge of structural adjustment in the post-war Belgian economy

   (C)   Dead weight: How Greater Belgium lost Flanders the industrial advantage

   (D)   Fiscal rally: How P.M. Martens found his legs

   (E)   Which way: Fickle government starves a state with too many choices

2.   The information in the beginning of the passage concerning the rise of Flanders over Wallonia serves to

   (A)   introduce the protagonist of the author's text early in the passage

(B) foreshadow the counterpoint between successful and unsuccessful policy-making

(C) introduce and demonstrate the idea of a compositional sea-change in the greater Belgian economy

(D) show how runaway development was ready to take hold of the Belgian economy before it was mismanaged and eventually recouped

(E) provide the reader with the factor responsible for driving away development in the greater Belgian economy

3. Select the sentence in the passage that illustrates one of the reasons that despite the world world wars, Flanders propped Belgian economy toward development.

4. The phrase "Against this grim backdrop" (line 16) used by the author to

(A) show that no matter how bad things are, a politician can make them worse.

(B) make light of Martens' genuine but misspent efforts to turn around the economy.

(C) show that Martens brought real change in the face of a formidable challenge.

(D) pardon Martens by showing that even the most expert of handlers could not have changed the hand Belgium was dealt.

(E) imply that there was no hope for Belgium.

5. The genre of the passage can be categorized as:

(A) Apologetic

(B) Historical

(C) Polemical

(D) Argumentative

(E) Encyclopaedic

6. In the passage, the author's use of the phrase "poor macroeconomic policies" (line 25) and the word "prop" in (line 28) regarding government subsidies suggests what about his opinion of government intervention in the economy?

(A) The government should not intervene in economic issues that can be handle privately.

(B) The government should not support industries that are ailing.

(C) The government can encourage sustainable progress without working with market forces.

(D) The government must be more decisive in its decision-making.

(E) The government cannot avoid being at the mercy of market fluctuations.

7. The author's critical portrayal of the Belgian government's reactions to the oil crises in the 1970's does not necessarily make its officials economically malfeasant because

   (A) no economist could have done better

   (B) economists are academics; politicians are pragmatists

   (C) this economic review of the Belgian economy is retrospective; the decisions made at the time were without the benefit of hindsight

   (D) there are no right or wrong answers in economics

   (E) administrators were giving the public what they wanted

8. Replacement of the word *masked* highlighted in the first paragraph with which of the following words would result in the LEAST change in meaning in the passage?

   (A) concealed

   (B) eluded

   (C) deceived

   (D) perplexed

   (E) mystified

4.10   Passage 10 (Craving for fast food: who to blame – behavior or the brain?)

Recent evidence from scientists has shown that eating "fast food" can be addictive in much the same way as using controlled substances can be. According to researchers, "fast food" such as hamburgers, processed sugar, and a wide range of deep fried foods can trigger a dependency in the brain that perpetuates a habit of further use. It is a view that is increasingly supported by
5   scientists who see a co-dependency between people's decisions and environmental influences *(including the wide availability of "fast food")* that have structural effects on human development. The proposed conclusions contend that the brains of overeaters experience chemical changes in response to unbalanced diets with a high content of processed sugar, salt, and saturated fats.

10
In time and in some cases, if people continue a pattern of consumption containing too much unhealthy food, their intake of this food will initiate changes in the brain that elevate the minimum level of ingestion the brain needs for satiation. Moreover, since high consumption of "fast foods" stimulates opiates in the brain *(substances which act as natural pain relievers)*,
15   large, recurrent doses of "fast food" can mimic the effects of opiates, albeit in a less intense form. Scientists raising rats on a diet of twenty-five percent sugar found that upon suddenly eliminating glucose from the rats' food supply, the animals experienced all the symptoms of withdrawal attributed to reducing traditional addictive opiates, including shivering and chattering teeth. Later, by treating rats with drugs that block opiate receptors, scientists were able
20   to lower the amount of dopamine in the nucleus acumen of rats' brains, an area linked with the dynamics of reward. Such neurochemistry can be seen in heroin addicts coping with withdrawal. By this reasoning, obesity, like other addictions, can be viewed as a disease beyond the control of those afflicted by it.

25   This has brought lawyers to argue that civil society has a responsibility to regulate food and educate people about the abuse of "unhealthy foods" in a way that is comparable to society's control of opiates and narcotics. Corporations that target this vulnerability in human beings can then be held liable for the sicknesses that result from the poor eating habits overwhelming their customers. Still, some scientists scoff at the lengths to which their colleagues seek to
30   separate the decision making process from people's behavior. For these researchers, the distinction between a habit and an addiction is not quantitative but qualitative. Their consensus is that individuals can still moderate their behavior to control the effects of what they eat on their systems.

1.   The passage seems to suggest that scientists who see a co-dependence between people's decisions and environmental influences would affirm that

   (A)   human decision-making has unconscious, chemical influences

   (B)   human beings have a responsibility to control their surroundings

   (C)   overeaters are not responsible for their behavior and their eating disorders

   (D)   obesity is a public health crisis

   (E)   overeaters continue to eat because they are unable to overcome the difficulties of withdrawal

2. Lawyers defending corporations against the findings of researchers on the effects of "fast food" would likely argue that: Indicate all that apply.

   A   obesity is a pre-existing condition in individuals

   B   the distinction between a habit and an addiction is "not quantitative but qualitative"

   C   corporations were not aware that "fast food" caused chemical dependency because the science confirming it is so new

3. By labeling obesity as a disease, the scientists in the passage seek to point out that

   (A)   the obese need to obey a strict diet

   (B)   the obese are more vulnerable to the health hazards of chronic consumption of "fast food" than those who are not obese

   (C)   obesity is a condition that targets those with a genetic precondition to it

   (D)   obesity is a result of factors that cannot be understood solely as the results of the behavior of individuals

   (E)   obesity exists in an individual whether or not they overeat

4. Some scientists in the passage who dispute the conclusions of their colleagues who link obesity with chemical factors find fault with their colleagues'

   (A)   findings

   (B)   expertise

   (C)   assumptions

   (D)   methodology

   (E)   comparisons between data

5. Select the sentence in the III paragraph that illustrates dissenting scientists' objection to the assumption that addictive behavior has nothing to do with behavior and choices and is dependent only on chemical imbalances in the brain.

6. From the passage, the role of dopamine in the rats' brain seems to

   (A)   reduce food intake

   (B)   block opiates

   (C)   replace opiates when they are blocked

   (D)   punish rats when opiates are received

   (E)   instruct the rat to eat more

7. As presented in the passage, lawyers who would seek to take "fast food" restaurants to court for damaging public health would agree with which of the following?

   (A) The government is not knowledgeable enough to safeguard public health.

   (B) Corporations are responsible for the consequences of their products.

   (C) The responsibility to determine what a good product is should be determined by the market.

   (D) People who suffer from obesity are victims of governmental incompetence.

   (E) People should take responsibility for their own diets.

4.11 Passage 11 (Masks & gas attacks during WW II)

The attack on Pearl Harbor by the Japanese introduced America to the world theater of World War II. What was unique about this battle was that American citizens experienced it as the first attack on American soil in what was then recent memory. Throughout World War I, Americans mostly felt secure in their homes. However, the changing times and the audacity of nationalis-
5 tic world powers, raised questions as to the need for civilian defense.

The highest priority was the protection of children from possible attack. The escalation of World War II already involved lengthy campaigns of civil terror waged by opposing powers. No power with a soldiering part in the war was immune or blameless. Germany unleashed the
10 lengthiest bombing campaign of the war on the people of London primarily to weaken British morale. Later, the Allied Forces would fire bomb on the German city of Dresden. Dresden had housed an almost entirely civilian population and had incidental wartime production.

Early on, Britain and the United States enacted an emergency measure to protect their youth
15 population. A leading concern was the exposure to gas attack, an effective measure against un-witting urban dwellers. Immediately after Pearl Harbor, thousands of military training masks were rushed to people living on the islands. However, the available equipment was unsuitable for protecting children. Instead, Hawaiian officials produced an expedient made up of bunny ears and a hood. This would lead to further improvisation in the protection of the child civilian
20 population. The Sun Rubber Company designed a mask based on the universal Walt Disney cartoon figure Mickey Mouse. The Mickey Mouse gas mask was then approved by the Chemical Warfare Service of the U.S. Department of Defense, with the assumption that other winning designs could follow the success of this first run. The popularity of these masks was depen-dent on internalizing their use in children by making their presence part of a perceived game.
25 This potentially reduced the element of fear that the masks conveyed on their recipients. If the element of fear could be diminished, gas masks might be employed by their owners more quickly in the event of an attack, and also worn without interruption.

All of this would increase the chances of survival of the youth population, of no small concern
30 to a nation with large numbers of its working age males facing the perils of combat overseas.

1. According to the passage, the main distinction between World War I and World War II for Americans was:

   (A) The lengthy campaigns of civil terror

   (B) The blame shared by all participating powers

   (C) The mobilization of civilian factories for military use

   (D) The first violation of national security in several generations

   (E) The threat of nationalism from foreign aggressors

2. The purpose of national armies engaging in civil terror as presented by the passage is: Indicate all that apply.

   A to destroy the civilian wartime infrastructure

     B   to destroy the enemy's willingness to continue fighting

     C   to kill key people

3. The design of gas masks to look like a cartoon character was intended to

    (A) make the war seem less omnipresent to children

    (B) make children less afraid of a foreign attack

    (C) induce children to learn how to use the mask properly

    (D) increase sales of gas masks to families

    (E) bring a level of normalcy back to everyday life

4. Select the sentence in paragraph III and IV that illustrates the concern that the special efforts were taken to consider the need to protect the youth population:

5. The topic of the passage can best be described as:

    (A) The coordination of the wartime economy to meet civilian defense

    (B) The special efforts to protect children in response to heightened civilian vulnerability

    (C) The need for all nations to engage in civilian terror tactics

    (D) The incorporation of popular images in the tools of war

    (E) The resourcefulness of the American military machine in meeting wartime production

6. In paragraph 3, in the sentence beginning with (line 18): "Instead, Hawaiian officials...," the word "expedient" most nearly means

    (A) a dire consequence

    (B) a cleaning agent

    (C) a response to an urgent need

    (D) a terror tactic

    (E) a placebo

7. The benefit of internalizing the use of these masks in children was that

    (A) they would wear them to bed

    (B) they would take the masks to school

    (C) they would encourage friends to use them

    (D) they would lack fear upon wearing them

    (E) they would love the cartoon character Mickey Mouse

8. It can be inferred from the passage that a significant avoidable danger of a wartime terror attack is

   (A) enemy propaganda

   (B) the youth of the civilian population

   (C) poor decision making on the part of unprepared civilians

   (D) plunging civilian morale

   (E) lack of warning of an attack

4.12   Passage 12 (Lord Dalhousie's uniform rate of postage in India)

Lord Dalhousie is credited with the creation of the modern postal system in India. Dalhousie, who held many roles in the administration and internal development of the region, contributed to the Indian postal system by sweeping away the fabric of its past obstructions and levying a uniform rate of postage.

5

All letters weighing less than a prescribed amount in weight would require the same postal fee (half an Anna) regardless of their destination or origin. This idea of instituting a uniform unit of weight and of charge for the whole of the vast Indian empire seemed sheer folly to many orthodox financiers of his time. It was, they said, pushing Rowland Hill's scheme of a-penny

10 postage for England to an extreme. For these onlookers, Dalhousie's plan was not so much an extension of the English penny postage scheme, as a reductio ad absurdum of the reform that had been effected in Great Britain. What could be more extravagant or more unjust than to levy the same charge on two letters, one of which was to be delivered to the adjoining street, and the other to the opposite side of India?

15

Lord Dalhousie was not significantly deterred by the criticism. Because of the uniform rate of postage, the old wrangle over the payment for delivery of every letter, from which the rural postman invariably managed to squeeze something additional for himself at the expense of the recipient, could be replaced by a simple system of postage stamps. The system was more

20 reliable for the person mailing the letter, and encouraged increased patronage.

The proof of his success was the renewal of the postal system as a self-sustaining organization rather than its continuance as a chronic drain on British colonial finances. The social results were even more important. It has been said that the half-penny post that Lord Dalhousie put

25 in place in India was more consequential than the telegraph, the railway and even Public In-struction for reversing the isolation which predated it.

1.   The objections to the uniform postal rate in India were related to

   (A)   the fact that it was not fair to charge the same rate for different degrees of service

   (B)   the fact that it was an unproven method

   (C)   the fact that it conveyed a lack of trust in postal workers

   (D)   the inability of the letter delivery service to handle a flood of cross-India mail

   (E)   an attempt by critics to put their own recommendations in place

2.   Select the sentence in the passage that illustrates the main benefit of the half-penny post scheme in India as an increase in the rate of communication throughout the subconti-nent.

3.   It can be inferred from the results of Dalhousie's revisions of India's postal system that: Indicate all that apply.

   A   the only way to see whether something will be successful is to put it into practice

  B if something works on a small scale, it is likely to work on a large scale as well, if executed judiciously

  C disorganization and unreliability may be more costly than charging at uniform and low rates

4. One lesson that can be taken from Dalhousie's success is that

  (A) personal experience can be more informed than extensive theoretical knowledge

  (B) postal systems are one example of goods that are not subject to supply and demand curves

  (C) there had been British mismanagement

  (D) long term social gains can compensate for short term capital losses

  (E) for Britain's purposes, the penny postage scheme should have preceded the telegraph, the railway, and public instruction

5. In the middle of the second paragraph (line 11), the term "reductio ad absurdum" most closely means

  (A) to misunderstand the purpose of an idea

  (B) to simplify an idea while losing its key elements

  (C) to extend an idea to a scale beyond which it is practical

  (D) to make a functional premise seem ridiculous

  (E) to apply an idea to an unrelated problem

6. The passage specifies that simplifying the mail system compensated the post office for the costs of uniform postage by

  (A) reducing staff

  (B) increasing patronage

  (C) increasing reliability

  (D) creating postage stamps

  (E) creating a market for written communication

7. The most decisive evidence of Dalhousie having made the right decision in instituting his postal system is:

  (A) Increased reliability

  (B) Reduced corruption in India

  (C) Its previous success in England as Rowland Hill's postal system

  (D) The attainment of a financially sound postal system

  (E) The quieting of critics

8. The experience of Lord Dalhousie in the passage demonstrates that

    (A) larger markets may experience increased transaction costs

    (B) transaction costs are negligible

    (C) postal workers are always corrupt

    (D) letters are the most efficient means of communication

    (E) standardization has the ability to reduce transaction costs

4.13   Passage 13 (Sustainability of homo sapiens)

The positioning of human beings as one of the species with the largest biomasses on earth, and as the leading influence on earth's ecosystems, is the result of the ecological processes which brought about their migration from the African Savannah, and geographically dispersed them throughout the world. It can be said the most rudimentary measure of the success of
5 the species is its position near the top of the aggregate biomass scale. Biomass is the total mass of all living members of a species. For human beings, it is a reflection of their claim on territory, and their consumption of resources as a species. It might be short-sighted to belittle the success of an emerging species or breed for being small in number if it is evident that the members of the species are elegant and well-adjusted. However, the ability to adapt one's
10 habitat to the largest ecosystem, while still retaining the flexibility to deal with local demands on the population may be considered high art in the annals of successful adaptation. It is here that human beings have had nearly unparalleled success (insects being larger in worldwide biomass). As a result human beings exist in huge numbers. It is the fact that human beings have remained in a generally undifferentiated form that allows them to rank highly as a single
15 successful species.

The whole world has been tenanted with life. Human beings are considered unique as they retain their form as they travel from environment to environment. Historically, human beings, like all organisms, may be driven into new areas, or a new environment may spring up around
20 them as a result of drought, competition or geological changes.

Still, human beings have been able to adjust their behavior sufficiently to avoid having nature make such extensive piecemeal adjustments to them that entirely distinct workable alternatives of the same model occupy the new space. It was through such piecemeal adjustments
25 that dinosaurs yielded to pigeons, primitive fish to amphibians and then eventually to whales, even Homo sapiens partially to Neanderthals for a time.

In all cases, these offshoots and also-rans of each species had to co-exist alongside their preceding heritage. Thus, it can be said that many species, through one of their members, were
30 able to succeed in carrying the genetic information of the group into another ecosystem. But eventually, each derivation became classified as something other than its ancestor. In this way, the transfer of genetic material circles the globe, and a species takes on scientifically unique identities at different times and in different places. Humans thus remain distinct not because they are the first to exist in so many habitats, and take advantage of so many resources, but in
35 that they have become one of the relatively few organisms to accomplish widespread population of different habitats while being able to exchange genetic material with others from their group, even if they had been largely geographically isolated over many generations.

1. According to the passage, the high ranking of human beings on a planetary biomass scale directly demonstrates which aspects of their success?

    (A)   their position at the top of the food chain

    (B)   their ability to eat almost anything and engineer their environment

    (C)   their ability to navigate their evolution

    (D)   their consumption of resources and claim on territory

    (E)   their mobility

2.   What makes human beings unique in their colonization of Earth is that

    (A)   they have existed at the same time in several genetic forms

    (B)   genetically they followed a similar path to that of dinosaurs

    (C)   they withstood dispersal while becoming the only surviving species in their genus

    (D)   they are the highest ranked organisms on the biomass scale

    (E)   they carried their genetic code to all parts of the world

3.   According to the passage, what characteristic has allowed human beings to avoid splitting into different species?

    (A)   their ability to reproduce with all the members of their species

    (B)   minimal exposure to geographic isolation

    (C)   the death of all their competing species

    (D)   their ability to adjust their behavior to fit their environment

    (E)   the presence of a very diverse genetic code with many permutations in a large population

4.   The passage quantifies success of any species in terms of

    (A)   the length of time a species has been in its state

    (B)   the population density of a species

    (C)   the population size of a species

    (D)   the global dispersion of its genetic code

    (E)   the degree of adaptation to its environment

5.   In the passage, an important factor in the success of a species is

    (A)   geographic dispersion

    (B)   the elimination of all but a few members of an original species

    (C)   the age of the preceding species

    (D)   mutation

    (E)   sexual selection

6.   In the first sentence of the third paragraph (line 28), "In all cases, ...preceding heritage.," the word "preceding" means

    (A)   existing at the same time

    (B)   receding from

    (C)   diminishing with every generation

    (D)   previous

    (E)   migratory

7. Select the sentence in the passage that discusses genetic material in regard to migration of species.

8. The style of the passage may be considered: Indicate all that apply.

    A   explanatory

    B   argumentative

    C   balanced

4.14 Passage 14 (Abortion law)

The question of legalized abortion in America has largely been considered in terms of moral objections resulting from competing perceptions of human rights and freedom of choice. While the representatives of these views have been influential actors for whom lawmakers must tweak any legislation pertaining to abortion, economists now offer tangible evidence that the abortion issue must be evaluated with some very practical considerations as well. While the importance of the life of a fetus brought-to-term is never a forgotten aspect of the debate on abortion, the relevance of the abortion issue to the lifestyle opportunities for all of society has yet to be weighed heavily in the debate.

However, in their retrospective examination of many years' evidence, John Donahue and Steven Levitt, researchers from Harvard University and the University of Chicago, have pointed out that a suggested correlation between the passage of Roe vs. Wade, the integral piece of abortion empowerment legislation, and reported crime statistics twenty years later can in fact be noted. This is because the period during which most perpetrators engage in the majority of any society's illegal activity is when they are in their late teens and early twenties. Adolescent and young adult males are considered to be the most likely to engage in illegal activity. Their relative inexperience in the world, the paucity of opportunities and their group relationships make them more prone to violence and defiance than women or older males. The researchers note that within a few years of the U.S. Supreme Court Roe vs. Wade decision, up to a quarter of all pregnancies in the United States resulted in abortions. Also, they observe that crime rates between 1985 and 1997 declined. The researchers note that children who would have otherwise been born in the early years after the Roe vs. Wade decision would be reaching their late teen years between 1985 and 1997. However, they were not born, and crime decreased in this time frame. These researchers interpret the termination of an unwanted pregnancy as the rational response of a woman who is not prepared to care for a child. Going forward with an unwanted pregnancy presumably confers on the woman too great a challenge in raising a child she is poorly prepared for, and provides the child with an upbringing that is suboptimal, making him more vulnerable to be party to illegal conduct.

These numbers signify less crime as a result of letting more mothers choose when to have a baby. Crime is financially costly to taxpayers as well. Lawmakers may take heed of this evaluation if they consider Donahue and Levitt's calculation that the economic benefit to society from the termination of unwanted pregnancies may be as high as $30 billion annually. As the ideological arguments over abortion refuse to abate, it may be time for hamstrung legislators to consider new sources of information to simplify their decisions about reopening the question of abortion reform and government aid.

1. The primary difference between the original abortion debate and the present one presented by the researchers is that

   (A) the original debate was subjective while the present debate is objective

   (B) the previous debate was based on ethics while the present debate is based on religion

   (C) the original debate was between completely oppositional parties while the present debate has more heterogeneous participants

      (D)   the previous debate was phrased ideologically while the present debate is concerned with practicality

      (E)   the original debate was supported scientifically while the present debate does not involve science

2. The style of the passage may be

      (A)   persuasive

      (B)   encyclopedic

      (C)   historiographic

      (D)   scientific

      (E)   journalistic

3. One fact which would strengthen the claims of the researchers would be if

      (A)   there was also a sharp decrease in white collar crime during the period of reported statistics

      (B)   there was a decline in the economy during the period of reported statistics

      (C)   states which legalized abortion first saw earlier decreases in crime during the period of reported statistics

      (D)   young males were shown to be avid watchers of violent programming

      (E)   states which legalized abortion first saw increases in crime during the period of reported statistics

4. The implication of the passage regarding unwanted pregnancies is that

      (A)   they are more common in poor families

      (B)   they are more likely to yield males

      (C)   they are more common with women likely to be criminals

      (D)   they are unwanted for a good reason

      (E)   the children resulting from unwanted pregnancies are raised by women

5. What is the assumption of the author regarding the historical abortion debate when presenting Donahue and Levitt's research as the premise for legislative decisions?

      (A)   Both sides were equally wrong.

      (B)   It is not the role of the state to make decisions based on the personal politics of its citizens.

      (C)   The research is weighed as heavily as either of the ideological arguments in the debate.

      (D)   Moral debates on economic issues like abortion cannot ever help in formulating legislation.

      (E)   Legislators view the ideological abortion debate as politically irresolvable for practical purposes.

6. In the last sentence of the last paragraph (line 33) beginning "As the ideological ... gov-
    ernment aid," the author seeks to do what to the abortion debate?

    (A) confine the debate to a small audience

    (B) emphasize its complexity

    (C) increase the influence of narrow interest groups

    (D) argue for a return to a debate on ideological grounds

    (E) simplify the dialogue

7. Which of the following, according to the researchers, depict the practical consideration
    of abortion? Indicate all that apply.

    A   More abortions due to unwanted pregnancies will result in less crime

    B   Crime decreases and money is saved when women have freedom of choice

    C   Abortions of non-violent female children are an unavoidable consequence of allow-
        ing women the right to an abortion

8. In the last sentence of the second paragraph (line 27), the word "suboptimal" could be
    replaced with which of the following without changing its contextual meaning

    (A) inadequate

    (B) almost perfect

    (C) inefficient

    (D) economically advantaged

    (E) second best

9. Select the sentence in paragraph II that provides evidence for the hypothesis that says
    adolescent and young adult males are considered the most likely to engage in illegal
    activities.

4.15   Passage 15 (Surveillance)

While clandestine observation has always played a part in investigation, the most important difference between modern database surveillance and traditional legwork is the proliferation of surveillance of the systems of mundane transactions and of social behavior. No less foreboding is analysis through calculations of regression and methods of associated comparison,
5   to broaden scientifically the range of 'suspicious' behavior in order to justify the oversight of new types of actors, and an increased number of actors. These abilities are being incorporated into a policy about which the public is not aware, and one, which is outside the scope of current legislation.

10   Given that most people regard themselves as 'law abiding,' and that the avoidance of crime, drug abuse and other quality of life infractions rates highly in citizens' priorities, the development of improved surveillance systems is widely seen as a benign invasion that improves policing. This sort of perception has led the U.K., after it was able to pinpoint two young men as being the culprits in the murder of a young boy, to be the country with the most widespread
15   use of surveillance cameras. The impracticality of, and lack of interest in, prosecuting every transgression caught by the system obscures its threat to individual liberty. But while this may keep the disadvantages of surveillance from bringing people to vocal dissent, what should be raised in the public consciousness is that what surveillance changes is the amount of leverage a minority of actors (authorities, bureaucrats, or system managers) receive over the general pop
20   ulation. In any encounter in which one individual must confront the state, the state achieves an advantage by having so many more 'leads' on the individual with which to use bullying tactics, and by engaging in non-judicial activities such as Secret Service searches, the disbanding of rallies, and the detention of political and foreign activists.

25   Compiling a file of criminal activities engaged in by a subject under surveillance is routine. But there can also be an insinuation of an activity that a government uses politically to undermine the position of a subject. That action changes the direction of prosecution, reiterating the importance of, and the reasoning behind, such safeguards as the Miranda acts, designed to protect suspects from incriminating themselves in the absence of their lawyer. The greatest
30   danger is that the rules of criminal justice can be controlled by a bureaucratic, authoritarian organization to prolong detention, and to control the flow of information under conditions of the confinement of a subject, in order to improve the ability of investigators to aid the prosecution. The monopoly which public bureaucracies have on prosecution and investigation allows them to use or disregard official rules in ways that are not transparent to a defendant.
35   It has been shown that increasing the level of surveillance in the public arena does not improve the ability to identify offenders, but improves the ability of the government to operate extra-judicially. This offers authorities the opportunity of manufacturing opportunities for themselves to control behavior in ways that are beyond redress.

 1.   The main concern of the passage regarding improvements in surveillance is

   (A)   the ability to record the activity of everybody

   (B)   the lack of knowledge many people have regarding their surveillance

   (C)   the ability of the government to influence prosecution

   (D)   the disbanding of rallies and detention of political prisoners

(E)   the fact that surveillance is technically illegal

2.   The passage suggests that which of the following is true of most people? Indicate all that apply.

   ☐A They have consented to surveillance

   ☐B They consider that surveillance is more widespread than it was in the past

   ☐C They are unaware of the details of surveillance

3.   According to the passage, which of the following is the most important benefit of improved surveillance for the state?

   (A) It makes it possible to identify and punish criminals far more effectively than before.

   (B) It makes it possible to improve the case against suspects.

   (C) It makes it possible to track down many more criminals.

   (D) It increases the number of jobs available in the public sector.

   (E) It limits the power of the police.

4.   The author would be most likely to agree with which of the following?

   (A) Government should be able to police itself to avoid overstepping its powers.

   (B) Government has a need to protect itself from criminals.

   (C) Government power lies partly outside the law.

   (D) Government is only as trustworthy as its people.

   (E) Government fulfills the wants of the people it represents.

5.   In the passage, the biggest danger of improved surveillance to the public has to do with

   (A) falsely identifying criminals

   (B) allowing the government to act without a process of review

   (C) empowering a minority of the public

   (D) reversing democracy

   (E) increasing costs

6.   It can be inferred from the passage that the author believes that the example of the boys from the U.K. collared in the murder case

   (A) is a good example of the need for surveillance

   (B) validates the use of surveillance

   (C) is not sufficient evidence of the value of surveillance

   (D) is an extreme and isolated case

   (E) is a reproducible result

7. Select the sentence in the last paragraph of the passage that shows that the laws have been passed to safeguard the rights of defendants in case they cannot avail external help to fight for themself.

8. One problem the passage sees with the capacity of government to contribute to the prosecution is

   (A)   the unreasonable punishment of offenders

   (B)   the inability of government to prove its case

   (C)   the monopoly of the government over prosecuting offenders

   (D)   the lack of press access to a case

   (E)   the inability of the public to regulate government

4.16   Passage 16 (Reforms in the European education system)

Universities in Europe are increasingly under the influence of the globalization movement, with examples of this trend widespread across the continent. European universities must answer the perceived needs of multinational corporations, as these firms aspire to draw on an employee base that is borderless, and highly mobile. The system of German engineering schools
5 provides a lucid example for understanding the logic behind transforming European education from a system of segmented and self-contained schools into a system with much more inter-reliance among institutions. Engineering schools are good examples of the myopia of many European institutions because of the common misreading by these schools that they are safe in exclusively focusing on the engineering content of their programs while claiming inde-
10 pendence from political transformations taking place outside their one specific discipline; in outlining the alternative view, a clear example of how closely linked educational environments are to their coursework is provided.

The attitude that professional schools only need to be concerned with the immediate issues
15 pertaining to students' core competencies raises objections from corporate onlookers and many international educators across the engineering fields. Leading concerns for critics of the German university system are that there is limited intercourse between different academies, and that too few courses are taught in English.

20 The lack of availability of English courses in German engineering schools contributes to there being a paucity of international students in German programs. In addition, German engineering students can find themselves painted into a corner midway through their studies if they seek to change the direction of their education. This is because they have limited experience in taking courses in other German universities, and taking engineering courses abroad is the
25 exception, never the rule. Moreover, if these students were to transfer to another school, it is commonplace that much of their course history would not count towards a future degree in a different program. For these reasons, engineering education has come under well-lit scrutiny by businessmen, educators and government officials.

30 In response, engineering administrators have developed a better head for global issues that pertain to their students' desire for varied post-university employment, as well as their students' access to borderless knowledge during their university years. These issues have jointly led educators to identify the need for a new Magna Carta of universities in order to transfer their awareness into solutions. The outcome of this collective attention is the Bologna Dec-
35 laration. Its recommendations are fourfold: to establish a system of comparable degrees to facilitate international competitiveness, to adopt the two cycle (undergraduate and graduate) system of schooling, to establish a standard credit system for classroom work, and to find a way to ensure the quality of programs offered Europe-wide. These improvements in European education increase the international marketability of matriculating students. However,
40 of equal importance, they also increase the mobility of students during their university years.

1. Mention of German sociology programs was probably not included in the passage because

   (A) they do not have the same difficulties as other programs

   (B) they are by nature peopled by a diverse and interactive student body

   (C) their discipline has a heightened focus on external conditions

   (D) one example is sufficient for the purposes of the passage

   (E) multinational corporations have little interest in the graduates of sociology programs, and exert no pressure on the heads of these programs

2. Critics of German university programs seem to prefer that more courses be taught in English in order to

   (A) make German students less likely to attend foreign schools

   (B) make students better qualified to accept employment positions throughout Europe

   (C) make more research available to German students

   (D) make it easier for students from abroad to get credit for German university courses

   (E) encourage more students from abroad to take courses in Germany

3. The term "well-lit scrutiny" in the last sentence of paragraph 3 (line 27) implies

   (A) criticism that is overdue

   (B) critique under the worst of conditions

   (C) critique from many sources is the most thorough

   (D) critique that is deserved

   (E) thoroughly executed critique with many perspectives

4. Select the sentence from paragraph II or III that illustrates that due to few courses taught in English in German university system, there are only a few international students in German programs.

5. The author would most likely agree with the principle that

   (A) the purpose of education is to raise active citizens

   (B) the purpose of education is to create well-rounded individuals

   (C) education should provide students with the flexibility they need to function effectively later in life in whatever field they choose

   (D) education ought to ease cultural tensions

   (E) education should encourage students to work outside of their national origins

6. The Bologna Declaration, mentioned in the middle of the last paragraph, declares the
    goal of: Indicate all that apply.

    A promoting English in European schools

    B ensuring quality of programs offered Europe-wide

    C allowing students to pursue a greater selection of vocational opportunities

7. The author's primary concern about the unlikelihood of engineering students ever chang-
    ing their course of study is best expressed in which statement?

    (A) Engineering degrees should not count towards a variety of credit programs.

    (B) Engineering schools should not be reformed.

    (C) Engineering schools are obligated to prove their competitiveness.

    (D) Engineering schools can no longer overlook the potential in other fields of study.

    (E) It is important to facilitate a variety of choices for students.

8. According to the passage, the importance of students being mobile during their univer-
    sity years is related to

    (A) the need for students to choose a city they like in which to study

    (B) the attractiveness of engineering as a career

    (C) the fact that too few cities have engineering schools

    (D) the desire for an amalgamation of engineering schools

    (E) the need for multinationals to have access to such a labor pool

4.17   Passage 17 (The U.S.'s Nuclear Energy Program)

In 1957, the United States invested in mining the atom for its stores of energy, and funneling this cache into an engineering and military revolution. Wartime uses of atomic energy went largely towards the development of more powerful weapons of mass destruction, though the Department of Defense also utilized it as a more efficient means of long-range propulsion for
5 warships and submersibles. At the same time, the United States Atomic Energy Commission (AEC) created what it would later call the "Plowshare Program." This initiative was intended to develop peaceful applications of modern nuclear power, then under feverish development by scientists primarily for Cold War armaments, and to develop domestic energy sources "too cheap to meter."

10

In August of 1958, scouts from the AEC conducted something of a reconnaissance of Point Hope, in Northwest Alaska. They had selected Ogotoruk Creek in this region as a possible site for the detonation of an atomic bomb. The logic behind the detonation was political and practical. The AEC had decided to bowdlerize the discussion of nuclear weapons by teaming
15 nuclear arms with civil engineering. If the science of Cold War defense could be a proven boon to civil engineering, the AEC felt it could dilute the intense public skepticism towards above ground nuclear testing. Romanticizing their ingenuity, the AEC identified their plan as "Operation Plowshare," alluding to the Biblical panegyric of a world after war when men may someday "beat their swords into plowshares." Atomic technology was presented as being an
20 engineering wonder, the driver of the future instead of the idle sentry needed for John Marshall's Mutual Atomic Destruction policy.

The need for something positive to add to the discussion on the nuclear weapons program came as Russia's successful launch of the Sputnik I satellite into space induced shallow breath-
25 ing in members of America's scientific and engineering elite. The immediate reaction, in the name of one-upmanship, was that "earth excavation" would be the surest demonstration of impressive and beneficial applications of America's existing nuclear capabilities. Their preferred advice was to detonate a 2.4 megaton atomic device on the northwest coast of Alaska, to create a deep water hole facilitating the shipping of coal, timber and oil, while developing
30 Alaska's coast, with obvious benefits for the 48 mainland U.S. states. This proposal would be accepted by the AEC, who designated it 'Project Chariot'. It was marketed to Alaska's financial community and lawmakers, but they remained unconvinced of the plan's commercial viability. The AEC then attempted to sell the plan to the U.S. Congress as a unique opportunity to uncover scientifically the benefits of nuclear energy. However, local unit objected and wrote to
35 President John F. Kennedy of their unease about heavy metals leaching and radiation (a plea backed by detractors in the continental United States). In turn, the AEC came to reconsider the reaction backing their proposed demonstration would realistically earn them. Project Chariot was shelved indefinitely and replaced by less visible undertakings which would be declassified decades later.

   1.   According to the passage, the AEC's purpose of "Operation Plowshare" was to

   (A)   find cheaper ways to produce energy for export

   (B)   innovate in the field of mechanical engineering

   (C)   improve the reputation of the nuclear arms program

   (D)   partake in weapons development

    (E)   diversify export industries

2.   The phrase "obvious benefits for the 48 mainland states" in the mid of third paragraph probably refers to: Indicate all that apply.

    A   a more respectable nuclear arms program

    B   better access to Alaska's resources

    C   political undermining of the arms program's opponents

3.   The selection of Ogotoruk Creek as a site for the detonation was the result of

    (A)   resistance from surrounding populations

    (B)   executive fiat

    (C)   a scan of the area

    (D)   cartographic research and topographical comparisons of Northwest Alaska

    (E)   political decisions

4.   The passage regards American scientists as thinking of Sputnik I as

    (A)   an international political statement

    (B)   a scientific achievement

    (C)   proof of Russia's scientific superiority

    (D)   specious showmanship

    (E)   a precursor to the escalation of the arms race

5.   The attitude of American citizens regarding nuclear weapons testing can be inferred to be

    (A)   doubtful

    (B)   gung-ho

    (C)   competitive

    (D)   inventive

    (E)   complacent

6.   The unwillingness of the AEC to proceed with Project Chariot as planned was the result of

    (A)   disapproval from president Kennedy

    (B)   its inability to achieve its original purpose

    (C)   financial impracticality

    (D)   better technological opportunities in undisclosed plans

    (E)   the politics by detractors

7. The decision by the AEC to name their plan "Operation Plowshare" was related to which characteristic?

    (A) political shrewdness

    (B) humor

    (C) irony

    (D) anticipation

    (E) realism

8. In the context of "Operation Plowshare," what does "beat their swords into plowshares" (line 19) best mean?

    (A) making ugly look pretty

    (B) turning evil into good

    (C) molding useless to useful

    (D) transforming lethal into blunt

    (E) transforming blunt into lethal

4.18   Passage 18 (Mechanized production systems in Europe)

The 1870s were a time of drastic technological challenges to industrializing nations. These challenges resulted in stark differences in the path of development pursued by economies organizing themselves for productive capacity. Manufacturing centers reacted differently to the opportunities blooming in these challenges, each assessing the benefits of rationalization and taking stock of their relevance to its production process. But while scores of industries in a variety of countries predicted some benefits from mechanization, the opportunity to increase production while reducing costs was rightly subject to pervasive debate.

German printing and textile firms showed why industrialization was not a cut and dried process. German and Austrian companies appeared to acknowledge certain impetuses to move over to mechanical production of a particular category of printed cotton handkerchiefs. The production of these handkerchiefs was reliant on the handiwork of individual workmen. These handcrafted articles were the pride and joy of certain regional manufacturers who settled in this niche of the international market. Select German firms obtained the ability to double and triple production while reducing their work force. But risks accompanied this methodology. While this rationalization did bring a substantial fall in the total remuneration of labor, it also significantly lowered the sale price and presented risks of overproduction. Head over heels production of items, with lowered regard for the ability of the market to absorb such production, had latent negative features.

The case of 'double printing' of 'Turkish bonnets' provides one example of why the adoption of fast, cheap production techniques was not a forgone conclusion for established manufacturers. In the case of these bonnets, a sudden, unpredictable drop in the demand for these items, faster than producers could react to changed preferences, concurrent with a monetary crisis in eastern markets, produced friction in the industry, opening up public debate as the relationship between bosses and workers became strident.

Reaction to production innovations was regional. It seemed as if the American system of production, from the start, sidestepped some dangers. It was precisely the American system that had drawn European attention to standardized production, which did offer an increase in profits while containing labor costs and unpredictability. American production was synonymous with standardization, mechanization and mass production. But in actuality, the American system was not uniquely immune to the conditions of the world market. Manufacturers of watches in Switzerland, of scarves in Germany and weavers in 19th century Glarus were reserved about their approval of change. Class disparity and capital rigidity would become built-in pressure points on the American economy. These were just the things that also kept many European producers from settling around a consistent, reproducible pattern of mechanization.

1. The central theme of the passage is that

   (A) the American economy is better equipped to withstand the rigidity of standardization

   (B) negotiation is important in selecting a path of development

   (C) many businesses have failed in their attempt to industrialize

   (D) employed labor is an unavoidable contributor to the development path of companies

(E)   european companies' responses to early industrialization were mixed – some were camphor and some were wet wood

2. With which of the following would the author of this passage would most likely agree? Indicate all that apply.

    [A]   Protectionism can be a valuable asset in industrial development

    [B]   Firms should consider the risks of overproduction

    [C]   Firms should consider the local market situation

3. For the author, the proof of the relevance of considering the local situation is expressed by

    (A)   the example of the American Great Depression

    (B)   the number of watches produced in Switzerland

    (C)   the type of cotton used in handkerchiefs

    (D)   the design of Swiss watches

    (E)   the problems in the bonnet market because of an Eastern currency crisis

4. In the passage, the threat posed by standardization involves

    (A)   lack of variety in color

    (B)   lack of detail

    (C)   elimination of regional differences

    (D)   overproduction

    (E)   alienation of the workforce

5. Select the sentence in the last paragraph of the passage that best illustrates that European companies went sporadically to industrialization.

6. The passage presents the difficulties eventually faced by American industrialization as being

    (A)   the quirks that needed to be ironed out of an unprecedented opportunity

    (B)   unforeseen by American capitalists

    (C)   issues irrelevant to a decision to standardize production

    (D)   a danger of standardized industrialization anticipated by some European industrialists

    (E)   unavoidable

7. One lesson the author might impart to his readers is that

   (A) innovation must overcome the resistance of many self-interested parties before it can rationalize the work process to cut expenses.

   (B) labor will always reduce the rate of progress for socialized countries.

   (C) a benefit can also be a cost down the line.

   (D) national systems of industry are compelled to industrialize by competitive pressure from industrializing nations.

   (E) social agendas should not stand in the way of progress.

8. An appropriate title for this passage might be:

   (A) American industrial pressure on the European regional economy

   (B) Examples of industrial growth and industrial decline

   (C) Discussion on the sporadic start of industrialization in Europe

   (D) Avoiding the American mistake: why industrial innovation will create unemployment and unrest

   (E) Industrial rationalization: getting more for less

4.19   Passage 19 (Gangsta rap)

Gangsta rap is a genre of rap music, with lyrics based on the violence, hedonism and misogyny inherent in the gangster lifestyle. Gangsta rap is typically identified with the American West Coast, while the broader Hip Hop music phenomenon is a potpourri of different styles. While it is unclear whether the violence in gangsta rap is actually based on real violence, the imagery
5 and "thug" iconoclasm of gangsta rap, when packaged with smooth technical production, enabled West Coast rap to distinguish itself within Hip Hop music.

Gangsta rap brought recognition to California as a legitimate music scene capable of African-American social commentary. Ultimately, Gangsta rap embraced a commercial production
10 style, which differentiated it from the music's roots in East Coast rap. The combination of Los Angeles' advanced technical production methods (Los Angeles had an extensive music post-production industry making wide use of synthesizers) and socio-economic and racial messages effectively branded Gangsta rap as a uniquely West Coast style of music. A brash and militant attitude born out of the experiences of disadvantage and racism differentiated West Coast
15 artists from their East Coast counterparts.

While initially all West Coast rap was pigeonholed as Gangsta rap, audiences' appreciation of Gangsta rap as a genre in itself made it possible for Hip Hop to solidify its foothold in American music.

20

Hip Hop had historically evolved among the economically challenged inner cities of the American East Coast. Previously, music of this style, characterized by a heavy emphasis on rhyming with a syncopated beat, had been universally labeled Hip Hop. This definition was challenged by rap group N.W.A.'s Straight Outta Compton. The album's aggressive, stripped-down sound
25 defied the traditional conventions of rap. The group's lyrical celebration of indulgence and unrelenting criticism of an American society which produced a culture of disadvantage for American blacks indicated that the old categories were not sufficient to classify its style.

Ironically, such social commentary found commercial and critical success despite the music's
30 highly commercial production style. Rap aficionados who valued conventional Hip Hop for its authenticity and "street cred" still respected the music despite its slick production techniques. Rappers were thus able to diversify, continuing to appeal to traditional rap audiences, while courting a mainstream bank of fans. Artists such as Dr. Dre, once a young Turk of West Coast rap and the most enduring of the region's vocalists, made use of funk music,
35 notwithstanding its disco lineage, to find a sound that overlaid his message with the "canned beat" post-production style popular in the region's studios. The combination allowed Hip Hop to reach a more heterogeneous audience, an audience that had already become familiar with West Coast production methods. This coupling allowed audiences to contextualize this style of Hip Hop, facilitating the listener's ability to appreciate Gangsta rap's lyricism and musical
40 production style on its own terms rather than solely against the yardstick of East Coast rap. Once West Coast rap was acknowledged as a unique style, fans were able to compare apples to apples, in evaluating the quality of East Coast and West Coast rap.

1. Reason(s) why Gangsta rap became commercially successful is because it

    [A] distinguished itself from East coast rap through rhyming

    [B] synthesized commercial production techniques and biting social observations

    [C] freed vocalists from the drudgery of post-production work

2. The passage suggests that images of violence associated with Gangsta rap led to what outcome?

    (A) It further confused audiences.

    (B) It earned rap commercial success but critics were nonplussed.

    (C) It made rap solely black art with a surprisingly limited range of topics.

    (D) It differentiated Gangsta rap within Hip Hop.

    (E) It coupled indulgence with social activism.

3. The militant, misogynistic and self-indulgent imagery of Gangsta rap was linked to a machined post-production process with what effect?

    (A) It made it possible to understand Gangsta rap in contrast to Hip Hop.

    (B) It alienated audiences.

    (C) It made it possible to discuss Gangsta rap as a new style.

    (D) It did not garner a wide enough audience of followers to achieve critical mass.

    (E) It maintained its street credibility.

4. The attitude of the author towards the hedonism and misogyny of rap lyrics seems to

    (A) be in favor of "Gangsta rap"

    (B) view these characteristics as a means to an end

    (C) doubt the sincerity of their use in rap songs

    (D) dispassionately acknowledge a relationship between the national rise of Gangsta rap and its hedonism and misogyny

    (E) be a non-judgmental observation of the way other people live

5. The importance of "canned beat" (line 35) to the appeal of rap to a more diverse audience implies what about rap's growing listener base?

    (A) They listen to rap's sound more carefully than its message.

    (B) They are not interested in the challenges facing inner city blacks.

    (C) They prefer to listen to a sound they are familiar with.

    (D) They are only willing to support revolutionary ideas if they are impressed by the even-tempered reviews big business can offer.

    (E) They consider the merging of hedonism and politics to be an attack on to their political sensibilities.

6. Select a sentence in last two paragraphs that identifies the origination of Hip Hop music in America.

4.20   Passage 20 (Women's contraceptives)

In the marketing of any new product, the number of potential consumers is not the only variable that a responsible corporation needs to take into consideration in its analysis of potential profits. Even though a given product may have numerous possible uses and a willing market of consumers, the effect of that product on a corporation's image and the public's good will is
5 not guaranteed to be in direct correlation to its commercial success. While some corporations use loss-leader products to increase the profits of unrelated products through their benefits to branding, corporations are equally wary of successful products that will hamper the sales of other product lines and the ability of the corporation to function politically in its market.

10 This reality is most striking in the American contraceptive industry, where endless surveys of women reveal that more choices always seem to equate to more satisfied consumers. Still, there appears to be as many as 100 new contraceptives trapped between development and market. Consider that when we speak of research and development in the contraceptive industry, it is products for females that we concern ourselves with almost exclusively. The un-
15 willingness of corporations to supply female consumers with their products of choice makes a statement about the political inferiority of these women as consumers. Undeniably, while men have a single, relatively simple and effective measure for contraception, women are afforded a cornucopia of alternatives that suit their lifestyles, sexual appetites, and personal habits. However, for women's sake, this patchwork of options should never be viewed as too varied
20 or as colorful enough.

Since it is women who are at risk of an unwanted pregnancy, not men, women have an interest in protecting themselves from the result of their sexual relations. Being proactive about contraception is a safer course of action than relying on the benevolent consideration of their partner
25 and uncertain availability of his "wallet condom." However, while American women spend 3/4 of their reproductive lives evading unwanted pregnancies, and 60% of pregnancies remain unplanned, evidence suggests that Americans view sex in political discourse with weak stomachs even as women privately search for options to protect themselves from unintended circumstances. Based on this, it is evident that conservative pharmaceutical corporations are laden
30 with fear over the reaction of extremist pro-life groups, religious organizations and prominent members of the Republican Party to increased research and even successful marketing of contraceptive alternatives. The enormous market of consumers who would welcome convenient alternatives to the daily "pill," such as a patch, monthly hormone injections, or intrauterine devices, continue to wait much longer than necessary for such products on account of the in-
35 timidating presence of a minority of well-organized non-consumer groups dominating product availability. The solution to this paradox is not only to preach that corporations need to pursue the orthodoxy of their own free market rewards, but also to create open communication about the real sexual lifestyles of women and to organize women around a possible bounty of consumer choices by criticizing their opponents' self-appointed flag-planting missions to a
40 private moral high-ground.

1. The passage states that which of the following can be considered more important than a certain product's profitability?

   (A) corporation's safety

   (B) cost of development

   (C) managerial complications

   (D) supply chain risk

   (E) publicity

2. Select a sentence in paragraph II that conveys that the corporations could bring new contraceptives to market but chose not to.

3. The passage presents the decisions of pharmaceutical corporations and their marketing campaigns as a function of

   (A) corporate responsibility

   (B) canny marketing

   (C) risk taking

   (D) a lack of information

   (E) risk averseness

4. The logic behind the author's presumption that women are under-served by the birth control market is that

   (A) women have less disposable income than men do

   (B) women are unwilling to buy new contraceptive products

   (C) women are more likely than men to sue manufacturers

   (D) women are less uniform than men in their contraceptive needs

   (E) women are not swayed by advertising

5. With which of the following assessments of pharmaceutical market would the author likely agree? Indicate all that apply.

   A   It must be deregulated so that women will have all the choices they need

   B   It must not be subjected to the political influence of extra-market actors

   C   It could provide women with many of the sources of contraceptives they seek

6. Which of the following would be a plausible step, in light of the passage, to increase the willingness of pharmaceutical companies to offer more contraceptive products to women?

   (A) Normalizing discussions on sex through televised discussions

   (B) Increased purchasing of available contraceptive products by women

   (C) Passing legislation that would have men take more responsibility for the consequences of sex

   (D) A demand that pharmaceutical companies lower their prices

   (E) Banning advertising of contraceptive products

7. In the sentence (line 23): "Being proactive about contraception is a safer course of action than relying on the benevolent consideration of their partner and uncertain availability of his wallet condom," the term "uncertain availability" most nearly means

   (A) likelihood

   (B) poor chance

   (C) voluntarism

   (D) good chance

   (E) reliability

8. Which of the following best describes the tone of the author?

   (A) exploratory

   (B) biased

   (C) neutral

   (D) appreciative

   (E) opinionated

4.21   Passage 21 (Influence of the British Poetry of World War One)

Perhaps the most persistent myth about British poetry of World War One is that it became progressively more realistic as soldier-poets learned more about the horrors of modern trench warfare. According to this orthodoxy, the pastoral patriotism of Brooke soon gave way, in the mud and blood of Flanders, to the angry realism of Sassoon and Owen. Thus when we
5 think of World War One poetry today, the poems that instantly come to the minds of most readers are those angry and satirical anti-war poems, such as Sassoon's " Base Details" and "Blighters" and Owen's " Dulce et decorum est," the last being probably the most famous, certainly the most widely anthologized, poem of the War. The problem with this view is that it is based on a relatively small group of poems that, despite their indisputable excellence, are in
10 many ways atypical of the bulk of poetry, including much of the good poetry, written during the War. That poetry was deeply indebted to the nineteenth-century poetic tradition running from Wordsworth and the Romantics through the major Victorian poets to Hardy and beyond. The majority of the war poets worked within this tradition to produce, as has been recently argued, the trench lyric. But it is not just much of the poetry of World War One that belongs
15 to this tradition. The last two paragraphs of what many regard as one of the best memoirs to come out of the War, Siegfried Sassoon's "Memoirs of a Fox-Hunting Man" (1928), emerge from the same tradition and constitute a prose version of the trench lyric composed by the solider-poets.

20 At first glance, a work by the author of some of the bitterest and most angry anti-war poems of World War One may seem an unlikely place to observe the conventions of Romantic poetry, but the ending of "Memoirs of a Fox-Hunting Man" reveals just how insistently the Romantic lyric imposed its form and structure on the imaginations of the writers of World War One.

25 Sassoon, like Rosenberg, does not abandon a set of worn-out poetic conventions so he can write directly and realistically, and hence originally, about it. Rather he translates a pre-existing model into local terms. Even literary memoirists, who are expected to respect the facts, can only be as realistic as the artificial literary conventions available to them will allow them to be. Writers write realistically not by directly " telling it like it is," but by telling it like
30 it's told in literature. They must, as Northrop Frye told us half a century ago, find, or adapt, a set of literary conventions, and out of this old paradigm create a new literary form.

1. The author is mainly concerned with

    (A) repudiating a historical misconception

    (B) discussing the different aspects of the great British poets of the war era

    (C) proving how Sassoon influenced most of the poets and writers of the British war era

    (D) highlighting the importance of nineteenth century Romantics and Victorian poets

    (E) establishing that new paradigms in literature are not created through existing conventions

2. With which of the following options is/are the author most likely to agree? Indicate all that apply.

A   That the most famous poem of the War is not an archetype of the bulk of the War poetry

B   That prose written during the War is inspired by the nineteenth century poetic tradition

C   That poetry did not grow a more and more realistic new style as soldiers got into modern warfare

3. Which of the following options present(s) the author's reasons for believing that the World War One poetry did not become more realistic into a different literary form? Indicate all that apply.

A   The bulk of the poems written during the war poets worked within the nineteenth century poetic tradition to produce literary conventions of trench lyric

B   The pastoral patriotism soon gave way, in the mud and blood of Flanders, to the angry realism of war poets, which led to the formation of trench lyric

C   Writers don't write realistically by abandoning the conventions, but adapting it in literature, while sticking to literary conventions

4. In the passage, the highlighted phrase That poetry refers to

(A) Sassoon's " Base Details" and "Blighters" and Owen's " Dulce et decorum est"

(B) Poetry written by Wordsworth, the Romantics and the major Victorian poets

(C) Angry and satirical anti-war poems

(D) The bulk of poetry written during the War

(E) World War One poetry

5. According to the context of the passage, which of the following can serve as the closest alternative to the highlighted word pastoral ?

(A) Serene

(B) Realistic

(C) Divine

(D) Satirical

(E) Conflicting

6. In which of the following sentences of the passage do/does the author demonstrate that Sassoon's work "Memoirs of a Fox-Hunting Man" is in keeping with the nineteenth century poetic tradition of the Romantics and Victorian poets? Indicate all that apply.

A   I sentence/III paragraph: "Sassoon, like Rosenberg, does not ... and hence originally, about it"

B   Last sentence/I paragraph: "The last two paragraphs of what many ... composed by the solider-poets"

C   I sentence/II paragraph: "At first glance, a work by the ... the writers of World War One"

7. Which of the following best describe the author's attitude towards the view that increasingly modern warfare rendered poetry of the war more and more angry and sarcastic?

    (A) Qualified enthusiasm

    (B) Utter disgust

    (C) Healthy regard

    (D) Cautious dubiety

    (E) Arrant disapprobation

8. Select a sentence in the second or third paragraph in which the author quotes another author to prove that writers create new forms using adaptation.

4.22   Passage 22 (New Evidence Clears a Long Puzzle)

Scientists have long speculated as to why animal species didn't burgeon sooner, once sufficient oxygen covered the Earth's surface. Animals first appeared and began to prosper at the end of the Proterozoic period, about 600 to 700 million years ago—but the billion-year stretch before that, when there was also plenty of oxygen, no animals. Evidently, the air was
5   not oxygen-rich enough then. The oxygen levels during the billion or more years before the rise of animals were only 0.1 percent of what they are today. While there is no question that genetic and ecological innovations are ultimately behind the rise of animals, there is also no question that for animal life to flourish a certain level of oxygen is required.

10 The evidence was found by analyzing chromium isotopes in ancient sediments from China, Australia, Canada and the United States. Chromium is found in the Earth's continental crust, and chromium oxidation, the process recorded by the chromium isotopes, is directly linked to the presence of free oxygen in the atmosphere. Specifically, samples deposited in shallow, iron-rich ocean areas were studied, near the ancient shoreline and compared with other sam-
15 ples taken from younger shoreline locales deposited in similar settings but known to have higher levels of oxygen.

The question about the role of oxygen in controlling the first appearance of animal has long vexed scientists. Previous estimates, which put the oxygen level at 40 percent of today's condi-
20 tions during pre-animal times, were based on very loose constraints, leaving open the possibility that oxygen was already plenty high to support animal life, and shifting the absence of animal life before the end of the Proterozoic to other controls. Oxygen levels were highly dynamic in the early atmosphere, with the potential for occasional spikes. However, it also seems clear that there are first-order differences in the nature of Earth surface chromium cycling before
25 the rise of animals versus the time interval coincident with their first appearance—implying vanishingly small oxygen conditions before. These differences are recorded in a dramatic shift in the chromium isotope data, with clear signals of cycling beneath a more oxygen-rich atmosphere at the time the animals appear.

1. Which of the following provides the most accurate inference implied by the new evidence?

   (A) Animal species had flourished sooner than is believed by the scientists

   (B) There was plenty of free oxygen before the end of the Proterozoic period

   (C) The evidence from Canada and US proves the existence of chromium cycles in the Proterozoic period

   (D) Before the end of the Proterozoic period, the atmosphere contained much less oxygen than had been estimated

   (E) Before the end of the Proterozoic period, the atmosphere contained oxygen level at 40 percent of today's level

2. Which of the following, if true, would weaken the claim made in the final paragraph?

   (A) Chromium oxidation is the only reliable indicator of oxygen levels poetry

   (B) Oxygen levels required to sustain animal life are far higher than currently believed

    (C)   Plant life evolved much before animal life did

    (D)   Chromium samples from other continents matches the samples from Australia

    (E)   Shoreline locales are not quite representative of the rest of the landform

3. Which of the following best describes the role of the second paragraph in the whole passage?

    (A)   Disputing the concept mentioned earlier

    (B)   Elaborating on the contents given in the first paragraph

    (C)   Buttressing the claim in previous paragraph

    (D)   Detailing an alternative explanation

    (E)   Offsetting the theory of the first paragraph

4. Which of the following explains the chief concern of the passage?

    (A)   Refuting a novel theory

    (B)   Discussing a scientific phenomenon

    (C)   Explaining the origin of life

    (D)   Supporting an original hypothesis

5. Which of the following was/were believed to be true by scientists? Indicate all that apply.

    A   Oxygen level was 40 percent of what it is today

    B   Animals first appeared 600 to 700 million years ago

    C   Oxygen level did not influence the appearance of animals

6. Select a sentence in passage in which the author presents latest estimate of oxygen levels.

7. According to the passage, which of the following statements is/are still considered true? Indicate all that apply.

    A   Oxygen is necessary for animals to prosper

    B   Oxygen levels were highly dynamic in the early atmosphere

    C   Atmosphere contained plenty of oxygen around the time the animals appeared

8. Which of the following would perfectly replace the highlighted word `burgeon` as used in the context of the passage?

    (A)   Flourish

    (B)   Dwindle

    (C)   Wane

    (D)   Change

    (E)   Evolve

4.23 Passage 23 (A new perspective on the classical black hole solution)

In a series of pioneering papers, starting in 1979, Leonard S. Abrams discussed the physical sense of the black hole solution. Abrams claimed that the correct solution for the gravitational field in a Schwarzschild space, an empty space filled by a spherically symmetric gravitational field produced by a spherical source mass, shouldn't lead to a black hole as a physical object.

5

It is certain that if there is a formal error in the black hole solution, committed by the founders of this theory, in the period from 1915-1920's, a long list of research produced during the subsequent decades would be brought into question. Consequently, Abrams' conclusion has attracted the attention of many physicists, since it directly challenges the classical solution

10 and the subsequent work.

Stephen J. Crothers, building upon the work of Abrams, was able to deduce solutions for the gravitational field in a Schwarzschild metric space produced in terms of a physical observable radius. Crothers' solutions fully verify the initial arguments of Abrams. Therefore, the claim

15 that the correct solution for the gravitational field in a Schwarzschild space does not lead to a black hole as a physical object requires serious attention.

The new solution, by Crothers, doesn't eliminate the classical " black hole solution," i.e. the line-element thereof, produced by the founders of the black hole problem, but represents the

20 perspective of a real observer whose location is in the real Schwarzschild space itself, inhomogeneous and curved, not by quantities in an abstract flat space tangential to it at the point of observation as it was previously, in the classical solution. Consequently, the new solution opens a doorway to new research on the specific physical conditions accompanying gravitational collapse in Schwarzschild space. This can now be studied in a reasonable manner both

25 through a purely theoretical approach and with the methods of numerical relativity.

1. According to the passage, which of the following can be inferred about the classical black hole solution? Indicate all that apply.

   A It discusses a line-element in its solution

   B Gravitational field in Schwarzschild space should cause black hole as a physical object

   C It represents perspective of an observer in an abstract flat space tangential to Schwarzschild space

2. According to the passage, which of the following would result, if the classical black hole solution is refuted?

   (A) Crothers and Abrams would be considered unworthy scientists

   (B) New research on specific conditions in gravitational collapse in Schwarzschild space will not occur

   (C) Theoretical approaches to the solution will fail

   (D) Research based on the classical solution will come under doubt

   (E) Abrams' conclusion will be disproved

3. Select a sentence in the passage in which the author voices the opinion about Crothers' solution with respect to the classical solution.

4. Which of the following most closely describes the role of the second paragraph in the context of the entire passage?

    (A) Add support to the work of Abrams

    (B) Discuss specifics of Crothers' work

    (C) Lay the foundation to introduce Crothers' work

    (D) Explain the implications of Abrams' work

    (E) Outline the actual interpretation by Abrams

5. Which of the following would be the most appropriate title for the given passage?

    (A) Pioneers of Schwarzschild space

    (B) Novel approach to the black hole solution

    (C) Work by Abrams and Crothers

    (D) Classical black hole solution

    (E) The Schwarzschild space paradox

6. According to the passage, which of the following is/are points of differences between the classical black hole solution and that proposed by Abrams? Indicate all that apply.

    A The vantage point of the observer

    B The nature of the space

    C The line-element

7. Which of the following would most likely come about if a physical black hole is not created from the correct solution for the gravitational field in a Schwarzschild space?

    (A) A symmetric gravitational field will be produced by a spherical source mass

    (B) Abrams and Crothers' work would be refuted

    (C) The classical black hole solution will emerge unaltered

    (D) A gravitational collapse in Schwarzschild space would not occur

    (E) Research on the classical solution will be open to challenge

8. Which of the following can be inferred as possible characteristics of the classical black hole solution? Indicate all that apply.

    A The observer is located in Schwarzschild space

    B The space is abstract and flat

    C It excludes line-element

Chapter 5

Answer Key

Passage 1

| (1) C | (3) C | (5) See solution | (7) A, B & C |
| (2) B | (4) E | (6) C | |

Passage 2

| (1) D | (3) B | (5) See solution | |
| (2) C | (4) A & C | | |

Passage 3

| (1) D | (3) E | (5) B | |
| (2) D | (4) A | | |

Passage 4

| (1) E | (3) A, B, & C | (5) D | |
| (2) See solution | (4) A | (6) A | |

Passage 5

(1) D	(4) A	(7) C	
(2) A	(5) C	(8) A	
(3) C	(6) See solution	(9) B	

Passage 6

(1) C	(3) See solution	(5) C
(2) C	(4) A & B	

Passage 7

(1) A & C	(3) E	(5) E	(7) C
(2) See solution	(4) A	(6) B	

Passage 8

(1) E	(3) A	(5) E	(7) C
(2) C	(4) C	(6) A	(8) B

Passage 9

(1) B	(3) See solution	(5) B	(7) A
(2) C	(4) C	(6) C	

Passage 10

(1) A	(3) D	(5) See solution	(7) B
(2) A, & B	(4) A	(6) E	

Passage 11

(1) D	(3) C	(5) B	(7) D
(2) B	(4) See solution	(6) C	(8) C

Passage 12

(1) A	(3) B & C	(5) C	(7) D
(2) See solution	(4) A	(6) B	(8) E

Passage 13

(1) D	(3) D	(5) A	(7) See solution
(2) C	(4) C	(6) D	(8) A & C

Passage 14

(1) D	(4) D	(7) A & B
(2) A	(5) E	(8) A
(3) C	(6) E	(9) See solution

Passage 15

(1) C	(3) B	(5) B	(7) See solution
(2) B & C	(4) C	(6) C	(8) C

Passage 16

(1) C	(3) E	(5) C	(7) E
(2) E	(4) B	(6) B	(8) E

Passage 17

(1) C	(3) C	(5) A	(7) A
(2) B	(4) A	(6) B	(8) B

Passage 18

(1) E	(3) E	(5) See solution	(7) C
(2) B & C	(4) D	(6) D	(8) C

Passage 19

(1) A & B	(3) C	(5) C
(2) D	(4) D	(6) See solution

Passage 20

(1) E	(3) E	(5) D	(7) A
(2) A	(4) D	(6) A	(8) E

Passage 21

(1) A	(3) A & C	(5) A	(7) D
(2) A B & C	(4) D	(6) C	(8) See solution

Passage 22

(1) D	(3) C	(5) A	(7) A
(2) E	(4) E	(6) A B & C	(8) See solution

Passage 23

(1) A B & C	(3) See solution	(5) B	(7) B
(2) D	(4) D	(6) A & B	(8) See solution

Chapter 6

Solutions

6.1 Passage 1 (Whistleblower laws)

Understanding the Passage

This is a long passage of low difficulty level on business policy and law.

Whistleblower laws are meant to encourage employees to expose corruption and mismanagement at the work level. The author gives an example of the role of a whistleblower in a factory in the manufacturing sector where a person may physically pull or blow a whistle to halt production in order to stop a faulty production process.

The federal government has passed legislation to provide incentives, as well as protection, to government employees who observe their co-workers and managers following unlawful practices or exercising abuse of their position.

Increasingly, the term whistleblower has been associated with somebody who informs about trustworthy co-workers. [*So, the people who tell the authorities about some employee's misconduct or unlawful behavior get branded as being untrustworthy and disloyal towards their group.*] However, whistleblower laws seek to change this public impression. The author expresses regret about the fact that government bureaucracy and state-financed corporations can at times appear to operate above the law, ignoring the administration, avoiding the discipline of a formal review, and doing their business while largely being able to hide themselves from public scrutiny. Because of these possible ill-effects, it is especially important that courageous employees should stand up on behalf of the voters to whom these institutions are answerable and bring out in the open any wrongful conduct in such organizations. Since an employee who decides to report illegal or unreasonable behavior to the authorities regularly finds that he is harassed with intense inquiry, or even with made-up charges if he continues to stay at his place of employment, it is necessary that the act of exposing unethical performance be appealing enough so that any harassment posed by angry co-workers and vengeful bosses should not sway the whistleblower from revealing the wrong-doing. Due to this threat, whistleblower laws often provide the whistleblower with a percentage of the money considered 'saved' by his honesty. Moreover, a settlement amount or court award is often paid to the successful whistleblower to compensate for the risk he has carried in exposing the co-worker.

Additionally, the whistleblower is simultaneously given protection against undue dismissal and other vengeful acts that a corporation or department might privately take against the claimant. These incentives were meant to make whistleblower laws both a progressive reform and effective legislation, so much so that the incentive aspects of whistleblower laws have not only brought many nervous employees forward to report co-workers, but has also encouraged some to go into the business of spying on suspicious employers with an intent towards reporting them to government investigators and collecting their incentive once a decision is reached.

The passage discusses whistleblower laws. It highlights the challenges an employee could face if he decides to report a co-worker of wrong-doing. The co-worker could be vengeful and the whistleblower employee's institution could even harass him. Whistleblower laws encompass measures to induce more upright employees to come forward by way of protecting their interest through incentives, court-settlement awards, and employment preservation.

Main point: Potent whistleblower laws are all-encompassing.

1. This is a Specific Detail question.

    A   This option is **correct**. One of the purposes of whistleblower laws is to encourage employees to report corruption in the workplace. This is clearly mentioned in the first sentence of the passage.

    B   This option is **incorrect** because whistleblower laws were not put in place to penalize corrupt practitioners; it is put in place to protect whistleblowers, encouraging them to report corruption. Penalizing corrupt practitioners is out of scope for the Whistleblower Laws.

    C   This option is also **correct**. It is supported by the sentence "...an employee who decides to report illegal or unreasonable behavior to the authorities regularly finds himself to be the subject of intense scrutiny, or even fabricated accusations, if he continues to stay at his place of employment, it is necessary to make the act of bringing unethical performance to light appealing enough to outweigh the disincentives posed by angry co-workers, punitive bosses..."

    The correct answers are A & C.

2. This is an Inference question.

    The reference of financial inducements, meaning incentives to whistleblowers is talked about in the last paragraph, so we must move directly to the last small paragraph.

    Lawmakers' concerns are supported by the sentence: *These (pecuniary, meaning 'financial') incentives were meant to make whistleblower laws both a progressive reform, and effective legislation.* Without these incentives, potential whistleblowers might be too scared of likely repercussions and not step forward at all.

3. This is a specific detail question.

    (A)   This option is **incorrect** because it is irrelevant; no such thing has been discussed in the passage.

    (B)   This option is **incorrect** because no such thing has been discussed in the passage.

    (C)   This option is **incorrect** because the question asks about the effectiveness of whistleblower laws, and not about how much they are realistic.

    (D)   This option is **incorrect** because patriotism in relation to whistleblowers is not discussed in the passage.

    (E)   This is the **correct** answer, as explained by the sentence (lines 31-36): "incentives were meant to make whistleblower laws both a progressive reform, and **effective** legislation, so much so that the lucrative prospects of being a whistleblower has not only brought many reluctant employees forward, but also has encouraged some to go into the business of poaching through phonebooks for dubious employers with an eye towards reporting them to government investigators and collecting their prize."

The correct answer is E.

4. This is an inference question.

   (A) This is the **correct** answer since the passage makes a distinction between legal reforms and effective whistleblower legislation to which lawmakers seek to attach financial inducements. The existence of ineffective legislation would imply that there have been laws passed but they have not had the full expected reach.

   (B) This option is **incorrect** because no such thing has been discussed in the passage.

   (C) This option is **incorrect** because it does not relate to the question asked.

   (D) This option is **incorrect** because it is irrelevant.

   (E) This option is **incorrect** because it is not relevant to the question asked.

The correct answer is A.

5. This is an inference question.

   Option E is the correct answer since 'oiling their machinery' typically means keeping the day-to-day means of the business functioning. Even if you do not know the meaning of 'oiling the machinery', you can infer it from the context of the passage. Its meaning must be in the range of working for the interest of self. Other options do not qualify as correct.

The correct answer is E.

6. This is a tone question from general category.

   Reading the passage, we can understand that the attitude of the author towards whistle-blower legislation is approving, or positive. Option B is the correct answer since all the other options designate a negative connotation to the author's attitude towards whistle-blower laws. The negative connotation is not supported by the passage. In addition, option B is supported by the sentences (Lines 13-19): "Government bureaucracy and state-financed corporations can at times.... Therefore, it is especially important to make it possible for courageous employees...." and the lines 31-36: "These incentives were meant.... but also have encouraged some to go into the business of poaching.... once a decision is reached."

The correct answer is B.

7. This is an inference question.

   Option C is the best answer since the plaintiff in this case refers to the person suing the business or government to obtain a claim or compensation or to correct a practice that he asserts is wrong.

The correct answer is C.

6.2   Passage 2 (The WTO and sustainable development)

Understanding the Passage

This is a short passage of low difficulty level on business and economics. A standard GMAT short passage asks you 3-4 questions, but we have asked you 5 questions in this passage. You should spend 2.5–3 minutes reading the passage and 60-75 seconds answering each question; so, in all, you should spend approximately 6 minutes on a short passage. For this passage, you should take approximately 8-9 minutes.

Environmental concern and development are inseparably linked *[This is the author's opinion]*. Experience demonstrates that environmental standards and cleaner production are compatible with and supportive of economic growth *[Basically, it is possible to have economic growth/profits while being environmentally conscious]*. Healthy people and ecosystems are more productive *[According to the author, being eco-conscious leads to more productivity]*. This link between economic growth and environmental improvement is enshrined, together with the commitment to development, in the World Trade Organization's Preamble, which includes sustainable development as a basic objective of the trading system *[The WTO also agrees that economic growth is linked to environmental consciousness]*. In endorsing this concept, despite some reservations, WTO members unanimously recognized that trade and the economic growth the WTO helps to create must be fostered in the context of sustainable development, which integrates economic, social, and environmental policies *[Initially, some members did not want to but eventually did recognize that all trade and economic prosperity has to come only after being eco-conscious. This is why the WTO's Preamble endorses this concept]*. Economic growth, sustainable development, and opportunity for citizens are fundamental goals of every society *[These should be goals of every society]*. And the record of the past five decades clearly shows how the trading system has helped us reach some of these goals. [For five decades, we, the people, have strived to reach some of these goals, but have not succeeded in all.]

Since 1960, the WTO has negotiated a 90% drop in tariffs and non-tariff barriers to trade have also been dramatically reduced *[So, the WTO has managed to attain a lot of economic growth]*. Moreover, market access for agriculture and services will be further expanded upon conclusion of the next Uruguay Round *[Further growth will be achieved in the economic sphere]*. Thus, since 1960 trade has grown fifteen-fold; world economic production has quadrupled; and world per capita income has more than doubled *[All in all, economic growth and opportunity goals of the WTO have come to bear fruit]*. However, has the World Trade Organization done enough to promote sustainable development and protect the environment? *[The author questions whether the WTO has succeeded in achieving economic goals while protecting the environmental.]* In reference to the concept of sustainable development, the Brundtland Commission Report of 1987 stated "we must meet the needs of the present without compromising the ability of future generations to meet their own needs." *[The author inserts some report's quote here to describe what is meant exactly by "sustainable development," probably to imply that it has not been achieved.]* Have any laws been made to make sustainable development mandatory? *[Again, this is a rhetorical question to imply that the WTO has probably not worked in a concrete way towards sustainability goals.]* The answer is yet to be presented by the WTO. [Thus, the author believes that the WTO has not kept up its promises for sustainability development.] Taking into account state practice, treaty law, international case law, and relevant legal literature, sustainable development is not yet a norm of international law *[So, nowhere is "sustainable development" mandatory or compulsory even though it is one of the main goals mentioned earlier].* Currently it reflects a policy goal of the international community *[It is given the status of only policy goal, but not mandatory law].* This method of taking a concept so important only as a precautionary guideline has brought the WTO's intentions regarding sustainable development into question *[The author believes that by not taking sustainable development importantly enough, because the WTO did not make it a mandatory law, the WTO's intentions about environmental consciousness are in doubt.].*

The author first introduces sustainable development and then explains the WTO's official position on it. Then data about the WTO's economic goals is given and the WTO's success at meeting them. The author then questions the WTO's lack of success at meeting sustainable development goals.

Main Point: While the WTO has met its trade and economic goals, it lacks in its environment goals.

1. This is a main purpose question from the general category.

    The question asks us to title the passage. For that, we must understand the purpose of the passage. The passage talks about the environment being linked to development. Then it introduces the WTO and its various functions, and its endorsement of the connection between sustainable development and economic growth. Later the passage explains how trade has grown dramatically because of the WTO's policies. However, in the second half of the second paragraph, the author raises questions about the WTO's environmental achievements. Thus, the author wishes to draw attention to the WTO's performance regarding sustainable development goals.

    Let us analyze each option one by one.

    (A) This answer is **incorrect** because it is too general and does not discuss the environmental concerns mentioned in the passage.

    (B) This answer is **incorrect** because it implies that the WTO has taken some actions to protect the environment, but the author implies otherwise.

    (C) This answer is **incorrect** because it's too general and does not even mention the WTO even though the author specifically discusses it.

    (D) This is the **correct** answer. It includes both the WTO and the environment, the two main areas in the passage.

    (E) This answer is **incorrect.** Though it correctly addresses the issue, it's too general and does not even mention the environment and the WTO, even though the author specifically discusses both.

    The correct answer is D.

2. This is a detail question.

The question asks us to look at a specific detail from the passage about the conditions under which the WTO endorsed the link between the environment and sustainable development. The answer to this question can be found in the first paragraph which states that the WTO accepts that care for the environment is compatible and interlinked with business and that sustainable development is one of its goals.

Let us analyze each option one by one.

(A) This answer is **incorrect** because it is too general and does not specifically mention sustainable or environmental development.

(B) This answer is **incorrect** because it is too extreme. The passage does not mention that the WTO committed itself only to environmental concerns.

(C) This is **correct.** It matches our deductions. The WTO members also recognized that the environment and development are interlinked and so added sustainable development as one of the WTO's goals.

(D) This answer is **incorrect** because there is no concept of temporary development discussed in the passage.

(E) This answer is **incorrect** because the WTO did not accept sustainable development as a goal only by understanding healthy ecosystems, but by recognizing that environment and development are interlinked.

The correct answer is C.

3. This is a function question from the general category.

To understand why the author presents that question, we must understand the point he is making. The author presents the given question and then defines sustainable development and presents another question. The gist of that entire part is that while the WTO is supposed to promote sustainable development, it hasn't. Thus, the role of the question in that paragraph is to introduce the idea that the WTO hasn't done enough for sustainable development.

Let us analyze each option one by one.

(A) This answer is **incorrect** because the author does not question the WTO to assess its actions, but rather to point out its lack of action towards the environment.

(B) This is the **correct** answer. This matches our deductions. The author does present the question to imply that the WTO hasn't kept up on its work towards sustainable development.

(C) This answer is **incorrect** because the author does not suggest anything to imply that sustainable development is not possible.

(D) This answer is **incorrect** because the author does not challenge the WTO, only its lack of action towards sustainable development.

(E) This answer is **incorrect** because the author does not question the WTO generally on its actions, but rather on its lack of action towards the environment.

The correct answer is B.

4. This is a specific inference question.

    We have to find an option with which the author would **agree.**

    Let us analyze each option one by one.

    [A] This option is **correct.** The author will agree with the statement that it is not necessary for a country or an organization to compromise its economic goals to achieve environmental goals; both can be achieved together.

    [B] This is the **incorrect** because the author would disagree with this statement. The author does not think that the WTO is NOT more motivated by business. In fact, the author thinks probably that the WTO is more motivated by business than by environmental concerns since the author thinks that WTO's sustainable goals are in question.

    [C] This option is also **correct.** The author would agree that the WTO has not been instrumental in protecting the environment.

    The correct answers are A & C.

5. This is a Specific inference question.

    This question asks us to fetch a specific sentence that illustrates that more reductions in tariffs and trading obstacles are going to take place. This is given in the second sentence of the second paragraph—*Moreover, market access for agriculture and services will be further expanded upon conclusion of the next Uruguay Round.* More reductions in tariffs and trading obstacles is implied by the use of the phrase*market access for agriculture and services will be further expanded.*

6.3 Passage 3 (Climate change due to volcanic eruptions)

Understanding the Passage

This is a short passage of high difficulty level on geology. A standard GMAT short passage asks you 3-4 questions, but we have asked you 5 questions in this passage. You should spend 2.5–3 minutes reading the passage and 60-75 seconds answering each question; so, in all, you should spend approximately 6 minutes on a short passage. For this passage, you should take approximately 8–9 minutes.

Previous studies on understanding the potential of Icelandic volcanic eruptions in modifying the environment have concentrated on the degree of induced climate change, but the complex interaction of the processes which control the atmospheric circulation patterns of the earth were imperfectly understood. Even with advanced equipment, they have proved difficult to model. *(There were previous studies which checked whether Icelandic volcanic eruptions have the potential to modify the environment. These studies concentrated on the degree of "induced" or brought-about climate change [as opposed to natural climate change]. However, even then, the complexities of the interaction processes that control the atmosphere were not fully understood. Even with advanced equipment, they were difficult to model into accurate conceptual details. The inference the author wants to drive home is that those studies would be, at best, limited, given the lack of understanding of the processes.)*

Documentary evidence suggests that during the Laki fissure eruption in 1783, severe acid damage to crops occurred in northern Europe, and acid pulses killed fish in Scotland.*(There is evidence that a volcanic eruption, in Laki [in Iceland], in 1783, acid probably caused crop damage and killed fish in Northern Europe, possibly modifying the environment.)* Although an induced climatic change was probably the primary mechanism responsible, the degree to which atmospheric circulation responds to volcanic forcinh is uncertain, so it is unsatisfactory to suggest that stress in the paleo-environmental record, associated with a volcanic eruption, has inevitably occurred in response to volcanic forcing of the climate. *(While we can say that it was not a natural climate change but an induced one that caused the damage, the degree to which the Laki volcano forced the change cannot be determined. So, we must not suggest that volcanic eruption forced the climate change and brought about a paleo-environmental (an environment at a period in the geological past) record change. Stress (power) [killing fish and damaging crops] was directly a result of that eruption).* The only volcanic eruptions which possess the theoretical ability to bring about climate change are those which emit substantial volumes of volatile gases. *(Not all, only some volcanic eruptions possess the ability to bring climate change. The ones that can change climate are those that emit substantial amounts of volatile gases.)* "Climate change theories" require that these be injected into the stratosphere and remain in the troposphere. *(Theories state that these emitted gases from such volcanic eruptions are injected into the stratosphere* (the second major layer of Earth's atmosphere, just above the troposphere) *and remain in the troposphere* (The troposphere is the lowest layer of Earth's atmosphere and the site of all weather on Earth.)). They must inevitably settle and be deposited on the surrounding sea and land rather than distant ecosystems.*(These gases will typically settle and be deposited on the surrounding sea of the volcanic eruptions and not in some distant land).* Despite plenty of excavations, such sedimentary evidence still eludes around the Laki central fissure. *(No sedimentation, the kind associated with the climate-changing volcanic eruptions, has been found around the Laki area. The inference being implied here is that it is unlikely Laki brought about the kind of climate change as is believed.)*

In the above passage, the author starts by introducing the concept that volcanic eruptions are thought to cause induced climate change but immediately presents the fact that there's not enough evidence to say so because the degree of complex atmospheric interactions isn't understood yet. He further makes this point using the Laki eruption, which is believed to have caused damage in Northern Europe, and possibly brought about climate change. However, the author explains that if the Laki eruption had brought about climate change, there would be volcanic emissions that would have settled around the sea and land. Such deposits haven't been found yet, so it is likely that the Laki eruption is not fully responsible for the climate change.

Main Point: To prove that volcanic eruptions are not very likely to cause induced climate change, and definitely not to the degree believed.

1. This is a main purpose question from the general category.

   Let's analyze the options one by one.

   (A) This option is **incorrect** because the author is not concerned with how eruptions work, but rather what their effects are.

   (B) This option is **incorrect** because the author does not discuss various theories as the main purpose. He merely presents them to make one point only. This is not his main purpose.

   (C) This option is **incorrect** because the author does not provide any evidence towards explaining climate change in Northern Europe, but merely explains that there is lack of such.

   (D) This is the **correct** answer. This matches our deductions.

   (E) This option is **incorrect** because the author does not discuss any controversial hypothesis at all.

   The correct answer is D.

2. This is a detail question.

   The question asks us to locate some detail about previous studies of volcanic eruptions. This is mentioned in the first paragraph. There were previous studies to check whether Icelandic volcanic eruptions had the potential to modify the environment. However, the complexities of the interaction processes that control the atmosphere were not fully understood. Even with advanced equipment, they were difficult to model into accurate conceptual details.

   Let's analyze the options one by one.

   (A) This option is **incorrect** because we cannot infer that the findings were necessarily refuted. The author calls them into question but does not conclusively refute them.

(B) This option is **incorrect** because the passage states that the eruptions were likely not responsible, rather than responsible, for the climate change.

(C) This option is **incorrect** because the previous studies were more likely accepted by existing theories than not. We cannot necessarily say that they were rejected.

(D) This is the **correct** answer. This matches our deductions.

(E) This option is **incorrect** because the passage states that the eruptions were likely not responsible for the climate change.

The correct answer is D.

3. This is a specific inference question.

We know that there is evidence that acid from a volcanic eruption in Laki in 1783 probably caused crop damage and killed fishes in Northern Europe, possibly modifying the environment. However, the degree to which the Laki volcano forced the change cannot be determined. So, we must not suggest that the volcanic eruption forced the climate change and brought about paleo-environmental stress [killing fish and damaging crops]. Also, no sedimentation has been found around the Laki area and thus there is no proof that Laki brought about the kind of climate change as is believed.

Let's analyze the options one by one.

(A) This option is **incorrect** because no such thing is mentioned in the passage.

(B) This option is **incorrect** because no such evidence is presented in the passage to infer this.

(C) This option is **incorrect** because the passage does not provide information to specifically infer this. It merely states that Laki emissions deposits, if there are any, haven't been found yet.

(D) This option is **incorrect** because this is the opposite of the implied inference. The author makes a case to suggest that the degree to which the eruption could affect change in the climate of Northern Europe is uncertain. The evidence in Laki also does not support it; hence, we cannot say that the eruption did so.

(E) This is the **correct** answer. This matches our deductions.

The correct answer is E.

4. This is a Reasoning question on weakening the conclusion.

The question asks us to prove the author incorrect and prove that Icelandic eruptions did bring about induced climate change. We need to find evidence to prove that. The author bases his claim that Icelandic eruption probably did **not** bring about induced climate change on the lack of sedimentation associated with the climate-changing volcanic eruptions around Laki area. Thus, to prove that Icelandic eruptions did bring about induced climate change, we need to prove either that the Laki volcano emitted volatile gases that were injected into the stratosphere and troposphere that eventually got deposited in surrounding land and sea. Such evidence would prove the author incorrect.

Let's analyze the options one by one.

A — This is the **correct** answer. This matches our deductions.

B — This option is **incorrect** because this is out of scope. Mere climate fluctuations do not necessarily prove the author wrong that volcanic eruption causing those fluctuations and eventually leading to climate change. Climatic fluctuation is a temporary phenomenon, and climate change is permanent.

C — This option is **incorrect** because this is too generic. Environmental records of Europe will only show events but not necessarily prove that those events happened because of volcanic eruption in Laki.

The correct answer is A.

5. This is a function question from the general category.

We are asked to find the purpose of the first paragraph with respect to the second paragraph, i.e. what is the first paragraph explaining and what is the connection to the second paragraph. The second paragraph proves the point that the Icelandic eruption probably did **not** bring about induced climate change. The first paragraph discusses the belief that the Icelandic eruption did bring about induced climate change only to later say that there's not enough evidence to say so because the degree of complex atmospheric interactions isn't understood yet. Thus, the author makes a point in first paragraph and then explains it in detail in the second paragraph. So, the first paragraph served as a sort of introduction to the details in the second paragraph.

Let's analyze the options one by one.

(A) This option is **incorrect** because the author does not discuss multiple theories at all.

(B) This is the **correct** answer. This matches our deductions.

(C) This option is **incorrect** because the author makes the opposite point that the climate change was not the result of the volcanic eruption completely.

(D) This option is **incorrect** because this point is being made in the second paragraph. The first paragraph merely states this point but the second paragraph **proves** it. This is a tricky option.

(E) This option is **incorrect** because the author implies the opposite of this in the entire passage.

The correct answer is B.

6.4 Passage 4 (Stock options in CEO pay)

Understanding the Passage

This is a short passage of intermediate difficulty level on business policy.

Defenders of runaway CEO pay argue that market forces are at work determining executive compensation levels and CEOs are rewarded for increasing their company's stock prices. *(CEO pay is runaway, i.e. shot up very high. However, there are defenders of this trend. These defenders argue that the rising pay is nothing but market forces at work. The CEOs should be paid highly because they increase their company's stock prices.)* But are America's CEOs entitled to such lucrative pay deals based on their performance? *(The author poses a rhetorical question asking whether CEOs actually deserve such lucrative deals, implying that he believes that the pay is too high.)* In 1998, the business press exploded with stories of pay for mediocrity *(In 1998, press started criticizing this trend of high pay for CEOs by stating that even mediocre CEOs who are not deserving are getting paid too much.)*: When it comes to executive pay, stock option grants appear to have the Midas touch*(CEOs and such executives are getting paid by mode of stock options. Stock options are as valuable as gold.)* . As the stock market has broken record after record, they have become an increasingly popular form of executive compensation. *(As the stock market is booming and breaking records, more and more CEOs are getting paid by stock options in the companies.)*

According to compensation analysts, stock options make up two-thirds of a CEO's pay, up from one-third in the 1960s. *(So, in 1960s, 1/3rd of a CEOs pay was through stock options, whereas now it is two-thirds, according to compensation analysts. Percentage share of stock options as part of CEO's pay seems to have risen dramatically.)* Instead of having to beat their competitors, CEOs with stock option-fueled compensation packages are graded on a curve: the rising stock market. *(Earlier, CEOs had to beat their competitors. Now, it seems that CEOs are graded against the stock market, given that their pay is linked to the stock market by way of stock options.)* As stock prices increase generally, even mediocre CEOs can realize large gains from their options. *(The stock prices always increase, as a general trend, even with no effort on the part of the CEO. Thus, even an average-performing CEO can earn lots of money through stock options without putting in much effort at all.)* Analysts estimate that only a quarter of option grants awarded to CEOs contain any sort of link to performance, such as premium-priced or indexed stock options. *(Analysts estimate that only a 25% of the stock options given to CEOs are actually linked to their performances. The remaining 75% of the stock options are just part of pay for being a CEO.)* But executive equity incentive plans can hurt shareholders. *(Such pay trends can hurt shareholders, according to the author.)* Recent research examined the largest U.S. companies by adjusting for the value of their executive's stock options. *(A study on the biggest companies in the U.S. was conducted by taking into account the value of their executive's stock options.)* The study found that 11 firms went from profit to loss, and 13 had their profits halved. *(The report found that 11 firms went into loss, and 13 companies had profits halved.)* In addition, the study found that the average potential dilution of shareholder value from stock options is 9.2 percent for S&P 500 companies. *(Also, this trend of paying CEOs in stock options diluted shareholder value by 9.2 percent for the top 500 companies.)*

The author starts by introducing the current trend in CEO pay–that pay is rising and is more and more composed of stock options. He then presents a rhetorical question asking whether this is justified. He then presents statistics and research to prove that CEO pay is too high and is hurting the shareholders.

Main Point: To conclusively prove that CEOs should not be entitled to compensation through the mechanism of stock-options and that this trend will hurt the shareholders and the company.

1. This is a main purpose question from the general category.

    We have derived the main point already; let's analyze the options one by one.

    (A) This option is **incorrect** because the author does more than just explain CEO's stock option-linked compensation packages. He makes an effective case against them as part of a CEO's pay. Had the option been "to explain the **demerits of** CEOs stock option-fueled compensation packages," it would have been correct.

    (B) This option is **incorrect** because the author did not explicitly express that he has an issue with the excessive pay of CEOs. The author has an issue with the mechanism of payment–stock options. Perhaps the author is fine with the excessive pay if it is linked to profit of the company or another indicator rather than stock prices.

    (C) This option is **incorrect** because the author does not discuss lack of parity (equality) among CEO compensation packages. In fact, he implies that all CEOs, even the mediocre ones, get paid too highly.

    (D) This option is **incorrect** because the author does not argue against **bonuses**. He argues against excessive pay. This is a tricky option because the author does suggest that performance-linked pay is not as bad as pay given for stock market performance of the company. However, he does not argue as much against bonuses as against compensation packages.

    (E) This is the **correct** answer. This matches our deductions. He does criticize the rising pay of CEOs via stock options. He quotes examples of companies undergoing losses, and dilution of shareholder value.

    The correct answer is E.

2. This is a Detail question from the General category.

    There are three sentences that may qualify. Let's discuss them in by one.

    (1) *But are America's CEOs entitled to such lucrative pay deals based on their performance?*: This is merely a question and does not answer itself; the questions asks for a sentence that unequivocally [that is, without any ambiguity, or with full clarity] demonstrates the absurdity, which is not served by the questions.

    (2) *In 1998, the business press exploded with stories of pay for mediocrity—when it comes to executive pay, stock option grants appear to have the Midas touch.*: This is the **correct** answer. The phrase—stories of pay for mediocrity— clearly and unequivocally demonstrates the absurdity of mediocre CEOs unjustified package.

(3)   *As the stock market has broken record after record, they have become an increasingly popular form of executive compensation.*: If taken in isolation, it is only a statement telling about increasingly popularity of executive compensation. It does not say it is absurd or unjustified!

3.   This is a Detail question.

The author proves that stock option compensation packages are illogical in the second paragraph. Thus the flaws against it are mentioned in that paragraph. The author has many issues against the stock option compensation packages. He states that percentage share of stock options as part of CEOs pay has risen dramatically. It is wrong to pay CEOs through stock options because stock prices always increase, as a general trend, even with no effort on the part of the CEO towards progress of the company. Thus, even a mediocre CEO can earn lots of money through stock options without putting in much effort at all. He further states that only a quarter of the stock options given to CEOs are actually performance linked. The remaining 75% of the stock options are just part of pay for being a CEO. Such pay trends can hurt shareholders. Also, paying CEOs in stock options diluted shareholder value by 9.2 percent for the top 500 companies. So, the author mainly discusses CEOs stock-option compensation packages can undermine the value of shares.

Let's analyze the options one by one.

A   This option is **correct** because the author disapproves the fact that stock-options are becoming more and more popular and that pay is rising disproportionately and is not linked to performance at all.

B   This option is also **correct** because the author does suggest that the CEOs get paid for the stock price rising but have to put no effort in improving the company performance.

C   This option is also **correct** because the author mentions twice that shareholders get hurt and that the potential dilution of the value occurs because of stock option compensation packages.

The correct answers are A, B, & C.

4.   This is a specific inference question.

This question asks us to find an option regarding stock option compensation packages with which the author would agree.

Let's analyze the options one by one.

(A)   This is the **correct** answer. The author would agree with this because this is the point the author has mainly made when he criticized stock option compensation packages. He states that it is wrong to pay CEOs through stock options because stock prices always increase as a general trend, even with no effort on the part of the CEO. Thus, even a mediocre CEO can earn lots of money through stock options without putting in much effort at all. He further states that only a quarter of the stock options given to CEOs are actually performance linked. The remaining 75% of the stock options are just part of pay for being a CEO. Thus, the author would agree that currently, companies consider their stock performance more important than actual performance.

(B) This option is **incorrect** because the reference of two-thirds comes from the first sentence of the second paragraph: "*stock options make up two-thirds of a CEOs pay*" which is unrelated to the option statement. We have no way of knowing whether the amount of compensation packages has risen by two-thirds. All we know is that stock options made up one-third of CEO pay earlier but now make up two-thirds of CEO pay.

(C) This option is **incorrect** because the author would not suggest this. While he may suggest that CEO's pay should be performance-linked, he wouldn't suggest that **all** of it be through premium-priced or indexed stock options.

(D) This option is **incorrect** because while this option might be factually true, this is not the author's intention. This option implies that stock option compensation packages should not be awarded to CEOs when the company performs well in the markets. The author does not suggest that. He suggests that CEOs should be awarded for improving the company's performance and **not only** for a company's stock price rising, which is very likely anyway.

(E) This option is **incorrect** because the passage does not suggest that stock option compensation packages enhance stock market figures. The passage suggests that due to rising stock prices, the CEOs benefit.

The correct answer is A.

5.   This is a tone question from the general category.

This question asks us the author's attitude towards stock option compensation packages. We know that the author's statistics and research show that CEO pay is too high and is hurting shareholders. His main point seems to conclusively prove that CEOs are not entitled to such compensation and this trend will hurt the shareholders and the company. Thus, his attitude seems very negative towards stock option compensation.

Let's analyze the options one by one.

(A) This option is **incorrect** because the author does not show only restrained (limited) criticism. He is fully against stock option compensation packages. He does not mention even a single point in favor of stock option compensation packages and hence we cannot say that he has limited criticism towards it.

(B) This option is **incorrect** because the author does not mention even a single point in favor of stock option compensation packages and hence we cannot say that he has at all any approval towards it.

(C) This option is **incorrect** because there is no disgust on the part of the author. He merely makes an unemotional case against stock option compensation packages.

(D) This is the **correct** answer. This is the author's tone because the author finds stock option compensation packages of today completely unacceptable and that's why he presents such a strong case against them.

(E) This option is **incorrect** because the author disapproves of stock option compensation packages but not in an unjustified manner. He presents proper research and statistics to make his case.

The correct answer is D.

6. This is a specific inference question.

The question asks us to find an option that can be inferred from the passage.

Let's analyze the options one by one.

(A) This is the **correct** answer. This can be inferred from the given passage. The passage states that in the 1960s, stock options made up only one-third of the CEO's pay. Today, they make up two-thirds of a CEO's pay. The author states that today the potential for shareholder value dilution because of CEO compensation packages is 9.2%, at two-thirds. Thus, it follows that, in the 1960s, at one-third, the potential for dilution because of CEO compensation packages was less.

(B) This option is **incorrect** because we cannot say that shareholders did not get hurt at all by companies in the 1960s. All we know is that in the 1960s, stock options made up only one-third of a CEO's pay. Today, they make up two-thirds of a CEO's pay. Thus, the potential for hurting shareholders through stock option compensation packages is greater today than it was in the 1960s.

(C) This option is **incorrect** because no such implication is made in the passage.

(D) This option is **incorrect** because while the author suggests that CEOs should be paid according to performance, he does not imply that the profits will be necessarily higher.

(E) This option is **incorrect** because It is the other way around. The passage rather suggests that "A CEO's pay should **NOT** be linked to the company's performance in the stock market."

The correct answer is A.

6.5   Passage 5 (Rising health care costs & medical malpractice)

Understanding the Passage

This is a short passage of intermediate difficulty level on business policy *(medical practices)*.

In 1990, a Harvard Medical Practice study cited the fact that 95,000 deaths a year in the U.S. are due to medical malpractice; an additional 700,000 individuals are subject to injury as a result of medical malpractice. These numbers are alarming. To hit our senses with the disproportionately high number of casualties due to medical malpractice, the author compares it with the casualties a jumbo jet would have caused had it crashed every day for a year. Despite this, barely 2,100 doctors a year are penalized in connection with a malpractice claim. [*The author implies that lot more than 2100 doctors are committing malpractice but they are not being charged or punished.*] Of those health care providers *(used to refer to "doctors & other health care professionals")* that do come under scrutiny and contempt, sadly the majority of them are subject to sanctions *(penalties)* on the grounds of substance abuse *(also known as "drug abuse")* or fraud, rather than medical malpractice *[meaning, malpractice goes either unnoticed or unpunished, possibly leading to more carelessness. The doctors committing malpractice get charged for different reasons, and not malpractice.]*. In the meantime, federal legislators are considering mechanisms to limit the claim amount a patient can get as compensation for damages incurred as a result of medical malpractice. *[However, legislators think that the amount of money a patient can win against a doctor accused of malpractice should be capped/limited, to reduce the cost of insurance overall.]*

Lawmakers hope that in capping jury awards *(Claim amount that a patient can win if he files a case against a doctor for malpractice)* to plaintiffs *(Claimants/patients)*, it may be possible to reduce rising health care costs. Since those costs are ultimately charged to patients in the form of insurance premiums, the reigning *(topmost/main)* logic implies that limits on claim amounts will save the patient money, and bring the cost of high quality healthcare within the reach of more Americans. [*The claim money that any patient/claimant wins against any doctor/hospital charged with malpractice is ultimately paid by insurance companies. These companies eventually make insurance more costly to pass on the high cost to the customer again.*] However, the soundness of this approach is in doubt when we consider that a congressional budget office report found that only 1% of national health care costs results from the expense of medical malpractice insurance premiums being passed on to the patient. [*Actual facts show that malpractice claim money costs only 1% of the health care costs.*] However, accidents, misdiagnosis, and conflicting prescriptions cost the nation nearly $60 billion a year. [*Actual malpractice costs more. So, the author wishes to imply that capping the claim money that a patient can win against a doctor for malpractice is pointless because it's not the real reason insurance premiums and healthcare is so costly. The real problem lies with the actual expenses caused by malpractice itself, and not cases suing for malpractice.*]

Even with these losses imposed on patients and on taxpayers yearly, less than 1/2 % of all civil cases pursued actually charge doctors with medical malpractice. [*The author implies that the malpractice issue is not being taken seriously enough, despite the loss and cost to patients.*] The 2000+ doctors who are penalized each year amount to hardly 1% of all acting health care providers. [*The author implies that even though only 1% of doctors are charged, there must be more committing malpractice, and they don't get charged or punished.*] Thus the amount of money going back into the hands of victims is a relatively petty contribution to the overall cost of health care in America when compared to the cost of compensation for the harm of malpractice. *[So, even if some patient/claimant wins a big amount in a case of malpractice against some doctor, it is negligible compared to the actual cost to make up for the wrong caused by the malpractice.]* Rising health care costs may more predictably be reduced by improving the way in which the policies of the health care industry are laid and by removing untrustworthy doctors from practice. *[The author provides a recommendation on how to deal with doctors accused of malpractice and how to have a better healthcare industry.]*

The passage is about reducing the rising cost of healthcare in the U.S., and understanding its components. Federal legislators are considering a plan to peg down the claim amount as a result of medical malpractice; it can possibly reduce rising health care costs. However, this approach doubtful; a report found that only 1% of health care costs results from the expense of medical malpractice insurance premiums being passed on to the patient. The author concludes that rising health care costs may be reduced by sound health care policies and by removing untrustworthy doctors from practice.

Main Point: Disciplining doctors and formulating sound health care policies can more predictably reduce rising health care costs.

1. This is a main purpose question from the general category.

    We have already derived the main point; let's analyze the options one by one.

    (A) This option is **incorrect** because it only partially covers the scope of the passage. Moreover, "widespread policing" is too vague a term. This option does not even mention doctors' practices with regard to malpractice.

    (B) This option is **incorrect** because it is too generic, vague, and wide in scope. It does not even mention that the problem is "rising health care costs" and not just "health care costs."

    (C) This option is **incorrect** because the author pinpoints that one of the major sources of high health care costs is the practices of undisciplined doctors.

    (D) This is the **correct** answer. This option talks about the role of doctors and patients. It rightly addresses the issue that rising health care costs have more to do with the malpractice of doctors than with the behavior of patients. Additionally, the passage affirms that malpractice claims from patients have been shown to have only a minor impact on health care costs.

    (E) This option is **incorrect**. It is too narrow in scope and it does not address the main point of the passage at all.

    The correct answer is D.

2. This is a function question from the general category.

    The passage states that over 95,000 people die due to malpractice every year. Many times, we are not able to react to the degree of severity because the number–95,000 or, say, 950,000–does not have any shape. The author uses the example of casualties caused by a jumbo jet so that a reader can visualize the figure of 95,000. A jumbo jet with a capacity of 200-250 would have to crash 365 times to make 95,000 casualties. It is a dramatic way of telling us the severity.

With the above analysis, option A is the correct answer. Though option B is close, the purpose of comparing the number of malpractice victims to the number of jumbo jet accident casualties is missing; it merely states "what" the author says in the example but not "why" the author gave us that example. The question asks us not "what" the point is but "why" the author made that point.

The correct answer is A.

3.   This is a specific inference question.

Refer to paragraph 1 (line 6): "*fewer than 2,100 doctors a year are disciplined in connection with a malpractice claim.*" The author implies that even though only 1% of doctors are charged, there must be more committing malpractice, and they don't get charged or punished. Also the conclusion recommends firing more doctors. So the inference is that too few doctors are penalized.

(A)   This option is **incorrect** because the passage did not mention that penalties are given out for the wrong reasons.

(B)   Similarly, this option is **incorrect** because the passage did not mention that penalties given out are not severe enough.

(C)   This is the **correct** answer. It follows our deductions.

(D)   Like option A and B, this option is **incorrect** because the passage did not mention that penalties are given out to wrong offenders.

(E)   This option is **incorrect**. It is a rephrased version of option B.

The correct answer is C.

4.   This is a specific inference question.

Option A is the correct answer because the passage states that a congressional report (refer to paragraph 2) found that malpractice claims account for only a minor portion (1%) of health care costs. Other options do not qualify to be inferred as they are either against the stated/implied facts (options B and C) or are out of scope of the passage (options D and E).

The correct answer is A.

5. This is an Inference question.

The passage speaks directly about the role of doctors in inflating the costs of health care through malpractice and patients not having sufficient opportunity or ways to recoup those costs– likely inference with which the author will agree is that malpractice of the doctors and unwillingness of authorities to charge such doctors is responsible for the rising health care costs.

|A| This option is **incorrect** because the author does not intend to mean that insurance companies will deliberately try to inflate their rate of return on premiums.

|B| This option is **incorrect** because the author does not mention expensive treatments. This option is not "must be true."

|C| This is the **correct** answer. It follows our analysis.

The correct answer is C.

6. This is a Function question from the General category.

The question asks to cite a fact, displaying Congress' policies. Two sentences should be discussed.

Let us analyze both the sentences:

(1) *Despite the multitudes of people who die or suffer as a result of medical malpractice, fewer than 2,100 doctors a year are disciplined in connection with a malpractice claim:* This is the **correct** answer. It clearly cites fact and figure. The discrepancy in Congress's policy of limiting the compensation to patients dues to malpractice overlooks the fact that by far a greater number of people die due to malpractice. This proves that the Congress is operating on a false premise.

(2) *These facts resurface at a time when federal legislators are considering measures to limit the monetary amount a patient can claim as compensation for damages incurred as a result of medical malpractice.:* This sentence is not a fact itself. It merely refers to the fact cite above. Moreover it is a rephrased version of the question.

7. This is a reasoning based question on assumption.

Conclusion: Greater policing of doctors will reduce the incidence of malpractice and drive down costs.

Let us predict the assumption. Why does the author conclude that greater policing of doctors will reduce the incidence of malpractice and drive down costs? There is an underlying assumption here: greater policing will ensure that doctors err less and improve their performance, thereby reducing the cost. He thinks that the policing will have a deterrent effect. Let us see the options one by one.

(A)   This option is **incorrect** because even if most doctors are responsible, they can still commit malpractice. The issue at hand is to reduce negligence and improve performance so that malpractice can be reduced.

(B)   This option is **incorrect** because it does not address the issue of malpractice.

(C)   This is the **correct** answer. It matches our deduction.

(D)   This option is **incorrect** because it is opposite of the conclusion. If doctors will never protect one another from investigation in case one commits malpractice, then there is no need for greater policing, which is against the conclusion.

(E)   This option is **incorrect** because it addresses the issue of corruption and not malpractice.

The correct answer is C.

8.   This is an Inference question.

Read the sentence (lines 13-14): "*It is the hope of lawmakers in capping jury awards (claim amount) to plaintiffs (claimants) that it may be possible to reverse the tide of rising healthcare costs.*"

In view of this sentence, option A is the most appropriate because the idea that jury awards should be reduced is connected to the idea that patients are claiming too much in the way of compensation.

The correct answer is A.

9.   This is a tone question from the general category.

We have to choose an option that is the most inappropriate; it means that 4 options relate to the tone of the author and the correct option does not. Let us understand the tone of the author. The author presents the content in an analytical fashion. He discusses the facts, and sees the pros and cons of the issue. We also find that he is critical of the Congress policy of capping jury awards to the patients. His tone is critical and disapproving. The author describes the issue well, so there is a shade of descriptive tone too.

Now let us discuss each option.

(A)   Distraught means upset and worried. The tone of the author is certainly distraught; he is upset and worried with the healthcare policy being discussed in its present form. So this option does relate to the tone of the author.

(B)   Apathetic means indifferent and uninterested. The author seems to be very concerned about the issue of malpractice and is subjective in places. He is not apathetic to the issue. This is the **correct** answer.

(C)   Infuriated means very angry. The author is certainly angry with the healthcare policy being discussed in its present form. So this option does relate to the tone of the author.

(D)   Dire means extremely concerning. The tone of the author implies that ignoring the much wider role of doctors in malpractice will have dire consequences in the time to come. This option does relate to the tone of the author.

(E)   Disparaging means criticizing, and critical. As discussed above, the passage does have traits of a disparaging tone. This option does relate to the tone of the author.

The correct answer is B.

6.6   Passage 6 (Sales force automation)

Understanding the Passage

This is a short passage of low difficulty level on business. A standard GMAT short passage asks you 3-4 questions, but we have asked you 5 questions in this passage. You should spend 2.5–3 minutes reading the passage and 60-75 seconds answering each question; so, in all, you should spend approximately 6 minutes on a short passage. For this passage, you should take approximately 8-9 minutes.

Companies don't fully succeed in holistic implementation of Sales Force Automation (SFA), because they miss the most important factor critical for success – the users' efficacy to fully utilize the capability of SFA. In setting up SFA system technology, the implementation team assumes the intended users have only low literacy in computer use proficiency. However, the users have computer literacy but lack technological knowledge about SFA. This leads the trainers to use unsuitable training techniques *meant for users with low computer literacy.* In reality, today's sales departments are mostly made up of users who have been exposed to computers, and are, therefore, *computer literate,* but who have never had to use them consistently and who struggle to grasp how much strategic value SFA will have *(therefore, they are not well-versed in optimum technology use).* An SFA project's success hinges on creating a situation where both sales representatives and managers can reap the benefits of the SFA tools, but all too often they haven't relied on technology as a strategic tool to meet objectives. *[The author feels this aspect should be taken into account in the training programs to maximize the returns from SFA and use it optimally.]*

Their compensation and job performance are very quantifiable, based on how well they do against a set of revenue targets. Inevitably they tend to define SFA in terms of its usefulness handling the transactions they normally work on *[The sales teams cannot fully comprehend the extent to which they can utilize SFA and end up using it to only handle transactions].* The SFA market has done a good job of selling the benefits of SFA tools to drive sales performance, but having convinced companies to purchase systems *[the SFA systems],* there is intense pressure to achieve a strong return on investment *[for the companies who spend money to buy the SFA systems].* To ensure a successful SFA implementation, companies need to set realistic expectations and consider issues that are unique when deploying the system. *[Thus, according to the author, what companies should do to ensure optimum use of SFA is set realistic targets and consider the company's characteristics in implementing the SFA system]*

Main Point: Poor implementation of SFA systems: incorrect approach, and how to correct it so that companies can better use SFA and reap its full benefits.

1.   The question asks us to understand the main purpose of the paragraph. The author starts by straight away introducing the topic of the discussion – that companies don't implement SFA properly. He explains how the companies fail to do so – by ignoring the literacy level of users about computers. He goes on to explain how SFA can be properly implemented and used much better than it is today. All in all, he discusses the inadequate implementation of SFA and points out that if SFA is implemented and used

properly, it can be used for meeting strategic goals.

Let us analyze the options one by one.

(A)   This option is **incorrect** because this is one of the many possible concerns for the company but not the main purpose in writing this passage.

(B)   This option is **incorrect** because the author merely discusses advantages and possible benefits of SFA and not its disadvantages. The author does point out that companies are concerned about the cost factor (by discussing their worries with return on investment), but this concern is not his main purpose.

(C)   This is the **correct** answer. The author discusses the poor implementation and the recommended method for correct implementation of SFA so that companies can better use and implement SFA and reap its full benefits.

(D)   This option is **incorrect** because the author does not imply that the onus of training the users lies on the SFA market. Though the author brings the issue of lack of skills for using SFA, he does not criticize the SFA market for not having trained the users well enough in SFA.

(E)   This option is **incorrect** because the author points out the opposite of this. The author explains that SFA can be much more useful than it is now.

The correct answer is C.

2.   This is a question on specific detail.

The question asks us to locate a specific detail in the passage, namely why traditional training approaches are inappropriate for SFA projects. The answer lies in the first three sentences of the passage, which state that companies miss out on succeeding at SFA projects because the implementation teams assume that the users are relatively illiterate in computer proficiency, but they are not. On the contrary, they lack skill from a technological aspect. This assumption causes the training programs not to be as effective as possible. The passage states that the trainers misjudge the computer literacy of the potential SFA users and consequently use the wrong training techniques.

Let us analyze the options one by one.

(A)   This option is **incorrect** because the number of SFA users is not mentioned anywhere in the passage.

(B)   This option is **incorrect** because the passage does not state that the management teams lack experience in defining goals.

(C)   This is the **correct** answer. It matches our deductions.

(D)   This option is **incorrect** because the author suggests the opposite of this – that the users are more computer literate than they are thought to be.

(E)   This option is **incorrect** because the passage states that the users do use SFA for transactions, thus implying that they are capable of helping users to define transactional goals.

The correct answer is C.

3. We are asked to infer about SFA for its optimal use and select a suitable sentence presenting the thought. We know that the author feels that the SFA is not utilized to its potential. Also, the author feels that SFA can be used better than it is now.

    There are two sentences that may be considered for the answer.

    (1) Last sentence/I paragraph: *An SFA project's success hinges on creating a situation where both sales representatives and managers can reap the benefits of the SFA tools but all too often they haven't relied on technology as a strategic tool to meet objectives.*

         The II clause of the sentence... *but all too often they haven't relied on technology as a strategic tool to meet objectives.* clearly expresses author's advice—SFA be used " optimally" to meet objectives. Thus, this sentence is the correct answer.

    (2) Last sentence/II paragraph: *To ensure a successful SFA implementation, companies need to set realistic expectations and consider issues that are unique when deploying the system* does expresses author's advice, but on setting realistic targets, and addressing issues, not about its optimal use.

4. This is a question on "Specific Inference."

    The question asks us to infer about holistic implementation of SFA. The passage states that companies miss out on succeeding in SFA projects because the implementation teams assume that the users are illiterate in computer use, but they are not. They lack in technology. This assumption causes the training programs to not be as effective as possible. The passage states that that the trainers misjudge the computer literacy as low of the potential SFA users and consequently use the wrong training techniques. Thus, it follows that SFA could be successfully implemented if the training programs did not assume the users to be illiterate in computer use, and correctly assess that they lack only in technology aspect, and trained them in a different way for using SFA to the maximum. In a way, the sales teams could not fully comprehend the extent to which they can utilize SFA. Thus, options A & B are correct.

    Option C is incorrect because the literacy level of SFA trainers isn't in question, rather the method of training is. The author in fact states that the training teams assume the computer literacy levels of users as much lower than it actually is. Thus the literacy level is definitely not a problem.

The correct answers are A & B.

5. This is a question on specific inference.

The question asks us to find a specific inference about successful implementation of SFA. To maximize the benefit of SFA, training programs need to be changed. However, for successful implementation of SFA, the author, in the second paragraph and especially in the last line, mentions that SFA can be successfully implemented if realistic goals are set after a company identifies its unique situation and understands it. Thus, a company needs to assess itself and set achievable targets.

Let us analyze the options one by one.

(A) This option is **incorrect** because the training of training staff in not an issue; the issue is training the sales staff on the technological aspect of SFA.

(B) This option is **incorrect** because the author mentions that this is already being done with SFA and that this alone isn't enough. SFA should be used for more than just this.

(C) This is the **correct** answer. This matches our deductions.

(D) This option is **incorrect** because the author mentions this as explanation for why the companies use SFA for keeping track of the transactions. However, this is not how he suggests that the SFA will bring about a more positive outcome.

(E) This option is **incorrect** because no such thing is mentioned in the passage.

The correct answer is C.

6.7   Passage 7 (Rising European Union and the U.S.)

Understanding the Passage

This is a long passage of high difficulty level on business and economics.

The European Union's (EU) world market is growing exponentially. Only the E.U. has the economic power to challenge the United States over international trade policies, but the U.S. is reluctant about E.U. proposals, which address the issues of labor regulations, the opening of consumer forums, and concerns for the environmental. Interest groups asking for these developments have been ignored in the process over trans-Atlantic economic unification (spanning and crossing the Atlantic Ocean); those with an interest in these groups see a trend towards liberalizing the rules for corporate advantage in the economic co-ordination that has evolved between the United States and Europe. Much of the current communication between the United States and the European Union is focused on establishing an agreement that forms the rules of trans-Atlantic trade and, on the extent of trade conducted between the U.S. and Europe, is much greater than what is happening between any other pair of regions in the world.

The bone of contention between the United States and the European Union on this issue came up when the U.S., Mexico, and Canada joined together and made the agreement known as the North American Free Trade Agreement: NAFTA. NAFTA is meant to standardize industrial and labor regulations between the United States and its neighboring countries so that tariffs can be reduced, international transport encouraged, and corporate investment diversified. Though standards of production will raise the quality of production and the level of cooperation across the continent, it creates a hurdle and makes a contradiction to European expectations of international regulation. To tackle this problem, the E.U. has proposed TAFTA– the Trans-Atlantic Free Trade Agreement, but the United States has repeatedly hesitated regarding the TAFTA proposal as it seeks to protect its dominance in the Western Hemisphere (America, the western part of Europe, and Africa). The U.S. can dominate the region and protect its factories and corporations from comparable European production and demanding practices.

Many interest groups have raised their voices over this issue and accused the U.S of maneuvering, protectionism, uncaring deregulation, third world exploitation, and anti-competitive practices. The route to economic expansion is an important issue in both the U.S. and the European Union; some interest groups repeatedly oppose this just to safeguard their own interest in the region while ignoring better world order.

The passage is about the rising economic power of the E.U. and its proposal of trans-Atlantic economic unification. On the other hand, the U.S. has an agreement–NAFTA–with its neighboring counties. Though it is good, it is a barrier for the E.U. in trade. To further its own interests, the E.U. has proposed TAFTA–the Trans-Atlantic Free Trade Agreement–but the US is reluctant regarding this agreement as it presumes that its dominance in the western hemisphere would cease to exist.

Main point: The ambivalent feelings of the U.S. in joining up with the potent E.U.

1. This is a function question.

    (A) This option is **incorrect** because, though it is factually correct, the intent of the author is not to merely demonstrate the difference between the past E.U. and the present E.U. in the context of the passage. He shows the difference in the E.U.'s standing to prove the E.U.'s considerable presence.

    (B) This option is **incorrect** because the passage does not need to clarify the number of parties in trans-Atlantic trade since it is clear in the passage that there are only two parties being discussed.

    (C) This is the **correct** answer because the first sentence seeks to introduce one of the most important economic powers worldwide.

    (D) This option is **incorrect** because though it seems correct, it is not necessarily true and the author does not show any belligerence on the part of the E.U. in the passage.

    (E) This option is **incorrect** because it is not relevant to the question.

    The correct answer is C.

2. This is an inference question.

    (A) This option is **incorrect** because it suggests no progress can be made. Impasse means deadlock. The passage does not suggest that a deadlock has been reached; the dialogue is ongoing, but consensus could not be reached. Impasse would mean that nothing can go further.

    (B) This is the **correct** answer because the exchange between the U.S. and the E.U. is a persistent disagreement over a certain topic.

    (C) This option is **incorrect** because 'shuttle diplomacy' refers to an explicit political process which is not identified in the passage. It means using an impartial third party to discuss terms between two concerned parties.

    (D) This option is **incorrect** because though some groups have accused the U.S. of brinkmanship in paragraph 3, it is not in the context of 'heated dialogue'. Brinkmanship is the political maneuver of taking things to an extreme to force the other party to accede.

    (E) This option is **incorrect** because the 'heated dialogue' between the U.S. and the E.U. is not occurring in a lighter vein; there are serious ramifications to it.

    The correct answer is B.

3. This is an inference question.

    Option C is the best possible answer, supported by lines 20-23: "While bringing standards of production into alignment is a goal that ought to raise the quality of production and the level of cooperation across the continent, it also creates an opportunity to establish a standard contra to European expectations of international regulation." The E.U. fears that NAFTA's standards may be incompatible with that of Europe's, hence the E.U. proposed TAFTA.

Other options are either not worth considering because they are out of scope or they are not supported with justifiable reasoning.

The correct answer is C.

4. This is an inference question.

    The question means that from the perspective of the E.U., production and environmental standards should be higher than those of North America. If they are lower, it is disadvantageous to the E.U.. We have find the best reason out of the 5 options.

    Option E is the correct answer because lower production and environmental standards, for example, could make doing business cheaper for U.S. companies than for other companies. The passage mentions "the United States is noncommittal on E.U. proposals calling for the alignment of labor regulations, the opening of consumer forums and the offer of an audience to environmental groups." The inferences given in other options cannot be made as no such things were mentioned in the passage. Also, the U.S. seems unwilling to agree to TAFTA because it wants to continue its dominance in the region. If it gives in to TAFTA, the E.U.'s higher standards will have to be met or business will go to the E.U..

    The correct answer is E.

5. Uncaring attitude of the US is a serious charge and keeping in mind the development of the issue in the passage, we can infer that the charge of " deregulation driven by Uncaring attitude of the US" should be discussed in the later part of the II paragraph or the II paragraph.

    The correct sentence: *These issues have resulted in the plethora of interest groups with a voice in the matter simultaneously **accusing** the U.S of brinkmanship, protectionism, **callous deregulation**, third world exploitation and anti-competitive practices.* accuses the US of callous deregulation, implying uncaring attitude.

6. This is an inference question.

    Option C is the correct answer since the last sentence (line 32) of the passage states: "The route to economic expansion is a prominent issue in both the U.S. and the European Union, and some (groups) with a say in the matter repeat these protests as a screen (shield) for their own plans to tip the balance of economic advantage towards their own region at the expense of all other involved parties in the process of exploring for parity." Thus, the author believes that some groups in both the U.S. and the E.U. are "biased" toward maintaining their dominance in the region.

    The correct answer is C.

7. This is an Inference question.

All the options are correct. The U.S. is unwilling to engage in any new agreements with EU but simultaneously seeking keen interest in NAFTA shows that the US is noncommittal with TAFTA.

The correct answers are A, B, & C.

6.8   Passage 8 (In-fighting Indian princes and the rise of the British)

Understanding the Passage

This is a long passage of low difficulty level on history.

For 17th century Europeans, the history of Eastern empires was stereotyped. India's historical events were predictable customs of unrefined and stereotypical traditional stories. According to the traditional story, typically, the founder of an empire would be a brave soldier and a frantic conspirator who would topple corrupt scions of a more ancient empire. The founder's son might inherit some of his talent; but in two or three generations, descendants become immoral and corrupt and are dethroned by some new adventurer. *[Thus, in the minds of the British, whenever anyone is dethroned in Eastern empires, it is justified because, according to them, the person sitting on the throne is a descendent of a brave person but does not have the appropriate qualities to rule correctly and should be overthrown/removed from the throne.]* Thus an upright rebellion will dethrone a corrupt empire and subsequently be dethroned by another rebellion. *[This is how they rationalize creating and orchestrating rebellions to remove the existing rulers.]* This practice was ongoing. This led to the recurrence of civil war and anarchy at fixed intervals. Due to these anarchistic practices, Britain's rulers could visualize their might in the subcontinent. *[Using such tactics, the British were virtually in control because they removed the rulers who could potentially disagree with the British and put in such rulers who would end up being puppets in British hands, thereby ensuring British interests.]* The British wished to avoid the bloodshed periodically occurring during the toppling of an empire and this led them to gain the favor of India's local empires. *[They played a diplomatic game by removing the current ruler and backing a new ruler, and they thus avoided actual wars but gained favors from the newly installed ruler.]*

The British were able to impose a proxy rule over India by setting up native princes in positions of power. It is to be noted that Indian empires used to follow the law of "doctrines of lapse," which means that if the ruling king dies without any sons *(heirs)*, any of the related princes *(nephews)* could lay claim to the empire. The British used to support anyone of the princes, and help maintain his power as long as it was in their interests. *[If there are two possible candidates for the throne, they would support the one who would further their interests the most and put him on the throne.]* In this way the princes became practically obliged to cooperate with the British, and the result was two generations of trivial tyrant princes, protected by the British. These tyrant princes spent their lives in apathetic dishonesty, cruelty, and oppression. *[The rulers chosen by the British were always bad ones who could not be removed because they were protected by British might.]*

The passage is about how the British could enforce their rule over India, their strategy, and tactics. The British took advantage of in-fighting among princes to claim the empire once the leadership to it lapsed. The British used to support a prince and make him the king, and, by doing this, the new king would be obliged to the British. Unfortunately the king under the shadow of the British would become corrupt and cruel.

Main Point: In-fighting among the princes of the Indian Empire and tactics by the British to impose proxy rule in India.

1. This is an inference question.

    Option E is the best answer because the passage speaks of the British in the following way: "Their methods took advantage of existing "doctrines of lapse," and made use of what was already the declared law in cases of heredity. By intervening on behalf of one prince or another, both of whom may have been equally suited to claim the right to the throne in cases in which the rights to leadership lapsed, they put themselves in a position to support a leader they selected, and to maintain his power as long as it was in their interests. In this way the princes became practically obliged to cooperate with the British.." So, they ruled by proxy *(indirectly)* by making the ruler obliged to them. Thus, their proxy rule can be attributed to the "doctrine of lapse."

    Other options are not discussed in the passage and so cannot be necessarily inferred.

    The correct answer is E.

2. This is Inference question.

    A   This option is **incorrect** because the reverse of this option is true. On the contrary the author may disagree with the statement that British intervention in India was a positive influence on India. The scheming done by British sustained their favorite, yet corrupt and incapable kings at the monarchies for a long period, during which these unsuitable king would have been dethroned by brave, upright rebellions.

    B   This option is **incorrect** because it is too extreme and cannot be inferred from the passage.

    C   This is the **correct** answer. The passage suggests that had British not intervened, the cycle of change of power would have taken place at a fixed interval, and at least periodically, India would have a competent king followed by corrupt kings. But because of British's supporting of their favorite, yet corrupt and incapable kings at the monarchies for a long period to change of leadership did not happen. Thus, British interference led to a necessarily bad king, whereas without British India would have had good kings sooner or later So, the author would agree that India would have been better off without British intervention.

    The correct answer is C.

3. This is a tone question from the general category.

    (A)   This is the **correct** answer because the author laments the constant decline of kings into "feeble inheritors"; he notes that feeble inheritors fostered by the British have done more bad than good for India.

    (B)   This option is **incorrect** because the author endorses the belief that change of power by a rebellion is the remedy to get rid of cruel kings. He does not despair of it or give it up.

    (C)   This option is **incorrect** because the author is not skeptical of the prevailing cycle of rule. He, in fact, acknowledges it.

(D)   This option is **incorrect** because 'matter of fact' is a neutral phrase. The author is certainly opinionated about the cycle of rule in Asia. He doesn't treat it merely neutrally.

(E)   This option is **incorrect** because we can't say that he necessarily approves of the cycle of rule. He acknowledges it as something that has worked out fairly well but that does not mean he likes it and approves of it. He may believe that there might be a better way. All we can say is that he certainly disapproves of British interference and that he accepts that the cycle of rule works better when left alone, but we can't say that he approves of it necessarily.

The correct answer is A.

4.   This is an inference question.

(A)   This option is **incorrect** because the British allowed princes to take over power, albeit the prince of their choice.

(B)   This option is **incorrect** because, according to the passage, the people were not supposed to choose their leader; it's the hereditary cycle of rule that choose the leader.

(C)   This is the **correct** answer because the last two sentences of the passage (line 21) endorse this: "The result was two generations of petty despots, insulated from the consequences of misrule by British bayonets. The despots spent their lives in listless debauchery, broken by paroxysms of cruelty and oppression." The British safeguarded their favorite, yet cruel, kings and did not let rebellions oust them, causing damage to the subcontinent. Thus, the rule continued because the Indian people did not have the sort of strength needed to overcome British power.

(D)   This option is **incorrect** because the passage did not talk about the demoralization of the Indian identity.

(E)   This option is **incorrect** because while this is the reason the despot rulers were put on the throne, it is not necessarily damaging. The British can exploit the doctrine of lapse and put a prince on the throne but this does not have to be damaging, if they had put a good ruler there. However, the British were greedy and sought to have an indirect rule over India, so they always chose the leaders with low morals. Thus, we can attribute the damage to the British attitude towards India or to their greed, but not necessarily to the way they put people in power.

The correct answer is C.

5.   This is an inference question.

Option E is the best option as it is exemplified by the British policy of coordinating with princes in need of support because their interest was to rule the Indian subcontinent by proxy and without bloodshed. Thus they cooperated when it was in their best interests to do so.

Other options are either not discussed in the passage or cannot necessarily be inferred.

The correct answer is E.

6. This is an inference question.

    (A) This is the **correct** answer because the British aided princes who were vulnerable and were competing with another prince. This action required little up front British influence in order to determine the outcome of the dispute, while making Britain the effective "kingmaker" in the region and allowing the British a great deal of influence later. This means that they had some amount of influence.

    (B) This option is **incorrect** because the British did not take over the leadership role themselves but put in rulers through whom they could rule by proxy.

    (C) This option is **incorrect** because the British were not helping the princes to discuss their dispute.

    (D) This option is **incorrect** because the British influence in the area was not impartial, but self-interested.

    (E) This option is **incorrect** because there were local candidates for leadership.

    The correct answer is A.

7. This is a tone question from the general category.

    Option C is the correct answer as is demonstrated by the British decision to seek to advance their own interests in India when it was possible to do so during times of disorder. Nothing else is possible to be attributed to the British in the given passage from among the options.

    The correct answer is C.

8. This is a Function question.

    Let us understand the usage of the word *despotism*; it is used in the sentence: *Thus rebellion and deposition were the correctives of* `despotism`*, and therefore, a recurrence, at fixed intervals, of able and vigorous princes through the medium of periodical anarchy and civil war, occurred.*

    The previous sentence to the above sentence—*His son may inherit some of the talent of the father, but in two or three generations, luxury and indolence do their work, and the feeble inheritors of a great name are dethroned by some new adventurer, destined to bequeath a like misfortune to his de- generate descendants.*—talks about the luxury and indolence (laziness, inactive) of inheritors and rebellions were hailed for toppling these inheritors' autocratic rule, thus it can be inferred that `despotism` is used with reference to the oppressive rule of the inheritors, which also means tyranny, thus the correct answer is option B.

    Though option A—stubborn (headstrong, willful), and option D—debauchery (depravity, immodesty) are negative in characteristics, they cannot be ideal replacements for despotism . We cannot necessarily infer that the degenerate inheritors are stubborn or debauched.

The correct answer is B.

6.9   Passage 9 (The Belgian economy: from devastation to restoration)

Understanding the Passage

This is a medium length passage of medium difficulty level on business policy and economics.

For 200 years until WW I, the Wallonia area of Belgium was a technically advanced industrial region, while the Flanders area was predominantly agricultural. *[Both Wallonia and Flanders are in Belgium.]* After WW II this difference between Wallonia and Flanders faded because Belgium had its industrial infrastructure remain relatively intact, and this set the stage for rapid development, particularly in Flanders. The older and traditional industries in Wallonia began to lose their competitive edge during this period. However, because the world economy was growing, there were no immediate effects on Belgium's economy, at least not until 1973. Unfortunately, the oil price shocks between 1973 and 1979 and the resultant demand and supply equation of oil brought the Belgian economy into a period of protracted recession *(economic slump)*.

All this contributed to Wallonia losing its primacy and Flanders growing in importance for Belgium. In the 1980s and 1990s, the economic progress of the country started coming from Flanders. In the early 1980s, Belgium faced a difficult period of structural adjustment caused by declining demand for its traditional products, worsening economic performance, and neglected structural reform. Consequently, the recession from 1980-82 devastated Belgium in many ways–unemployment rose, social welfare costs increased, personal debt rose, the government deficit touched 13% of GDP, and national debt, although mostly held domestically, thrived. This was the time for quick and effective action. To fight this slump, in 1982 Prime Minister Martens' government formulated an economic recovery program to promote export-led growth by enhancing the competitiveness of Belgium's export industries. As a result, economic growth rose from 2% in 1984 to a peak of 4% in 1989. In May 1990, the government linked the Belgian currency, the franc, to the German currency, the mark. However, as German interest rates rose after 1990, Belgian rates subsequently increased and this resulted in a decline in the economic growth rate of Belgium again.

Belgium, otherwise a wealthy country, had spent more but collected fewer taxes for years. Belgium reacted to the 1973 and 1979 oil price hikes with poor macroeconomic policies: it absorbed the workers who were laid off in the private sector into the public sector and subsidized ailing industries–coal, steel, textiles, glass, and shipbuilding–in order to support the economy. But due to this, debt reached 121% of GNP by the end of the 1980s. However, thanks to Belgium's high personal savings rate, the Belgian Government managed to finance the deficit mainly from domestic savings. This minimized the damaging effects on the overall economy.

The passage is about the devastated economy of Belgium and how it rose after WWII. The Flanders region of Belgium led the growth of Belgium, but the oil price shock in 1973-73 pushed Belgium into an extended slump. During the early 80s, it faced many economic challenges from structural adjustment caused by low demand of its products and poor economic performance. In 1982, PM Martens started an economic recovery program led by export-oriented growth. Economic growth rose from 2% to 4% in 1989. In 1990, the government linked the Belgian currency (the franc) to the German currency (the mark), but the move resulted in a decline in the economic growth rate. The author blames Belgium's damaged economy on the fact that Belgium reacted to the 1973 and 1979 oil price hikes with poor macroeconomic policies: it supported and subsidized ailing industries. Due to this, debt reached 121% of GNP by the end of the 80s. The author ends the passage on a positive note, pointing out that the Belgian economy could finance the deficit mainly from domestic savings it had accrued over the years, thus minimizing the damaging effects on the overall economy.

Main Point: Surmounting the challenges of the devastated Belgian economy through structural reforms after WWII.

1. This is a main point question from the general category.

   (A) This option is **incorrect** because the passage is not about Flanders and its rise to a leadership position in Belgium, it is about the Belgian economy.

   (B) This is the **correct** answer because the passage discusses the Belgian economy under structural readjustment. This option correctly addresses the challenges the Belgian economy had to face after WWII.

   (C) This option is **incorrect** because the passage is not about Flanders but is about the Belgium economy.

   (D) This option is **incorrect** because the passage only mentions P.M. Martens as influencing economic restructuring; it narrowly covers the scope of the passage.

   (E) This option is **incorrect** because the topic of the passage is not just the damage inflicted by the government.

   The correct answer is B.

2. This is a function question.

   (A) This option is **incorrect** because the passage is not about Flanders but is about the Belgian economy.

   (B) This option is **incorrect** because the passage does not demonstrate how all of Belgium could have followed Flanders's example in order to prevent economic hardship. Flanders' rise after the war was coincidental, and not a deliberate plan that brought success.

   (C) This is the **correct** answer because the success of Flanders in some sectors and the decline of Walloon in other sectors exemplify the change in the economy as a whole.

   (D) This option is **incorrect** because it is not demonstrated that Belgium was in a position to experience "runaway" economic growth. In fact, the damaged situation in the Belgian economy is discussed throughout the passage.

   (E) This option is **incorrect** because there is no single factor that drove down growth in the Belgian economy.

   The correct answer is C.

3. This is Inference question.

    Since the questions concerns about the role of Flanders, which is referred to only in paragraph I, we must seek an answer only in paragraph I.

    The sentence: *When Belgium emerged from World War II with its industrial infrastructure relatively* **undamaged**, *the stage was set for a period of rapid development, particularly in Flanders.* is the correct answer. It says that in Flanders, the industrial infrastructure were relatively unharmed and this led Flanders to contribute to the Belgian economy.

4. This is a function question.

    (A) This option is **incorrect** because Martens is not treated in the passage as only a source of mismanagement. He is shown to have shored up Belgium's economy after the shock the oil price hikes wreaked on Belgium's economy.

    (B) This option is **incorrect** because the passage does not consider Martens' efforts to be misspent. He managed to bring Belgium up a bit.

    (C) This is the **correct** answer because the passage seeks to show that the progress Martens made was amid genuine economic difficulty even if it lacked a macroeconomic perspective.

    (D) This option is **incorrect** because the passage does credit Martens with improving aspects of the Belgian economy. Also, the author does criticize Martens' lack of macroeconomic perspective.

    (E) This option is **incorrect** because the Belgian economy did improve after a bad run.

    The correct answer is C.

5. This is a tone question from the general category.

    (A) This option is **incorrect** because the passage does not seek to apologize or paint poor actions in a good light.

    (B) This is the **correct** answer because it provides a historical interpretation of the actions taken during a period.

    (C) This option is **incorrect** because the passage does not seek to assert a political position or discuss a controversy.

    (D) This option is **incorrect** because the passage does not seek to argue against an interpretation of the facts.

    (E) This option is **incorrect** because the passage is better understood as a historical interpretation rather than all-encompassing account of events.

    The correct answer is B.

6. This is an inference question.

    (A) This option is **incorrect** because the passage mentions ways in which the government responded advantageously using its power.

(B) This is the **correct** answer because the passage suggests that it is economically inefficient to aid ailing industries. The author mentions that the subsidizing drove up the government's debt to 121% of GNP, suggesting that the author personally does not agree with this measure.

(C) This option is **incorrect** because the passage does not suggest the market can be ignored.

(D) This option is **incorrect** because the passage does not accuse the government of making decisions too slowly.

(E) This option is **incorrect** because the passage seeks to demonstrate the need to structure the economy in a way that is appropriate to minimize the effects of market fluctuation.

The correct answer is B.

7. This is an inference question.

(A) This option is **incorrect** because it is too broad, and unsubstantiated.

(B) This option is **incorrect** because the passage does not assert that economists are not pragmatists.

(C) This is the **correct** answer because the piece is a historical interpretation and makes assessments of the correct course of action after the fact, which is different from making decisions at the time of an issue.

(D) This option is **incorrect** because the author does assert that correct answers cannot be found in economics.

(E) This option is **incorrect** because the passage does not mention that the policy decisions were politically motivated.

The correct answer is C.

8. The word *masked* is used in the sentence: *The older, traditional industries of Wallonia, particularly steelmaking, began to lose their competitive edge during this period, but the general growth of world prosperity* **masked** *this deterioration until the 1973 and 1979 oil price shocks and resultant shifts in international demand sent the economy into a period of prolonged recession.*

From the sentence, we can deduce that though a few traditional industries of Wallonia, started declining, the general growth of world prosperity offset the ill-effects on Belgian economy. In other words, we can say that *the general growth of world* helped the poor state of a few traditional industries of Wallonia unexposed, or concealed the deterioration. Thus, option A is the **correct** answer.

Other options do not qualify for the replacement of **masked**, as mystified & perplexed mean confused–not apt in meaning in this context; eluded means baffled/dodged–inappropriate in the given context; and deceived means cheated–again improper word in this context.

The correct answer is A.

6.10 Passage 10 (Craving for fast food: who to blame – behavior or the brain?)

Understanding the Passage

This is a medium length passage of medium difficulty level on medical science and human behavior.

A finding by scientists has shown that consuming more "fast food" *(food with a high content of processed sugar, salt, and saturated fats)* can be addictive, just like other controlled substances *(heroin, narcotics, etc.).* According to researchers, fast food can trigger an addiction in the brain, causing it to ask for more fast food. *[Scientists conclude that fast food is addictive and the addiction demands regular feeding.].* Many scientists see a relationship between people's decisions to choose fast food as their preferred food and influencing factors in the environmental such as the wide availability of fast foods. *[Scientists believe that people want to eat fast food mainly because of permissive culture, environment, and easy availability of fast food]*; it leads to detrimental effects on human health and development. The researchers conclude that the brains of overeaters of fast foods experience some chemical changes triggering more appetite for the unhealthy food. *[The scientists believe that as one starts eating fast food regularly, the brain undergoes changes and craves more and more fast food.]*

If people continue to eat too much unhealthy food, it will initiate changes in the brain that raise the minimum level of eating the brain is usually satisfied with. *[Eating addictive stuff, or fast food, follows the law of diminishing returns, i.e. the amount that one needs to eat to get satisfied keeps increasing over time.]* Moreover, high consumption of fast foods stimulates opiate receptors in the brain *[opiate receptors are distributed widely in the brain; they act as natural pain relievers and eating fast food mimics this effect.).* Due to this, frequent and bigger doses of fast food feign some effects of opiates. *[Scientists contend that an uncontrolled amount of unhealthy food makes changes in the brain's response. The brain is only satisfied with bigger and more frequent feedings. Since the effect of fast food is similar to that of opiates, or pain relievers, people crave more to get the same psychotropic effect.].* Scientists performed an experiment on rats. They fed rats a sugar-rich diet; when they stopped the sugar-rich diet, they found that the rats showed the symptoms of withdrawal– shivering and chattering teeth. Their behavior was comparable to opiate addicts when the supply of opium is reduced to such addicts. When the rats were given the drugs that block opiate receptors *(natural pain relieving areas in the brain),* the dopamine levels in their brains *(an area linked with the dynamics of reward-reward is used for "craving for more food" and responsible for keeping a person addicted)* looked similar to those in heroin addicts. The scientists concluded that obesity can be viewed as a disease beyond the control of those affected by it *(just as addiction is beyond the control of addicts).* *[Scientists contend that propensity to eat more unhealthy food and get fatter is not truly related to one's behavior, but rather to changes in the neurochemistry of the brain.]*

Lawyers argue that society has a responsibility to regulate food and educate people about the abuse of unhealthy foods. Fast food companies should be held accountable for the ill-effects arising from unhealthy food. Still, some scientists are skeptical about the degree to which some researchers attribute the addiction to unhealthy food as the cause of neurological disorder rather than people's behavior. *(Some skeptics think that it is not right to blame neurochemistry alone for fast food addiction. People choose to eat fast food and so choice should be factored in, too.)* They contend that a habit and an addiction can be differentiated on qualitative parameters and not on quantitative parameters. *[These scientists think that some people habitually eat fast food but never overeat while others overeat fast food repeatedly, and this difference is not just the quantity of fast food consumed by both.]* The scientists think it's a qualitative difference, i.e. the qualities of these people differ. The ones who eat fast food regularly do not throw caution away and eat all they want but those who become addicted overrule common sense and eat more than is justified. These scientists think we cannot blame neurochemistry changes alone for differences between habitual fast food eaters and addicted overeaters.

The author cites a finding made by a few scientists claiming that unhealthy food, if consumed regularly and in large proportion, will make some neurological disorder in the brain, which in turn will ask for more food to satiate it. This leads to its ill-effects such as obesity. They contend that obesity may not be tackled only by exercising discipline in eating, as the brain will not be satisfied and will ask for more of such food. It needs to be treated like any other addiction disease. Some scientists are skeptical as to the degree of this claim.

Main Point: Addiction to unhealthy food is triggered more by the brain and less by undisciplined behavior, but some scientists remain unconvinced.

1. This is an inference question.

    (A) This is the **correct** answer because the passage demonstrates that people can be affected by environmental influences that create a cycle of addiction though they may not be aware that a chemical imbalance may have unconsciously affected their decision-making.

    (B) This option is **incorrect** because the scientists who see the relationship between decisions and environment note that it is not always possible to control surroundings once decision-making skills have been compromised.

    (C) This option is **incorrect** because the passage makes a distinction between being vulnerable to a cycle of addiction and having no responsibility over one's own behavior with an eating disorder. The passage does not suggest that overeaters are not responsible for their behavior. It just states that overeaters cannot control their impulse to overeat because their neurochemistry is affected. However, they still remain responsible for what's happening to them. They need to be treated like any other addict.

    (D) This option may be correct, but it is not affirmed in the passage. It's out of scope.

    (E) This option is **incorrect** because the passage does not say that overeaters are unable to overcome the difficulties of withdrawal. It does not even suggest that they try to withdraw from something.

    The correct answer is A.

2. This is Reasoning based question on strengthening the argument.

    The questions asks for the likely argument(s), lawyers would likely to put forth to defend corporations against the findings of researchers on the effects of "fast food." There may be one or more correct arguments.

    A   This option is a **likely** argument because arguing that obesity is a pre-existing condition in individuals, companies can claim that obesity is not caused because of their products.

    B   This is also a **likely** argument because it eliminates the threat of an addiction caused by the product by establishing that obesity is a result of consumer habits and not addiction to products. This will prove that overeating is not a result of neurochemistry altering effects of the company's products. This option will put the responsibility on the consumer *(by implying that moderation is a choice)* and free the company from the blame of making addictive products.

    C   This is an **unlikely** argument because if corporations claim that they are not liable for the unforeseen damage caused by their products, as they got to know now that "fast food" causes chemical dependency in people. I am conceding that there indeed is a link between fast food and addiction, even if I am not to blame for it now. I can be held liable now onwards or even retrospectively.

    The correct answers are A, & B.

3. This is an inference question.

    (A) This option is **incorrect** because while it may be true, the purpose of the scientists, as presented in the passage, is not to argue about strict diets.

    (B) This option is **incorrect** because it is not necessarily true. Even those who are not obese can be equally vulnerable to the health hazards of chronic consumption of fast food. The passage does not support such a deduction.

    (C) This option is **incorrect** because one does not necessarily have to have a genetic predisposition to obesity in order to contract the disease. This is out of scope.

    (D) This is the **correct** answer because treating obesity as a disease allows people to understand that obese people suffer from their behavior in a way that people without the disease may not. There are factors other than solely individual behavior, such as chemical imbalance, that may be considered responsible for obesity. Scientists do think that environmental factors and neurochemistry changes are responsible for obesity.

    (E) This option is **incorrect** because it is not true and is not stated by the scientists mentioned in the passage.

    The correct answer is D.

4. This is a detail question.

    (A) This is the **correct** answer because the researchers object to the conclusions reached based on the evidence *(findings)* found by their colleagues. *(Refer to the* *first sentence of the passage.)* The skeptics believe that data may exist on neurochemistry being altered, but the extent to which individual choices determine obesity should not be discounted. Thus the skeptics disagree with the conclusion of the researchers.

(B) This option is **incorrect** because there is no mention in the passage that suggests that the researchers doubted the expertise of their colleagues. They certainly were skeptical about the findings presented by their colleagues.

(C) This option is **incorrect** because there is no mention of the proponents making any assumptions that the skeptics disagreed on.

(D) This option is **incorrect** because there is no mention of the method, or of the opponents' objection to it, in the passage.

(E) This option is **incorrect** because the researchers do not contest the validity of the data collected.

The correct answer is A.

5.   This is a Function question.

The correct sentence: *For these researchers, the distinction between a habit and an addiction is not quantitative but qualitative.* is the **correct** answer because opponents view consumption choices ("qualitative") as primarily behavioral and not primarily chemical problems ("quantitative"). So, it follows that those skeptics would object to the assumption that addictive behavior has nothing to do with behavior and choices and is dependent only on chemical imbalances in the brain.

6.   This is an inference question.

(A) This option is **incorrect** because dopamine makes rats happier as they pursue consumption *(reward)*, and therefore they feel encouraged to eat more. Refer to the latter part of the second paragraph: "*Later, by treating rats with drugs that block opiate receptors, scientists were able to lower the amount of dopamine in the nucleus acumen of rats' brains, an area linked with the dynamics of reward.*" The word "reward" is used here for "more food." It can be inferred that by lowering the level of dopamine, the desire for more food reduces, so the role of dopamine would be to make one long for more food *(and to reward oneself)*.

(B) This option is **incorrect** because dopamine does not block opiates. The passage talked about opiate-blocking drugs that helped to lower dopamine levels.

(C) This option is **incorrect** because opiates are not replaced by dopamine.

(D) This option is **incorrect** because, on the contrary, dopamine is linked to the reward mechanism which activates when rats receive opiates.

(E) This is the **correct** answer since rats are encouraged to eat more. It follows from the deduction made in option A's explanation.

The correct answer is E.

7. This is a detail question.

   (A) This option is **incorrect** because we cannot infer from the passage that the lawyers' position implies that the government lacks knowledge.

   (B) This is the **correct** answer because the passage states that lawyers argue that there is a responsibility to regulate food and educate people about the abuse of "unhealthy foods" in a way that is comparable to society's control of opiates and narcotics. Corporations (fast food restaurants) that target this vulnerability (addiction to fast food) in human beings can then be held liable. . .'

   (C) This option is **incorrect** because lawyers are arguing that it is the responsibility of corporations, and not the market, to keep consumers informed, and to account for damage caused by their products.

   (D) This option is **incorrect** because the lawyers do not assume governmental incompetence. Moreover, the lawyers wish to make fast food restaurants, and not the government, accountable for damaging public health.

   (E) This option is **incorrect** because by placing the responsibility for a good diet on the individual, the lawyers' objective to make fast food restaurants liable will get diluted.

The correct answer is B.

6.11   Passage 11 (Masks & gas attacks during WW II)

Understanding the Passage

This is a short length passage of low difficulty level on wartime history.

World War II exposed America to the need for security of its citizens. Unlike in WW II, in WW I its citizens were never attacked.

The highest priority for the U.S. was the protection of children from possible attack. WW II had a history of participating nations attacking civilian areas. It was started by Germany on London, and then the Allied Forces retaliated with attacks on the German city of Dresden.

A leading concern for Britain and the U.S. was the exposure to gas attacks upon the youth population. Immediately after Pearl Harbor, thousands of military training masks were rushed to people living on the islands. However, these masks were unsuitable for protecting children. Hawaiian officials produced an expedient *(a temporary means to an end)* made up of bunny ears and a hood. The Sun Rubber Company designed a relatively acceptable mask based on the universal Walt Disney cartoon figure Mickey Mouse. The adoption of these masks made them popular among children and this in turn potentially reduced the element of fear of masks.

This measure would increase the chances of survival for youth; it was important to protect them because a large number of working age males were vulnerable to losing their lives fighting overseas.

The passage is about the mechanism of protecting the youth population of the U.S. from possible gas attacks during WW II. The author discusses the importance of protecting them, the challenges with masks, and the popularity and adoption of innovatively-designed masks for children.

Main Point: Challenges and a mechanism to protect youth from gas attacks during WW-II.

1.   This is a detail question.

   The first paragraph of the passage mentions that World War II exposed America to the need for security of its citizens. Unlike in WW II, in WW I, its citizens were never attacked. Option D is the only answer mentioned in the passage distinguishing World War I from World War II.

   Option E—The threat of nationalism from foreign aggressors—is extreme and cannot be inferred.

   The correct answer is D.

2. This is a Function question.

   A   This option is **incorrect** because there was no such intent of destroying the civilian wartime infrastructure was reflected in the passage.

   B   This is the **correct** and the best answer as stated in the sentence: "Germany unleashed the lengthiest bombing campaign of the war on the people of London primarily to weaken British morale."

   C   This option is **incorrect** because nothing of this sort was stated in the passage.

   The correct answer is B.

3. This is a function question.

   Option C is supported by line 23-27: "The popularity of these masks was dependent on internalizing their use in children …This potentially reduced the element of fear. If the element of fear could be diminished, gas masks might be employed by their owners more quickly in the event of an attack, and also worn without interruption."

   The design of gas masks to look like Mickey Mouse was intended to encourage children to wear the masks and wear them properly so that they were safe against possible gas attacks.

   Other options are either not supported by the passage or are irrelevant.

   The correct answer is C.

4. This is a Detail question.

   We need to choose a sentence that contains both special efforts and concern exhibited towards protecting the youth population.

   The last sentence of the passage is the **correct** answer. "All of this would increase the chances of survival of the youth population, of no small concern to a nation with large numbers of its working age males facing the perils of combat overseas."

   In other words, the measure of protecting children from possible gas attacks would increase the chances of survival of the youth population; it is important to protect the youth because a large numbers of working age males were vulnerable as they could lose lives fighting overseas. (important concern)

5. This is a main Point question from the general category.

   We have derived the main point in the Understanding the Passage section.

Main Point: Challenges and a mechanism to protect youth from gas attacks during WW II.

Option B is the best answer since the passage primarily discusses the role of civilian terror tactics and the provisions needed to protect children from those tactics.

Other options are either not supported by the passage or are irrelevant.

The correct answer is B.

6. This is a detail question.

    Option C is the correct answer since an expedient is something used as a temporary means to an end, and is helpful or useful in a particular situation.

    The correct answer is C.

7. This is a function question.

    Option D is correct since the passage states: "The popularity of these masks was dependent on internalizing their use in children by making their presence part of a perceived game. This potentially reduced the element of fear that the masks conveyed on their recipients. If the element of fear could be diminished, gas masks might be employed by their owners more quickly in the event of an attack ..."

    Other options are either not supported by the passage or are irrelevant.

    The correct answer is D.

8. This is an inference question.
    (A) This option is **incorrect** because enemy propaganda as a danger is not discussed in the passage.
    (B) Like option A, this option is **incorrect** because the youth of the civilian population itself is not the danger.
    (C) This is **correct** since the point of providing gas masks in a familiar form is to allow civilians to make the correct decisions by being prepared to act correctly.
    (D) This option is **incorrect** because it is not supported by the passage. Though the attack of Germany on Britain was meant to weaken British morale, the author did not ratify it as a significant avoidable danger of a wartime terror attack.
    (E) This option is **incorrect** because it is not supported by the passage, and lack of warning of an attack is not an avoidable danger.

    The correct answer is C.

6.12   Passage 12 (Lord Dalhousie's uniform rate of postage in India)

Understanding the Passage

This is a short passage of low difficulty level on the topic of business sociology.

Lord Dalhousie is credited with the creation of the modern postal system in India. He implemented the practice of levying a uniform rate of postage throughout India, irrespective of origin or destination.

Many critics ridiculed Dalhousie's idea. It was, they said, pushing Rowland Hill's scheme of penny postage for England to the extreme in India. They viewed it as a "reductio ad absurdum" of the reform that had been effected in Great Britain. [*It was termed as extreme as the area of India was far more than that of England implying uniform rate is devoid of any logic; it was absurd!*].

Lord Dalhousie was firm in his decision of levying the uniform rate of postage. Earlier there had been an argument over the payment for delivery of every letter, and the rural postman used to charge additional money to the recipient for his service. But Dalhousie's intention was that with the new simplistic system of postage stamps, petty bickering with postmen would cease to exist, and people would be assured of reliable service.

His postal system became a self-sustaining organization, from which the financial outlay for postal services could be recouped. The social results were even more important. It has been said that the half-penny postage system of Lord Dalhousie was more significant in bridging the gap between the various parts of India than earlier developments such as the telegraph, the railway, and other formal systems.

The passage is about the implementation of Lord Dalhousie's innovative but absurd-seeming postal scheme in India, which proposed to charge a uniform rate of postage throughout India, irrespective of origin or destination. The passage talks about its success owing to its simplicity and the social benefit it caused.

Main Point: The success of Lord Dalhousie's uniform rate of postage scheme in India.

   1.   This is a detail question.

        Option A is the correct answer and is demonstrated by the description in the passage of perceived injustice which opponents saw in the new Indian post system. Lord Dalhousie implemented the scheme of levying a uniform rate of postage throughout India irrespective of origin or destination, which was ridiculed by many critics. It seemed absurd and unreasonable to charge for a letter going a long distance the same amount as for a letter going a short distance.

        Though option B deserves a thought, it can be inferred from the passage that the proposed postal scheme by Lord Dalhousie was not unproven – it was applicable in England, but looking at the vast geographical area of Indian, it looked rather unreasonable. Critics were opposed not because it was unproven, but because it seemed illogical.

Other options are either not discussed in the passage or are irrelevant.

The correct answer is A.

2. This is a Detail question.

    The apt sentence is expected to be found in paragraph III or IV as para I in more of an introduction and para II is the critique of the scheme.

    The **correct** sentence is the last sentence of the passage: *It has been said that the half-penny post that Lord Dalhousie put in place in India was more consequential than the tele-graph, the railway and even Public Instruction for reversing the isolation which predated it.".* Thus, the system facilitated increased communication. This sentence is preceded by the sentence, which states that the social benefit was more important. Thus, it can be considered the main benefit - which the question asks us to find.

3. This is an Inference question.

    | A | This option is **incorrect** because it is extreme and devoid of any solid reasoning. |

    | B | This option is **correct** because the scheme succeeded at both the places—small scale (England: smaller geographical area compared to India), and large scale (India), so we can infer that that if something works on a small scale, it should work on a large scale as well, if executed properly. |

    | C | This option is also **correct** because the passage observes that benefits provided by uniform postage were the elimination of wrangling with the local postman and the creation of reliability. If the result of these changes in the system was increased postage, then the disorganization caused by the previous system may have been more costly than shipping a letter across India at a set rate irrespective of cost because it allowed the postmen to get unwarranted cuts of their own and increased mistrust among people, reducing their use of the postal services. Thus, Dalhousie proved that charging uniform, lower rates was a much better proposition in the longer term for postal system than not. |

    The correct answers are B & C.

4. This is an inference question.

    (A) This is the **correct** answer because it can be deduced from the experience of Dal-housie in different roles in the administration and internal development of the region, as well as his willingness to disregard the criticism of traditional financiers, whom we might assume were using traditional methods of problem resolution. He didn't see India's vastness as a detriment to a scheme that had worked in a smaller place successfully.

(B)   This option is **incorrect** because there is no evidence to support this.

(C)   This option is **incorrect** because there is no evidence to support this.

(D)   This option is **incorrect** because it cannot necessarily be deduced.

(E)   This option is **incorrect** because though the objective of bridging the gap between different parts of India was achieved through the postal scheme, other objectives could have been met through the telegraph, the railway, and public instruction, which were of equal importance.

The correct answer is A.

5.   This is a detail question.

Option C is the correct answer because "reductio ad absurdum" literally means to reduce something to an absurd degree, or to extend something to an absurd degree. However, if you are not sure about the meaning, you can still infer it from the context.

Let us examine the sentence and infer the meaning. *"For these onlookers, Dalhousie's plan was not so much an extension of the English penny postage scheme, as a reductio ad absurdum of the reform that had been effected in Great Britain."*

It is clear that critics found the idea of implementing the postal scheme as absurd simply due to its success in England. They were of the opinion that extending the same scheme to much larger geography was absurd! Clearly option C is the correct answer.

The correct answer is C.

6.   This is a detail question.

Option B is the correct answer as indicated in the sentence (line 19) stating "The system was more reliable for the person mailing the letter, and encouraged **increased patronage**."

Other options are either not discussed in the passage or are irrelevant.

The correct answer is B.

7.   This is a detail question.

Option D can be seen as the correct answer from the sentence (line 22) stating "The proof of his success was the renewal of the postal system as a self-sustaining organization rather than its continuance as a chronic drain on British colonial finances."

Other options are either not discussed in the passage or are irrelevant.

The correct answer is D.

8. This is an inference question.

  (A) This option is **incorrect** because, in fact, it is the other way around. Uniform rate of postage irrespective of distances shows that transaction costs may not increase substantially even in larger markets.

  (B) This option is **incorrect** because it is an extreme answer. We cannot infer this from the passage.

  (C) This option is **incorrect** because it is an extreme answer. We cannot infer this from the passage. Though there was mention of postmen wrangling over the charges to deliver letters and trying to squeeze some extra money from the recipient, calling them "always corrupt" is an extreme reaction.

  (D) This option is **incorrect** because it is an extreme answer. The passage does not have supporting evidence to infer that letters are the MOST efficient means of communication.

  (E) This is the **correct** answer because wrangling (disputing/bickering) with local postman appeared costly as it limited the reliability of the system. This unreliability decreased patronage and raised costs. However, when rates were standardized, patronage increased to the extent that the postal system became self-sustaining and did not need the British government's financial intervention. So, this can be inferred.

The correct answer is E.

6.13   Passage 13 (Sustainability of homo sapiens)

Understanding the Passage

This is a long passage of high difficulty level on the topic of biology.

Biomass is the total mass of all living members of a species. Considering all the species, human beings are one of the largest biomasses on earth [*Insects have the most biomass*]. They are the leading influence on earth's ecosystems, and, as a result of ecological processes, they inhabit most areas throughout the world. A species has a great chance of survival if its aggregate biomass is at the top compared with other species. Since the biomass of human beings is on top, they claim their territory *(habitats)*, and have control of resources. [*For a species to survive, it must compete with other species and have influence, thereby leveraging on sustainable resources*]. It might be short-sighted to belittle the success of an emerging species or breed for being small in number if it is evident that the members of the species are elegant and well-adjusted [*The author says that while the aggregate biomass is one of the determinants of the species' success, it is not wise to think less of species with less biomass if they have good adaptations that allow them to adjust well to the environment*]. A species' ability to adapt to their habitat in the ecosystem, yet being able to vary according to the needs of the environment, is considered very beneficial. Human beings have had nearly unparalleled success compared to other species in successful adaptation. As a result, human beings exist in huge numbers. It is a fact that human beings have remained in a generally undifferentiated form that allows them to rank highly as a single successful species. [*Human being did not branch out in many different sub-species; they adapted themselves well and remain Homo sapiens. Usually when a species changes, its habitat or the environment around it has changed, and the species is forced to adapt to the new surroundings and often adapts and changes so much that it is no longer like the earlier species, and becomes a new variant.*]

Compared to other species, human beings are considered unique, as they retain their form as they travel from environment to environment. [*Other species, if adapted successfully, may lose their form.*] Despite challenges in the environment and adapting to new environments, human beings have been able to adjust their behavior sufficiently to avoid having nature make such extensive piecemeal adjustments to them that entirely distinct workable alternatives of the same model occupy the new space. [*It means that humans withstood nature's default adjustment of splitting a species into similar yet different variants of surviving species.*] And with these adjustments, other species such as dinosaurs transmogrified to pigeons, primitive fish to amphibians and then eventually to whales, even Homo sapiens *(human begins)* partially to Neanderthals (a similar yet different species of human) for a time. [*All these are examples of when nature stepped in to help a species to adapt to survive better and the final result was drastically different from the original one.*]

Surviving and extinct variants of each species had to co-exist alongside their parental species [*Original species and newly-adapted and developed species live side-by-side*]. Many surviving species, with successful reproduction with other members, move into another ecosystem. Following this, each variant species was considered a different species from its parent species [*Each variant becomes nearly completely different from the original ones – and probably can no longer mate with the original species*]. In this way, the exchange of genes among members occurred across the globe, and a new species takes on a scientifically unique identity at different times and in different places. But humans remain a distinct species [*compared to other species, humans did not branch out to many variant species*] not because they are the first to exist in so many habitats and take advantage of so many resources, but for the reason that they have become one of the relatively few species to inhabitat different parts of the world in great numbers while being able to exchange genetic material [*sexual reproduction*] with others from their group, even if they had been largely geographically isolated from other groups over many generations. [*Humans are different because while they populated different habitats all over the world, unlike other species they did not undergo such drastic changes that they could not continue to mate with other human beings from different places. So, human beings are one of the most successful species ever.*]

Main Point: Survival of the supreme species Homo sapiens.

1. This is a detail question.

    Option D is the correct answer supported by the sentences given in the first part of paragraph 1 (lines 4-7): "*It can be said the most rudimentary measure of the **success of the species** is its position near the top of the aggregate biomass scale... For human beings, it is a reflection of **their claim on territory, and their consumption of resources as a species.**"*

    Option A is classic case of mixing up words. The passage states "*It can be said the most rudimentary measure of the success of the species is **its position near the top of the aggregate biomass scale**," and* <u>not at the top of the food chain</u>.

    Other options are either not stated in the passage or are inconclusive.

    The correct answer is D.

2. This is a detail question.
    (A) This option is **incorrect** because, on the contrary, the passage states otherwise. The second sentence of the second paragraph (line 17) states "*Human beings are considered unique as **they retain their form** as they travel from environment to environment.*"
    (B) This option is **incorrect** because though the passage mentions that even Homo sapiens partially yielded to Neanderthals for a time through piecemeal adjustments, it does not make human beings unique in their colonization of the Earth. What makes human colonization unique, and unlike that of other species, is that while spreading to different habitats they did not adapt to the extent of becoming different from the original species. Most species change and adapt so much when they move to new habitats that they no longer resemble the original species.
    (C) This is the **correct** answer. It is supported by (line 17): "***Humans thus remain distinct** (unique) not **because** they are the first to exist in so many habitats, and take advantage of so many resources, but in that **they** have become one of the relatively few organisms to **accomplish widespread population of different habitats while**

being able to exchange genetic material with others from their group, even if they had been largely geographically isolated over many generations." This implies that unlike other species, humans could withstand splitting into different groups yet were able to habituate themselves densely in diversified habitats. Thus, they survived as one species despite their dispersal all over the world, and did not get differentiated and fragmented into different sub-species.

(D) This option is **incorrect** because though it is correct that human beings are one of the highest ranked organisms on the biomass scale, it does not make human beings unique with respect to the colonization aspect. Also, insects are ranked higher than human beings on the biomass scale.

(E) This option is **incorrect** because this is opposite of the fact given in the passage. Refer to the last part of the last paragraph (line 17); the gist is: Humans thus remain distinct (unique)... because... they accomplish widespread population of different habitats while being able to exchange genetic material with others from their group, <u>even if they had been largely geographically isolated over many generations.</u>

The correct answer is C.

3. This is a detail question.

Option D is the correct answer. Since human beings had the ability to adjust themselves according to their environment, they could withstand the genetic splitting into different species. It is supported by: *"Still, human beings have been able to adjust their behavior sufficiently to avoid having nature make such extensive piecemeal adjustments to them that entirely distinct workable alternatives of the same model occupy the new space."* It means that humans withstood nature's default adjustment of splitting a species into a similar yet different variant of a surviving species by adjusting their behavior to suit the environment in which they were put.

Other options are either not stated in the passage or are not supported.

The correct answer is D.

4. This is a detail question.

(A) This option is **incorrect** because it is not mentioned in the passage.

(B) This option is **incorrect** because it is also not mentioned in the passage. How densely any species is populated is not mentioned.

(C) This is the **correct** answer since the passage notes that it is the *"widespread population of different habitats (population size) while being able to exchange genetic material with others from their group"* which the passage notes as 'distinct' in terms of success over other species. That is how biomass is defined and success of a species is how much biomass it has accumulated.

(D) This option is **incorrect** because the passage mentions that genetic code is dispersed around the world for any given species, but the ability of that species to retain its genetic code is one of the criteria for success and not merely the global dispersion of its genetic code.

(E)   This option is **incorrect** because as shown by the sentences *"It might be short-sighted to belittle the success of an emerging species or breed for being small in number if it is evident that the members of the species are elegant and well-adjusted. However, the ability to adapt one's habitat to the largest ecosystem, while still **retaining the flexibility to deal with local demands on the population may be considered high art in the annals of successful adaptation."*** There are two factors to be taken into account for success, one: the ability to adapt, and two: being flexible in dealing with local demands of the population. Thus, the degree of adaptation to its environment by itself cannot be quantified as success.

The correct answer is C.

5.   This is a detail question.

The passages measures success through many parameters: species biomass (insects on the top, and humans near the top), capability to claim territory and consume resources, and adaptation in different environments. Option A is the correct answer since the passage discusses the effect of ecological change driving species into different habitats, which is related to geographic dispersion.

Other options are either not mentioned or are not inferable from the passage.

The correct answer is A.

6.   This is a detail question.

Option D is the correct answer since the passage discusses the fact that some species had to co-exist alongside their predecessors or previous forms.

The correct answer is D.

7.   This is a Function question.

The last and the lengthiest sentence of the passage is the correct answer because the passage discusses the movement of human genetic material as human beings migrated across the earth. Refer to the sentence: the gist is: *"Humans thus remain distinct(unique)... because...they accomplish widespread population of different habitats while being able to **exchange genetic material (or, migration of species) with others from their group, even if they had been largely geographically isolated** over many generations."* Any other sentence discusses either only genetic material or only migration but not both.

8.   This is a Tone question.

Options A & C are the correct answers since the passage is a detailed, fact-driven, objective, and impartial discussion of a topic, thus explanatory. It is not critical of the facts presented in the passage, thus not argumentative. Thus, it can be best expressed as balanced & explanatory.

The correct answers are A & C.

6.14   Passage 14 (Abortion law)

Understanding the Passage

This is a medium length passage of low difficulty level on the topic of socio-economics.

The debate on the legalization of abortion in America has been advocated on the grounds of human rights and freedom of choice. The supporters of these views want lawmakers to alter any legislation pertaining to abortion. Moreover, economists also want lawmakers to alter any legislation pertaining to abortion by looking at the issue from some practical point of view. While it is important to note that the life of any unborn child matters, the economic relevance of bringing up an unwanted child and depriving him of an adequate life-style must also be considered when looking at legislation pertaining to abortion. [*Apart from looking at the abortion issue on moral grounds, it should also be looked at from an economics point of view.*]

However, researchers have pointed out that there is a correlation between the Roe vs. Wade abortion empowerment legislation and reported crime statistics twenty years after an unwanted child is born. They suggest that when abortion is not allowed, the crime rate increases. This conclusion is based on findings that within a few years of Roe vs. Wade's abortion legislation, up to 25% of all pregnancies in the United States resulted in abortions. Also, they observe that crime rates between 1985 and 1997 declined. The researchers note that due to the implementation of abortion legislation, a significant number of illegitimate children were not born, and this led to a decrease in crime during this time frame. It mentions a 20 year period because it is the age at which most wrongdoers engage in the majority of any society's illegal activity. Since those illegitimate children are relatively inexperienced (and thus don't get gainful employment), lack moral values, are deprived of societal support and adequate opportunities to grow from, they are more prone to violence and rebelliousness compared to women or adult males. The researchers realize that abortion by a woman is a practical and sensible step if she is not prepared to care for an unwanted child. Raising an illegitimate child is a great challenge. This in turn deprives the child of adequate resources to grow, and exposes him to the likelihood of illegal conduct in society.

A low crime rate signifies that giving a choice to a woman when to have a baby is a welcome move. Another aspect to the abortion debate is that crime is financially costly to taxpayers. According to one estimate, taxpayers would lose as much as $30 billion annually because of crimes committed by teen-aged illegitimate children who had not been aborted, thereby creating an even higher crime rate. Though ideologists have been arguing against abortion, legislators must look into abortion reform from all aspects so that they can reach a rational decision, especially from an economic angle.

The passage is about reforms aimed at abortion legislation. Though the demand to legalize abortion has been argued from a moral point of view–human rights and freedom of choice, there is another aspect discussed in the passage–economics (the cost society pays due to letting unwanted children be brought up in society.). The passage argues that illegitimate and unprivileged teenaged children indulge in crimes and society has to pay dearly for it. To sum up, the author advocates that legislators look into this aspect while reforming abortion law.

Main Point: Reform abortion law: it's time to look at it from a financial and safety point of view.

1. This is a detail question.

   Option D is the best option since the passage claims the difficulty lawmakers have with contending with the abortion debate problem relates to their inability to see past ideologies (moral issues), while the benefit offered by the researchers is information on the practical results of abortion for society (a lower crime rate, and annual savings as high as $30 billion).

   While option A is too general and vague, other options do not qualify to be in the reckoning.

   The correct answer is D.

2. This is a tone question from the general category.

   While reading the passage, we find that the author is clearly of the opinion that reform on abortion legislation must take place. Apart from lawmakers being influenced from the point of view of human rights and freedom of choice, he cites the economic aspect–the cost and crime due to abortions that do happen. There are indicators in the passage that imply that the author is in favor of the reforms such as *"As the **ideological arguments** over abortion **refuse to abate**, it may be time for **hamstrung legislators** to consider new sources of information **to simplify their decisions** about reopening the question of abortion reform and government aid."* Option A is the correct answer.

   The closest option could be journalistic, however it is incorrect because he is not merely reporting various aspects and facts. He is not unbiased (as journalism is supposed to be) but is in favor of reforms in abortion laws and conveys such ideas implicitly. He is quite clearly not a disinterested party given the last sentence, *"it may be time for hamstrung legislators to consider new sources of information to simplify their decisions about reopening the question of abortion reform and government aid"*; he suggests that action be taken on this from a practical point of view. A journalistic argument will not present an opinion but merely present the various aspects.

   However, the author quite clearly wants us to be persuaded about reform in abortion laws. Thus, he is "persuasive" in his passage.

   The correct answer is A.

3. This is a strengthen the argument question from the reasoning question category.

   Let us understand the claim of the researchers.

   Claim: There is an economic cost society has to pay (an annual cost to the tune of $30 billion because of crime committed by illegitimate teen-aged children) due to anti-abortion.

Let us look through each option one by one and see which option supports or strengthens the claim made by the researchers.

(A) This option is **incorrect** because it is irrelevant. The researchers are concerned about the crime committed by illegitimate and unprivileged teenaged children, and not by white-collar workers (professionals and office workers).

(B) This option is **incorrect** because the aspect of the economy is out of scope; the economic cost arising from an issue and the economy itself are two different things.

(C) This is the **correct** answer since reduced crime at an earlier stage in states which first legalized abortion could show that the birth of unwanted babies in other areas is correlated with higher crime in those areas for the length of time that abortion was illegal in those states. This will directly support the researchers' claims that allowing abortion reduces crime rates.

(D) This option is **incorrect** because it is irrelevant.

(E) This option is **incorrect** because it would instead weaken the claim.

The correct answer is C.

4. This is an inference question.

Option D is the correct answer since the passage claims that anti-abortion legislation results in higher crime because mothers are unable to care for babies they are legally compelled to have. It is suggested that mothers do not want babies they are not ready to raise in part because they are incapable of raising them. Also, the researchers who claim that unwanted pregnancies lead to increases in crime specify that such crimes are conducted by males, and not females. Thus, those researchers assume that the un-aborted babies are more likely to be males than females, and that these males, when not properly cared for by their unwilling mothers, will resort to crimes in their adolescence or early youth.

Other options are either irrelevant or not discussed in the passage.

The correct answer is D.

5. This is a function Question.

(A) This option is **incorrect** because the author clearly supports the position of the researchers for reforms in abortion legislation.

(B) This option is **incorrect** because it is irrelevant.

(C) This option is **incorrect** because the author does not seem to weigh any of the position vis-a-vis others.

(D) This option is **incorrect** because it is an extreme option. Though the author assumes that moral debates on economic issues like abortion cannot solely help in formulating legislation, it does not mean that they cannot help in any way in formulating legislation.

(E) This is the **correct** answer because the passage notes that the abortion debate has ideological contentions that do not abate, and a simpler method of resolving the problem may be useful.

The correct answer is E.

6. This is a function question.

Let us look at the given piece: *"As the ideological arguments over abortion refuse to abate, it may be time for hamstrung legislators to consider new sources of information to simplify their decision about reopening the question of abortion reform and government aid."*

Let us understand the gist: The author is against the position taken up by ideologists–anti-abortion proponents. He seems to be trying to persuade restrained legislators to consider the pro-abortion position and reach a decision on abortion reform and government aid using persuasive economic data. Thus, his main purpose seems to be to get some useful legislation made and for the debate to end.

(A) This option is **incorrect** because it is irrelevant.

(B) This option is **incorrect** because it is the other way around. The author seeks to simplify the abortion debate.

(C) This option is **incorrect** because it is irrelevant.

(D) This option is **incorrect** because it is the other way around. The author is against the position taken up by ideologists–anti-abortion proponents, and wants the debate to rather end sooner than later.

(E) This is the **correct** answer. It falls in line with what we analyzed earlier.

The correct answer is E.

7. This is an Inference Question.

A   This option is **correct** because abortions of unwanted babies that researchers assert can be reasonably correlated with lower crime.

B   This option is also **correct** because it clearly articulates what researchers imply: crime decreases and money is saved when women have the freedom of choice to not to give birth to unwanted children.

C   This option is **incorrect** because neither the passage nor the researchers mention the role of non-violent female children as a practical consideration in the abortion debate.

The correct answers are A & B.

8. This is a main point question from the general category.

Let us look at the piece where the word "suboptimal" is used. *"Going forward with an unwanted pregnancy presumably confers on the woman too great a challenge in raising a child she is poorly prepared for, and provides the child with an upbringing that is* **suboptimal***, making him more vulnerable to be party to illegal conduct."*

Option A—Inadequate—is the correct answer since the passage communicates a condition in which children are not being provided a sufficient standard of living to assure quality of life and are poorly prepared to decline illicit opportunities for gain.

While almost perfect, economically advantaged, and second best do not have negative undertones, inefficient is an incorrect substitute in the present context.

The correct answer is A.

9.   This is a Detail question.

We have to select the sentence that provides **evidence** for the hypothesis that says adolescent and young adult males are considere the most likely to engage in illegal activities.

Three sentences can be discussed.

1. *This is because the period during which most perpetrators engage in the majority of any society's illegal activity is when they are in their late teens and early twenties.*: This is **incorrect** because it is a hypothesis but not evidence.

2. *Their relative inexperience in the world, the paucity of opportunities and their group relationships make them more prone to violence and defiance than women or older males.*: Again, this is **incorrect** because it is a hypothesis but not evidence.

3. *Also, they observe that crime rates between 1985 and 1997 declined.* This is **correct** because it does present evidence for the hypothesis mentioned in the question.

6.15 Passage 15 (Surveillance)

Understanding the Passage

This is a medium length passage of medium difficulty level on the topic of law and policy.

Secretly observing suspects has always been a tool in investigation activities over the years, but the most important difference between modern practices of surveillance and traditional practices is that in the past, the everyday routine of the accused and his social behavior were monitored, whereas currently almost everyone who is considered even remotely suspicious or likely to commit a crime is subjected to intense and unrelenting scrutiny without being aware of it. [*The author seems critical of the fact that in modern day surveillance, according to him, the extent of surveillance on the suspects is a breach of privacy.*] No less foreboding is analysis through calculations of regression and methods of associated comparison that broadens scientifically the range of 'suspicious' behavior in order to justify the oversight of new types of actors, and an increased number of actors. [*The author asserts that analyzing suspect's behavior based on his past activities and on his associations to try to estimate the current scenario is a dangerous trend. When scrutinizing a person's behavior, there may be nothing wrong with what he is currently doing, but the analysis shows that he had negative associations in his past or was close to committing a crime in the past. This is the justification that governmental agencies use to survey more and more people, bringing those people under their expanding definition of "suspicious." The author is highly critical of this behavior on the part of the government.*] These abilities are being incorporated into a policy about which the public is not aware, and one which is outside the scope of current legislation. [*People are not aware of these new trends of unscrupulous surveillance; moreover it is outside the scope of current legislation, that is, it would be considered illegal if someone other than the government were doing so.*]

Given that most people regard themselves as 'law abiding,' and that the avoidance of crime, drug abuse and other quality of life infractions rates highly in citizens' priorities, the development of improved surveillance systems is widely seen as a benign invasion that improves policing. [*Most people see themselves as 'law abiding' citizens, and though they view the increased surveillance on their life as an invasion of their privacy, they consider that it is done with noble intentions.*] In a famous incident in the UK, two young men were put under surveillance (because they had appeared suspicious as per the analyses) and were discovered to be the culprits in the murder of a young boy; following this, people in the UK began to feel that surveillance served a purpose. Since then, the most widespread use of surveillance cameras has occurred in the UK. The impracticality of, and lack of interest in, prosecuting every transgression caught by the system obscures its threat to individual liberty. [*Most people feel that it is nearly impossible to track every person's each and every activity and so feel that the invasion on their privacy is minimal.*] But while this may keep the disadvantages of surveillance from bringing people to vocal dissent [*since they feel their privacy is not really being invaded, they do not protest against the huge increase in surveillance*], what should be raised in the public consciousness is that what surveillance changes is the amount of leverage a minority of actors (authorities, bureaucrats, or system managers) have over the general population [*but they are not aware that this surveillance is impacting the negotiating/defending powers that any individual or group has against the government*]. In any encounter in which one individual must confront the state, the state achieves an advantage by having so many more 'leads' on the individual with which to use bullying tactics, and by engaging in non-judicial activities such as Secret Service searches, the disbanding of rallies, and the detention of political and foreign activists. [*The state resorts to bullying tactics and non-judicial activities such as Secret Service searches on individuals to frame charges against them; the state can even exercise the same on political figures and foreign activists. Thus, using surveillance, any governmental authority can establish that any person "seems" suspicious and then go on to intimidate that person, even if no actual proof of any wrongdoing is present.*]

Compiling a file of criminal activities engaged in by a subject under surveillance is routine. But there can also be an insinuation of an activity that a government uses politically to undermine the position of a subject. [*Though keeping a record of criminal activities of people is routine, at times the authorities use the surveillance records to imply that someone has done something wrong without any actual proof of anything at all.*] That action changes the direction of prosecution, reiterating the importance of, and the reasoning behind, such safeguards as the Miranda acts, designed to protect suspects from incriminating themselves in the absence of their lawyer. [*Due to these kinds of practices, the intention of prosecution takes the wrong course, and the very purpose of the Miranda acts (which are designed to prevent suspects from incriminating themselves in the absence of their lawyer) is lost because just doing anything can be construed as suspicious by the government and held against the person, thereby restricting the person's freedom and rights.*] The greatest danger is that the rules of criminal justice can be controlled by a bureaucratic, authoritarian organization to prolong detention and to control the flow of information under conditions of the confinement of a subject, in order to improve the ability of investigators to aid the prosecution. [*The greatest danger of these practices is that the rules of criminal justice can be controlled and influenced by authorities; these authorities unduly harass suspects and try to manipulate the case in order to aid the prosecution by using the surveillance records to delay the freeing of the persons and keeping them in jail, etc. to help the police and prosecuting lawyers in making a better case.*] The monopoly which public bureaucracies have on prosecution and investigation allows them to use or disregard official rules in ways that are not transparent to a defendant. [*These new trends of unscrupulous surveillance do not pay respect to the official rules and, sadly, it is not known to the accused that they are being cheated on account of this, since effectively it is the government breaking the rules, and the public isn't aware of such thing.*] It has been shown that increasing the level of surveillance in the public arena does not improve the ability to identify offenders, but improves the ability of the government to operate extra-judicially. This offers authorities the opportunity of manufacturing opportunities for themselves to control behavior in ways that are beyond redress. [*On the contrary, it has been noticed that increasing the level of surveillance on the public does not improve the state's ability to identify offenders, but it unjustifiably improves the ability of the government to operate above the law and force people into legal battles against which the people have barely any defenses.*]

The passage is about government and authorities exercising extra-judicial power in the guise of increased surveillance on people. They influence the case against the defendants. By way of increased surveillance, the authorities invade the privacy of people. The author is clearly against the current trend. The innocent people are not aware of the fact that the state does not have any right to infringe upon their lives and make use of evidence collected through unauthorized means against them.

Main Point: The state exercising extra-judicial power in the guise of increased surveillance on people and influencing prosecution.

1.   This is a main point question from the general category.

This is a main point question. We have extracted the main point already. The passage notes that the biggest danger posed by the government regarding defendants is its ability to aid the prosecution in ways which are outside the realm of legal review.

Let us review each option one by one.

(A)   This option is **incorrect**. Though it is correct that the author is concerned about the ability of the state to record the activity of everybody, it is not the main concern. The repercussions arising from the ability to record the activity of everybody is the main concern– the ability of the government to influence prosecution.

(B)   This option is **incorrect**. Like option A, though it is correct that the author is concerned that people are unaware about the surveillance performed on them, it is not the main concern. The repercussions arising from the ability to record the activity of everybody is the main concern– the ability of the government to influence prosecution.

(C)   This is the **correct** answer. It follows the analysis we made earlier.

(D)   This option is **incorrect**. It is a concern of tertiary importance.

(E)   This option is **incorrect**. Like option D, it is a concern of tertiary importance.

The correct answer is C.

2.   This is a Detail question.

[A]   This option is **incorrect**. The passage does not support exactly this. Though people view increased surveillance as a benign invasion, it does not construe as a consent from them. They do see it as an invasion, though benign, thereby implying that they would rather not have it.

[B]   This option is **correct** because the passage states people view **increased surveil-lance**, thus we can infer that they consider that surveillance is no more widespread than in the past.

[C]   This option is also **correct** because it is supported by the statement that people are unaware of all aspects of the policy of government surveillance and how it can be used to manipulate legal battles between individuals and the state.

The correct answers are B & C.

3.   This is a detail question.

Option B is the correct answer since the passage notes that the power of the government in the area of prosecution lies in its ability to work around safeguards and to manipulate bureaucracy against a suspect's legal rights. The passage also shows concerns over the ability of the government to influence prosecution. The passage states that the increased surveillance does not aid in tracking down more criminals.

Option A is close but incorrect because the author implies that the surveillance is being used unfairly against citizens who are suspects, not just against criminals. Thus, we cannot infer option A.

Other options are either not stated in the passage or are not inferable.

The correct answer is B.

4. This is an inference question.

Option C is the correct answer. It is supported in the passage by the statement: "*the state achieves an advantage by having so many more 'leads' on the individual with which to use bullying tactics, and by engaging in non-judicial activities.*" It implies that the state partially operates outside the law.

Option A not does not qualify to be inferable because, though the author is concerned about the extra-judicial power of the state, it does not mean that the government should be able to police itself to avoid overstepping its powers. However it can be inferred that government should not resort to unreasonable surveillance. In fact, the author seems to prove that the government has not been able to correct itself, and has resorted to using this illegal means to get control over suspects.

Other options are either non-inferable or are irrelevant.

The correct answer is C.

5. This is a detail question.

Option B is the correct answer. It is supported by the statement that the state improves its ability to "operate extra-judicially" and act in ways that are without redress. Also, the author calls the "state-actors, government authorities" the minorities, that is, a small part of the population. He accuses the minority of using surveillance to infringe upon the rights of the unaware public.

Other options are either not stated in the passage or are not inferable.

The correct answer is B.

6. This is an inference question.

(A) This option is **incorrect** because though after the UK boy's murder case most peo-ple in the UK approved of increased surveillance on them, it is invalidated by the author. He believes that the public is unaware of the real danger of increased surveillance by the government.

(B) This option is **incorrect**. As discussed in option A, the use of surveillance is invalidated by the author.

(C) This is the **correct** answer because the passage mentions the murder case as an example of the 'perception' of the public in regard to the benefits of surveillance in contrast to the reality of the state being able to improve its ability to prosecute the defendants it has caught. The author then goes on to explain why increased surveillance is not for the best. So, clearly, the author feels that the catching of the murderers is not a good enough reason for the government to resort to such surveillance.

(D) This option is **incorrect** because we cannot infer this.

(E) This option is **incorrect** because it is the opposite of what the author implies. The author feels that the increased surveillance does not help identify and track more criminals but is used by the state to intimidate and incriminate helpless citizens. Thus, the author is more likely to think that the case in which two murderers were apprehended is a one-off incident and not a reproducible result.

The correct answer is C.

7. This is a Detail question.

It is supported by the statement: *That action changes the direction of prosecution, reiterating the importance of, and the reasoning behind, such safeguards as the **Miranda acts**, designed to protect suspects from incriminating themselves in the absence of their lawyer.*

The author states that increased surveillance is used by government to aid the prosecution and that it makes laws like Miranda acts useless. Thus, laws like Miranda acts are intended to safeguard the defendants in case they cannot avail the services of a competent lawyer.

8. This is a detail question.

(A) This option is **incorrect** because we cannot construe that unjustifiably increased surveillance will render unreasonable punishment to offenders.

(B) This option is **incorrect** because it is not inferable.

(C) This is the **correct** answer. It is mentioned in the passage where it shows the relationship between the monopoly over prosecution and investigation and the ability that this monopoly gives to authorities to disregard official rules and manipulate the defendant. Increased surveillance without public permission and use of that to intimidate the citizen and detain him are examples of the government using its monopoly to help the prosecution.

(D) This option is **incorrect**. It is not mentioned in the passage.

(E) This option is **incorrect**. Like option D, it is not mentioned in the passage.

The correct answer is C.

6.16   Passage 16 (Reforms in the European education system)

Understanding the Passage

This is a long passage of low difficulty level on the topic of education systems.

European universities are increasingly adapting to global standards of education. The need to adapt to global standards stems from the fact that multinational corporations recruit human resources that are versatile, and not limited to a country and culture in terms of experience. German engineering schools have understood this dynamic better and are transforming themselves to the compelling need. Engineering schools elsewhere in Europe were shortsighted in assuming that engineering programs were immune to any upheaval from outside as they exclusively focused on engineering content. This shortsightedness is a clear example of how educational systems are governed by the coursework provided.

Professional schools must be concerned with their myopic attitude towards their courses. Some corporations and many international educators across engineering fields have observed some gap between students' core competencies and current needs. The main concerns of the German university system are that the courses are isolated and devoid of any interaction among the courses. Another important issue is that too few courses are taught in English. Due to the lack of availability of English courses in German engineering schools, too few international students opt for German programs. Another drawback is that if German engineering students seek to change the course midway, they feel disadvantaged. This is because they have limited experience in taking courses in other German universities, and taking engineering courses abroad is a rare possibility. Moreover, if these students were to transfer to another school, much of their course credits (points accumulated though previous programs) would not count towards a future degree in a different program, meaning they would have to start from the beginning in any new course. For these reasons, engineering education is being analyzed by all segments of society– businessmen, educators, and government officials.

To address the issue, engineering administrators have started developing course curriculum to suit the global and ever dynamic needs of students. These issues have jointly led educators to identify the need for a new Magna Carta of universities in order to turn their awareness into solutions. The outcome of this collective attention is the Bologna Declaration. [*The Magna Carta Universitatum is a document to celebrate university traditions and encourage bonds amongst European universities, though it also serves as a universal inspiration and is open to universities throughout the world. It was proposed by the University of Bologna in 1986, and has been signed by 755 universities from 80 countries*] Its recommendations are fourfold:

(1) Establish a system of comparable degrees (degrees that can be related to other international degrees) so that students can compete for other international programs.

(2) Adopt a two-tier, internationally acknowledged and widely popular system of schooling– undergraduate and graduate programs.

(3) Establish a standard credit system for classroom work.

(4) Find a way to ensure the quality of programs offered Europe-wide.

These improvements not only increase the international marketability of students, but they also increase the flexibility of students in case they choose to change direction during their university years.

The passage is about the transformation taking place in the European education system to equip students to adapt to the international education system and international market. The passage discusses the status quo in the European education system by looking at the situation in German universities–how German students face challenges with non-standardized courses offered by their universities, how a lack of courses based on the English language hampers the attractiveness of these schools for foreign students in Germany, and how compelling pressure from multiple corners–multinational corporations, international educators, and other bodies – has forced Germany to adapt to international standards.

Main Point: Reformation in the European education system to adapt to the international education system and international market.

1. This is an inference question.

   (A) This option is **incorrect** because as per the information given in passage, we cannot infer that sociology programs do not have the same difficulties as other programs.

   (B) This option is **incorrect** because nothing of this sort was mentioned in the passage.

   (C) This is the **correct** answer because the passage notes that German engineering programs are a good choice for the change because they operate according to a logic which says that they do not need to pay heed to external conditions. Thus, a discipline such as sociology, which studies a range of social conditions, would be less useful as an example, since it will pay attention to external conditions and accordingly adapt.

   (D) This option is **incorrect** because it is devoid of any logic.

   (E) This option is **incorrect** because nothing of this sort was mentioned in the passage.

   The correct answer is C.

2. This is detail question.

   Option E is the correct answer because the passage states that a major problem with the lack of instruction in English in engineering courses is that it makes it harder for students from abroad to take courses in German universities. It is supported by the passage (line 20): *"The lack of availability of English courses in German engineering schools contributes to there being a paucity of international students in German programs."* Other options are out of scope of the passage.

   The correct answer is E.

3. This is a detail question.

    The sentence is (line 27): *"For these reasons, engineering education has come under well-lit scrutiny by businessmen, educators, and government officials."*

    Option E is the correct answer because it duplicates the adjectival nature of the phrase which relays a notion of observation enacted through diligent examination by many interested parties. Also, the fact that the sentence includes diverse people like businessmen, educators, and government officials shows that the issue is being examined from multiple aspects.

    The correct answer is E.

4. This is a Detail question.

    There are two sentences in the reckoning.

    1. *Leading concerns for critics of the German university system are that there is limited intercourse between different academies, and that too few courses are taught in English.*: This a trap answer as the testmaker, deliberately, picked similar words from the sentence to frame the question—too few courses are taught in English.—however this is not the answer as the sentence means that due to few courses taught in English in German university system, there is limited intercourse between different academies. We need a sentence that shows that because very few courses are taught in English, very few international students are found in Germany.

    2. *The lack of availability of English courses in German engineering schools contributes to there being a paucity of international students in German programs.*: This is the correct answer as it provides what the question asks for.

5. This is an inference question.

    Option C is the correct answer since the passage asserts that the vocational inflexibility in the German education system makes it difficult for German students to be mobile outside the system. The author advocates that students must have liberty to even change the direction of their course. Thus, the author feels that courses should be flexible enough to allow students to interact with other disciplines, and even switch to another field if they wish so.

    Option A, B, and D are not discussed in the passage. Regarding option E, the author does not mean that by advocating to provide flexibility in choosing courses, and by incorporating courses in English, that students should be encouraged to work outside of their national origins. It implies that students must have flexibility in choosing their career effectively and nothing should impede that.

The correct answer is C.

6. This is a Detail question.

    We listed Bologna Declaration's recommendations in understanding the passages section; in short the four recommendations were:

    1. Establish a system of comparable degrees
    2. Adopt two tier system of schooling—undergraduate and graduate programs
    3. Establish a standard credit system for classroom work
    4. Find a way to ensure the quality of programs offered Europe-wide

    A   This option is **incorrect** because nothing of this sort was under the purview of Bologna Declaration.

    B   This option is the **correct** option as listed above.

    C   This option is **incorrect** because vocational opportunities were not listed in Bologna Declaration.

7. This is an inference question.

    We have to choose an option that articulates the author's concern about "the unlikelihood of engineering students ever changing their course of study."

    (A) This option is **incorrect** because the author states otherwise.

    (B) Like option B, this option is **incorrect** because the author states otherwise.

    (C) This option is **incorrect** because nothing of this sort is inferable.

    (D) This option is tricky, but **incorrect** because the author does not imply that engineering schools need to be concerned with the potential in other fields of study. Other fields may have potential, but so does the engineering field. The author advocates that if students wish to opt out of engineering courses, they must have flexibility in doing so.

    (E) This is the **correct** answer because it correctly expresses the concern.

    The correct answer is E.

8. This is a detail question.

    The reference to 'mobile' was made in the first part of the first paragraph (line 2): *"European universities must answer the perceived needs of **multinational corporations**, as these firms aspire to draw on an employee base that is borderless, and highly **mobile**."*

    Option E is the correct answer because some of the main actors with an interest in re-evaluating the German education system are large corporations in need of having access to a wide labor pool, and students who seek to increase their options in the workforce. Other options are out of the scope of the passage.

The correct answer is E.

6.17   Passage 17 (The U.S.'s Nuclear Energy Program)

Understanding the Passage

This is a long passage of low difficulty level on the topic of nuclear energy.

In 1957, the U.S. invested in mining the atom to make it useful as a source of energy, and for engineering and military revolution. Up to that point, atomic energy was utilized for the development of more powerful weapons of mass destruction, warships, and submersibles. The U.S. Atomic Energy Commission (AEC) took the initiative to develop peaceful applications of modern nuclear power (a source of abundant energy for domestic use). Moreover, under the guise of noble intentions, scientists could carry out other development, primarily to manufacture Cold War armaments. The AEC later named the partly noble and partly treacherous program the "Plowshare Program"–implying noble intentions.

In Aug 1958, the AEC selected Ogotoruk Creek as the site for the detonation of an atomic bomb (*A gulf was chosen to test an atomic bomb*). The rationale behind testing an atomic bomb was political and practical. The AEC had decided to disguise the discussion of nuclear weapons by pairing nuclear arms with civil engineering. They reasoned that if nuclear energy could prove to be a boon to civil engineering, then using nuclear energy for Cold War purposes – such as making nuclear weapons – and nuclear ground testing could be portrayed positively and the public's negative opinion towards these things could be reduced. The AEC played clever and named their plan "Operation Plowshare." The name "Plowshare" was deliberately chosen as it referred to the holy prose–"beat their swords into plowshares." [*It is a concept in which military weapons or technologies are converted for peaceful civilian applications. The plowshare is often used to symbolize creative tools that benefit mankind, as opposed to destructive tools of war, symbolized by the sword, a similar sharp metal tool with an arguably opposite use–that of plowing the earth and farming.*] The AEC presented atomic technology as an engineering wonder, the driver of future development in the U.S..

Russia's successful launch of the Sputnik I satellite into space panicked the U.S. To outdo Russia, America's scientific and engineering team proposed an "earth excavation" program to demonstrate the U.S.'s impressive and beneficial applications of America's existing nuclear capabilities. It advised detonating a 2.4 megaton atomic device on the northwest coast of Alaska. The supposed purpose was to create a deep water hole to facilitate the shipping of coal, timber, and oil from one part to another. The detonation had the apparently noble intention of developing Alaska's coastal state. This proposal was accepted by the AEC, who named it 'Project Chariot'. The plan was marketed to Alaska's financial community and lawmakers, but they remained unconvinced of the plan's commercial viability. The AEC then attempted to sell the plan to the U.S. Congress as a unique opportunity to impress the Congress with what nuclear energy could do for the country. However, a local unit objected to the plan and wrote to the President about not continuing with the plan as they were skeptical about heavy metals leaking into the ground and water, and about radiation in the environment. Due to this, Project Chariot was dumped and replaced by less visible projects (thus less under public scrutiny) and these projects would be revealed to the common public many decades later.

Main Point: The highs and the lows of the U.S.'s maiden nuclear energy program.

1. This is a detail question.

    Option C is the correct answer because the passage mentions that the AEC sought to "bowdlerize" (line 14) (censor) the contemporary discussion on nuclear weapons. The implication is that they wanted to increase the positive comments regarding nuclear weapons by naming it "Operation Plowshare"–implying a program of noble intentions, and reduce the public's negative sentiments against it.

    Options A, B, and E are out of scope and option D is opposite of what is meant after naming the program "Operation Plowshare."

    The correct answer is C.

2. This is a Detail question.

    The phrase is used here: *"Their preferred advice was to detonate a 2.4 megaton atomic device on the northwest coast of Alaska, to create a deep water hole facilitating the shipping of coal, timber and oil, while developing Alaska's coast, with obvious **benefits for the 48 mainland U.S. states.**"* The detonation was mean to provide much better access to coal, timer, and oil (resources) with the use of under-water tunnel.

    Option B is the only correct answer because the sentence refers to the development of Alaska's coast. Other options are irrelevant.

    The correct answer is B.

3. This is a detail question.

    Option C is the best answer since the passage discusses the AEC conducting a "recon-naissance" (inspection) of the area, a physical scan by reconnaissance personnel on location.

    Option D is close, but incorrect as the passage does not mention anything about cartographic research and topographical comparisons for the selection of the creek. So, we cannot assume that option D is necessarily true.

    The correct answer is C.

4. This is an inference question.

    (A) This is the **correct** answer because if scientists interested in Sputnik's successful launch wanted to engage in "one-upmanship," it can be assumed that the statement being made about the Sputnik accomplishment is the thing which these actors consider important. The American scientists felt the need to retaliate (as a reply) by showing America's superiority in nuclear science. Thus, the American scientists clearly viewed Sputnik I as a political claim by the Russians on the world stage, as part of the one-upmanship game in the Cold War era.

(B) This option is **incorrect** because the scientists were not limited to regarding Sputnik I as merely a scientific achievement; they did engage in "one-upmanship" with a counter nuclear program.

(C) With the same reasoning as cited in option B, this option is **incorrect**.

(D) This option is **incorrect** because the scientists did regard Sputnik I seriously (not as specious [fake] showmanship). They did engage in "one-upmanship" with a counter nuclear program.

(E) This option is **incorrect** because nothing of this sort can be inferred from the passage.

The correct answer is A.

5. This is a tone question from the general category.

Option A is the correct answer because the AEC was seeking to improve the reputation of nuclear weapons. This implies that the American public had a negative perception of nuclear weapons and testing. The AEC felt that teaming nuclear arms with civil engineering could dilute the intense public skepticism towards above ground nuclear testing. This implies that people in general were doubtful (skeptical) about nuclear weapons testing and held it in a negative light.

The correct answer is A.

6. This is a detail question.

(A) This option is **incorrect** because it is not evident from the passage that President Kennedy disapproved of the project.

(B) This is the **correct** answer because the passage notes that the AEC shut down the program because they had reconsidered the reaction their project would earn them, thus implying that they would not be able to carry pro-nuclear favor from continuing their program and thus should not continue "Operation Plowshare" by pursuing Project Chariot. This is also evidenced by the great number of negative reactions they received, thus dashing the AEC's hope of whitewashing the nuclear programs issue.

(C) This option is **incorrect** because only after being termed commercially unviable was the project sent to the president for consideration.

(D) This option is **incorrect** because nothing of this sort was discussed in the passage.

(E) This option is **incorrect** because it cannot necessarily be inferred from the passage. We know that there are negative opinions expressed by detractors of the programs, but not necessarily that they indulged in politics.

The correct answer is B.

7. This is a tone question from the general category.

Option A is the correct answer because the inventors of "Operation Plowshare" were politically motivated in "spinning" the perception of nuclear weapons with positive images,
and thus were seeking politically savvy (shrewd and clever) methods of influencing the
discussion on nuclear weapons.

The correct answer is A.

8. This is an application question from the reasoning category.

We discussed in the "Understanding the Passage" section that the AEC played clever and
named their plan "Operation Plowshare." The name "Plowshare" was deliberately chosen
as it referred to the holy prose–**"beat their swords into plowshares"**. [*It is a concept in
which military weapons or technologies are converted for peaceful civilian applications.*
***The plowshare is often used to symbolize creative tools that benefit mankind, as
opposed to destructive tools of war, symbolized by the sword, a similar sharp metal
tool with an arguably opposite use.*** *Thus, a plowshare refers to using a negative, or evil,
object, such as a sword and turning it into an object of good, such as a plow, meant to
yield good deeds like farming.*]

From the above analysis, it is evident that "beat their swords into plowshares" means
"turn evil (sword: a destructive tool) into good (plowshare: a useful tool):."

The correct answer is B.

6.18   Passage 18 (Mechanized production systems in Europe)

Understanding the Passage

This is a long passage of medium difficulty level on the topic of business and processes.

During the 1870s, industrializing nations went through radical technological challenges. However these nations followed drastically different approaches to leverage on their productive capacity and carry on industrial development. Manufacturing companies decided that their best bet was to rationalize the production process and thus weighed the pros and cons of mechanization of production. However, such mechanization debates had no clear winning side and were subject to numerous debates.

Though many industries in many countries anticipated some benefits from mechanization (production with the help of machines and a mass production process using assembly lines rather than only manual input, i.e. labor making each article personally), the rationality of increasing production while reducing production costs was still debated. The mechanization side of the debate was not winning with a clear margin.

German printing and textile firms showed why industrialization was not a cut and dried process (a simple process that is followed according to a plan, set procedure, or formula). *[It implies that there is no standard procedure to augment industrialization and such a decision cannot be taken lightly]*. In the meantime, German and Austrian companies transitioned to mechanical production from hand-work of printed cotton handkerchiefs (handcrafted articles).

These great handcrafted articles made by certain regional manufacturers let them make their mark in the international market. Few German firms obtained the ability to double and triple production while reducing their work force; however, there were some risks in adopting mechanization. While this new mechanized order did bring a substantial drop in the total remuneration of labor (reduced salary costs), it also significantly lowered the sale price and raised risks of overproduction. *[Though machination reduces labor cost, it usually results in mass production, resulting in overproduction. Such developments lead to a fall in sale prices, and can also cause demand to fall because of oversupply.]* Head over heels *['Head over heels' is now most often used as part of 'head over heels in love'. When first coined, it wasn't used that way though, and referred exclusively to **being temporarily the wrong way up**. It is one of many similar phrases that we use to describe **things that are not in their usual state - 'upside-down',** **'topsy-turvy',** etc.]* (Topsy-turvy) production of items *[excessive production of items]* did not pay attention to the ability of the market to absorb such overproduction, and this resulted in negative impressions about products on the market. *[The author implies that when companies rushed into mechanization, replaced labor, and started producing items at double the speed, they did not pay attention to the market (specifically the demand and other factors that factored into the demand). This oversupply and lack of attention to the market brought about negative impressions about those products (which would result in falling demand)].*

The failure of double-printed 'Turkish bonnets' (a kind of skull cap) in the marketplace is an example of why fast and cheap production techniques are not necessarily the best means of production for established manufacturers. The market experienced a sudden unpredictable drop in the demand for these bonnets. Before manufacturers could react to the changed preferences of customers (due to mass production through mechanized process), a large in-ventory was already there in the market with no takers for the same, resulting in huge losses. The crisis was aggravated due to a monetary crisis in eastern markets. This led to unrest in the industry, and stakeholders started contemplating the efficacy of the new production order.

Only a few regions adopted mechanization because the sentiment towards it was skeptical. The American production system was solely based on standardization, mechanization, and mass production and it did not seem to face the problems that others had, and the American system had drawn European attention to standardized production, which did offer an increase in profits while reducing labor costs and control unpredictability in production. The lessons from the case of the 'Turkish bonnets' imply that the American system of production, since its inception, overlooked some pitfalls arising from standardization, mechanization, and mass production techniques. However, the American system was abreast of the conditions of the world market and was not untouched by them. Unlike printing and textile firms in Germany and Turkey, manufacturers of watches in Switzerland, of scarves in Germany, and weavers in Glarus did not adopt the new mechanized American system. This differential adoption of the manufacturing process *(in which some adopted mechanization and some did not)* brought about "class formation" *[mechanized classes and unmechanized ones]* and caused class disparity. It also resulted in capital rigidity *(when there are two choices with no obvious better one, instead of choosing one of the two choices, the investors choose neither and capital is either frozen or unavailable–capital rigidity)*. This class disparity and capital rigidity would become built-in pressure points on the American economy *(that is, eventually the American economy would face these challenges as well)*. Also due to these challenges, many European producers could not develop a consistent, reproducible system of mechanization. *[This incomplete adoption of mechanization prevented Europe from developing a uniform production method.]*

Main Point: Europe's response to mechanization in the industrialization process.

1. This is a main Point question from the general category.

   We have already derived the main point of the passages. Option E is the correct answer because the passage discusses the pros and cons of strategies of industrialization.

   Option E is the correct answer because the passage discusses varied responses from Eu-ropean companies to industrialization. "Some were camphor and some were wet wood" is used as a metaphor which implies that a few companies were like camphor (camphor catches fire instantly), meaning that a few German and a few Austrian companies adopted industrialization quickly while Switzerland and Glarus were like wet wood, im-plying that they did not adopt industrialization (wet wood has a hard time catching fire)."

   Other options are either too narrow in scope or are irrelevant.

   The correct answer is E.

2. This is an Inference question.

   A   This option is **incorrect** because we cannot infer that the author would agree that industries must exercise protectionism, implying no-need to change and interfering in the markets to protect domestic companies. The author advocates that industries must evaluate whether industrialization or mechanization is beneficial for them or not. If it benefits an industry, the industry must follow it.

   B   This option is **correct** because the passage discusses the risk of overproduction in the middle of second paragraph—*"But risks accompanied this methodology— presented risks of **overproduction.**"*

   C   This option is also **correct** because it was cited through the example of "Turkish bonnet." The problem was exacerbated when demand fell and preferences changed. So, the author used the example of the bonnet market in Turkey to explain how local markets and preferences can be unfavorable for industrialization.

   The correct answers are B & C.

3. This is a detail question.

   Option E is the correct answer because the passage shows that a monetary crisis in eastern markets caused problems in the industry. It was cited in the example of "Turkish bonnets." The problem was exacerbated when demand fell and preferences changed. So, the author used the example of the bonnet market in Turkey to explain how local markets and preferences can be unfavorable for industrialization.

   Other options are not relevant to the question.

   The correct answer is E.

4. This is a detail question.

   Option D is the correct answer since the section of the passage discussing bonnets, which were produced using standardized mass production techniques, refers to overproduction as a major problem the producers faced.

   Option E is incorrect as the alienation of the workforce resulted due to low demand and high supply of bonnets. It is not the threat posed by standardization.

   The correct answer is D.

5. This is a Function question.

   The **correct** answer is the sentence: *These were just the things that also kept many European producers from settling around a consistent, reproducible pattern of mechanization.*

Though there are a couple of sentences that seemingly qualify, they are incorrect such as

Reaction to production innovations was regional.: It does hint an element of "sporadic," but it talks about production innovations, and not about industrialization.

Manufacturers of watches in Switzerland, of scarves in Germany and weavers in 19th century Glarus were reserved about their approval of change.: Though we can infer that few manufactures in Switzerland, Germany, and Glarus were averse to industrialization, the sentence itself does not answer that few other manufacturers adopted industrialization.

6. This is an inference question.

   Option D is the correct answer because the last part of the passage states (line 32): *"the American system was not uniquely immune to the conditions of the world market. Manufacturers of watches in Switzerland, of scarves in Germany and weavers in 19th century Glarus were reserved about their approval of change."* This implies that America faced problems in standardizing industrialization. Not all European manufacturers went for standardized industrialization because they were aware of these potential dangers.

   Other options do not qualify to be correct.

   The correct answer is D.

7. This is an inference question.

   (A) This option is **incorrect** because the opinion of self-interested parties was not discussed in the passage.

   (B) This option is **incorrect** because the passage does not discuss the impact on socialized countries.

   (C) This is the **correct** answer because through the example of the bonnet, the passage states that technological improvements can create economic difficulties as well, something that was unanticipated initially.

   (D) This option is **incorrect** because competitive pressure from industrializing nations is not discussed in the passage.

   (E) This option is **incorrect** because social agendas are out of the scope of the passage.

   The correct answer is C.

8. This is a main Point question from the general category.

   We have already derived the main point of the passage: "Pros and cons of the evolution of industrialization in Europe."

   We will discuss each option one by one.

(A) This option is **incorrect** because it focuses more on America, while the passage focuses on comparing industrial models.

(B) This option is **incorrect** because it would be a good title for a passage discussing different examples of industry in detail, rather than comparing the pros and cons of industrial models.

(C) This is the **correct** answer because the passage discusses uneven responses from European companies to industrialization. "A few German and a few Austrian companies adopted industrialization quickly while Switzerland and Glarus did not adopt industrialization."

(D) Like option A, this option is **incorrect** because it focuses more on America than on industrial models.

(E) This option is **incorrect** because it would be an appropriate title for a passage discussing the advantages of industrial rationalization, rather than discussing the advantages and disadvantages of standardization for different industries.

The correct answer is C.

6.19   Passage 19 (Gangsta rap)

Understanding the Passage

This is a long passage of medium difficulty level on the topic of society and culture.

Gangsta rap is a form of gangster lifestyle rap music; its lyrics are based on violence, pleasure-seeking behavior, and hatred against women. Usually Gangsta rap is found on the American West Coast, but the term "Hip-hop" is broader and encompasses a mixture of many styles. It is unclear whether the violence in gangsta rap is actually based on real violent incidents. *[the discussion of graphic violence and a "don't-care-about-society's-rules" attitude are trademarks of gangsta rap]*. When such traits were packaged with smooth technical production, it helped West Coast rap to distinguish itself within Hip Hop music.*[Hip Hop music is a mixture of different styles.]*

Gangsta rap made California famous in music circles by demonstrating that it could be the birthplace of music with lyrics that are based on societal issues prevalent in African-American society. With great music, it made its mark on people. Traditionally, rap was rooted on the East Coast, but Gangsta rap differentiated itself from East Coast rap with the use of commercial production style. (Los Angeles had an extensive music post-production industry making wide use of synthesizers). The combination of Los Angeles' advanced technical production methods and lyrics based on socio-economic and racial messages branded Gangsta rap as a uniquely West Coast style of music. Gangsta rappers had an impatient and militant attitude which arose from the bitter experiences of facing disadvantage and racism. However this helped them to be differentiated from the East Coast artists.

Initially all West Coast rap was branded as Gangsta rap, but audiences appreciated Gangsta rap as a distinguished form of rap music. This made it possible for Hip Hop to solidify its foothold in American music.

The evolution of Hip Hop music occurred among the economically lower class in smaller downtown areas of the American East Coast. Previously, this style of music, with a heavy emphasis on rhyming and high decibel beat, had been universally identified as Hip Hop. But this identity was challenged by the rap group N.W.A.'s Straight Outta Compton's different style. Compton's aggressive, minimalist sound were much different from the traditional conventions of rap. Compton's lyrics were based on living on excesses and merciless criticism of American society. It is alleged that American society exploited American blacks who were always at a disadvantage, and these unfair realities were reflected in the group's songs. This led to a very different style of Hip Hop, something which could not be classified into what was traditionally considered Hip Hop.

Despite such hate messages towards American society and the highly commercial production style of this music, Gangsta rap became a commercial hit. However, rap fanatics who valued conventional Hip Hop for its authenticity and popularity respected Gangsta rap music despite its being heavily dominated by smooth, modern production techniques (something that traditional Hip Hop had stayed away from). These rappers started attracting a huge fan base, expanding into the mainstream while maintaining its traditional fan base. One of the artists, Dr. Dre, used funky music that had originated in disco. He mixed it with a "canned beat" (a heavy sound that was popular in California) with which he blanketed his message (lyrics) which made him reach the general public. The combination helped Hip Hop to appeal to a more varied audience. This helped listeners to appreciate Gangsta rap's lyricism and musical production style on its own terms rather than solely measuring it against the yardstick of East Coast rap. Once West Coast rap was acknowledged as a unique style, fans were able to compare the quality of East Coast and West Coast rap.

Main Point: The evolution of the American West Coast's maverick Gangsta rap.

1. This is a detail question.

   A This option is **correct** because the passage discusses rhyming as a characteristic of Gangsta rap as one of the reasons why Gangsta rap became commercially successful, distinguished from East Coast Rap.

   B This option is also **correct** because Gangsta rap became successful by integrating both these factors—commercial production techniques and biting social observations—into its music.

   C This option is **incorrect** because the passage does not discuss the work done by vocalists in post-production.

   The correct answers are A & B.

2. This is a detail question.

   (A) This option is **incorrect** because the passage does not mention that audiences were confused by gangsta rap.

   (B) This option is **incorrect** because the passage does not mention any disconnect between critical and commercial success for gangsta rap.

   (C) This option is **incorrect** because the passage does not talk of gangsta rap as only black art. Lyrics were based on problems faced by blacks but that does not mean that the genre was exclusively made up of black artists.

   (D) This is the **correct** answer because the passage mentions that the imagery of violence "enabled West Coast rap to distinguish itself within Hip Hop music" and develop into a complete genre by itself.

   (E) This option is **incorrect** because it was the coupling of indulgence and social activism which resulted in the "gangsta rap" moniker.

   The correct answer is D.

3. This is a detail question.

   (A) This option is **incorrect** because gangsta rap was a part of Hip Hop; it differentiated itself within Hip Hop but did not contrast with Hip Hop.

   (B) This option is **incorrect** because the passage does not discuss the alienation of audiences.

(C) This is the **correct** answer. Refer to the first paragraph (line 3): *"While it is unclear whether the violence in gangsta rap–,when packaged with* **smooth technical production, enabled West Coast rap to distinguish itself within Hip Hop music."** It is clear that it made it possible to discuss gangsta rap as a new style.

(D) This option is **incorrect** because gangsta rap appealed to a more heterogeneous audience and achieved commercial success.

(E) This option is **incorrect** because the street credibility of gangsta rap was maintained despite its use of slick production techniques.

The correct answer is C.

4. This is a tone question from the general category.

(A) This option is **incorrect** because the author does not argue for or against gangsta rap; he is not judgmental or opinionated.

(B) This option is **incorrect** because the author does not view the hedonism and misogyny of gangsta rap merely as tools to achieve the purpose of gangsta rap. He does not suggest any such thing.

(C) This option is **incorrect** because though the author questions whether these aspects of gangsta rap have a real basis, he does not question the sincerity of their use in songs.

(D) This is the **correct** answer because the author dispassionately acknowledges a relationship between these aspects of gangsta rap and its rise.

(E) This option is **incorrect** because it is too general a statement.

The correct answer is D.

5. This is an inference question.

(A) This option is **incorrect** because it is not supported by the passage.

(B) This option is **incorrect** because it is not supported by the passage.

(C) This is the **correct** answer because the passage indicates that the music industry in L.A. was long established and made use of such methods, thus it can be concluded that this style had been popularly received and was useful in establishing "Gangsta Rap" as a popular medium. Also, the passage gives the example of Dr. Dre using canned beats despite their origins in disco because he knew it was familiar for the audience and a good vehicle for his message.

(D) This option is **incorrect** because it makes a connection between synthesized beats and corporate oversight that is not supported by the passage.

(E) This option is **incorrect** because it is not mentioned in the passage.

The correct answer is C.

6. The first sentence of second last paragraph explicitly talks about the evolution of Hip Hop. It is: *Hip Hop had historically evolved among the economically challenged inner cities of the American East Coast.*

6.20   Passage 20 (Women's contraceptives)

Understanding the Passage

This is a long passage of medium difficulty level on the topic of health and wellness.

When an organization launches a product, the number of potential consumers is an important aspect to assess the potential of profits. However, it is not the only variable that needs to be taken into consideration. Even though a given product may be very useful and people could be willing to buy it, the effect of that product on a corporation's image and the public's goodwill towards that product is not a guarantee to make it commercially successful. *[It is contrary to normal belief that if a product is desirable and people at large long for it that when it makes great sales, a company's image will increase in direct proportion.]* Some corporations use loss-leader products to increase the profits of unrelated products through their benefits to branding. *[A loss leader is a pricing strategy where a product is sold at a much lower price to stimulate other sales of more profitable goods or services. For example, in some countries where the advertising of liquor products is restricted, companies advertise and sell music CDs with the same brand name as a popular brand of liquor at throw-away prices with the hidden objective of promoting their liquor brand.]* Corporations are equally aware of the fact that successful products which can hurt the company's image will hurt the sales of other products, and thereby the corporation may fail to grow in a market due to political interference from pressure groups that have political clout.

The above phenomenon is observed in the American contraceptive industry. Research indicates that women need more choices of contraceptives. Despite dire need, corporations deliberately do not launch many contraceptives on the market and leave them hanging in the R&D phase. The corporations' ploy not to launch a variety of female contraceptives shows that females are neglected and not treated on par with male consumers. Unlike men, who have a single, relatively simple, and effective measure of contraception, women have varied needs so many alternatives must be made available to them to suit their lifestyles, sexual appetites, and personal habits.

Unlike men, it is women are at risk of an unwanted pregnancy, so they are more worried about protecting themselves from the result of their sexual relations. For a woman, it is better to be prepared with her own contraceptive than to rely on her male partner's likelihood of carrying a condom with him. Despite the fact that women have pressing needs, Americans do not wish to talk about sex as a routine thing. This makes women search for options privately to protect themselves from unintended circumstances (i.e. unwanted pregnancy). Based on this, conservative pharmaceutical corporations do not make and market innovatively designed female contraceptives as they are scared about the reactions and political influence of anti-contraceptive extremist pro-life groups, religious organizations, and prominent members of the Republican party. Such political groups can affect a corporation's success with other products or even make it politically difficult for the corporation to exist freely in the market. Women are deprived of many innovatively designed contraceptives due to the intimidating presence of a minority of well-organized non-consumer groups determining product availability *[Women do not get the contraceptive choices that they should because the conservative groups who are pro-life and such political organizations control the political power and indirectly keep the companies from releasing the products through intimidation].* The solution to this paradox *[the paradox is that there is a demand that is not met with apt products.]* is not only to preach that corporations need to pursue the orthodoxy of their own free market rewards *[that means one should not just say that free-market ideology is best, but should also practice free-market ideology in which the market demands **only** determine what products a company makes and provides].* *[Thus,]* corporations must also create an open environment to talk about the real sexual lifestyles of women, and make available for women products of their choice while ignoring the pressure groups–extremist pro-life groups, religious organizations,and prominent members of the Republican party.

Main Point: The unavailability of varied choices of female contraceptives despite a dire need.

1. This is a detail question.

    Option E is the correct answer since the passage notes that while loss leader products are valuable for the branding (publicity) of surrogate products though they lose money, corporations are wary of profitable products that have negative effects on other products, which is why many companies don't provide contraceptives even though there is a huge demand for such products (because they fear the negative publicity associated with it).

    The correct answer is E.

2. This is an Inference question.

    The implication of the author in the sentence *"Still, there appears to be as many as 100 new contraceptives trapped between development and market"* is that the corporations could bring new contraceptives to market but chose not to.

3. This is an inference question.

    Option E is the correct answer. It is supported by the sentence (line 29): *"Based on this, it is evident that conservative pharmaceutical corporations are laden with fear over the reaction of extremist pro-life groups, religious organizations, and prominent members of the Republican Party to increased research and even successful marketing of contraceptive alternatives."*

    Pharmaceutical corporations feel that it is a risk to introduce and market new products, as they fear the reaction from pressure groups. And because of their unwillingness to bear that risk (i.e. they are averse to risk), the products never enter the market even though there is a demand for such products.

    The correct answer is E.

4. This is an inference question.

Option D is the correct answer because it can be derived from the sentences (line 17): *"women are afforded a cornucopia (many) of alternatives which suit their **lifestyles, sexual appetites, and personal habits**. However, for women's sake, this patchwork of options should never be viewed as too varied or as colorful enough."* Thus, the author feels that, owing to women's physiological differences, women need plenty of contraceptive choices, and there aren't enough on the market.

Other options are not supported by the passage.

The correct answer is D.

5. This is an Inference question.

| A | This option is **correct** because the author propagates the free-market ideology in the end. |

| B | This option is also **correct** because the author agrees that political influence such as the Republicans, and others stifle the market of much needed contraceptives Thus, he would want the market freed of external influences. |

| C | This option is also **correct** because it can be accounted for by the sentence *"The enormous market of consumers who would welcome convenient alternatives to —continue to wait much longer than necessary for such products on account of the intimidating presence of a minority of well-organized non-consumer groups."* |

The author advocates that women are deprived of varied contraceptives because the corporations are scared of the backlash and negative publicity.

The correct answers are A, B, & C.

6. This is a detail question.

(A) This is the **correct** answer since the passage is concerned with the inability of Americans to discuss sex in a natural way. This allows anti-contraceptive groups to have a more vocal and organized presence that prevents more contraceptive products from entering the market.

(B) This option is **incorrect** because increased purchasing of current products may not encourage corporations to diversify.

(C) This option is **incorrect** because if men took more responsibility for sex it would presumably be less risky for women to be sexually active, given that the passage indicates that one reason women need an array of contraceptive options is because it is unsafe to rely on their partners for contraceptive availability.

(D) This option is **incorrect** since it would discourage companies from offering more products.

(E) Like option D, this option is **incorrect** since it would discourage companies from offering more products.

The correct answer is A.

7.   This is a detail question.

   (A)   This is the **correct** answer since the phrase refers to the possibility that the man may have a contraception alternative. The author wants to say that "being proactively safe is better than depending on the **possibility** (not impossibility) of a wallet condom." Thus, "likelihood" is the best choice.

   (B)   This option is **incorrect** because the phrase intends to convey uncertainty, but not a particular degree of uncertainty.

   (C)   This option is **incorrect** because it is completely out of place.

   (D)   Like option B, this option is **incorrect** because the phrase intends to convey uncertainty, but not a particular degree of uncertainty.

   (E)   This option is **incorrect** because reliability refers to the quality of the contraceptive and not just whether it is available or not.

The correct answer is A.

8.   This is a tone question from the general category.

   (A)   This option is **incorrect** because the author does not explore new things. He merely presents the observations and negative consequences for women with a solid but judgmental reasoning.

   (B)   This option is **incorrect** because the author presents the observations and difficulties of women with a solid reasoning. He is not unduly biased towards women's needs. He supported the cause with facts and figures.

   (C)   This option is **incorrect** because the author does express his opinion and is aggrieved due to ignorance of women's dire need.

   (D)   This option is **incorrect** because the author is rather critical of the current scenario.

   (E)   This is the **correct** answer because as discussed in the other options, the author is opinionated. He presents a case and discusses all its aspects and firmly and explicitly mentions his opinions on the matter that the companies are not right in delaying contraceptives and that the pressure groups are to blame.

The correct answer is E.

6.21   Passage 21 (Influence of the British Poetry of World War One)

Understanding the Passage

This is a long passage of higher difficultly level on Critical Commentary on Historical Literature.

Perhaps the most persistent myth about British poetry of World War One is that it became progressively more realistic as soldier-poets learned more about the horrors of modern trench warfare. *{There is a stubborn myth. Myth is that the British poetry during WWI became more and more realistic, as soldiers, who were the poets, got deeper and deeper into modern type of warfare, known as trench warfare.}* According to this orthodoxy, the **pastoral** patriotism of Brooke soon gave way, in the mud and blood of Flanders, to the angry realism of Sassoon and Owen. *{According to this orthodox belief, calm and serene patriotic poems written by Brooke decreased and angry, realistic poems, possibly depicting the muddy, bloody situation in Flanders (a place), written by Sassoon and Owen increased.}* Thus when we think of World War One poetry today, the poems that instantly come to the minds of most readers are those angry and satirical anti-war poems, such as Sassoon's " Base Details" and "Blighters"and Owen's " Dulce et decorum est," the last being probably the most famous, certainly the most widely anthologized, poem of the War. *{This is why when we think about WWI poetry, the angry, sarcastic poems written by Sassoon and Owen come to mind. Owen's " Dulce et decorum est," is possibly the most famous and most widely anthologized (published) poem of that time.}* The problem with this view is that it is based on a relatively small group of poems that, despite their indisputable excellence, are in many ways atypical of the bulk of poetry, including much of the good poetry, written during the War. *{There is a problem with this myth/view. The problem is that such angry poems were made but these angry poems represent a minority proportion of WWI poetry. The bulk of WWI poetry, which includes most of the good poetry from that time, is not typically angry or sarcastic.}* **That poetry** was deeply indebted to the nineteenth-century poetic tradition running from Wordsworth and the Romantics through the major Victorian poets to Hardy and beyond. *{That bulk poetry is inspired from 19th century poetic style from Wordsworth (of Romantic style) to Hardy (of Victorian style). Thus, the bulk of WWI poetry was made in 19th century Romantic and Victorian style.}* The majority of the war poets worked within this tradition to produce, as has been recently argued, the trench lyric. *{Majority of the war's soldier-poets worked in this 19th century Romantic and Victorian style and created a new style called trench lyric (the new style was called "trench" because the soldiers were conducting "trench" style of warfare, some form of modern warfare.)}* But it is not just much of the poetry of World War One that belongs to this tradition. *{However, it is not only that WWI poetry was made in this 19th century Romantic and Victorian style. Some WWI prose too followed this style.}* The last two paragraphs of what many regard as one of the best memoirs to come out of the War, Siegfried Sassoon's "Memoirs of a Fox-Hunting Man" (1928), emerge from the same tradition and constitute a prose version of the trench lyric composed by the solider-poets. *{The last two paragraphs of Sassoon's memoirs also follow the 19th century Romantic and Victorian style. This book is considered the best memoirs of WWI.}*

At first glance, a work by the author of some of the bitterest and most angry anti-war poems of World War One may seem an unlikely place to observe the conventions (rules and methodology) of Romantic poetry, but the ending of "Memoirs of a Fox-Hunting Man" reveals just how insistently the Romantic lyric imposed its form and structure on the imaginations of the writers of World War One. *{Initially, it may seem not possible that a bitter and angry, anti-war poem* *will contain 19th century Romantic and Victorian style; however, in the ending of that memoir demonstrates that 19th century Romantic and Victorian style was very deeply embedded in the minds of WWI poets and writers.}*

Sassoon, like Rosenberg, does not abandon a set of worn-out poetic conventions so he can write directly and realistically, and hence originally, about it. Rather he translates a pre-existing model into local terms. *{Both Sassoon and Rosenberg write realistically using the same poetic conventions. They do not ditch the conventions completely. Instead, Sassoon uses the existing convention and customizes to his need.}* Even literary memoirists, who are expected to respect the facts, can only be as realistic as the artificial literary conventions available to them will allow them to be. *{Even professional memoirists use existing conventions, and so definitely soldier poets will too (Memoirs — a style of biography; memoirists — biographers).}* Writers write realistically not by directly " telling it like it is," but by telling it like it's told in literature. *{Writers are realistic not by writing reality but by writing conventionally about reality.}* They must, as Northrop Frye told us half a century ago, find, or adapt, a set of literary conventions, and out of this old paradigm create a new literary form. *{Writers adapt conventions to make new forms.}*

Main Point: British poetry did not become more and more realistic during WWI; Trench lyric was formed by adapting existing style, not by creating a new one.

1. This is a Main Purpose question from the General category.

The question asks us to choose the primary purpose of the passage.

The author first presents a myth about British poetry of the war and then explains why she believes that the myth is incorrect. She provides examples to make her point and ends the passage with a generalized idea of what actually the war poetry is. Thus, she wishes to debunk the myth that the war poetry became more and more realistic when soldiers who were poets learned about modern warfare and that earlier poetic convention was replaced by new one.

Let's analyze the options one by one.

(A) This is the **correct** answer. This can be accurately described as the primary purpose.

(B) This option is **incorrect** because the author's intention isn't just to discuss the British war poetry but to negate a particular myth about it.

(C) This option is **incorrect** because the author does not discuss Sassoon as a main point. Sassoon is mentioned as an example.

(D) This option is **incorrect** because the author discusses nineteenth century Romantics and Victorian poets only as a basis for war poetry and not as a point in itself.

(E) This option is **incorrect** because the author implies the opposite of this option. The author suggests that new styles are created by adapting existing styles and not by themselves.

The correct answer is A.

2. This is a Detail question.

    The question asks us to choose options with which the author will agree.

    Let's analyze the options one by one.

    A   This is the **correct** option because the author mentions that Owen's " Dulce et decorum est" is the most famous poem of the War and as an example of poetry that is not characteristic or representative of the bulk of war poetry.

    B   This is also the **correct** option because the bulk poetry (referred to as "That poetry") is influenced by nineteenth-century poetic tradition, which is defined by Wordsworth and the Romantics and also the major Victorian poets to Hardy and more. The majority of the war poets worked within this nineteenth-century tradition to produce the trench lyric.

    C   This is also the **correct** option because this is the main point of the author. The author implies that new styles are created by adapting existing styles and not by themselves, and specifically that the famous war poetry is derived from the nineteenth-century tradition.

    The correct answers are A, B, & C.

3. This is an Inference question.

    We have been asked to choose specifically those options that state the author's reason for believing that the World War One poetry did not become more realistic into a different literary form.

    Let's analyze the options one by one.

    A   This is the **correct** option because the passage states that the bulk poetry (referred to as "That poetry," highlighted in the passage) is influenced by nineteenth-century poetic tradition, which is defined by Wordsworth and the Romantics and also the major Victorian poets to Hardy and more. The majority of the war poets worked within this nineteenth-century tradition to produce the trench lyric.

    B   This option is **incorrect** because the author believes the opposite of this option. The author suggests that new styles are created by adapting existing styles and not by themselves. Thus, she wouldn't agree that pastoral patriotism gave way to the angry realism of war poets, which led to the formation of trench lyric.

    C   This is the **correct** option because this is suggested by the author in the last part of the passage. It states that Sassoon did not give up completely the poetic conventions of the nineteenth-century poetic tradition but that he adapted them according to circumstances and time. This adaptation is the "realistic" version of the earlier conventions, and not an original invention. The last part also states that writers adapt or develop supposedly new forms from old conventions.

The correct answers are A, & C.

4. This is an Inference question.

The answer to this question lies in the highlighted sentences (reproduced here) — "Thus when we think of World War One poetry ... much of the poetry of World War One that belongs to this tradition." In this part of the passage, the author explains that most people tend to think of World War poetry as the angry and satirical anti-war poems, but those angry poems are **atypical (i.e. not representative)** of the bulk of the War poetry. Then the author uses the term. That poetry and states that "that poetry" is grateful to the nineteenth century poetry, to which the majority of the war poetry is being attributed. Thus "That poetry" refers to the "bulk of the War poetry" but not to the "angry poetry," which is different from the bulk or war poetry. Also, we cannot say that the term "That poetry" can refer to all poetry from World War because then it would include the "angry poetry."

Thus, the correct answer is D.

5. This is a Function question.

We have been asked to find an alternative to the word pastoral as used in the passage.

Let's analyze the sentence: "the **pastoral patriotism** of Brooke soon gave way ... to the **angry realism** of Sassoon and Owen." Thus, "pastoral patriotism" was replaced by "angry realism." So, "pastoral" is relatively contradictory to "angry."

Let's analyze the options one by one.

(A) This is the **correct** answer. This can very well serve as a replacement for "pastoral" because it is contextually contradictory to "angry." "Serene" means "calm, undisturbed."

(B) This option is **incorrect** because it is not contextually contradictory to "angry realism."

(C) This option is **incorrect** because "divine — holy, godly" is out of context of the passage and the sentence.

(D) This option is **incorrect** because "satirical — sarcastic" is a negative word; "pastoral" is contextually positive.

(E) This option is **incorrect** because "conflicting" is out of scope for "pastoral."

The correct answer is A.

6. This is a Detail question.

We have been asked to choose a sentence in which the author **demonstrates** that Sassoon's work "Memoirs of a Fox-Hunting Man" is in keeping with the nineteenth century poetic tradition of the Romantics and Victorian poets.

While Sassoon's work "Memoirs of a Fox-Hunting Man" has been first mentioned in the previous sentence: "The last two paragraphs of what many ... composed by the solider-poets"; the author proves that it follows the nineteenth century poetic tradition in "At first glance, a work by the ... the writers of World War One," especially in the part "... the ending of "Memoirs of a Fox-Hunting Man" reveals just how insistently the Romantic lyric imposed its form and structure ...."

The sentence (option A) "Sassoon, like Rosenberg, does not ... and hence originally, about it" merely discusses connections between Sassoon's work and trench lyric but not to poetic tradition of the Romantics and Victorian poets.

Thus, only the sentence (option C) "At first glance, a work by the ... the writers of World War One" **demonstrates** that Sassoon's work "Memoirs of a Fox-Hunting Man" is in keeping with the nineteenth century poetic tradition of the Romantics and Victorian poets.

The correct answer is C.

7. This is a Tone question.

We have been asked to describe the author's attitude towards the view that increasingly modern warfare rendered poetry of the war more and more angry and sarcastic. This view is discussed by the author in the first sentence of the passage. The author calls this view "the most persistent myth." Thus, it is clear that the author does not believe in this view. However, we cannot say that she fully disagree with this view because she states that this myth is persistent as it is based on some (famous) poems that do not reflect the bulk of the war poetry. Thus, she believes that the myth holds true for some of the poems but not for the most of the poems or prose. Thus, her attitude towards the myth can be thought of as partial disagreement.

Let's analyze the options one by one.

(A) This option is **incorrect**. Qualified enthusiasm — Limited enthusiasm; using "enthusiasm," even if "limited," for partial disagreement is one step too far from the actual attitude.

(B) This option is **incorrect**. Utter disgust; the author does not bear complete disgust towards the myth. The author is quite objective; she logically disagrees with it and does not let emotions color her judgment.

(C) This option is **incorrect**. Healthy regard; this does not express any of her partial disagreement of the myth.

(D) This option is **correct**. Cautious dubiety — Controlled skepticism/doubt; this expresses the author's partial disagreement is the best way; the author is skeptical of believing the persistent myth.

(E) This option is **incorrect**. Arrant disapprobation — Utter disapproval; the author does not completely disapprove of the myth. The author is quite objective; she logically disagrees with it and does not let emotions color her judgment.

The correct answer is D.

8. This is a Detail question.

We need to find a sentence in which the author quotes someone else to prove that writers create new forms using adaptation. This is present in the final sentence in the passage in which the author quotes Northrop Frye.

The correct answer is: Last sentence/III paragraph: *They must, as Northrop Frye ... create a new literary form.*

6.22   Passage 22 (New Evidence Clears a Long Puzzle)

Understanding the Passage

This is a medium length passage of hard difficulty level on Life Sciences.

Scientists have long speculated as to why animal species didn't burgeon sooner, once sufficient oxygen covered the Earth's surface. *{Scientists have been unable to understand why animals did not thrive sooner, at the time when oxygen was adequate.}* Animals first appeared and began to prosper at the end of the Proterozoic period, about 600 to 700 million years ago–but the billion-year stretch before that, when there was also plenty of oxygen, no animals. *{Oxygen was sufficient for about a billion years before animals actually appeared. Animals appeared at the end of the Proterozoic period, about 600 to 700 million years ago, but there was plenty oxygen for an about a billion years before that.}*

Evidently, the air was not oxygen-rich enough then. The oxygen levels during the billion or more years before the rise of animals were only 0.1 percent of what they are today. *{The answer to this puzzle is that oxygen seemed like it was enough but it actually was not. Oxygen was only 0.1% of today's level.}* While there is no question that genetic and ecological innovations are ultimately behind the rise of animals, there is also no question that for animal life to flourish a certain level of oxygen is required. *{Thus, earlier oxygen estimates were incorrect. Based on the old, incorrect oxygen estimates, scientists would wonder whether oxygen is necessary. However, the latest data proves that a certain amount of oxygen is necessary, just as genetic and ecological adaptations are required for animals to flourish.}*

The evidence was found by analyzing chromium isotopes in ancient sediments from China, Australia, Canada and the United States. *{This new evidence showing actual estimates of oxygen level was found by analyzing chromium isotopes from four countries.}* Chromium is found in the Earth's continental crust, and chromium oxidation, the process recorded by the chromium isotopes, is directly linked to the presence of free oxygen in the atmosphere. *{Chromium isotopes are used because they are directly proportional to the amount of free oxygen. So, analyzing chromium isotopes can give a clue about the oxygen levels of the atmosphere .Chromium isotopes are created by oxidation; they are present in the Earth's crust.}* Specifically, samples deposited in shallow, iron-rich ocean areas were studied, near the ancient shoreline and compared with other samples taken from younger shoreline locales deposited in similar settings but known to have higher levels of oxygen. *{To get specific details, chromium isotopes from both old and new crusts were collected to get an idea of how much oxygen was present earlier and now.}*

The question about the role of oxygen in controlling the first appearance of animal has long vexed scientists. *{Based on the old, incorrect oxygen estimates, scientists would wonder whether oxygen is necessary.}* Previous estimates, which put the oxygen level at 40 percent of today's conditions during pre-animal times, were based on very loose constraints, leaving open the possibility that oxygen was already plenty high to support animal life, and shifting the absence of animal life before the end of the Proterozoic to other controls. *{Earlier estimates of oxygen levels, before chromium data, were based on loose constraints. This led to the estimate that oxygen level was 40% of today's level, but it actually was only 0.1%. Since, oxygen* *was thought to be sufficient, scientists began to think that later appearance of animals must be linked to some other factor or reason, and not oxygen.}* Oxygen levels were highly dynamic in the early atmosphere, with the potential for occasional spikes. *{Oxygen levels were very dynamic and given to changing easily, and occasionally spiked too.}* However, it also seems clear that there are first-order differences in the nature of Earth surface chromium cycling before the rise of animals versus the time interval coincident with their first appearance?implying vanishingly small oxygen conditions before. *{However, it is clear that oxygen was in vanishingly small amounts, not enough to support animal appearance or rise. Chromium cycling changed around the time of appearance of animals proving that earlier oxygen was insufficient.}* These differences are recorded in a dramatic shift in the chromium isotope data, with clear signals of cycling beneath a more oxygen-rich atmosphere at the time the animals appear. *{The differences in the chromium cycling data prove that oxygen became plentiful around the time the animals appeared.}*

Main point: New evidence solves a long-standing puzzle about relevance of oxygen in the appearance of animals.

1. This is an Inference question.

   We have to choose an option that provides the most accurate inference implied by the new evidence. The answer to this question lies in the final paragraph, which states that previous estimates were based on very loose constraints, leaving open the possibility that oxygen was already plenty high to support animal life, and shifting the absence of animal life before the end of the Proterozoic to other factors. Thus, the earlier estimates were incorrect, making the scientists feel that animals could have existed before end of the Proterozoic period. However, new evidence shows that oxygen levels were so dynamic and low that animals could not have existed then.

   Let's analyze the options one by one.

   (A) This option is **incorrect** because the passage proves the opposite of this ? that the animals could not have existed then.

   (B) This option is **incorrect** because the passage proves the opposite of this ? that oxygen levels were so dynamic and low before end of the Proterozoic period.

   (C) This option is **incorrect** because the passage does not set out to prove the existence of chromium cycles. This is not an inference, but is a stated fact.

   (D) This is the **correct** option. It matches our deductions. The passage proves that oxygen levels were so dynamic and low before end of the Proterozoic period and that the earlier estimates were incorrect and much higher than what they actually were.

   (E) This option is **incorrect** because the passage proves the opposite of this ? that oxygen levels were so dynamic and low before end of the Proterozoic period.

   The correct answer is D.

2. This is a Reasoning question on weakening the conclusion.

We have to choose an option that would weaken the claim made in the final paragraph.

The final paragraph states that previous estimates of oxygen were based on very loose constraints, leaving open the possibility that oxygen was plenty high to support animal life, and shifting the absence of animal life before the end of the Proterozoic to other factors. Thus, the earlier estimates were incorrect, making the scientists feel that animals could have existed before end of the Proterozoic period. However, new evidence shows that oxygen levels were so dynamic and low that animals could not have existed then. Therefore, the claim being made in the final paragraph is that animals did not exist before end of the Proterozoic period despite plenty of oxygen is that there was no plenty of oxygen. This claim is based on evidence in the second paragraph. Chromium oxidation cycles were studied from shoreline samples. We have to weaken the claim.

Let's analyze the options one by one.

(A) This option is **incorrect** because stating that Chromium oxidation is the only reliable indicator of oxygen levels strengthens the claim, which is based on those cycles.

(B) This option is **incorrect** because stating that oxygen levels required to sustain animal life are far higher than currently believed strengthens the claim, which stated that oxygen levels were lower than thought. Thus, if required oxygen level is higher than is thought, the lower than estimated oxygen could not have sustained animal life at all.

(C) This option is **incorrect** because stating that plant life evolved much before animal life did is irrelevant by itself.

(D) This option is **incorrect** because stating that Chromium samples from other continents matches the samples from Australia strengthens the claim, which is based on those levels.

(E) This is the **correct** option because stating that shoreline locales are not quite representative of the rest of the landform weakens the claim, which is based on Chromium samples from shoreline locales. On the basis of samples from shorelines, claims about oxygen and animal life were made. However, if shoreline areas are not representative of the rest of the land, the claims will not apply to the rest of the land, leaving open the possibility that oxygen could have been high enough to sustain animal life, thus weakening the claim in the final paragraph.

The correct answer is E.

3. This is a Function question.

We have to choose an option that best describes the role of the second paragraph in the whole passage.

In the first paragraph, author introduces that a particular question has always bothered the scientists - why animal species didn't flourish sooner, once sufficient oxygen covered the Earth's surface. The author explains the background for this question. In the second paragraph, the author presents some new evidence that begins to explain how the question can be answered. Thus, the second paragraph is providing evidence to answer the question presented in the first paragraph, to support the claim made in the last line of the first paragraph.

Let's analyze the options one by one.

(A) This option is **incorrect** because the second paragraph does not dispute the first one.

(B) This option is **incorrect** because the second paragraph presents new evidence, and does not elaborate on the things discussed in the first one.

(C) This is the **correct** option. It matches our deductions. The second paragraph is buttressing (supporting) the first paragraph.

(D) This option is **incorrect** because the second paragraph does not provide an alternative explanation. That is done by the third one.

(E) This option is **incorrect** because the second paragraph does not offset (negate) the theory of the first one.

The correct answer is C.

4. This is a Main Purpose question from the General category.

The question asks us to find the primary purpose of the passage.

Let's analyze the passage.

The author first introduces that a particular question has always bothered the scientists - why animal species didn't flourish sooner, once sufficient oxygen covered the Earth's surface. The author explains the background for this question. In the second paragraph, the author presents some new evidence that begins to explain how the question can be answered. In the final paragraph, it becomes clear that the question itself is incorrect because it relied on incorrect data. Thus, the author is concerned with refuting an old belief or a myth and providing new evidence to dispel that belief.

Let's analyze the options one by one.

(A) This option is **incorrect** because the passage does not refute any new theory. The author is concerned with refuting an old belief.

(B) This option is **incorrect** because the passage does not only discuss a scientific phenomenon but also provides new evidence to dispel an old belief.

(C) This option is **incorrect** because the passage does not explain origin of life, but discusses origin of animals.

(D) This option is **incorrect** because the passage does not provide any hypothesis or support for it.

(E) This is the **correct** option. It matches our deductions.

The correct answer is E.

5. This is an Inference question.

We have been asked to choose options that were believed to be true by scientists, that is, those statements that are no longer true, or have been disputed by the new evidence.

Let's analyze the options one by one.

A This is a **correct** option as this must have been believed to be true by scientists earlier. The second sentence of the third paragraph states that previous estimates put the oxygen level at 40 percent of today's conditions during pre-animal times. However, these estimates have been disputed. The oxygen levels during the billion or more years before the rise of animals were only 0.1 percent of what they are today.

B This is an **incorrect** option because the fact that animals first appeared 600 to 700 million years ago was never called into question and is still considered true.

C This is also a **correct** option as this must have been believed to be true by scientists earlier. The scientists had an inflated estimate of oxygen. Scientists had long been puzzling over why animals had not appeared sooner despite having plenty of oxygen. Thus, they must have believed that oxygen level did not influence the appearance of animals.

The correct answers are A, & C.

6. This is a Detail question.

We have been asked to present the latest oxygen levels estimate. There are two sentences with oxygen levels estimate – 40 percent and 0.1 percent, but only 0.1 percent is the latest one, and the correct one; it is given in the I paragraph of the passage – "The oxygen levels during ... only 0.1 percent of what they are today."

7. This is a Detail question.

We have to choose statements that are still considered true.

Let's analyze the options one by one.

A This option is **correct** because this is stated in the final sentence of the first paragraph – that there is no question that for animal life to flourish a certain level of oxygen is required.

B This option is also **correct** because this is stated in the third sentence of the third paragraph.

C This option is also **correct** because this is stated in the final sentence of the third paragraph – that there are clear signals a more oxygen-rich atmosphere at the time the animals appear.

The correct answers are A, B, & C.

8.   This is a Function question.

We have to find a replacement for the highlighted word burgeon as used in the context of the passage.   The sentence is "Scientists have long speculated as to why animal species didn't burgeon sooner, once sufficient oxygen covered the Earth's surface. Animals first **appeared** and began to **prosper** at the end of the Proterozoic period" So, animals appeared and prospered at the end of the Proterozoic period and scientists have wondered why they did not burgeon sooner. Thus, "burgeon" would be similar to "appear and prosper."

Let's look at the options one by one.

(A)   This is **correct** because "flourish" means "grow, thrive."

(B)   This is **incorrect** because "dwindle" means "decline in numbers."

(C)   This is **incorrect** because "wane" means "reduce."

(D)   This is **incorrect** because "change" is out of context.

(E)   This is **incorrect** because "evolve" does not necessarily mean "appear and prosper." It is closer in meaning to "change"; however, we need something similar to "thrive."

The correct answer is A.

6.23 Passage 23 (A new perspective on the classical black hole solution)

Understanding the Passage

This is a medium length passage of intermediate difficulty level on Astrophysics.

In a series of pioneering papers, starting in 1979, Leonard S. Abrams discussed the physical sense of the black hole solution. Abrams claimed that the correct solution for the gravitational field in a Schwarzschild space, an empty space filled by a spherically symmetric gravitational field produced by a spherical source mass, shouldn't lead to a black hole as a physical object.*{Abrams made some pioneering, novel studies. He presented a different solution for the gravitational field in a Schwarzschild space. He said that the solution should not create black hole as a physical object. Schwarzschild space is an empty space; it is filled with a spherical symmetrical gravity field; this field is created by a spherical object having mass.}*

It is certain that if there is a formal error in the black hole solution, committed by the founders of this theory, in the period from 1915-1920's, a long list of research produced during the subsequent decades would be brought into question. Consequently, Abrams' conclusion has attracted the attention of many physicists, since it directly challenges the classical solution and the subsequent work. *{If Abrams is right, then the earlier solution is wrong. If the earlier solution is wrong, then lot of research and studies based on the earlier solution would be weakened. This is why Abrams' work is attracting the attention of many scientists.}*

Stephen J. Crothers, building upon the work of Abrams, was able to deduce solutions for the gravitational field in a Schwarzschild metric space produced in terms of a physical observable radius. Crothers' solutions fully verify the initial arguments of Abrams. Therefore, the claim that the correct solution for the gravitational field in a Schwarzschild space does not lead to a black hole as a physical object requires serious attention.
textit{Another scientist, Crothers, has worked on Abrams' solution. Crothers has worked out the maths for Abrams' solution. So, Crothers' work supports and proves the initial points made by Abrams. Thus, it is very important that Abrams claim of no physical black hole be investigated.}

The new solution, by Crothers, doesn't eliminate the classical " black hole solution," i.e. the line-element thereof, produced by the founders of the black hole problem, but represents the perspective of a real observer whose location is in the real Schwarzschild space itself, inhomogeneous and curved, not by quantities in an abstract flat space tangential to it at the point of observation as it was previously, in the classical solution. Consequently, the new solution opens a doorway to new research on the specific physical conditions accompanying gravitational collapse in Schwarzschild space. This can now be studied in a reasonable manner both through a purely theoretical approach and with the methods of numerical relativity. *{Crothers' solution does not remove the line-element of the classical solution. In Crothers' solution, perspective is from an observer who is in the real Schwarzschild space itself, but in classical solution, the perspective is from an observer who is tangential to the abstract flat space. In Crothers' solution, space is inhomogeneous and curved and not abstract flat space as was in the classical. Thus, the new solution allows research on the physical aspects in Schwarzschild space, enabling* *study from theoretical and numerical way.}*

Main point: Crothers' and Abrams' work is a novel interpretation of black hole solution; it opens up a new research avenue.

1. This is an Inference question.

   We have to choose an option that is true about the classical black hole solution, according to the passage.

   Let's analyze the options one by one.

   [A]   This is the **correct** option because the first sentence in the last paragraph states that the classical solution includes a line-element. Thus, this can be inferred as true.

   [B]   This is also the **correct** option because the first paragraph states that Abrams suggested that gravitational field in Schwarzschild space should NOT cause black hole as a physical object, and also that Abrams challenged the classical black hole solution. Thus, we can infer that classical black hole solution argued for the opposite – that is, gravitational field in Schwarzschild space should cause black hole as a physical object.

   [C]   This is also the **correct** option because the last paragraph states that in the classical solution, perspective of an observer in an abstract flat space tangential to Schwarzschild space, as opposed to the new solution, which represents the perspective of a real observer whose location is in the real Schwarzschild space itself, inhomogeneous and curved.

   The correct answers are A, B, & C.

2. This is an Inference question.

   We have to choose an option that would result, if the **classical** black hole solution is refuted, according to the passage. The answer to this question lies in the second paragraph, which states that if the black hole solution is refuted, all subsequent research based on the black hole solution will come into question.

   Let's analyze the options one by one.

   (A)   This option is **incorrect** because the passage does not suggest any such thing. This is the opposite of what is likely because if the classical solution is refuted, both Crothers and Abrams would be considered worthy, not unworthy.

   (B)   This option is **incorrect** because the passage discusses the statement in this option only with respect to Abrams' research and not in direct connection to the black hole solution. Hence, this cannot be inferred.

   (C)   This option is **incorrect** because the passage discusses theoretical approaches only with respect to Abrams' research and not in direct connection to the black hole solution. Hence, this cannot be inferred.

(D) This is the **correct** option. It matches our deductions.

(E) This option is **incorrect** because the passage does state that Abram's conclusion will be negated. In fact, since Abrams intends to modify the black hole solution, if the black hole solution is negated Abrams' conclusions will probably be accepted.

Thus, the correct answer is D.

3. This is a Detail question.

We have to choose a sentence in passage in which the author puts forth his opinion about Crothers' solution with respect to the classical solution. Crothers' and Abrams' work has been discussed primarily in the first and the fourth paragraph. The correct answer is the first sentence of the last paragraph—*"The new solution, by Crothers, doesn't ... in the classical solution"*, which states that the new solution by Crothers may seem to challenge the classical solution, but in fact, it does not. Thus, the author voices possible opinion about Crothers' solution in this sentence with respect to the classical solution.

4. This is a Function question.

We have been asked to describe the role of the second paragraph in the context of the entire passage.

Let's analyze the passage.

In the first paragraph, the author immediately introduces the topic of discussion: a new interpretation of the black hole solution by Abrams. The black hole solution deals with Schwarzschild space.

In the second paragraph, the author explains the possible effects or repercussions of this new interpretation.

In the third paragraph, the author further substantiates the new interpretation by adding support of another scientist's work built upon the new interpretation.

In the fourth and final paragraph, the author deals with the specific differences between the new and the classical approach and explains why the new approach needs to be studied further.

Let's analyze the options one by one.

(A) This option is **incorrect** because this is the role of the third paragraph, not of the second.

(B) This option is **incorrect** because this is done in the final paragraph, not in the second.

(C)   This option is **incorrect** because no paragraph lays foundation for Crothers' work. It is directly discussed in the third paragraph.

(D)   This is the **correct** answer. It matches our deductions.

(E)   This option is **incorrect** because this is the role of the first paragraph, not of the second.

The correct answer is D.

5.   This is a Main Purpose question from the General category.

We have to been asked to choose a suitable title for the passage.

This is akin to finding the primary purpose. Let's analyze the passage. In the first paragraph, the author immediately introduces the topic of discussion: a new interpretation of the black hole solution by Abrams. The black hole solution deals with Schwarzschild space. In the second paragraph, the author explains the implications of this new interpretation. In the third paragraph, the author further substantiates the new interpretation by adding support of another scientist's work built upon the new interpretation. In the fourth paragraph, the author deals with the specific differences between the new and the classical approach and explains why the new approach needs to be studied further. Thus, the author is primarily concerned with the new approach to the black hole solution.

Let's analyze the options one by one.

(A)   This option is **incorrect** because the passage is not just about Schwarzschild space. Schwarzschild space in order to explain the black hole solution. Also, this option suggests that Schwarzschild space has been discovered by Abrams, but it is not so. The passage actually suggests a new interpretation of an already-known concept.

(B)   This is the **correct** answer. It matches our deductions.

(C)   This option is **incorrect** because the passage is not only discussing work by Abrams and Crothers in a general way. A specific approach by Abrams is being discussed in the passage.

(D)   This option is **incorrect** because the passage is not furthering classical solution but rather discussing the novel solution against classical solution.

(E)   This option is **incorrect** because the passage is not just about Schwarzschild space. Also, no paradox is discussed.

The correct answer is B.

6.   This is an Inference question.

We have to choose points of differences between the classical black hole solution and that proposed by Abrams. The actual solution is worked upon by Crothers but on the points made by Abrams. The differences between Crothers' solution and the classical one are given in the final paragraph.

Let's analyze the options one by one.

[A]   This option is **correct** because the final paragraph mentions that the vantage point (or perspective, viewpoint) of the observer is different in Crothers' solution. In Crothers' solution, perspective is from an observer is in the real Schwarzschild space itself but in classical the perspective is from an observer tangential to the abstract flat space.

[B]   This option is also **correct** because the final paragraph mentions that the nature of space is different. In Crothers' solution, space is inhomogeneous and curved and not abstract flat space as was in the classical.

[C]   This option is **incorrect** because the final paragraph distinctly mentions that Crothers' solution does not change the line-element of the classical black hole solution. Thus, this cannot be a point of difference between the classical black hole solution and that proposed by Abrams.

The correct answers are A, & B.

7. This is a Reasoning question.

We have been asked what would happen if a physical black hole is not created from the correct solution for the gravitational field in a Schwarzschild space. The statement that the correct solution for the gravitational field in a Schwarzschild space should not lead to a physical black hole is what Abrams proposed. Thus, if Abrams' work is proved, the classical solution would be questioned, as will the research based on the classical solution.

Let's look at the options one by one.

(A)   This option is **incorrect** because this merely presents the definition of Schwarzschild space.

(B)   This option is **incorrect** because Abrams and Crothers' work would be proved, not refuted, if a physical black hole is not created from the correct solution for the gravitational field in a Schwarzschild space.

(C)   This option is **incorrect** because the classical black hole solution will have to be altered, if a physical black hole is not created from the correct solution for the gravitational field in a Schwarzschild space.

(D)   This option is **incorrect** because this is not in keeping with the new solution, given in the final sentences of the final paragraph.

(E)   This option is **correct**. It matches our deductions.

The correct answer is E.

8. This is an Inference question.

We have to choose possible characteristics of the classical black hole solution. These can be inferred from the final paragraph.

Let's analyze the options one by one.

A   This option is **incorrect** because having the observer in Schwarzschild space is a characteristic of the new solution, by Crothers, not of the classical solution.

B   This option is **correct.** The new solution discusses space as inhomogeneous and curved, and not an abstract flat space. Thus, we can infer that the classical solution included an abstract flat space.

C   This option is **incorrect** because the classical " black hole solution" includes, not excludes, the line-element.

The correct answer is B.

Argument

Structure

Passages

Chapter 7

Argument Structure Passage (ASP) Concepts

7.1 What is an Argument Structure Passage?

Argument Structure Passage (ASP) based question is one of the two types of questions that make up the Reading Comprehension sub-section of the GRE. Argument Structure Passages are very short compared to typical reading comprehension passages, we have seen in the I part of the book. The length of passages typically range form 3 to 7 lines. An ASP comprises a logic-based argument and a specific instruction followed by five options, only one of which is correct. Unlike a typical RC passage, ASP is followed by only one question; you can expect 1-3 ASP per section.

What does a typical ASP question look like?

CR Argument

Premises "The new subway line, opened barely a year ago to alleviate traffic congestion, has already been deemed insufficient in satisfying demand. The State Transport Authority (STA), commissioned by the Mayor's office to come up with solutions, has admitted that even if more trains and carriages are added, the demand is such that only a 23% reduction in congestion would be feasible. **Conclusion** For this reason, the city council is now considering building a new highway linking the downtown business district with the East Canton suburbs."

Premise(s) + Conclusion = Argument

Question Stem Which of the following would most weaken the conclusion of the above argument?

Options

(A) One year is insufficient time to judge the viability of the subway.

(B)   A ride-sharing program has been successfully operating for more than a year.

(C)   The business district suffers from a chronic shortage of parking spaces.

(D)   Some residents in the business district are opposed to the program.

(E)   The cost of the proposed highway would severely strain the city's budget.

7.1.1   What is an Argument?

An argument is a composition of reasoning and conclusion designed to make some point. The writer of the argument is called the author. He is not to be confused with the test-maker—ETS. The author wants the reader to believe in a point called the **conclusion** and the reasoning on which he bases his conclusion is called the **premise.**

There could be more than one premise in an argument, but there could be only one conclusion in the argument—main conclusion. In some arguments, there could be two conclusions—main conclusion, and intermediate conclusion—but only one of them will function as the main conclusion

Let us take an argument to better understand this point.

> Companies Pinnacle and Acme provide round-the-clock e-mail assistance to any customer who uses their laptops. Customers send e-mails only when they find the laptop difficult to use. Since Pinnacle receives four times as many e-mails as Acme receives, Pinnacle's laptops must be more difficult to use than Acme's.

What is the purpose of writing this argument by the author?

The author provides information about two companies — Pinnacle and Acme. These companies provide 24/7 e-mail support to its customers on the uses of laptops. The author further states that the customers send e-mail only when they face problems in using the laptop.

The purpose of the argument is to _conclude_ that **Pinnacle's laptops must be more difficult to use than Acme's,** and the reasoning advanced by the author in support of that conclusion is that **Pinnacle receives four times as many e-mails as Acme** and that **the customers send**

e-mail only when they face problems in using the laptop. Since the customers send e-mails only when they face problem in using the laptops, more e-mails sent to Pinnacle implies that its laptops are more difficult to use than Acme's.

Break-Up of the argument

Background Information: *Companies Pinnacle and Acme provide round-the-clock e-mail assistance to any customer who uses their laptops.*

> **Role:** This statement is to introduce the reader to two companies, their businesses, and their service to their customers.

Premise1: *Customers send the e-mails only when they find the laptops difficult to use.*

> **Role:** This is a statement which tells the reader that the customers send e-mails only when they face problem. This is a **premise.** There is reasoning hidden in this statement. If this premise is missing, and one company receives more # of e-mails than the other from the customers, you cannot necessarily conclude that the e-mails are related to customer's concerns over laptop problems. You may assume that most e-mail maybe related to sales enquiry or for other purposes, hence the motive behind writing premise 1: **Customers send the e-mails only** when they find the laptop difficult to use is to help us to conclude something.

> **A Premise** is any **statement, information, fact, evidence, or viewpoint** the author uses to reach his conclusion.

Premise2: *Pinnacle receives four times as many e-mails as Acme receives.*

> **Role:** This statement is easy to understand. This is also a **premise.** It means that # of e-mails received by Pinnacle = 4* # of e-mails received by Acme. Based on this reasoning Pinnacle receives more e-mails than Acme receives, author concludes something.

Conclusion: *Pinnacle's laptops must be more difficult to use than Acme's.*

> **Role:** This statement is also easy to understand. This is the purpose or the **conclusion of the argument.**

Premises and Conclusion

Identify premises and conclusion

1. Humidity has been rising for the last 10 days. Therefore, sales of air-conditioners will rise in coastal areas.

Premise: Humidity has been rising for the last 10 days.
Conclusion: Therefore, sales of air-conditioners will rise in coastal areas.

2. The floods destroyed groundnut crops this season. A rise in the prices of oil is inevitable.

Premise: The floods destroyed groundnut crops this season.
Conclusion: A rise in the prices of oil is inevitable.

3. The floods destroyed onion crops this season. However, the neighboring country has achieved a record onion production. Hence, the inevitability of a rise in prices is false.

Premise 1: The floods destroyed onion crops this season.

Premise 2: However, the neighboring country has achieved a record onion production.

Conclusion: Hence, the inevitability of a rise in prices is false.

7.1.2 Placement of conclusion

How do you identify a conclusion? Is the conclusion last statement of the argument? Not really! Usually it is, but not always. It can be placed anywhere in the argument.

Let us see few examples of variously placed conclusions.

Conclusion at the end

The floods destroyed onion crops this season. However, the neighboring country has achieved a record onion production. **Hence, the inevitability of a rise in prices is false.**

Conclusion in the middle

The floods destroyed onion crops this season. **Hence, a rise in prices is likely.** However, a record production of onions achieved by the neighboring country might counter price rise.

Conclusion in the beginning

A rise in prices of onion is likely, as the floods destroyed onion crops this season. However, a record production of onions achieved by the neighboring country may counter price rise.

7.2 Drill - Identifying Premises and Conclusions

Q1- Steve was awarded Best Player of the Season by State Sports Committee. Steve will make his career in sports.

Q2- Now only rains can make things better for the country. Disappointed farmers have consumed their existing water resources to the fullest. The level of water in dams has reached a record minimum.

Q3- The new course curriculum of Midland High School is praiseworthy. The school maintains good mix of academics and sports. This is the need of the hour. Many schools have followed Midland.

Answers

Q1: Premise: Steve....committee. Conclusion: Steve will....sports.
Q2 : Conclusion: Only rains can...country. Premise 1: Disappointed....fullest. Premise 2: The....level.
Q3 : Premise 1: New.... praiseworthy. Premise 2: The school....sports. Conclusion: This....hour. Premise 3: Many.....Midland.

7.3 Markers of Conclusions and Premises

Markers are words and phrases that are commonly used to present premises and conclusion. In most of the arguments, these markers help a lot in determining the premises and the conclusion swiftly.

Below is a partial list of words and phrases that commonly precede the premises or the conclusion:

Premise Markers	Conclusion Markers
Since	Therefore
Due to	Hence
Owing to	It shows that
Because	It follows that
For	It can be concluded that
Given that	Thus
For example	so
As stated	Consequently
As reasoned	As a result
Besides	Clearly
In addition	Accordingly
Additionally	
Moreover	
Furthermore	

This list is not comprehensive and there is no need to mug up these markers. The purpose is to get an idea about the conclusion and the premises in the argument.

7.4   Counter-Premises

A few arguments may include premises that go against the conclusion of the argument.

What is the purpose of such premises? If the purpose of the argument is to formulate the conclusion and ultimately convince the reader about it, why does the author present some information that goes against his conclusion?

The author does so because his stated premises and conclusion may invite some counter-arguments. To safe-guard the conclusion, the author sometimes presents counter-premises himself and then argues against those counter-premises. A premise that goes against the con-clusion is called a **counter-premise.**

Let us see a counter-premise in an argument:

Credited with benevolent behavior, Mr. Jackson must not be fired from the company, though he mishandled the case.

What are the conclusion and the premise?

Conclusion: Mr. Jackson must not be fired from the company.

Premise: He is benevolent.

What role does the statement "*though he mishandled the case*" play?

The statement goes against the conclusion. Therefore, this statement is a **counter-premise.**

As we said above, the author presents counter-premise because the stated premises may invite some counter-arguments, and he wishes to prevent those from weakening his argument. One could have countered the argument by stating "Mr. Jackson must be fired from the company, because *he mishandled the case.*"

Without the counter-premise added, the argument may look weak. The author has strengthened his argument against the criticism by presenting the counter-premise. Conclusion is still valid as the premise counts more than the counter-premise.

7.5   Application of Basic knowledge in ASP questions

ASP questions require only basic knowledge to solve the questions. There is no bias towards an expert on worldly affairs or the one in possession of many facts about any particular subject.

ASP questions require basic knowledge that is is universally known and undisputed.

For example: a premise is *The tax rate for IT industry is doubled.* You should know that tax is a type of cost for the companies and it will negatively impact the profit; however, you cannot infer that the profit will go down for sure.

Another example: Consider this relationship:

$$Sales = Cost + Profit$$

This relationship among sales, cost, and profit is a fact and cannot be disputed. Therefore, this basic knowledge is used in GRE ASP.

Some key financial terms such as **budget** and **deficit** are expected as basic knowledge. However, high order financial terms and their implication are not expected. If they are used in the argument, the argument will either define them or if the argument does not define them, the question does not need that knowledge to solve the question. GRE does not expect you to know the difference between terms like **budgetary deficit and monetary deficit.**

7.6   Premises cannot be challenged, but the Conclusion can be

Most GRE ASP arguments comprise premise and conclusion. Some may have background information, premises, and a conclusion. Others may have background information, premises, counter-premises, intermediate conclusion, and a main conclusion. A few may have only premises.

GRE ASP questions are designed to assess your reasoning ability. You must not mix up real world knowledge with GRE ASP arguments. We have already stated that the premises play the role of facts. Since they are facts, we cannot challenge them.

However, we can question the conclusion. This is only because the conclusion is derived by the author after applying his reasoning to the facts—the premises. We also learnt that the conclusion can be drawn only by the author. So, in a nut shell, can we doubt the author—The answer is yes! But this does not mean that we doubt the author's integrity. We believe that the facts presented (premises, as well as counter-premises) are true, but author's reasoning could be wrong!

Premises, and counter-premises cannot be challenged.

Conclusions can be challenged.

Let us understand this with an example:

> Marijuana works well for arthritis and ailments; hence its controlled consumption should be legalized.

Premise: Marijuana works well for Arthritis and ailments.

Conclusion: Its (Marijuana) control consumption should be legalized.

In real world, you can dispute the premise: **Marijuana works well for arthritis and ailments,** but for the sake of this question, you cannot challenge it, you have to accept it as it is. However, you may doubt the conclusion: **Its (Marijuana) controlled consumption should be legalized,** since the conclusion is derived from the premise.

It is observed that test-makers craft the options in a few questions in such a way that it does not seem like the option is challenging the premise, and you may fall in the trap. Whenever there is an option which goes against the premise, you must discard it as inconsistent with the premises.

Let us see a premise and some statements. We will sort each statement on the basis of whether it is consistent or inconsistent with the premise.

Premise: Motorbikes with less than 150 cc capacity are worthless to speedsters.

Statement 1: Speedsters drive all types of motorbikes for adrenaline rush: less than 150 cc as well as more than 150 cc.

This statement is **inconsistent** as the premise clearly states that for speedsters motorbikes with less than 150 cc capacity are worthless, implying that they will not drive 150cc motorbikes for adrenaline rush. Whereas the statement says that the speedsters do not choose between less than 150 cc and more than 150 cc because they like to drive motorbikes for adrenaline rush. It goes against the premise, and hence inconsistent.

Statement 2: Many speedsters do not drive motorbikes with less than 150 cc capacity for adrenaline rush.

This statement is **consistent** with the premise.

Statement 3: Some speedsters drive motorbikes with more than 150 cc capacity for adrenaline rush.

This statement is also **consistent** with the premise.

Statement 4: Some speedsters drive 125-350 cc motorbikes for adrenaline rush.

This statement is also **inconsistent** with the premise. This statement is cleverly crafted with the usage of ambiguous quantity word "some" and an unqualified range: 125-350 cc motorbikes.

Let us see following argument which has two premises.

> Companies Pinnacle and Acme provide round-the-clock e-mail assistance to any customer who uses their laptops. Customers send e-mails only when they find the laptop difficult to use.

Premise 1: Companies Pinnacle and Acme provide round-the-clock e-mail assistance to any customer who uses their laptops.

Premise 2: Customers send e-mails only when they find the laptop difficult to use.

Statement 1: Number of sales enquiries through e-mail is significantly more for Acme than for Pinnacle.

This statement is **inconsistent** with premise 2. Premise 2: *Customers send e-mails only when they find the laptop difficult to use,* clearly states that customers send e-mails only when they find the laptop difficult to use, hence there is no question of e-mails sent by customers for any other purpose.

Statement 2: Acme is far more prompt in responding to customers' e-mails between 10 pm-6 am, while Pinnacle responds the e-mails next day between 6 am-8 am.

This statement is **inconsistent** with premise 1. Premise 1: *Companies Pinnacle and Acme provide round-the-clock e-mail assistance to any customer who uses their laptops,* clearly states that Pinnacle and Acme provide round-the-clock e-mail assistance to any customer, hence there is no question of not responding to the e-mails during the 10 pm-6 am period.

Statement 3: Some customers prefer to raise their concerns on the phone rather than send e-mails.

This statement is **consistent.** The statement does not conflict with any premise. Even though the premise 2 states that **Customers send e-mails only when they find the laptop difficult to use,** it does not mean that none can mail a letter or telephone the companies to discuss their concerns.

7.7   ASP question types

Argument Structure Passage arguments are followed by a question stem (Except in one question type; we will discuss it later). There are at the most 9 different types of ASP questions. The question stem, followed by the argument, determines which type of ASP question argument belongs. Each question type requires different type of strategy to solve, hence it very important to identify the question type.

We classify 9 different question types based on the family of question types they belong. GRE-ASP question types can be classified on three families.

(1) **Assumption based family:** Finding the Assumption is at the core of solving these questions. Four question types belong to this classification—Find the Assumption, Strengthen the Argument, Weaken the Argument, and Evaluate the Argument. While Strengthen the Argument, and Weaken the Argument question types are quite common in the GRE, Finding the Assumption questions have also appeared in the test, and Evaluate the Argument questions are rarely asked; however, we have provided sufficient number of questions on both the question types.

(2) **Structure based family:** Understanding the structure of the argument is the core to solving these questions. Two question types belong to this classification—Boldface (Role Play) questions, and Parallel Reasoning. Parallel Reasoning question types are super rare in the test, but we have provided four questions in the book.

(3) **Evidence based family:** Understanding the inference or the evidence from the argument is the core to solving these questions. Two question types belong to this classification—Inference questions, and Resolve the Paradox.

Complete the Argument question type does not belong to any family. This question type may have a mix of many question types.

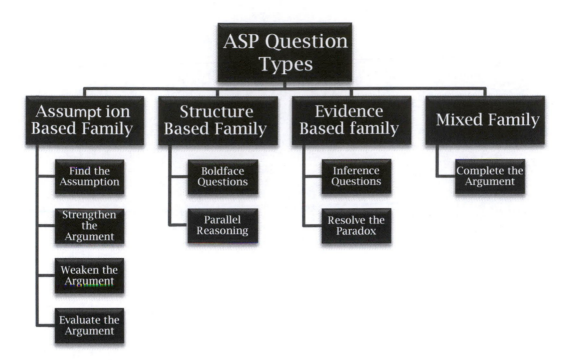

From next chapter onwards, we will understand, develop an approach to solve, and practice questions each question type.

Chapter 8

Find the Assumption

8.1   Find the Assumption question type

 Find the Assumption questions belong to assumption based family. The GRE has been occasionally testing this question type. These questions require us to identify the assumption made by the author to reach the conclusion.

An assumption in an argument is a premise that the author must assume to be true in order to draw the conclusion. However, the assumption is unstated in the argument.

In our daily lives, we also make many assumptions. Take a real life situation: *You have to fly from London to New York.* How many assumptions do we make during this travel?

You may assume: **The plane will take me to NY only; I will not be asked for additional money in the plane; the food available is reasonably good; trained pilots will fly the plane; my seat will not be broken.**

In a Find the assumption question, you have to find out the missing link between the stated premises and the conclusion. Your objective is to think "how can the premises and the unstated premise lead to the finite conclusion?" The act of finding out unstated premise implies finding out the assumption.

Look at the image below. There is a dialogue taking place between two persons. What do you think a necessary assumption here?

By replying: *Yes, I have cracked the GRE* to the question: *Can you solve this tricky question?*, there is an unstated assumption: ***Those who crack the GRE can solve tricky questions.*** This is the purpose of this question type.

See another example. What does the author of the below argument necessarily assume?

> *Messi will score Hat-Trick in the match. So, Barcelona will again be the winner.*

Premise: Messi will score a hat-trick in the match.

When a player scores a hat-trick, the team wins the match.

Conclusion: So, Barcelona will again be the winner.

Missing link = the Assumption

ASP arguments may have many assumptions. Any one assumption will not necessarily make the argument complete, but it will certainly make the conclusion more believable.

Let us see following argument.

> *Companies Pinnacle and Acme provide round-the-clock e-mail assistance to any customer who uses their laptops. Customers send e-mails only when they find the laptop difficult to use. Since Pinnacle receives four times as many e-mails as Acme receives, Pinnacle's laptops must be more difficult to use than Acme's.*

Let us first, deconstruct the argument.

Background Information: *Companies Pinnacle and Acme provide round-the-clock e-mail assistance to any customer who uses their laptops.*

Premise1: *Customers send e-mails only when they find the laptop difficult to use.*

Premise2: *Pinnacle receives four times as many e-mails as Acme receives .*

Conclusion: *Pinnacle's laptops must be more difficult to use than Acme's.*

Our job is to think about unstated assumption(s) (missing link) that connect premises and the conclusion.

In a Find the assumption question, there would be five options, out of which one is correct, but it is always recommended that you predict one or two assumptions on your own. There are two advantages to it. One, you will not be distracted by cleverly crafted options by test-makers, and two, you will better understand the argument.

8.1.1 Predicting Assumption

To predict unstated assumptions, we must keep an eye on the conclusion—how to make the conclusion more believable. Remember that you must not provide a new information to the argument. The assumption is something that is already there in the argument, but it is not stated by the author.

Conclusion: *Pinnacle's laptops must be more difficult to use than Acme's.*

What if Acme receives more letters of complaints through letters that Pinnacle does? The conclusion would seem less believable. So, there is a scope of an assumption.

Predictive Assumption 1: Acme does not receive more complaints through other means such as letters, and phones than Pinnacle receive.

What if Acme sells significantly less laptops than Pinnacle sells, it is obvious that Acme will receive less e-mails than pinnacle receives. The conclusion would seem less believable. So, there is a scope of one more assumption.

Predictive Assumption 2: Acme does not sell significantly less laptops than Pinnacle.

What if significant number of Pinnacle's customers are newbie, then it is obvious that Pinnacle will receive more e-mails than Acme regarding how to use the laptop.

Predictive Assumption 3: Pinnacle does not sell significantly more laptops to newbie than Acme.

Since the author compares laptops of two companies, hence their laptops must be comparable in terms of configuration, and features. If one company's laptop is high-end, and other is low-end, then the conclusion seems less believable.

Predictive Assumption 4: Both company's laptops are comparable in terms of configuration, and features.

There may be few assumptions that either do not matter or not necessary. Let us see couple of them.

Assumption 1: E-mails to Acme are more or less of same length, on average, as to Pinnacle.

Assumption 2: Acme and Pinnacle are in business for sufficiently long period of time.

Remember that assumptions should work toward the conclusion. In a typical assumption question, you may come across such statements, they may fall in the category of assumptions, but your job is to seek for **necessary assumption,** without which the argument is not believable.

Following illustration depicts your job for an Assumption type question.

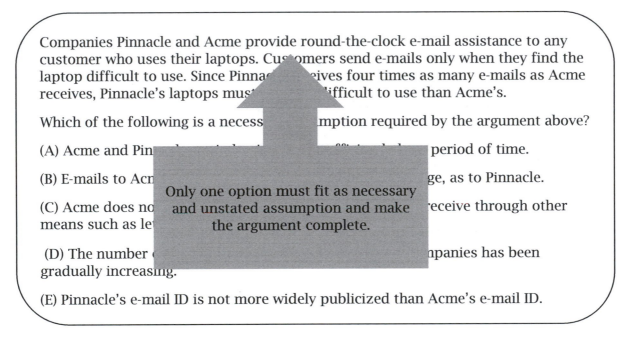

Companies Pinnacle and Acme provide round-the-clock e-mail assistance to any customer who uses their laptops. Customers send e-mails only when they find the laptop difficult to use. Since Pinnacle receives four times as many e-mails as Acme receives, Pinnacle's laptops must be more difficult to use than Acme's.

Which of the following is a necessary assumption required by the argument above?

(A) Acme and Pinnacle are in business for sufficiently long period of time.

(B) E-mails to Acme are more or less of same length, on average, as to Pinnacle.

(C) Acme does not get the e-mail that it should receive through other means such as letters.

(D) The number of laptops sold by both companies has been gradually increasing.

(E) Pinnacle's e-mail ID is not more widely publicized than Acme's e-mail ID.

Only one option must fit as necessary and unstated assumption and make the argument complete.

8.1.2   Beware of new information

Read the following statement.

Acme has three times the number of laptop customers that Pinnacle has.

The statement certainly makes the conclusion more believable, but the information given is additional information, and hence cannot be counted as assumption. For assumption questions, you have to extract the information hidden in the argument.

8.2 Process of solving ASP questions

There may be 1-3 questions based on ASP, and you have to solve them in less than 2 minutes per question. It is important to apply strategy to solve questions correctly.

An untrained student will do back and forth on the argument, question stem, and options few times. The student will re-read the argument each time he/she reads options. This will eat up his/her precious time and put a lot of pressure. We recommend 4-step approach to attempt an ASP question.

4-step approach

(1) Recognize the question type

(2) Understand the argument construction

(3) Predict the qualifier

(4) Process of Elimination

(1) **Recognize the question type**

As soon as you see a very short passage of only 3-7 lines, look at the "Question Stem" rather than the "Argument". Since there are around 9 types of ASP questions, it is necessary that you read the argument keeping in mind that you wish to seek out information from specific point of view. Once you have seen all 9 question types, your mind will be trained to read the argument from specific objective.

It is critically important to read the questions stem fully. Many times students read only the qualifying and selective word or phrase in the question stem and lose heavily. Read the following question stem partially and then read it fully and notice the difference.

Questions stem: Which of the following most strengthens the position of the critics against the claim of US government?

If you hurriedly read the stem and stopped at the word "Strengthen" and decided that is a question on "Strengthen the argument", you are in trouble. When you read fully, you realize that you have to strengthen the claim of critics. If the conclusion of the argument is written from US government's perspective, then you are supposed to weaken the conclusion. The same question may be a "Weaken the argument" question type.

Invariably GRE test-makers draft strengthen as well as weaken the argument options for each question type: "Strengthen the argument" and "Weaken the argument". So, be careful!

Recognizing the question type step should not take more than 5 seconds.

(2) **Understand the argument construction**

After identifying the question type, we must understand and analyze the argument. How to analyze the argument? It requires the understanding of Logical Structure of the argument; identifying background information, premises, and conclusion. We have covered these in previous chapter.

To understand the argument in bits and pieces, many students write notes on scratch-board. Some write only conclusion. Some don't, but most students do take some sort of notes. If you are a beginner, do start writing brief summary for a week and gradually start taking notes in short-hand. More questions you solve, less you write, and later you will write notes on the long-winded arguments only.

I show you my way of taking notes; rather how I used to take notes! I recall 'Pinnacle and Acme' argument once again.

> Companies Pinnacle and Acme provide round-the-clock e-mail assistance to any customer who uses their laptops. Customers send e-mails only when they find the laptop difficult to use. Since Pinnacle receives four times as many e-mails as Acme receives, Pinnacle's laptops must be more difficult to use than Acme's.
>
> Which of the following is a necessary assumption required by the argument above?

After reading the question stem, we identified that the question type is "Assumption" question type. Pl. see the image below.

On the scratch-board, write the question type in abbreviated form: here Assumption; write A; write all the 5 options A, B, C, D and E vertically. The first premise reads: *Companies Pinnacle and Acme provide round-the-clock e-mail assistance to any customer who uses their laptops.* You can write in short hand as Pinn. for Pinnacle, Cust. for customer, arrows to show relation between two objects or events. It is totally up to you how you write notes in short. You have to keep it alive for 2 minutes only. It is clear from the image that encircled C stands for conclusion: Laptop Difficult (Pinn. > Acme).

At this stage you will fully understand premises, the conclusion, and logical structure. Now your job is to find out 4th premise—assumption.

You must not spend more than 60 to 70 seconds on this.

(3) **Predict the qualifier**

Before jumping directly to options, predict the qualifier. What is a Qualifier? In this example, it the predictive assumption you can think of. If a question is Strengthen the argument type, you have to predict what could be Strengthener for the conclusion. Similarly, for Weaken the argument type, you have to predict what could be Weakener for the conclusion.

We have done this exercise for this question. I simply reproduce predictive assumptions for your ready reference. You may refer to "Predicting Assumptions" section for details.

> **Predictive Assumption 1:** Acme does not receive more complaints than Pinnacle receives through other means such as letters, and phones.
> See the the image below how you can write predictive assumption 1 in short.
> **Predictive Assumption 2:** Acme does not sell significantly less laptops than Pinnacle.
> See the the image below how you can write predictive assumption 2 in short.
> **Predictive Assumption 3:** Both company's laptops must be comparable in terms of configuration, and features.
> **Predictive Assumption 4:** Pinnacle does not sell significantly more laptops to newbie than Acme.

Predicting qualifiers may not be feasible for some question types, but is always a good practice to think of probable correct answer(s) from test-maker's point of view.

You must not spend more than 30 seconds on this.

(4) **Process of Elimination**

The best approach to reach the correct answer is going the options one by one, and either eliminate it there itself, if it cannot be an answer or hold it as probable with *?* mark. See the complete argument.

Companies Pinnacle and Acme provide round-the-clock e-mail assistance to any customer who uses their laptops. Customers send e-mails only when they find the laptop difficult to use. Since Pinnacle receives four times as many e-mails as Acme receives, Pinnacle's laptops must be more difficult to use than Acme's.

Which of the following is a necessary assumption required by the argument above?

(A) Acme and Pinnacle are in business for sufficiently long period of time.
(B) E-mails to Acme are more or less same length, on average, as to Pinnacle.
(C) Acme does not receive more complaints than Pinnacle receive through other means such as letters, and phones.
(D) The number of e-mails received by each of the two companies has been gradually increasing.
(E) Pinnacle's e-mail ID is not more widely publicized than Acme's e-mail ID.

Pl. see the image below.

The advantage of predicting a qualifier is that you may find a similarly worded option, and secondly, you will not be carried away with cleverly crafted wrong option as you have done your homework.

You must not think that your predicted qualifier must be present in options; it may or may not be present. For "Pinnacle and Acme" question, we predicted four assumptions; but in actual test, you will not be able to think more than two assumptions due to scarcity of time.

Quantity Words and Their Negation

Sometime you come across quantity words like Some, All, None, Few, Not All, Most, Many, Always, Never, and Significant. When you negate these quantity words, the knowledge of real world and the ASP perspective clash.

Refer to following table with the quantitative range of these quantity words and their opposites.

Quantity Words	Quantitative Range (In a sample of 100 people)	Opposite
Some	(1-100); 0 excluded	None
No/None	0	Some
All	100	Not All
Not All	0-99; 100 excluded	All
Never	0	Sometimes
Most/Many	Majority; Sizable; More than 50; 51-100	Minority; Not sizable; Less than 50; 0-50
Always	100	Not Always
Significant	Sizable; Considerable	Insignificant

Example

Questions

8.3 Examples

Example 1

Since less than 150 cc motorbikes are worthless to speedsters, the State Transport Officer plans to reduce the number of accidents committed by 18-21 age-group youth by restricting them to drive less than 150 cc motorbikes.

The State Transport Officer (STO) assumes that.......................................

(A) some natives find less than 150 cc motorbikes are not less prone to causing accidents than do more than 150 cc motorbikes

(B) speedsters drive all types of motorbikes—less than 150 cc and more than 150 cc

(C) all more than 150 cc motorbikes have disk-brakes as standard fitment inducing speedsters to drive fast

(D) imposing fixed penalty ticket on speedsters will decrease the number of accidents committed by speedsters

(E) speedsters do not drive motorbikes that are worthless to them

Argument construction

The State Transport Officer plans to reduce the number of accidents committed by 18-21 age-group youth by restricting them to drive less than 150 cc motorbikes.

Premise: Less than 150 cc motorbikes are worthless to speedsters.

Conclusion: Restricting 18-21 age-group youth to drive less than 150 cc motorbikes will reduce the number of accidents committed by them.

Predict an assumption

We can predict following assumptions based on the premise and the conclusion.

Based on the premise—less than 150 cc motorbikes are worthless to speedsters, STO plans to restrict 18-21 age-group youth to drive less than 150 cc motorbikes, so that # of accidents caused by them will be reduced. It implies that STO assumes that speedsters find more than 150 cc motorbike worth-driving.

Predictive Assumption 1: Speedsters find more than 150 cc motorbike worth-driving.

Another assumption may be that STO targets 18-21 age-group, it implies that STO assumes that most speedsters fall in 18-21 age-group.

Predictive Assumption 2: Most speedsters fall in 18-21 age-group.

STO also assumes that by imposing restriction on 18-21 age-group youth, the youth will comply with it.

Predictive Assumption 3: Speedsters will obey the restriction imposed on them.

Last, but not the least—STO assumes that less than 150 cc motorbikes are less prone to causing accidents than do more than 150 cc motorbikes.

Predictive Assumption 4: Less than 150 cc motorbikes are less prone to causing accidents than do more than 150 cc motorbikes.

Answer choices explanation

The above argument states that digital TV has posed a dilemma. There are advantages, but there are problems too. BBC, when it tried to go digital, decreased subscriptions to its analog channels. It also fired some program makers, impacting the quality. This upset the public, leading to a reduced viewer base. BBC is facing financial disaster. Because of this, many other channels have resisted trying to switch to digital.

The question on drawing an inference; it asks us to draw a conclusion on the basis of the argument, something that should be true from TV channels' perspective.

(A)   This option is **inconclusive**. 'Some' is a tricky quantity word. In real world, we may equate 'Some' to a significant number, but in ASP, 'Some' may range from anything between 0% to 100%; 0 is excluded, hence it is inconclusive. Had 'some' been replaced with 'Many', probably the statement would have qualified to be an assumption.

(B)   This option is **inconsistent**. It goes against the premise. No-one can challenge the premise, even if in real world, opposite may seem true. The premise already states that less than 150 cc motorbikes are worthless to speedsters, hence option C is against the premise, as it states that speedsters drive all types of motorbikes including less than 150 cc (worthless).

(C)   This option is **irrelevant**. Why speedsters drive fast is not relevant.

(D)   This option is out of scope. Penalty aspect is outside the scope of the argument. You must translate 'Restriction' to 'Penalty' of any sort.

(E)   This is the **correct** Answer. It is aligned with the predictive assumption 1.

The correct answer is option E.

Example 2

Edward was considered one of the upcoming Julian Assange, the infamous yet upright whistle-blower, till the US declared him a spy and issued a warrant against him. It is clear that if the warrant was justified, then Snowden was either an amateurish or else a traitor. Soon after the issue of warrant, however, it was clear that he had never been amateurish. Thus, one can conclude that Snowden must be a traitor.

Which one of the following states an assumption upon which the argument depends?

(A)   Edward was a low-profile intelligent officer.

(B)   A warrant for anyone who is a traitor would be justified.

(C)   Anyone whose warrant is justified is a traitor.

(D)   If someone is a traitor or amateurish, then his warrant is justified.

(E)   Edward's warrant was justified.

Argument construction

Edward was considered a whistleblower until the US declared him a spy and issued a warrant. If the warrant is justified, then Snowden is either amateurish or a traitor. After the issue of the warrant, it was clear that he had never been amateurish.

Conclusion: Edward must be a traitor.

Predict an assumption

This is a causal relationship type question.

If X occurs, then either Y or Z occurs. We can conclude that if Z has occurred, then X must have occurred.

The premise if the warrant **(X)** is justified, then Snowden is either amateurish **(Y)** or a traitor **(Z)**. Since he is not amateurish (Y), it is concluded that he is a traitor (Z), which means that his warrant (X) was justified.

Predictive Assumption: Edward's warrant is justified.

Answer choices explanation

(A)   This option is **irrelevant.**

(B)   This option is **out of scope**. The statement "A warrant for anyone who is traitor would be justified" is tricky. This option is wrong because it talks about anyone, and not specifically about Edward. The argument states the conditional declaration about Edward only.

(C)   This option is **out of scope**. Like option B, it focuses on anyone.

(D)   This option is **inconclusive**. It is a reverse statement of premise. We cannot conclude that if someone is a traitor or amateurish, then his warrant is justified. The premise does not state this. It states that if the warrant is justified, then Edward is either amateurish or a traitor.

"If A, then B" is not equivalent to "If B, then A"

(E) This is the **correct** answer. It is aligned with our predictive assumption.

The correct answer is option E.

Example 3

Because of the soaring number of fatalities incurred in accidents in major interstate high ways, the Interstate Highways Commission have put forward a proposal to be considered by the state government that only vehicles less than ten years old be allowed to use major interstate high ways. Under the terms of the proposal older vehicles would be confined to using minor interstate highways. Despite vocal opposition from particularly classic car clubs, the Commission has stated that such a reform would dramatically reduce the number of highway fatalities.

The conclusion drawn in the passage above depends on which of the following assumptions?

(A) The Interstate Highway Commission cannot pass laws without government approval.

(B) Vehicles older than ten years are less reliable than newer vehicles.

(C) Minor interstate highways are overused.

(D) Minor interstate highways are favored by high performance older vehicles.

(E) Major interstate highways have a design flaw.

Argument construction

Number of fatal accidents occurring in major interstate high ways is high. To reduce it significantly, Interstate Highways Commission(IHC) have proposed state government that only vehicles less than ten years old be allowed to use major interstate high ways (Major Highways), and older vehicles would be confined to using minor interstate highways (Minor Highways).

Conclusion: IHC claims that such a reform (only vehicles less than ten years old be allowed to use major interstate high ways) would dramatically reduce the number of highway fatalities.

Predict an assumption

The conclusion for which an assumption has to be found is that vehicles more than ten years old should be banned from major highways to reduce fatal accidents. This leads to our predictive assumption.

Predictive Assumption 1: Vehicles older than ten years are less prone to accidents than newer vehicles.

What if number of newer vehicles is significantly more than older vehicle? The move to restrict newer vehicles on major highway will not help reduce the accidents dramatically.

Predictive Assumption 2: Newer vehicles are not significantly more than older vehicles.

Answer choices explanation

(A) This option is **irrelevant**.

(B) This is the **correct** answer. It is aligned with our predictive assumption 1.

(C) This option focuses on minor highways rather major highways. This option is **out of scope**.

(D) Same as option C, this option focuses on minor highways rather major highways. This option is **out of scope**.

(E) This option is **out of scope**.

The correct answer is option B.

Example 4

The State Transport Authority (STA) have voted to strengthen their bid to transform the commuting habits of citizens regardless of the fact that both the inner city roads and access highways have become so clogged that some leading city officials have said that a radically new transport policy is necessary. Despite the high toll and purchase taxes levied on car owners by the STA, research has shown that the public transport system would have to be greatly improved and the price fixation at a nominal sum if more people are to be enticed out of their cars.

What assumption is the argument based on?

(A) Road and vehicle purchase taxes will be raised even higher.

(B) Taxpayers will rebel against more investment in public transport.

(C) Private transport is generally considered more convenient than public transport.

(D) The current public transport system is over used and therefore requires improvement.

(E) A new transport policy has been agreed upon.

Argument construction

Both the inner city roads and access highways have become clogged. City officials have said that a radically new transport policy is necessary. STA believes in the need to transform the commuting habits of citizens. Despite the high toll and purchase taxes levied on car owners by the STA, most prefer to use private cars. The research has shown that the public transport system would have to be greatly improved and the price to avail the services should be nominal if more people are to be appealed to avoid their cars.

Conclusion: Greatly improved public transport system and price fixation at nominal sum will make people use it and thus avoid cars.

Predict an assumption

Predictive Assumption: Greatly improved public transport system and the nominal price will make people use public transport system.

Answer choices explanation

(A)   This option is **irrelevant**. It does not relate to the conclusion and public transport system.

(B)   This option is **irrelevant**. It does not relate to the conclusion and public transport system.

(C)   This is the **correct** answer. From the premise—Despite the high toll and purchase taxes levied on car owners by the STA, it can be inferred that people still use cars. The obvious reason could be that private transport is generally considered more convenient than public transport.

(D)   We cannot assume from the argument that the public transport system is over used. The argument states that it needs improvement, but it does not mean that it is over used. Moreover, it does not impact the conclusion.

(E)   This option is **out of scope**. The policy agreement aspect is not considered in the argument.

The correct answer is option C.

Example 5

Derrango have come up with a central heating system that industry analysts predict will have to be adopted by other heating equipment manufacturers in order to successfully compete. Prior to this invention, gas burning central heating furnaces employed a system similar to the carburetors in automobiles, mixing air and gas, which is then fed into the burner. However, the Derrango engineers have invented a gas injection method that heats the air before it mixes with gas and thus raises volatility. The system reduces fuel consumption by almost 40% and should lead to an equivalent reduction in utility bills.

Which of the following represents a necessary assumption for the preceding argument?

(A)   Homeowners have voiced concern over rising utility bills.

(B)   Gas suppliers have warned of possible interruptions to services.

(C)   Central heating systems using conventional mechanisms are cheaper.

(D)   The new system creates a less humid environment than that created by conventional systems.

(E)   The Derrango system is as efficient as a conventional heating system.

Argument construction

The information given in the argument is details about the conventional and the new heating system.

Conclusion: The new heating system should lead to an equivalent reduction in utility bills.

Predict an assumption

Predictive Assumption: Heating the air before it mixes with gas and thus raising the volatility will reduce the fuel consumption by almost 40%.

Answer choices explanation

(A) This option is **out of scope.** It does not impact the conclusion.

(B) This option is **out of scope.**

(C) This option is **inconsistent**. Central heating systems do not use conventional mechanisms. It is against the premise—Derrango engineers have **invented** a gas injection method that heats the air before it mixes with gas and thus raises volatility. Two systems have different mechanisms.

(D) This option is **out of scope**. Humidity aspect is not under consideration.

(E) This is the **correct** answer. It compares two systems. The Derrango system must be as efficient as a conventional heating system to make the conclusion valid.

The correct answer is option E.

Example 6

Icarus Airline Manufacturing Corporation has continuously made greater profits by supplying airlines with quality airplanes which are equipped with increased seating capacity. In an effort to continue this financial trend, the company is set to launch a double-decker jumbo jet.

The plan of the company as described above assumes all of the following EXCEPT:

(A) The demand for air travel will increase in the future.

(B) Increased production expenses for the new jumbo jet will be offset by increased revenues.

(C) Passengers have no preference between the new double-decker jumbo jet and the previous models in the market.

(D) The new jumbo jet will be technologically reliable once in operation, yet resulting in unexpected costs or unrealized revenues.

(E) The new jumbo jet will not require substantial new training of the pilots or building new parking space at the airports.

Argument construction

Icarus Airline Manufacturing Corporation (IAMC) has been making greater profits with single-decker. It wishes to introduce double-decker jumbo jets so that it can serve more passengers and book more profits.

Conclusion: Double-decker jumbo jet will continue to make greater profits like single-decker jets have been doing.

Predict an assumption

The question is an EXCEPT kind of question. You must be careful while reading the qualifier word in the question stem. The difference between a regular Assumption kind of question and EXCEPT kind of question is that in case of latter, there would be four statements that can be assumed from the argument, while only one option cannot be assumed. You have to mark that as correct answer.

Predictive Assumption 1: IAMC will be able to sell the increased number of seats such that it makes more profits.

Predictive Assumption 2: IAMC is technically competent to manufacture double-decker jets.

Predictive Assumption 3: The cost to manufacture double-decker jets will be overcome by increased revenue in stipulated time frame.

Answer choices explanation

(A)   This is a correct assumption. It is almost aligned with our predictive assumption 1.

(B)   This is also a correct assumption. It is aligned with our predictive assumption 3.

(C)   This is also a correct assumption. Passengers must not have preference between the new double-decker jumbo jet and the previous models in the market so that both the models should have optimum sales.

(D)   This is the **correct** answer. It cannot be assumed that the new jumbo jet would incur unexpected costs or impede more revenue.

(E)   This is also a correct assumption. Training of pilots and new parking space are the cost that will eat up profit, hence it is necessary that no substantial new training of the pilots or building new parking space at the airports is required.

The correct answer is option D.

Example 7

Recent research into obesity suggests that although certain amphetamines are capable of quelling physical hunger pangs, they also have a mood altering affect that frequently leads to food binging. Of the 63 patients that took part in tests carried by Hopkins Institute scientists, 43 admitted to periodically binging to assuage depression and at the conclusion of the eight week trial were found to have gained weight. From these results, scientists have concluded that appetite quelling amphetamines are often counter-productive and should be prescribed to patients only in controlled environments.

The conclusion drawn by scientists is based on which of the following assumption?

(A) Amphetamines induce food binging.

(B) Controlled environments govern secret binging.

(C) Food binging causes depression.

(D) Obesity is worse than depression.

(E) Food binging is not always coupled with depression.

Argument construction

A research into obesity suggests that although certain amphetamines are capable of suppressing physical hunger pains, they also have a mood altering affect that frequently leads to food binging. Of the 63 patients that took part in tests carried by Hopkins Institute scientists, 43 admitted to periodically binging to soften depression and at the conclusion of the eight week trial were found to have gained weight.

Conclusion: Appetite quelling amphetamines are often counter-productive and should be prescribed only to patients in controlled environments.

Predict an assumption

Predictive Assumption: Patients will not be allowed to food binging in controlled environments.

Answer choices explanation

(A) This option is **inconsistent.** The argument states that certain amphetamines, not all, have a mood altering affect that frequently leads to food binging.

(B) This is the **correct** answer. It is aligned with the predictive assumption.

(C) This option is **inconsistent.** It is other way round 43 patients admitted to periodically binging to assuage depression. Depression causes food binging.

(D) This option is **irrelevant.**

(E) This option is **irrelevant.**

The correct answer is option B.

Example 8

The government of Akhlazia should stop permitting mafia run opium companies to subtract shipping expenses from their revenues in calculating the amount of kickbacks that go to the central government. These opium companies would have to pay a higher kickback. As a consequence they would have to raise the price of opium and this price would then discourage buyers on the world market from purchasing Akhlazian opium.

Which of the following is an additional premise required by the argument above?

(A)   Opium companies would not be able to offset the payment of extra kickbacks by reducing other operating expenses.

(B)   Opium companies would need governmental approval before they can change the price of opium.

(C)   Buyers on the world market have no other suppliers of opium other than Akhlazia.

(D)   The money the government would earn as a result of increased kickbacks would be used to educate the public about the dangers of drug addiction.

(E)   The increase in kickbacks would be equal to the additional income generated by the rise in prices.

Argument construction

The government of Akhlazia should not allow mafia run opium companies to subtract shipping expenses from their revenues while calculating the amount of payments that go to the central government. Since these opium companies would have to pay a higher kickback, hence as a consequence they would have to raise the price of opium and this high price would then discourage buyers on the world market from purchasing Akhlazian opium.

Conclusion: Akhlazia opium companies will have to raise the price of opium and the price rise would discourage buyers on the world market from purchasing Akhlazian opium.

Predict an assumption

As states earlier that assumption is a hidden premise. ASP may indirectly ask you an assumption question with a twist.

Predictive Assumption 1: World market can buy same quality opium from other markets at reduced price.

Predictive Assumption 2: The government of Akhlazia will not pass on any benefit to opium companies that can offset reduced profits.

Answer choices explanation

(A) This is the **correct** answer. Since opium companies would not be able to offset the payment of extra kickbacks by reducing other operating expenses, they would be compelled to raise the price resulting in anticipated loss of business.

(B) This option is **out of scope.**

(C) This option is **opposite.** It implies that world market have no choice, but to buy opium from Akhlazia. It weakens the conclusion.

(D) This option is **out of scope.**

(E) This option is **opposite.** It implies that opium companies can garner more revenue despite increase in price.

The correct answer is option A.

Practice

Questions

8.4   Practice Questions

8.4.1   Questions

Question 1

Although superstars are hailed as great actors, the truth is that superstar movies showcase action and drama. Therefore, superstars should not be considered great actors.

Which of the following is an assumption on which the argument depends?

(A)   Some great actors have acted in superstar movies.

(B)   Few superstars have degrees from Film Institute.

(C)   Movies that showcase only action and drama are not the only kind of movies to portray acting prowess for great actors.

(D)   Many have started respecting radio voice-over artists as actors.

(E)   Some superstars have acted in meaningful cinema.

Question 2

Among those automobile mechanics who own their own garages and completed a qualifying course at Main Street Technical School, 35 percent earn above $80,000 a year. Among those who own their own garages but did not complete the qualifying course at Main Street Technical School, only 10 percent earn above $80,000 a year. These figures indicate the importance of technical education in getting a higher salary.

The argument above depends on which of the following assumptions about the people mentioned in the statistics?

(A)   At least one-third of the group of people who did not complete the qualifying course would today be earning more than $80,000 a year if they had completed the course.

(B)   The group of people who did not complete the qualifying course and the group who did are comparable in terms of factors that determine how much people are paid.

(C)   Most of those people who did not complete the course did so entirely because of the cost of the course.

(D)   As a group, those persons who completed the course are more competent as mechanics than the group that did not.

(E)   The group of people who did not complete the qualifying course and today earn more than $80,000 a year are more capable than the group that completed the course.

Question 3

Mitchell Motor Company recently had a big jump in pick-up truck sales after hiring a new design team to give their pick-up trucks a more upscale look designed to appeal to a more affluent clientele. The company is now planning to launch a new line of sub-compact cars using the same concept.

The company's plan assumes that

(A) other sub-compact cars with an upscale look do not yet exist in the market

(B) an upscale clientele would be interested in a sub-compact car

(C) the same design team could be employed for both projects

(D) giving sub-compacts an up-scale look requires a design team

(E) customers who bought older pick-up trucks would be just as likely to buy the new upscale looking pick-up trucks

Question 4

Instead of blaming an automobile accident on driver error, insurance companies should first try to figure out why the error was made by analyzing flaws in road design, automobile designs and in criteria to determine eligibility for a driver's license. Only then will the insurance companies be able to effectively issue guidelines to prevent future accidents, instead of merely punishing the incidental driver.

Which of the following is a presupposition of the argument above?

(A) Driver error is not a significant factor in most automobile accidents.

(B) Automobile manufacturers should be the agents who investigate automobile accidents and not insurance companies.

(C) Stricter government regulation of the automobile and highway construction industries would make automobile travel safer.

(D) Investigation of automobile accidents should contribute to the prevention of future accidents.

(E) Most drivers who make errors in driving repeat those errors unless they are retrained.

Question 5

Two different cages of rabbits were given injections of mild toxins. In addition, the first cage was also exposed to cold temperature; three-fourths of the rabbits in this cage became sick. Only one-fifth of the rabbits in the normal temperature cage became sick. The lab technicians concluded that cold temperature increases the likelihood of illness in rabbits.

The technicians' conclusion logically depends on which of the following assumptions?

(A) The exposure to cold temperature acted as a catalyst for the toxins which made more rabbits in the first cage sick.

(B) The toxins given to the rabbits in the two cages were of same strength and same amount of dose were given to each rabbit.

(C) Injecting the rabbits with toxins does not make them sick.

(D) Even without the exposure to cold temperature, the rabbits in the first cage would have probably gotten sick.

(E) Even exposing rabbits to slight variances in temperature is likely to induce illness irrespective of which cage rabbits belong to.

Question 6

Now that the babies of the post-war baby boom have reached retirement age, there is a burgeoning population of elderly people yet despite a chronic lack of workers throughout the US, employers are still reluctant to take on elderly workers. Age Concern, an elder citizens' rights protection organization, campaigns for greater employment of those past the age of retirement. The Elder citizens' rights protection organization cites numerous examples of successful companies that have an active policy of employing elder citizens and therefore claims that employing older people is good for business.

The claim made by Age Concern organization is based on which of the following assumption?

(A) Since Company A adopted a policy of employing elder citizens, minor thefts by staff have decreased by 45%.

(B) Certain companies that employ elder citizens have a policy of supporting charitable causes.

(C) Some companies employing elder citizen report that their elder workers are more punctual than the younger workers are.

(D) All the companies employing elder citizens accept that output has declined but say this has been more than compensated for by the improvement in public image.

(E) Most elderly citizens in employment are willing to accept lower wages than those acceptable to young workers.

Question 7

This year, pollution levels particularly in downtown areas reached such alarming levels that city councils in several states established temporary exhaust control points on the highways feeding inner city areas. This led to an immediate drop in the number of people suffering from asthma. As a result, several councils have decided to make the exhaust control points a permanent feature.

The decision to make the exhaust control points a permanent feature on highways is based on which of the following assumption?

(A) All highways pass through outskirts of downtowns, uninhabitable areas.

(B) Prolonged sustenance with pollution causes asthma.

(C) A variation of Asian flu prevalent in down town areas has the same symptoms as acute asthma.

(D) A newly available mask does not reduce the risk of acquiring asthma from pollution.

(E) The company running the exhaust checks is paid according to the number of defective vehicles detected.

8.4.2 Answer-Key

(1) C	(4) D	(7) B
(2) B	(5) A	
(3) B	(6) E	

Solutions

8.4.3 Solutions

Question 1

Argument construction

Although superstars are hailed as great actors, the truth is that superstar movies showcase action and drama.

Conclusion: Superstars should not be considered great actors.

Predict an assumption

Let's look at the conclusion: Superstars should not be considered great actors.

Why does the author think that superstars should not be considered great actors? There must be a qualification that Superstars lack, yet great actors possess. What is that qualification? Well, it is not mentioned in the argument. All that is mentioned in the argument is that the superstars focus on the action and drama aspects of movie. It implies that great actors focus on more aspects of the movie than just action and drama.

Predictive assumption: Movies that focus only on action and drama is not the only domain of great actors.

Answer choices explanation

(A) This option is **irrelevant**. This option tells us more about great actors, but does not answer why superstars should not be considered great actors.

(B) This option is **out of scope**. Only few superstars having film course degree do not explain why superstars should not be considered great actors.

(C) This is the **correct** answer. This option is aligned to our predictive assumption Movies that focus only on action and drama is not the only domain of great actors.

(D) This option is **irrelevant**. Radio voice-over artists' aspect is not relevant.

(E) This option is **inconclusive**. As discussed in previous question, we cannot conclude anything based on quantity word—some.

The correct answer is option C.

Question 2

Argument construction

There are two groups of automobile mechanics who own their garage. One, with qualifying course at Main Street Technical School. Two, without qualifying course at Main Street Technical School.

Of the group one, 35 percent mechanics earn above $80,000 a year, and of the group two, only 10 percent mechanics earn above $80,000 a year.

Conclusion: Getting technical education helps in getting higher salary.

Predict an assumption

In order for the comparison of mechanics to imply something about the importance of technical education, the subject group being compared needs to be relatively homogenous in terms of factors which will affect their income as auto mechanics, otherwise the results we see do not clearly reflect how the course increases the ability of auto mechanics to earn a better income.

Predictive Assumption 1: Both the groups are homogenous in terms of comparison of income.

What if remaining 90% of group two mechanics, who earn less than $80000 earn significantly more than the remaining 65% of group one mechanics, who earn less than $80000 earn? The conclusion will be shattered. We cannot conclude that technical education helps get more salary.

Predictive Assumption 2: Remaining 90% of group two mechanics, who earn less than $80000 do not earn significantly more than the remaining 65% of group one mechanics, who earn less than $80000 earn.

Answer choices explanation

(A)   Statistically, it looks logical that 33.33% < 35%, but we cannot necessarily state this as both groups can be heterogeneous in terms of comparison of income.

(B)   This is the **correct** answer. It is aligned with the predictive assumption 1.

(C)   This is option is **out of scope.** Cost is out of scope.

(D)   This option is **inconclusive.** It focuses on competence, and not on salary.

(E)   This option works against the conclusion. It states that top 10% of group two mechanics earn more than group one mechanics.

The correct answer is option B.

Question 3

Argument construction

The argument is easy to comprehend. The conclusion is missing from the argument, but we can infer the implied conclusion.

Implied Conclusion: By hiring the same design team, and the concept, Mitchell Motor Company plans to launch sub-compact cars, and aspires to make good sales.

Predict an assumption

Predictive Assumption 1: Prospective clients will buy the car designed by the new design team.

Predictive Assumption 2: Mitchell Motor Company is competent to manufacture sub-compact car.

Answer choices explanation

(A) It is not a necessary assumption. Even if there are sub-compact cars in the market, still Mitchell Motor Company can plan to manufacture it. It does not impact conclusion.

(B) This is the **correct** answer. It is somewhat aligned with the predictive assumption 1. Since Mitchell Motor Company has loyal base of upscale clientele, they would be interested in a sub-compact car manufactured by their truck company—Mitchell Motor.

(C) This is option is **rephrase of premise**. It is already stated.

(D) This is option is **rephrase of premise**. It is already stated.

(E) This option is **out of scope**. It does not focus on cars.

The correct answer is option B.

Question 4

Argument construction

Usually insurance companies blame drivers for accidents. They must analyze the reasons of accidents by studying flaws in road design, automobile designs and criteria to determine eligibility for a driver's license. Only then the insurance companies will be able to effectively issue guidelines to prevent future accidents.

Conclusion: To effectively issue guidelines to prevent future accidents, insurance companies must analyze the reasons of accidents by studying flaws in road design, automobile designs and in criteria to determine eligibility for a driver's license.

Predict an assumption

Predictive Assumption: Flaws in road design, automobile designs and criteria to determine the eligibility for a driver's license are also significant factors in causing accidents.

Answer choices explanation

(A) The argument need not assume this. It does not say so. Driver error is certainly a factor apart from other factors in accidents.

(B) This option is **out of scope**. It talks about who should investigate accidents rather than causes of accidents.

(C)   This option is **out of scope**. It focuses on government regulation of the automobile and highway construction industries, and not on three factors mentioned in the argument.

(D)   This is the **correct** answer. It is a natural hidden premise in the argument.

(E)   This option is not hitting the bull's eye. It pretends to address the criteria to issue a driver's license, but the argument talks about the eligibility aspect and not about the training aspect.

The correct answer is option D.

Question 5

Argument construction

The argument is easy to understand. In cage one, rabbits were given injections of mild toxins, and were exposed to cold temperature simultaneously; because of this, 3/4th of the rabbits got sick.

In Cage two, rabbits were given injections of mild toxins, but were not exposed to cold temperature, so only 1/5th of the rabbits got sick.

Conclusion: Cold temperature increases the likelihood of illness in rabbits.

Predict an assumption

If more rabbits became sick in the cage where they were exposed to colder temperature, as opposed to the warmer cage where fewer rabbits became sick, after being injected with the same toxins, it can be assumed that the combination of cold temperature and the toxin makes more rabbits sick.

Predictive Assumption: The combination of cold temperature and the toxin makes more rabbits sick.

Answer choices explanation

(A)   This is the **correct** answer. It is aligned with the predictive assumption.

(B)   This option does not focus on cold temperature. It does not impact conclusion.

(C)   Like option B, this option too does not focus on cold temperature. It does not impact conclusion.

(D)   This option is **irrelevant.** Like option B & C, this option too does not focus on cold temperature. It does not impact conclusion.

(E)   This option is **inconclusive.** It talks about the impact of slight variances in temperature, which may be hotter than normal temperature too. The argument is concerned about the impact of only cold temperature.

The correct answer is option A.

Question 6

Argument construction

Though there is a growing population of elderly people, yet despite a chronic lack of workers throughout the US, employers are still reluctant to employ elderly workers. Age Concern organization campaigns for greater employment for elder citizens. Age Concern cites numerous examples of successful companies that have an active policy of employing elder citizens.

Conclusion: Employing older people is good for business.

Predict an assumption

The definition of Good for Business is somewhat vague. It can be interpreted as Profit, Revenue, Output, or Cost. We will have to go through options to pin-point the correct assumption. However, we can still predict couple of assumptions.

Predictive Assumption 1: Elder citizens have wide experience that employers can capitalize on.

Predictive Assumption 2: Elder citizens can be employed at significantly lower wages, yet their output is not significantly lower than that of young workers.

Answer choices explanation

(A) This option is **inconclusive.** It cites one of a case from company A. It cannot be generalized.

(B) This option is **opposite.** It goes against the conclusion. It states that the motive behind employing elder citizens is not because they can contribute, but organizations do so because organizations wish to do some charity implying that elder citizens are cost to the organizations.

(C) This option is **inconclusive.** It cites experiences of some companies. Number of companies may range from few to many. It cannot be generalized.

(D) This option is **inconclusive.** While decline in output is a loss, image building is a gain. We cannot conclude what weighs more.

(E) This is the **correct** answer. It is aligned with the predictive assumption 2.

The correct answer is option E.

Question 7

Argument construction

Because of pollution reaching alarming, particularly in downtown areas, city councils in several states established temporary exhaust control points on the highways joining inner city areas. This move led to an immediate drop in the number of people suffering from asthma living in downtown areas.

Conclusion: By making the exhaust control points a permanent feature on highways, asthma can be controlled significantly in downtown areas.

Predict an assumption

Predictive Assumption 1: Only pollution causes asthma in downtown areas.

Predictive Assumption 2: There is no other factor that led to an immediate drop in the number of people suffering from asthma.

Answer choices explanation

(A)   This option is **out of scope.** The option looks tempting, but it tries to establish that there people do not live in highway areas, hence, there is no ill effects due to exhaust in those area, whereas the argument is concerned with pollution, and asthma in downtown areas.

(B)   This is the **correct** answer. It is aligned with the predictive assumption 1.

(C)   This option is **opposite.** It tries to establish that the acute asthma may be due to Asian Flu, and not due to pollution.

(D)   This option is **irrelevant.**

(E)   This option is **irrelevant.**

The correct answer is option B.

Chapter 9

Strengthen the Argument

9.1 Strengthen the Argument Question type

 Strengthen the argument questions are one of the frequently asked question types in Argument Structure Passages.

Strengthen the argument questions also belong to assumption based family. Strengthener is an additional piece of information that supports the conclusion. Do not get confused with assumption and strengthener, as even though both make the conclusion more believable, they are different. In the last chapter, we have seen that an assumption is an unstated hidden premise that the author chooses not to state, but that is necessary to make the conclusion more believable. However, a strengthener is new information provided in the option that supports the conclusion and makes it more believable. The new piece of information will act as evidence that the assumption is valid. Both—assumption and strengthener make the conclusion more believable, but the strengthener is always NEW INFORMATION.

A strengthener, as additional support, has a wide range. The options could strengthen the argument to some extent, mediocre extent, or a great extent. You have to select the option that supports the argument to the greatest extent. You will find the usage of the word 'most' or an equivalent word in question stems so that there is no ambiguity while selecting the correct option.

Look at the image below. There is a dialogue taking place between two people. What do you think could be the strengthener here?

Let us see this argument: **Steve will get 300+ in his GRE.**

Assumption	Strengthener
Steve will appear for his GRE exam.	Steve has been consistently getting 300+ in his mocks.
Steve has prepared well for the GRE exam.	Steve has studied for over 100 hours for the GRE exam.
Maximum score for the GRE is more than 300.	Steve has scored well in similar high-pressure competitive exams.

Following illustration depicts your job for strengthen the argument question type.

Companies Pinnacle and Acme provide round-the-clock e-mail assistance to any customer who uses their laptops. C[...]rs send e-mails only when they find the laptops difficult to use. Since Pi[...] s four times as many e-mails as Acme does, Pinnacle's laptops mus[...]use than Acme's.

Which of the following, if true, [...] he argument above?

A. Acme and Pin[...] d of time.
B. E-mails to Ac[...] s to Pinnacle.
C. Acme does n[...] Only one option supports the conclusion [...] e through other means such as letter[...] the most, and strengthens it.
D. The number [...] es has been gradually increasing.
E. Pinnacle's e-[...] 's e-mail ID.

The Question Stem

All strengthen question stems include *'if true'* or equivalent words in the question stem. This means that you have to attempt the question keeping in mind that the information given in the options are unquestionable and to be taken as facts. Never judge the validity of the options, or their truth, only judge whether they most strengthen the given argument.

Typical 'strengthen the argument' question stem looks like this.

- Which of the following, *if true*, would most *strengthen* the argument against the automobile manufacturer's claim?

- Which of the following would most likely *support* the data's implication?

Strengthen the argument questions may sometimes skip the exact phrase 'if true', but some way or the other question stem will convey the similar meaning. In either case, do not get hung up on the phrase, because it is there only to imply that you should not doubt the options.

- Which of the following, *if feasible*, provides the *best basis* for the conclusion?

- Which of the following, *if effectively achieved*, provides *the best reason* for the conclusion?

- Which of the following, *if true*, provides *justification* for the conclusion?

9.2   Process Of Solving Strengthen The Argument Questions

The 4-step approach is same as mentioned in Find the Assumption chapter.

The 4-step approach

(1) Recognize the question type

(2) Understand the argument construction

(3) Predict the qualifier

(4) Eliminate incorrect options

First 2 steps are same for strengthen the argument questions. Let us jump to predict the qualifier.

9.2.1   Predict the qualifier

We already know what 'predict the qualifier' means. Let us see this from strengthener's point of view.

Let us see the 'Pinnacle and Acme' argument.

> Companies Pinnacle and Acme provide round-the-clock e-mail assistance to any customer who uses their laptops. Customers send e-mails only when they find the laptop difficult to use. Since Pinnacle receives four times as many e-mails as Acme receives, Pinnacle's laptops must be more difficult to use than Acme's.

Conclusion: *Pinnacle's laptops must be more difficult to use than Acme's.*

9.2.2   Predicting Strengthener

Our job is to strengthen the argument by providing new information.

Please read the following statement.

Acme has three times as many laptop customers as Pinnacle.

The statement certainly supports or strengthens the conclusion, and the information given is additional information, and hence it is not an assumption, but a strengthener. It strengthens the argument because it most clearly shows that even though Acme has more laptop customers than Pinnacle does, Pinnacle is the one getting more complaints. So, Pinnacle's laptops must really be more difficult to use.

Predictive Strengthener 1: Desktop computer users also find Pinnacle's desktop more difficult to use than Acme's.

Predictive Strengthener 2: Pinnacle's laptops are not based on a widely used OS—operating system.

Predictive Strengthener 3: Pinnacle also receives more complaints via letters, and phones.

Example

Questions

9.3 Examples

Example 1

Bio-chemists at Perck Pharma Corporation have discovered a new type of allergy. Their research confirms that it is not caused just by the pollen of a certain flower, as was thought. In addition, the flower has to be pollinated by a certain kind of bee to cause the allergy.

Which of the following, if true, would most likely support the data's implication?

- **(A)** In the absence of the bee, the pollination by other kinds of bees does not cause allergic reactions.

- **(B)** The bee has been shown to be a critical element in the reproduction of the particular flower.

- **(C)** Many cases of the allergy have been observed only in the presence of the bee.

- **(D)** In cases in which the allergy does not develop, the flower will grow without the presence of the bee.

- **(E)** The onset of the allergy is usually caused by the flower even if the pollen is not present.

Argument construction

Bio-chemists have discovered a new type of allergy. The allergy is not just caused by pollen of a certain flower. The flower has to be pollinated by a certain kind of bee to cause the allergy.

Conclusion: The flower pollinated only by a certain kind of bee causes the allergy.

Predict a strengthener

We have to strengthen the conclusion that not the flower itself, but the pollination by the certain kind of bee causes the allergy.

Predictive Strengthener 1: Pollination by other kinds of bees does not cause the allergy.

Predictive Strengthener 2: Flower itself does not cause the allergy.

Answer choices explanation

- **(A)** This is the **correct** answer. It is aligned with the both predictive assumptions 1 & 2. This option rules out that the flower itself causes the allergy when pollinated implying that the bee causes allergy.

- **(B)** This option is **irrelevant**. It does not address the source of allergy— whether the flower or the bee is responsible.

(C)   This option is a close contender. It is certainly a strengthener, but the question stem asks for the option that would support the data's implication the MOST. Also, if you critically analyze this option you cannot rule out that the allergy is not caused by the flower itself.

Imagine this: In an orchard, there are specific kinds of flowers—X; they were pollinated by certain kind of bee—Y. Many cases of the allergy were observed in the orchard. Who can you rightly blame? It may be that the flower itself is the source of allergy, not the bee.

The best way to conclude who is responsible for the allergy is by removing the bee and studying the pollination : exactly what option A does—the **correct** answer.

(D)   This option is **inconclusive**. It is a conditional statement. It cites the scenario if allergy is not developed and we are not concerned about the growth of the flower, but only about its allergenic effect.

(E)   This option is an **opposite** answer. It weakens the conclusion. It blames the flower for the allergy.

The correct answer is option A.

Example 2

Automobile manufacturers defend their substitution of steel frames in cars with cheaper plastic components by claiming that consumer demand for light cars with crumple zones rather than corporate profit motives led to the substitution. However, if this trend were true, carbon reinforced tubing, which is lighter than steel but stronger, would be available as an option. It is not.

Which of the following, if true, would most strengthen the argument against the automobile manufacturer's claim?

(A)   When carbon tubing was introduced in the market place, it was not yet commercially viable to produce it in large volumes.

(B)   Automobile companies are reluctant to invest in high volume industrial technology to produce carbon tubing until profits from the sale of small scale commercial carbon products, such as bicycle frames, have stabilized.

(C)   Some types of carbon tubing for sports equipment are in such high demand that there is a back log of several weeks for orders.

(D)   Because carbon tubing has completely different chemical properties from plastic frame components, new construction techniques will be required for automobiles.

(E)   Any valid comparison among steel, plastic and carbon frames must be based on identical performance measures.

Argument construction

Automobile manufacturers substituted steel frames in cars with cheaper plastic components. They claim that because of consumers' desire for light cars with crumple zones, they chose plastic and not because of profit motives. The counter view is that, if this trend were true, carbon reinforced tubing, which is lighter than steel but stronger, would be available as an option. However, it is not.

Conclusion: Substitution of steel frames in cars with cheaper plastic components is driven by profit motive.

Predict a strengthener

This question basically belongs to weaken the argument category. STRENGTHEN and WEAKEN are opposites. We are asked to strengthen the argument against the automobile manufacturer's claim. Alternatively, we can look at this question as?

Which of the following, if true, would most weaken the claim made by the automobile manufacturers?

Predictive Strengthener 1: The cheaper plastic used is not as strong as steel.

Predictive Strengthener 2: There are relatively expensive materials other than steel available in the market, materials that are lighter than steel yet stronger.

Answer choices explanation

(A) This option is a **weakener**. It provides a reason for why manufacturers were not able to use carbon tubing instead of cheaper plastic or costlier steel—because it was not commercially viable to produce the carbon tubing in large volumes.

(B) This is the **correct** answer. Automobile companies are unwilling to invest in high volume industrial technology to produce carbon tubing till their profits motives from other operations have steadied. This weakens the claim made by the automobile manufacturers or in other words, strengthens the argument against the automobile manufacturer's claim. It proves very emphatically that manufacturers are motivated entirely by profits in using the cheaper plastic in car frames.

(C) This option is a **weakener**. It presents another reason the manufacturers could not use carbon tubing because of short supply. The manufacturers are not at fault then.

(D) This option is a **weakener**. Another reason for manufacturers being unable to use carbon tubing because new construction techniques will be required to produce them for automobiles.

(E) This option is **inconclusive.** It does not conclusively state the merits and demerits of three materials or provide reasons for the use of any one of three materials.

The correct answer is option B.

Example 3

John, an expert in game theory, predicts that negotiations cannot be resolved unless one party is willing to concede a symbolic step. He also believes that when such a symbolic step of concession is taken, negotiations will be resolved. Other game theory experts, however, believe that these results do not take other variables into account.

Which of the following, if true, best supports the contention in the last sentence?

(A) Predicting the success of a particular negotiation requires specifying the goal of the negotiation.

(B) Judging the outcome of a particular negotiation requires knowing about other negotiations that have taken place in the past.

(C) Learning whether a certain negotiation strategy is good requires observing how that strategy works through several negotiating sessions.

(D) Parties who are willing to take a symbolic step are more likely to complete negotiations successfully for other reasons.

(E) Making a negotiation successful requires knowing the symbolic steps that a party in the negotiations might desire.

Argument construction

John, an expert in game theory, predicts that negotiations cannot be resolved unless one party is willing to concede a symbolic step. He also believes that when a symbolic step of concession is taken, negotiations will be resolved. However, other game theory experts believe that this theory do not take other factors into consideration. Thus, these other experts believe that John is not taking other factors into consideration that led to the resolution but is focusing only on the concession.

Conclusion: For a negotiation to be resolved, apart from symbolic step, other factors also play their roles in the resolution.

Predict a strengthener

This is truly a tough one. Let us simplify more.

John: Negotiations can be resolved when a symbolic step is taken.

Other Experts: Apart from the concession as a symbolic step, other factors also play important roles in the resolution.

It is tough to predict strengtheners in this question. We have to strengthen the other expert's claim—*other factors also play their roles*, so focus on other factors and any options that talk about other factors leading to the resolution of the negotiation.

Answer choices explanation

(A) Is 'specifying the goal'—a part of other factors? Maybe, maybe not...However, we are not concerned with "predicting the success" of negotiations. We are concerned with "concession of symbolic step" and its part in resolution of negotiations. Our goal is not success prediction of negotiation but its resolution.

(B) Is 'knowing about other negotiations that have taken place in the past'—a part of other factors? Maybe, maybe not. Again, "judging the outcome" is not our goal. Hence, even if "knowing about other negotiations" is a factor for "judging the outcome", we're not concerned with it because our goal is "resolution of negotiation" not "judging" whether the negotiation will get resolved.

(C) This option talks about the process of negotiation. It is not relevant to resolution of negotiations.

(D) This option seems to hit the bull's eye. Out of 3 options seen so far, this one is the best. It clearly mentions "other reasons" as a driving force in the resolution of the negotiations.

(E) This option tells more about the symbolic step rather than the other factors. It is not a strengthener for other factors. It may strengthen John's case.

The correct answer is option D.

Example 4

Finance Minister: Last year was disastrous for our manufacturing sector, which has traditionally made up about 75 percent of our national budget. It is therefore encouraging that there is evidence that the IT sector is growing stronger. Taxes from the IT sector accounted for 15 percent of our national budget, up from 8 percent last year.

On the basis of the statements above, which of the following best supports the above conclusion?

(A) The increase in taxes from the IT sector could have merely been the result of new laws imposed on the IT sector.

(B) The profits of the IT sector remained at a steady level despite the fact that it paid more taxes to the national government.

(C) The rise in the percentage of taxes that the IT sector contributed to the national government was insignificant in actual dollar terms.

(D) It is difficult to determine whether the jump from 8—15 percent tax contribution by the IT sector will be on-going.

(E) The information given above does not fairly compare the contribution of taxes paid by different industries to the national government.

Argument construction

Finance Minister states that last year was disastrous for manufacturing sector. Manufacturing sector had traditionally contributed about 75 percent of national budget implying that it is significantly lower than 75% now.

The minister further states that it is therefore encouraging that the IT sector is growing stronger. Taxes from the IT sector accounted for 15 percent of our national budget, up from 8 percent last year.

Conclusion: IT sector is growing stronger.

Predict a strengthener

Basically, we need to support the conclusion by proving that either the IT sector will continue to grow more or at least grow steadily at the current pace. We can prove that by proving that the demand for the nation's IT services is increasing. We can also achieve the same effect by demonstrating that the IT sector growth is based on a solid foundation and will remain unaffected.

Predictive Strengthener 1: IT sector has been making greater profits for last few years consistently.

Predictive Strengthener 2: World market sees the nation as one of the most competent IT services provider.

Answer choices explanation

(A)   This option is a **weakener.** It rules out the conclusion that IT sector is going strong, and the increased percentage of tax from 8 to 15% is due to another factor—new law.

(B)   This option is the **correct** answer. Despite paying more taxes, profits of the IT sector remained at a steady level—clear evidence that the sector is growing strong and will continue to add to the national budget and income.

(C)   This option is **inconclusive**. It implies that the tax in dollars is nearly the same as before, but we are clueless whether the IT sector is growing and whether it will continue to grow.

(D)   This option is **inconclusive**. This option implies that one cannot conclude whether the rise in contribution of IT sector from 8 to 15% is sustainable. The statement has bi-polar nature; the swing on either side will strengthen the argument on one end, and weaken on the other.

(E)   This option is **irrelevant**. Comparing the contribution of taxes with different industries does not impact the conclusion because regardless of the taxes paid by other industries, the contribution of the IT industry will remain what it is.

The correct answer is option B.

Example 5

The fact that many large women's rights organizations consist almost entirely of white middle-class women has led many black feminist critics to question the seriousness of those organizations in speaking out on behalf of the needs of all women in general.

Which of the following generalizations, if justified, would support the criticism implied in the statement?

(A)   The ideology of an organization tends to supersede the particular desires of its members.

(B)   The needs of black women are substantially similar to the needs of white middle-class women.

(C)   Organizations are more capable of resolving issues that individuals alone cannot.

(D)   White middle-class women are more likely to join feminist groups than black women are.

(E)   The interest of individuals in an organization tends to supersede the objective of organization.

Argument construction

Many black feminist critics question the seriousness of many large women's rights organizations consisting of almost entirely of white middle-class women. They doubt whether these organizations will speak out on behalf of the needs of all women (whites and black) in general. They feel that since the other ethnic groups and economic classes are not represented in those groups, the rights of those missing groups will be ignored.

Conclusion: Many large women's rights organizations consisting of almost entirely of white middle-class women will not be able to address the rights and the issues of black women in general.

Predict a strengthener

Predictive Strengthener 1: The needs and issues of white women and black women are different.

Predictive Strengthener 2: The organization is biased toward whites.

Answer choices explanation

(A)   This option is a **weakener**. The ideology of the organization is to speak for the rights of all women in general and not to differentiate between black and white women. If the ideology of an organization tends to supersede the particular desires of its members, it means that the organization is upright and unbiased and will help black as much as it will help whites.

(B)   This option is a **weakener**. It is opposite of predictive strengthener 1.

(C)   This option is **irrelevant**. It does not discuss the "black/white" debate at all.

(D)   This option is **inconclusive**. It does not impact the conclusion. Just because white women tend to join the groups more does not mean the rights of all get focused on in the organization.

(E)   This option is the **correct** answer. If people tend to join organizations that serve their interests, then the fact that many large women's rights groups consist almost entirely of white middle class women indicates that these groups do not serve the interests of people with other ethnic backgrounds or economic positions. This would mean that the groups will focus on the needs of the white middle-class women and not any other group.

The correct answer is option E.

Example 6

After losing the 5-set final of the Open Tennis Tournament, the runner up Maddy blamed the partisanship of the spectators for his loss. Against the advice of his trainer, he appealed to the Tennis Association for the result to be annulled and the final to be re-staged. As evidence to support his case, Maddy explained he had already won the first two sets, 6-1 and 6-2, when the audience began to loudly support his opponent, Alex. Maddy claimed that the deafening noise had hampered his concentration, causing him to lose the match.

Which of the following, if true, would provide justification for Maddy's case?

(A)   Maddy's unforced errors, losing shots due to own blunders rather than the opponent's brilliance, were far more in set 3 than in sets 1 & 2.

(B)   A pre-match TV report had predicted that Maddy would win.

(C)   Alex's ace serve average over the whole match was 50% more than Maddy's.

(D)   The highest serve speed of the match was achieved by Maddy.

(E)   Maddy's standing in the international tennis rankings was above Alex's.

Argument construction

The argument is easy to comprehend. Maddy claims that he would have won the match had the audience not started vocally and loudly supporting his opponent Alex from the third set onwards.

Conclusion: Due to the deafening noise, Maddy lost his concentration, causing him to lose the match.

Predict a strengthener

The case requiring strengthening is that Maddy lost not through his own mistakes but because of circumstances set against him, making the match unfair. Perhaps the quickest way to solve such questions is to sort the options into positive and negative categories, in that the correct option, as a strengthener for Maddy's case, must show bias towards Alex or against Maddy.

Predictive Strengthener: Evidence proving that Maddy lost concentration in the third set onwards and not before.

Answer choices explanation

(A)   Compared to sets 1, and 2, Maddy made more unforced errors in set 3. This makes his case strong that he lost concentration set 3 onwards. This sets the possibility that it was not Alex's skill but something else that made Maddy lose set 3 onwards. This option is a contender. We hold this till we find better one.

(B)   This option is **inconclusive**. A TV report, without further qualification, is not a case-builder.

(C)   This option is a **weakener**. This supports Alex.

(D)   This option is **irrelevant**.This does not support Alex or Maddy.

(E)   This option is **inconclusive**. Just because Maddy has a higher ranking does not mean he must win whenever he plays against a player of lower ranking.

The correct answer is option A.

Practice

Questions

9.4 Practice Questions

9.4.1 Questions

Question 1

Despite many innovative features, the speed of the new Suzuki, like that of all bikes, is still dictated by a delicate ratio involving weight, power, air resistance and height. Whatever speed increase has been achieved has been made possible by the fine tuning of these variables to such an extent that one is forced to wonder whether the optimum ratio has finally been reached and any further increase would require a brand new frame and engine.

Which of the following, if unquestionable, would most validate the conclusion drawn above?

(A) A reduction of all the variable factors increases speed.

(B) The ratio governing speed consists of four factors only.

(C) The speed could be increased by increasing the weight while decreasing wind resistance.

(D) The speed could be increased by retaining the current ratio but strengthening the engine and frame.

(E) Many new innovations would make an increase in speed possible.

Question 2

Nearly 1,000 coronary patients at a Utah hospital were subjects in a trial that judged the power of prayer on recovery. Half were chosen to receive remote, intercessory prayers for 28 days from community volunteers given only the first names of the chosen people. Progress or decline of all the patients was charted daily and, at discharge or death, each was given a summed numerical score. It was found that the patients for whom intercession had been requested had a 10% higher score, a fact used by certain doctors now to claim as evidence of existence of god.

Which of the following, if true, provide the best basis for the claim of the doctors?

(A) Coronary disease is frequently fatal.

(B) The community volunteers imparting intercessory prayers were noble souls.

(C) 62% of all the patients were aged over sixty.

(D) National Medical authorities accept that the results of the trial were statistically significant.

(E) The intercessory prayers were supervised by representatives from three different religions.

Question 3

The Cheetah, the fastest animal on land, uses its incredible maneuvering and acceleration capability when it hunts its prey. It gets the acceleration by exerting approximately five times more power than does the famous sprinter Usain Bolt. In a study of 368 chases that were predominantly hunting, scientists found that on most hunting chases cheetahs attained about 30 to 35 mph, a speed close to half of their peak speed. Therefore, cheetahs rely more on maneuvering than on their speed to hunt.

Which of the following, if true, would most support the conclusion?

(A) For cheetahs, speed has never been an issue and it is the result of some special physical characteristics that enable it to survive as a predator.

(B) Alan Wilson, a veterinarian, followed five cheetahs in the wild for a year and found that the cheetahs accelerated and changed direction rapidly, and that they ran very fast occasionally—close to a peak speed of 60mph.

(C) Study has found that cheetahs could increase their speed by nearly 7miles per hour in a single stride.

(D) Cheetahs have a very strong grip and can even rip the ground as they run.

(E) It was the use of the animals' claws that enabled them to accelerate and decelerate very quickly according to the study.

Question 4

The incessant monsoon rains are adding to the misery of urban dwellers. As the water level of Yamuna River constantly rises, panic in low-lying areas is growing. More water was released from Hathnikund barrage on Monday, and it will reach the Yamuna by Tuesday evening. The district administration is contemplating evacuation of over 50,000 people from the low-lying areas.

Which of the following, if true, would most support the decision being contemplated by the district administration?

(A) By crossing 205 meter level mark in the state, Yamuna River surpassed highest water level mark it had ever crossed in the last decade.

(B) The district administration of neighboring state was late in evacuating over 20,000 people, causing 44 deaths.

(C) Over 50 boats, 68 divers and a unit of Disaster Management Force have been deployed to encounter any eventuality.

(D) The city government plans to set up over 160 relief camps to tackle the threat of the aftermath of flood.

(E) Yamuna River crossed the danger level mark.

Question 5

Medicare has announced the introduction of a computer system to streamline the registration of new applicants throughout the US. The system will eliminate the possibility of fraudulent claims by cross-checking the names of applicants against past work records and birth certificates. Government officials claim that, once it is up and running, the new system will be able to save more than $500M every year currently paid for assorted medication that is then sold to individuals ineligible to receive Medicare assistance.

Which of the following, if true, most strengthens the claim of the government officials?

(A) The computer system will take approximately $900M to set up and another $100M to implement and run smoothly.

(B) The way the computerization of services is taking place in the US, medical services cannot be left behind.

(C) The computerized registration system will not stop all fraudulent claims.

(D) Many doctors have expressed concern that Medicare staff cannot be fully trained in the handling of the new system.

(E) Critics claim that the new system will prevent many impoverished patients from receiving vital medication.

Question 6

Advertisement: The Adosis tennis racket will revolutionize the entire game. Due to its unique hyper-strengthened lightweight fiber glass frame and super tension strings, even an amateur player can strike a ball so that the ball attains speeds of over 100 mph. Amaze your friends and improve your game overnight. Buy the Adosis racket today.

Which of the following, if true, most supports the message of the advertisement?

(A) The material from which the frame is made is also used to strengthen bathroom fittings.

(B) The strings of the racket can be adjusted manually.

(C) Many players would find the weight of the frame optimum.

(D) The tension of the strings and strength of the racket are the only factors dictating speed.

(E) All sports shops stock the Adosis racket.

9.4.2 Answer-Key

(1) B	(3) B	(5) A
(2) D	(4) E	(6) D

Solutions

9.4.3 Solutions

Question 1

Argument construction

In short, the argument is: the speed of the new Suzuki, like that of all bikes, is a function of weight, power, air resistance and height for the same frame and the engine. To further increase the speed, one would require a brand new frame and engine.

Conclusion: Maximum possible speed of bikes has been achieved by fine tuning a delicate ratio involving weight, power, air resistance and height.

Predict A Strengthener

Read the variation in the question stem, you may find such differently expressed phrases, but similar in meaning to "if true" and "strengthen".

Predictive Strengthener: Variation in any 5th factor will not increase the speed for the given frame and the engine.

Answer choices explanation

(A) This option is **inconsistent.** The premise states that the delicate ratio of four variables has been exploited to the maximum. Stating that the reduction of all the variable factors increases speed is against the premise.

(B) This option is the **correct** answer. If there are only 4 factors governing speed, the conclusion is strengthened. It rules out the possibility that any other factor may increase the speed for the given bike frames and engines.

(C) This option is **inconsistent.** As stated earlier that the delicate ratio of these 4 variables has been exploited to the maximum. Stating that the speed could be increased by increasing the weight while decreasing wind (air) resistance is against the premise.

(D) This option is **out of scope.** The argument is concerned with increasing speed with the same frame and the engine. This option alters the frame and the engine and thus becomes pointless towards this argument.

(E) This option is **out of scope.**

The correct answer is option B.

Question 2

Argument construction

Nearly 1,000 coronary patients were subjects in a trial that judged the power of prayer on recovery. Nearly 500 were chosen to receive remote, intercessory prayers for 28 days from community volunteers. The volunteers were given only the first names of the chosen subjects.

Progress or decline of all the subjects was monitored daily and, at discharge or death, each subject was given a total numerical score. It was found that the subjects for whom intercession had been requested had a 10% higher score. Based on this certain doctors now claim that there is evidence of the existence of god.

Conclusion: God exists.

Predict A Strengthener

Predictive Strengthener 1: 10% is a significant number to act as proof of existence of god.

Predictive Strengthener 2: 500 patients who received prayers were not given any special medical treatment by doctors, and not received by the other 500 patients.

Answer choices explanation

(A) This option is **irrelevant.** The argument is concerned with the summed numerical score and the finding that those who received prayers got a higher score, *whether the subject died or recovered.* Hence, whether the diseases are mostly fatal is irrelevant since the argument is not regarding whether prayers saved the subjects from death.

(B) This option is **inconclusive.** *Noble soul* is an ambiguous qualification. This neither strengthens nor weakens the argument.

(C) This option is **irrelevant.** Again, since patients were judged on the basis of their final numerical scores, their age is irrelevant to the "power of prayer".

(D) This option is the **correct** answer. It is aligned with the predictive strengthener. This option lends support to the trial by negating the possibility that the trial is an oddity and affirms that the trial is possibly representative.

(E) This option is **irrelevant.** The argument does not discuss the religion of the god or of the patients. It deals with prayers and its effect on coronary patients regardless of the religion.

The correct answer is option D.

Question 3

Argument construction

The argument is about cheetah's ability to maneuver and accelerate when it hunts its prey. There are two aspects mentioned about cheetah's maneuvering, and acceleration, its ability to increase speed while hunting.

Further, the argument states how the cheetahs accelerate up to approximately five times than sprinter Usain Bolt. It is noteworthy that in most of the chases that were predominantly hunting, cheetahs attained only 30-35 mph, and did not reach their peak speed.

Conclusion: - Cheetahs rely more on maneuvering than on their speed to hunt.

The conclusion is based on the fact that despite having the capability to increase speed—acceleration—to their advantage, cheetahs do not exploit that capability to the fullest, yet they are very successful predators. The contributing factor must be their tactical maneuvering since the argument mentions that a cheetah *uses its incredible maneuvering and acceleration when it hunts its prey,* implying that there are only two factors under consideration.

Predict A Strengthener

Predictive Strengthener: Evidence proving that cheetahs rely more on maneuvering than on their speed to hunt.

Answer choices explanation

(A)   This option is **irrelevant.** It focuses on speed and cheetah's capability of attaining more speed. The option does not focus on why the cheetah does not use its maximum possible speed when it hunts.

(B)   This is the **correct** answer. This option is evidence that states that the cheetahs accelerate and change direction rapidly, but that they run very fast only occasionally. This provides further proof for the study by talking about specific acceleration and changing direction—a possible maneuvering tactic. If the cheetahs succeeded at hunting without exploiting their capability of speed to the fullest, they must have maneuvered successfully. In other words they relied more on maneuvering than on speed.

(C)   Like option A, this option is **irrelevant.** It also focuses on speed.

(D)   This option is **out of scope.** There's no discussion of the effect of their speed on the ground.

(E)   Like option A, this option is **irrelevant.** It also focuses on speed.

The correct answer is option B.

Question 4

Argument construction

This is a pretty simple argument in understanding. The argument is about panic created in low-lying areas caused by the rising level of Yamuna River.

Conclusion: Over 50000 people from the low-lying areas should be evacuated.

Answer choices explanation

(A)   This option is **inconclusive.** While we are told that the river crossed the 205-meter level mark, highest in the last decade, we do not know whether this mark is dangerous to begin with. It may be quite an ordinary level. This would mean that Yamuna was not ever and is not now either a threat to life.

(B) This option is **out of scope.** Situation in the neighboring state cannot mirror the situation in this state. The argument does not state that the two states are similar or that both face danger from Yamuna's rising water levels.

(C) This option tells us about the preparedness of the unit of Disaster Management Force to address any eventuality. This option does strengthen the conclusion to some extent; however, being prepared to encounter any eventuality does not provide concrete proof that over 50,000 people should be evacuated. Any state, regardless of existing danger, should be prepared with a disaster management unit prepared to help in eventualities. We can keep this option in the reckoning till we get the best answer.

(D) This option tells us how the city government will temporarily accommodate the flood-hit people. Like option C, this option also strengthens the conclusion to some extent; however, planning for setting up relief camps to tackle the threat the aftermath of flood does not provide support to a decision that involves over 50,000 people and their evacuation. We keep this option in the reckoning till we get the best answer.

(E) This is the **correct** answer. A danger-level mark is a qualifying mark to execute some anticipatory action. Although the preventive action may not necessarily be evacuation, among three probable options, this one most supports the reason that evacuation exercise should be carried out.

The correct answer is option E.

Question 5

Argument construction

The argument is easy to understand.

Conclusion: Once the computer system is up and running, the system will be able to save more than $500M a year.

Predict A Strengthener

The claim that needs to be strengthened is that the new system will save money by reducing fraud.

Predictive Strengthener 1: The cost of new system is not disproportionately high.

Predictive Strengthener 2: It is possible to implement the system and train the staff to use the system to prevent frauds.

Predictive Strengthener 3: The new system is competent enough to stop most fraudulent claims.

Answer choices explanation

(A)   While the new system set up and execution is costly, the new system will pay for itself and start saving millions within two years. This is a close contender. If no better than this option is found, this is the **correct**answer.

(B)   This option is **irrelevant.** Medical services or computerization in general is not part of the argument.

(C)   This option is a **weakener.** This is against predictive strengthener 3.

(D)   This option is a **weakener.** This is against predictive strengthener 2.

(E)   This option is a **weakener.** This is against the objective of the new system.

The correct answer is option A.

Question 6

Argument construction

Conclusion: New Adosis tennis racket has unique hyper-strengthened, lightweight fiber glass frame, and super tension strings that can enable a player strike a ball to raise the ball's speeds to over 100 mph.

Predict A Strengthener

The racket has three qualities—strength, light-weight and strings with super-tension. Based on these qualities, the advertisement claims that a player can raise the ball's speeds to over 100 mph.

Predictive Strengthener: Many veteran players have tested the racket and they endorse the claim.

Answer choices explanation

(A)   This option is **inconclusive.** We do not have any clue about the strength of bathroom fittings. Even if we infer that the material is of high strength, it is not new information. The argument already mentions this. We need to test the validity of the racket's qualities influencing the ball's speed.

(B)   That the strings can be adjusted manually is a good feature to adjust the tension of strings, but it does not help support the conclusion—that the racket can make the struck ball attain 100 mph speed.

(C)   This option is **inconclusive.** If many players find the weight of the frame optimum, they would prefer to use it, but it does not help support the conclusion—that the racket is designed can make the struck ball attain 100 mph speed.

(D)   This option is the **correct** answer. If the tension of the strings and strength of the racket are the only factors dictating velocity, Adosis racket is qualified to make the struck ball attain 100 mph.

(E)   This option is **out of scope.** It does not address the speed issue.

The correct answer is option D.

Chapter 10

Weaken the Argument

10.1 Weaken the Argument Question type

 Like strengthen the argument questions, weaken the argument questions are one of the frequently-asked question types in Argument Structure Passages.

Weaken the argument questions also belong to assumption based family. Weakener is an additional piece of information that shatters the conclusion, making the conclusion illogical. The new piece of information will work against the evidence and make the assumption invalid.

Look at the image below. There is a dialogue taking place between two people. What could be a weakener here?

Let us see this argument: **Steve will get 300+ in his GRE.**

Assumption	Weakener
Steve will appear for his GRE exam.	Steve has been inconsistent in getting 300+ in his mocks.
Steve has prepared well for the GRE exam.	Steve has prepared poorly for the GRE exam.
Maximum score for the GRE is more than 300.	Steve has scored poorly in similar high-pressure competitive exams.

Following illustration depicts your job for weaken the argument question type.

Companies Pinnacle and Acme provide round-the-clock e-mail assistance to any customer who uses their laptops. Custo   s send e-mails only when they find the laptops difficult to use. Since Pinn   our times as many e-mails as Acme does, Pinnacle's laptops must   than Acme's.

Which of the following, if true,   en the argument above?

A.   Acme and Pin   iod of time.
B.   E-mails to Acr   as to Pinnacle.
C.   Acme does no   eive through other
      means such a
D.   The number o   nies has been
      gradually incr
E.   Pinnacle's e-m   me's e-mail ID.

Only one option weakens the conclusion most, and makes it illogical.

Question Stem

All weaken question stems include 'if true' or an equivalent phrase in the question stem. This means that you have to attempt the question keeping in mind that the information given in the options is unquestionable and to be taken as fact.

Typical 'weaken the argument' question stem looks like this.

· Which of the following, if true, would most seriously weaken the argument against the automobile manufacturer's claim?

· Which of the following, if true, would cast the most serious doubt on the validity of the argument?

Weaken the argument questions may sometimes skip the phrase 'if true', but the question stem will still convey similar meaning.

· Which of the following, if true, most strongly calls the conclusion into question?

- Which of the following, if true, most seriously undermines the claim?

- Which of the following, if true, makes the conclusion flawed?

- Which of the following, if true, is most damaging to the conclusion?

- Which of the following, if true, is ill-suited to the plan?

- Which of the following, if true, makes the argument most vulnerable to criticism?

- Which of the following, if true, most criticizes the conclusion?

10.2   Process Of Solving Weaken The Argument Questions

The 4-step approach is same as in Find the Assumption chapter.

The 4-step approach

   (1) Recognize the question type

   (2) Understand the argument construction

   (3) Predict the qualifier

   (4) Eliminate incorrect options

First 2 steps are same for weaken the argument questions. Let us jump directly to predict the qualifier step.

10.2.1   Predict the qualifier

We already are familiar with this step. Let us see this applying to "weakeners".

Let us see the 'Pinnacle and Acme' argument.

> Companies Pinnacle and Acme provide round-the-clock e-mail assistance to any customer who uses their laptops. Customers send e-mails only when they find the laptop difficult to use.Since Pinnacle receives four times as many e-mails as Acme receives, Pinnacle's laptops must be more difficult to use than Acme's.

Conclusion: *Pinnacle's laptops must be more difficult to use than Acme's.*

10.2.2   Predicting Weakener

Our job is to weaken the argument by providing new information. The optimum approach in predicting weakeners is to shatter assumptions. If you are able to predict assumptions, just work against those assumptions.

Let's see how.

Pinnacle has four times the number of laptop customers as Acme.

Since Pinnacle has four times the number of laptops customers as Acme, it is obvious that there would be significantly more number of e-mails sent to Pinnacle. The statement certainly weakens the conclusion. The information given is additional information that weakens the conclusion; a weakener.

Predictive Weakener 1: Desktop computer users find Pinnacle's desktop more user-friendly than Acme's.

We already discussed the following predictive weakeners in Find the Assumption chapter; we reproduce it. What if a significant number of Pinnacle's customers are newbies? Then obviously Pinnacle will receive more e-mails regarding how to use the laptop than will Acme. This information will make the conclusion illogical.

Predictive Weakener 2: Pinnacle sells a significantly higher number of laptops to newbies than does Acme.

What if Acme receives more queries for help through letters than Pinnacle does? The conclusion would seem less believable.

Predictive Weakener 3: Acme receives more complaints through letters and phones.

Example

Questions

10.3 Examples

Example 1

The new subway line, opened barely a year ago to alleviate traffic congestion, has already been deemed insufficient of satisfying the demand. The State Transport Authority (STA), commissioned by the Mayor's office to come up with solutions, has admitted that even if more trains and carriages are added, the demand is such that only a 23% reduction in congestion would be feasible. For this reason the city council is now considering building a new highway linking the downtown business district with the East Canton suburbs.

Which of the following, if true, would most weaken the conclusion of the above passage?

(A) A year is insufficient time to judge the viability of the subway.

(B) A ride-sharing scheme has been successfully operating for more than a year.

(C) The business district suffers from a chronic shortage of parking spaces.

(D) Some residents in the business district are opposed to the scheme.

(E) The cost of the proposed highway would severely strain the city's budget.

Argument construction

The new subway line was opened hardly a year ago to reduce traffic congestion, but it has been deemed insufficient of handling the traffic load. STA has admitted that even if more trains and carriages are added, the traffic load can be reduced by up to 23%. For this reason the city council is now contemplating building a new highway road linking the downtown business district with the East Canton suburbs.

Premise 1 - The new subway line was opened barely a year ago to reduce traffic congestion has been deemed insufficient of handling the traffic load.

Premise 2 - More trains and carriages will reduce the traffic load by only up to 23%.

Conclusion: Whether to build a highway because of the current congestion on the roads and the inadequacy of the subway system.

Predict a Weakener

We have to weaken the argument. Let us predict some statements that will weaken the conclusion.

Predictive weakener 1: Proposed new highway road will reduce the traffic load by less than 23%.

Predictive weakener 2: Proposed new highway road will pose unfathomable and insurmountable challenges.

Predictive weakener 3: Other alternative to address the problem in hand will fare better than the proposed solution of linking highway road.

Answer choices explanation

(A)   This option is **inconsistent**.The statement is not consistent with the premise 1. It is evident from the premise 1 that present system is inadequate. You cannot **ever** challenge premise, but the conclusion can be challenged.

(B)   This option is **irrelevant**. Even though ride sharing scheme has been operating for a year, it hasn't eased congestion.

(C)   This is the **correct** answer. This option is aligned to our predicted weakener 2. A problem that cannot be easily overcome is encountered with the proposed plan—The business district suffers from a chronic shortage of parking spaces. It weakens the conclusion that we should build a highway.

(D)   This option is **inconclusive**. We have discussed in ASP concepts chapter that the quantity word "some" ranges from 1-99%. We tried to measure quantity words- all, many, some, few, and none. Had the option said, "Most residents in the business district are opposed to the scheme" it would have made a little sense. However, despite using quantity word most, this option lacks a solid reasoning on why residents are opposed to the linking highway. Opposed to this, option C clearly cites the problem and effectively weakens the conclusion.

(E)   This option is **out the scope**. The cost factor is beyond the scope of this argument.

The correct answer is option C.

Example2

Acme University receives 2,000 applications a year from high school students who wish to attend college. The university's admission committee would like to ensure constant standards of quality in the incoming class each year. The admissions committee has decided, therefore, to accept for admission each year only the best 200 students, selected on the basis of the quality of their personal statements.

Of the following, if unquestionable, the best criticism of the admission committee's plan is that:

(A)   The universities cannot accept all of the students who seek admission in a given year.

(B)   The total number of applications will remain at approximately 2,000 in the coming years.

(C)   Each applicant deserves to be considered seriously for admission.

(D)   The best 200 personal statements will be difficult to assess.

(E)   It is difficult to judge the quality of an applicant based on personal statements alone.

Argument construction

The argument is easy to understand. To standardize quality of the classes, the university will select 200 best candidates, judged so by the quality of their personal statements.

Conclusion: Selecting best 200 students on the basis of the quality of their personal statements (SoP) will ensure constant standards of quality.

Predict a Weakener

Predictive Weakener 1: Assessing the quality of students on the basis of only SoP is flawed.

Predictive Weakener 2: Students have mastered the art of writing great SoPs regardless of their personal qualities.

Answer choices explanation

(A)   This option is **irrelevant**. The university only wants to accept 200 students.

(B)   This option is **irrelevant**. It implies nothing relevant towards the conclusion.

(C)   This option is **inconclusive**. It does not impact the conclusion because the argument does not state that in judging the applicant the university won't consider each applicant seriously.

(D)   This option is a possible **weakener**. This option is tricky. It focuses on difficulty in assessing SoPs, whereas the argument is concerned with the difficulty in assessing the quality of students. It does weaken the conclusion, but compared to option E—the best criticism, we eliminate this option.

(E)   This is the **correct** answer. This option challenges the authenticity of selecting best 200 on the basis of SoP alone. If some average students with great SoPs got selected, the quality of the university will be in question. It is aligned with predictive weakener 1.

The correct answer is option E.

Example 3

Companies that launch asteroid mining robots from the moon have a distinct advantage over earth-based asteroid-mining robotic systems because of the moon's lower gravity. The higher the gravity of the object from which the company launches its systems, the more money it has to spend on fuel and on rocket systems that can carry the extra fuel required to enter orbit. In order to be as competitive as the lunar based Apollo Mining Company (AMC), Terra Now Mining Corporation (TNMC), located near the equator in South America, has decided to build a space elevator that will connect an orbiting artificial satellite with the ground base via a super-thin, super-strong cable.

Which of the following, if true, makes the argument most vulnerable to criticism?

(A)   The cable is composed of a carbon-based material that is yet to be tested against the effect of thermal changes.

(B)   The high cost of building the cable will negate any cost-savings in launching mining robotic systems into orbit for the foreseeable future.

(C)   Over its expected lifetime, the cable will cut the cost of placing robots in orbit by 95%.

(D)   The mining robots are flexible enough to be sent up and down via thin cable.

(E)   The market for elements mined from asteroids is expected to decrease in size over the next fifty years.

Argument construction

Compared to earth, the moon has lower gravity; hence companies that launch asteroid mining robots from the moon have a distinct advantage over earth-based robotic systems. The higher the gravitational force on the object, the more money the company has to spend on fuel and on rocket systems that can carry the extra fuel required to enter orbit.

TNMC is located near the equator in South America. In order to be as competitive as the moon based AMC, TNMC has decided to build a space elevator that will connect an orbiting artificial satellite with the ground via a super-thin, super-strong cable.

Conclusion: TNMC's plan to launch robots from earth by building space elevator will be as competitive as AMC's, making a level-playing field for both in the market.

Predict a Weakener

Predictive Weakener 1: Cost of building the space elevator will be so disproportionately high that TNMC cannot compete with AMC.

Predictive Weakener 2: TNMC will encounter insurmountable technical challenges in building the space elevator.

Answer choices explanation

(A)   This option is **inconclusive**. Carbon-based material may or may not withstand the effect of thermal changes. We cannot conclude from this option that the thermal changes will definitely hamper the space elevator.

(B)   This is the **correct** answer. It is aligned with predictive weakener 1. It shows a definitive reason for TMNC to not build a space elevator.

(C)   This option is a **strengthener**. We do not know the current cost of production. The option states the scenario which focuses on future.

(D)   This option is a **strengthener**. This adds information that shows a reason the space elevator will be helpful.

(E) This option is **out of scope**, but a tricky option. It does seem to discourage the company to invest in the robotic systems because if the markets were to decline, spending stupendous sums on a project does not make sense. However, it has two issues. One is that we cannot assume that the markets will decline to such an extent that the project is unviable, and two is that a fifty year period is a long-term period; the money invested in the project could be recovered in this period. Moreover, compared to option B, we can easily eliminate this option.

The correct answer is option B.

Example 4

Investing in the Jones & Weston Munitions Company would be a great way to increase the value of one's stock portfolio at the current time. Clock and Roll, a gun enthusiasts' magazine, conducted a survey which indicated that 75 percent of its readers want to buy a second gun within a year. This is a great time for the gun industry. The new study also shows that the gun industry could only provide 55 percent of the total population with a new gun a year.

Which of the following, if true, reveals a weakness in the evidence cited above?

(A) The manufacturing of guns requires very precise industrial processes.

(B) Gun manufacturers are not evenly distributed across the country.

(C) The number of people who want a second gun has been increasing each year for the past ten years.

(D) Readers of Clock and Roll are more likely than most people to want a second gun.

(E) Gun magazines include articles about owning a gun as well as articles about hunting.

Argument construction

The argument states that investing in the stocks of JWM Company would increase its value. Clock and Roll, a gun enthusiasts' magazine, conducted a survey which indicated that 75 % of **its** readers want to buy a **second gun** within a year. The new study also shows that the gun industry could only provide 55 % of the total population with a new gun each year.

Conclusion: This is a great time for the gun industry.

Predict a Weakener

This question deals with biased population samples. While it may be true that the readers of that magazine want to buy a gun within a year, what needs to be established is whether the readers of the magazine are representative of the general population. Say, out of 1M people, there are only 100,000 readers of the magazine. In such a scenario, saying that because 75% of those readers want new guns, we can expect gun sales to increase significantly is not a valid statement. There's also the fact that currently the industry can provide for 55% of the **population** and not just 55% of the readers. A weakener would most likely be an option that points out this inconsistency in the samples used for making the claims.

Predictive Weakener 1: People who read magazines about guns will tend to be more likely to buy or want a second gun than those who don't read such magazines.

Predictive Weakener 2: The government is going to pass a resolution under which no one would be allowed to carry second gun.

Answer choices explanation

(A)   This option is **irrelevant** to the conclusion that gun sales will increase.

(B)   This option is **inconclusive** and implies nothing about gun sales going either up or down.

(C)   This option is **strengthener** for the conclusion.

(D)   This is the **correct** answer. It is aligned with predictive weakener 1. It establishes that the general population will not buy guns as the readers of the magazine would. Thus the expected sales are not going to be as much.

(E)   This option is **irrelevant**.

The correct answer is option D.

Example 5

Which of the following, if true, would undermine the validity of the investment advice in the argument above?

(A)   Some gun owners are satisfied with only one gun.

(B)   About half of the people who buy guns also purchase large cartridge magazines.

(C)   About half of the people who buy guns do so to protect their families.

(D)   Only a quarter of the guns that are made are sold within the first four weeks.

(E)   Only a quarter of those who claim that they want a second gun actually end up purchasing one.

Argument construction

Investment Advice: Invest in the stocks of JWM.

Predict a Predict an Invalidator

The investment advice is that investing in Jones & Weston would increase the value of one's stock portfolio. This advice implies that the author expects the company to make a large profit, by selling more of its product, namely guns. An option that demonstrates that the demand for guns is not as high as the magazine claims will undermine the validity of this advice.

Predicative invalidators are same as weakeners in the previous question.

Answer choices explanation

(A)   This option is **inconclusive**. **"Some"** a quantity word range 1 to 99%. We cannot conclude on the basis of some.

(B)   This option is a **validator**. This option shows that sales will rise and provides reason to buy shares of JWM.

(C)   This option is **irrelevant** because the reason people buy guns does not make a difference to whether they will buy more as predicted.

(D)   This option is **inconclusive**.This option is cleverly crafted. The tone of the option suggests negative prospects for gun industry, but we cannot conclusively state this because we don't know when the remaining 75% guns are sold or which period of sale is miserable.

(E)   This is the **correct** answer. It shows that only 25% of those who claim they want a second gun end up buying one. Hence, the predictions are inflated and based on flimsy data, which undermines the validity of the investment advice.

The correct answer is option E.

Example 6

Recently, there was a huge flood in Hunan, China, during the rice-growing season. This will lead to doubling of the price of rice this season and ultimately to the cost of making rice-cakes becoming expensive. Unfortunately, rice-cake consumers in Hunan will now have to pay more for rice-cakes.

Which of the following, if true, is most damaging to the argument above?

(A)   The recent flood was not as severe as the scientists had predicted.

(B)   Regions other than Hunan also supply rice to rice-cake manufacturers in Hunan.

(C)   Ingredients other than rice are used in the production of rice-cakes.

(D)   Last year the price of rice was actually lower than the average price over the past ten years.

(E)   The price of rice will eventually be too high for most consumers because of inflation.

Argument construction

Due to a huge flood in Hunan, during the rice-growing season, the price of rice will double. It will make rice-cakes more expensive.

Conclusion: Due to doubling of the price of rice, consumers in Hunan will now have to pay more for rice-cakes.

Predict a Weakener

Our task is to weaken the conclusion that the price of rice-cakes will rise. The author concludes that the huge flood in Hunan will cause the price of rice to double. He assumes that the flood will destroy a significant amount of rice crops and that shortage of rice crops will lead to the price rise. This price rise will mean making rice-cakes becomes more expensive.

The author seems to imply that the rice used in Hunan is supplied entirely by Hunan growers itself. What if Hunan is not the only source of rice? Hunan could import rice from other parts of the country, and possibly at almost normal price.

Predictive Weakener 1: Rice produced in Hunan is not the only source of rice for Hunan.

Predictive Weakener 2: Due to flood, the damage to rice crops in Hunan is not significant.

Answer choices explanation

(A)   This option is **inconsistent**. From this option, we cannot infer whether the rice crops were not destroyed significantly. Note that the predictive weakener 2 is different from this option.The option states that the flood was not severe (inconsistent with the premise), whereas predictive weakener 2 states that damage to the rice crop is not significant, but the floods are, as the premise claimed, severe.

(B)   This is the **correct** answer. It is aligned with predictive weakener 1.

(C)   Major proportion of rice-cake has to be rice; hence, the impact due to the prices of other ingredients will not be significant.

(D)   This option is **irrelevant**. Last year's price does not impact the conclusion dealing with current and future prices.

(E)   This option is **out of scope** and much too general.

The correct answer is option B.

Example 7

Enshrined in the US Constitution, a clause protecting the right of the citizen to bear arms remains the most potent argument used by the gun lobby in their resistance to those wishing to ban possession of handguns. Their opponents cite the most recent UN statistics that prove conclusively that globally there exists a clear correlation between the number of violent gunfire incidents and the laxity of gun control legislation.

Which of the following, if true, would LEAST support those wishing to ban the possession of hand guns?

(A) Iceland, with the strongest gun laws, has too small a population to be statistically significant for US.

(B) Financial support for the gun lobby has decreased considerably over the last two years.

(C) Since its adoption, the US Constitution has proved extremely resilient to change.

(D) Instances of violence have fractionally increased in at least one country that adopted harsh gun possession legislation.

(E) The UN statistics took more than two years to compile.

Argument construction

Argument of gun lobby: Every citizen has right to possess gun to protect oneself. It is written in the US Constitution. Their position is—do not ban gun possession.

Argument of opponents: The most recent UN statistics proves that globally there exists a clear correlation between the number of violent gunfire incidents and the leniency of gun control legislation. Their position is—ban gun possession.

Conclusion: Ban gun.

Predict a Weakener

The language of the question stem is unusual. You have to pick an option that would LEAST support opponents. Since the conclusion is drawn from gun opponents' point of view, hence we have to look for the option that weakens the conclusion—Ban gun!

In GRE ASP questions, you have to read "LEAST support" as one that weakens, and "LEAST challenge" as one that strengthens.

So, we have to cite a reason that justifies possession of guns.

Predictive Weakener: There is sizable number of deaths caused by criminals of the people who could not protect themselves because they did not have guns.

Answer choices explanation

(A) This option is **out of scope**. It presents neither support nor challenge.

(B) This option is **irrelevant**. Finances of the gun lobby are irrelevant.

(C) This is the **correct** answer. If the US Constitution has proved extremely resistant to change the Constitution, then the amendment to ban gun will not take place.

(D) This option also weakens the conclusion, but not to the extent option C does because of the use of its word "fractionally" and "one country".

(E) This option is **inconclusive.**Two-year time for compilation is voluminous data to reach the conclusion, it may be inferred that the data is out-dated, so we cannot infer from this option.

The correct answer is option C.

Example 8

A company QuickBite buys free-holiday coupons from people who earned these coupons from Magic Holidays for holidaying frequently at Magic Holidays destinations. QuickBite sells these coupons to the people who pay less for the coupons than they would pay by buying holiday packages from Magic Holidays. This reselling of coupons results in loss of revenue to Magic Holidays.

To discourage the buying and selling of free holiday coupons, it would be best for Magic Holidays to restrict the following.

(A) use of the coupons to those who earned the coupons and their family members

(B) number of coupons that a person can earn in a particular year

(C) seasons in which the coupons can be used

(D) time period within which the coupons can be used after they are issued

(E) number of holiday destinations for which persons can use the coupons

Argument construction

QuickBite buys free-holiday coupons from frequent vacationers who earned these coupons from Magic Holidays for holidaying at Magic Holidays destinations. QuickBite sells these coupons to the people who pay significantly less for the coupons than they would have paid had they bought the full holiday package from Magic Holidays. This sale of coupons is the loss of potential business for Magic Holidays.

Conclusion: This reselling of coupons results in loss of revenue to Magic Holidays.

Predict a Solution

We have to discourage the trading of free holiday coupons by the Magic Holidays patrons. We need to find a solution that will keep the marketing going but will stop the loss of revenue for MH.

Predictive Solution: Restrict the use of the coupons to the patrons who earn them.

Answer choices explanation

(A)   This is the **correct** answer. It is aligned with the predictive solution. By restricting the usage of the coupons to the patrons and their family members, the trading of coupons will be stalled, yet the patrons will either use the coupons for themselves or for their family members.

(B)   The move to restrict the number of coupons that a person can earn in a particular year will not address the issue. Even the limited number of coupons can still be traded. Moreover, with this move, the objective of free-coupon-reward to the patrons will be defeated. Our problem remains.

(C)   Like option B, the move to restrict the seasons on which the coupons can be used will not address the issue. The coupons can still be traded for those restricted seasons. Our problem remains.

(D)   Again, like option B, the move to restrict the time period within which the coupons can be used after they are issued will not address the issue. The coupons can still be traded in the restricted time period. Our problem remains.

(E)   The move to restrict the number of holiday destinations for which persons can use the coupons will not address the issue. The coupons can still be traded for the restricted number of holiday destinations. Our problem remains.

The correct answer is option A.

Example 9

Because of new developments in electric accumulators, the way has been opened to the marketing of practical and economically viable electric automobiles. Citing such developments and the urgent need to encourage environmentally friendly transport systems, Washington State Senator Brenda Sheperton has proposed the adoption of a state law that would offer state subsidies to propel auto manufacturers to reduce the prices of their range of electric vehicles and auto retailers to sell one electric powered vehicle for each gasoline powered vehicle sold in the state.

Which of the following, if true, best explains why the authors' reasoning is vulnerable to criticism?

(A)   Not all environmental groups have welcomed the proposal.

(B)   The price of electric powered vehicles is much higher than that of conventional vehicles.

(C)   Only a few gas stations in the state have battery-charging facilities.

(D)   Only top four automobile manufacturers have the capability to manufacture electric car.

(E)   Auto retailers have limited space in the showrooms to accommodate more vehicles.

Argument construction

New developments in electric accumulators have led to the marketing of practical and economically viable electric automobiles. A Washington State Senator has proposed a state law that would offer subsidies to the state so that the state can compel: one, auto manufacturers to reduce the prices of their range of electric vehicles and two, auto retailers to sell one electric powered vehicle for each gasoline powered vehicle sold in the state. Basically, the senator is pushing for more electric automobiles sales.

Predict a Weakener

What assumptions does this argument contain?

Predictive assumption 1: Electric vehicles are environment friendly because they are better than gasoline-powered vehicles.
Predictive weakener 1: Electric vehicles, though not emitting carbon emission, have other detrimental effects to the environment.

Predictive assumption 2: Subsidies given on electric vehicles are ample enough to encourage the customers to buy electric vehicles over gasoline-based vehicles.
Predictive weakener 2: Benefits given on electric vehicles are NOT ample enough to encourage the customers to buy electric vehicles over gasoline-based vehicles.

Answer choices explanation

(A)   This option is **inconclusive**. Just because some environmental groups haven't welcomed the proposal does not mean the proposal is flawed. They may have other reasons to reject the proposal. Anyway, this option does not show any inherent vulnerability in the reasoning. It merely shows some groups' response to the proposal, which by itself cannot constitute a weakness in any plan.

(B)   This option is **inconclusive.** We cannot conclude whether subsidies given on electric vehicles are ample enough to offset the difference in the price of electric vehicles and conventional vehicles.

(C)   This is the **correct** answer. Scarcity of battery-charging facilities would severely cripple the plan to promote electric vehicles. Because people will not buy the electric cars until this problem is resolved regardless of how affordable the electric cars are.

(D)   This option is **inconclusive.** We cannot conclude whether top four manufacturers can manufacture ample number of electric vehicles to meet the requirements of the state. If they can, this statement is valid. In the absence of data, this option cannot be pinned down as a damaging to the argument.

(E)   This option is certainly a **relevant** and a tricky option, but the argument states that the retailer will have to sell one electric vehicle for every conventional vehicle. It does not necessarily translate to scarcity of space in the showrooms. The dealers can replace some of the conventional car displays with electric car ones to overcome this problem. The plan is to sell one electric car but not necessarily after putting it on display.

The correct answer is option C.

Practice

Questions

10.4 Practice Questions

10.4.1 Questions

Question 1

Although Milton international school provided competent teachers and a revamped course, social science and geography scores for grade 10 students failed to reach the expected level. Therefore, parents suggested to the principal that social science and geography subjects be taught in the native language instead of in English.

Which of the following, if true, would cast a serious doubt on parents' proposal?

(A) Social science and geography subjects are taught by a teacher, whose competence in native language is profound.

(B) A few students can speak fluent native language.

(C) Currently final examinations are conducted in English language; the status quo is not going to change in near future.

(D) Many grade 10 students were born and brought up in either a town or culturally similar surrounding areas.

(E) Students of Milton International School are consistently scoring satisfactorily in their native language subject.

Question 2

The city's transport authorities have proposed a new contract to union negotiators that would decrease the number of trains in service and do away with guards but would increase the salaries of subway car drivers by 16%. However, the proposal is facing stiff opposition from rank and file members. It is not so much the increased pay offer, although this falls well short of the figure agreed upon by the arbitration council, but more the fear that guard-less trains would lead to mass redundancies despite the statutory obligation on the authorities to maintain full employment of all union members.

Which of the following would do the most to relieve the fears of the union members?

(A) All those made redundant would receive 50% of their annual bonus entitlement.

(B) The redundancies would be kept to a minimum.

(C) Competent redundant guards would be trained as drivers.

(D) Management would receive a 16% cut in their salaries.

(E) The authorities would adhere to contractual stipulations.

Question 3

People with modern views believe that a genuine belief in astrology is a proof of a naive and an unscientific mindset. However, in the past, people with great intellect and scientific wisdom accepted astrology wholeheartedly. Therefore, there is no scientific basis for not accepting astrology.

The argument is most vulnerable to criticism on which one of the following grounds?

(A) Since it has been debated for ages whether astrology has any scientific merit, any evidence to show that it has a method of proof will be fallacious.

(B) There has been a rapid progression of intelligence in modern people.

(C) The implied assumption that everyone with modern views does not believe in astrology is false.

(D) A faith can be consistent with the available proofs and accepted scientific notions at one time but not with the accepted proofs and notions at a later time.

(E) There might be authentic nonscientific basis for not accepting astrology.

Question 4

Statistics demonstrate that children who are beaten usually grow up believing that it is appropriate to beat their children as well. This cycle is just one instance of violence perpetuating violence. A certain religious sect claims, however, that beating children is a form of discipline, not violence, and that this discipline is necessary to develop certain good habits in children, because children are too emotional and not capable of responding to situations with reason and logic until they reach adolescence.

Which of the following, if true, make the conclusion flawed?

(A) Young children often, for no apparent reason, burst into fits of tears or laughter thereby showing mixed emotions at times.

(B) If beaten properly, there should be no permanent marks left on children.

(C) Even at an early age, children are capable of differentiating right from wrong and understanding why things should or should not be done.

(D) Even at an early age, children who are more intelligent are beaten for different reasons than less intelligent children are.

(E) Child-beating is an acceptable social practice in many countries.

Question 5

This year UK's tax hike on tobacco and alcohol places Britain at the head of, what many experts call, a worrying global trend. The government has defended the rise, which now makes the UK proportionally the world's leading collector of excise tax, as being the only effective deterrent against tobacco and alcohol abuse. However, critics claim that such policies are a sham and intrinsically flawed as the vast sums gathered annually finance so many governmental activities and expenses that if tobacco and alcohol consumers were really deterred, the government would have collapsed.

Which of the following most challenges the position of critics against the UK government?

(A) The high taxes fund medical and other services in the country.

(B) By pretending to be interested in tobacco and alcohol deterrence, the government is increasing the wealth of Britain.

(C) Extreme tobacco and alcohol use is common in many impoverished countries; hence the high tax is justified.

(D) Incremental tax rises compensate for the gradual decrease in tobacco and alcohol use and the derived revenues.

(E) Some of the critics are paid lobbyists for the tobacco and alcohol industries.

Question 6

To claim that computer-industry revenues are declining is overstated. It is a fact that the computer manufactures' share of the industry revenues declined from 75 percent three years ago to 60 percent today, but for the same period companies selling computer parts had their share increase from 15 percent to 25 percent and service companies, such as dealers, resellers, and repairers had their share increase from 10 percent to 15 percent.

Which one of the following, if true, best indicates why the data given above provides no evidence to support the conclusion?

(A) There is no explanation given for why the revenue shares of three sectors of the industry changed.

(B) It is likely that the data for manufactures' share of revenues came from a source, which is different from the sources of data for computer parts and service companies.

(C) Computer manufactures and parts companies depend for their revenue on dealers' success in selling computers.

(D) The change computer industry's overall revenues is experiencing does not matter; the total of all shares of these revenues is 100 percent.

(E) Although revenue is an important factor, it is not the only factor in determining profits.

Question 7

The wholesale price of mustard has increased substantially in the last six months, whereas that of groundnut has decreased. Thus, although the retail price of mustard oil at grocery shops has not yet increased, it will predictably increase.

Which of the following, if true, is ill-conceived while drawing the conclusion above?

(A)   The operating costs of the grocery shops have been constant for the last three quarters.

(B)   The wholesale price of mustard is usually less than that of groundnut.

(C)   The cost of processing of mustard oil has decreased in the last year.

(D)   The cost of harvesting mustard has decreased in the last two quarters.

(E)   Per capita consumption of mustard oil has not changed significantly over last two years.

Question 8

Workers of a particular community X in the company raise a doubt over the bias against them in the recruitment. However, the record shows that nearly 65% of the applicants belonging to the community X have been employed in the company against nearly 55% of the applicants not belonging to community X. This, therefore, shows that the company is not biased against the community X.

The argument is vulnerable to which of the following criticism?

(A)   Nearly 85% of the applicants belonging to the community Y have been employed in the company.

(B)   According to the experts, nearly only 35% of the applicants not belonging to community X should have been employed.

(C)   There are a large number of workers employed in the company not belonging to community X.

(D)   The majority of the resumes of the workers belonging to the community X reach the company through an outside recruitment consultant.

(E)   Despite having large number of resumes of non-recruited applicants belonging to community X, the company invites applications from the workers not belonging to community X.

10.4.2 Answer-Key

(1) C	(4) C	(7) C
(2) E	(5) D	
(3) D	(6) D	(8) B

Solutions

10.4.3 Solutions

Question 1

Argument construction

Milton international school employs competent teachers and teaches through a revamped course curriculum. Still the social science and geography scores for grade 10 students are not satisfactory.

Conclusion: Social science and geography subjects should be taught in the native language.

Predict A Weakener

Predictive Weakener 1: Many students do not understand native language well.

Predictive Weakener 2: Competent text books on social science and geography are not available in the native language.

Predictive Weakener 3: Competent teachers who can teach social science and geography in native language are not available.

Answer choices explanation

(A) This option **strengthens rather than weakens** the argument. If the teacher's competence in native language is profound, it supports parent's suggestion.

(B) From the statement we cannot infer either that only a few students understand native language well or that more students understand native language well. It is not clear from the statement whether many students understand the native language well. This option is relevant, but **inconclusive.**

(C) This is the **correct** answer. If the final examination continues to be conducted in English language, social science and geography must be taught through English language only to allow the students to score. This option weakens the conclusion.

(D) This option **strengthens rather than weakens** the argument. If many grade 10 students in Milton International School were born and brought up in a town or culturally similar surrounding areas, it is likely that they must be well versed in the native language.

(E) The argument is concerned about social science and geography only and not about any other subjects. This option is **outside the scope** of the argument.

The correct answer is option C.

Question 2

Argument construction

The city's transport authorities have proposed following new contract to union negotiators:

1. Decrease the number of trains in service.
2. Do away with guards.
3. Increase the salaries of subway car drivers by 16%.

Objection to the proposal by union members is:

1. Not so much about the increased pay offer.

2. More the fear that guard-less trains would lead to mass redundancies despite the statutory obligation on the authorities to maintain full employment of all union members.

Note that the union does not voice any objection to accidents that may occur because of trains running without guards.

Conclusion: The new proposal will leave the guards jobless.

Predict A Weakener

The fear of the union members that needs to be relieved is that they will be left unemployed despite the obligation of the transport authorities to maintain full employment. This question asks us to weaken the fears of the union.

Predictive Weakener: Redundant guards will be absorbed at the same scale of pay that they are currently.

Answer choices explanation

(A)   The bonus offer will not get back the jobs. The guards would still be redundant.

(B)   Minimum redundancies are not zero redundancies. This will not alleviate the fears of the union. As long as there are redundancies, the union would protest.

(C)   This option may seem to address the fear to some extent, but not completely because only the competent redundant guards would be trained as drivers and retained in the job. This means that some guards who are deemed incompetent will be made redundant and will lose their jobs. This will not pacify the unions.

(D)   This option is **irrelevant.** This does not deal with either the unions or the guards.

(E)   This is the **correct** answer. The authority would adhere to contractual stipulations implies that the management will retain the jobs of guards, even though the capacity in which the guards will be retained is not mentioned. This is what union wants.

The correct answer is option E.

Question 3

Argument construction

People with modern views believe that those who have genuine belief in astrology are naive and unscientific in their mindset. But in the past, people with great intellect and scientific wisdom accepted astrology wholeheartedly. So, this marks a contrast in the thinking of two kinds of people.

Conclusion: There is no scientific basis for not accepting astrology.

Answer choices explanation

(A)   Debating for long whether astrology has any scientific base or not does not mean that any evidence that attempts to prove that it has evidence will be fallacious. This option is **inconclusive.** It sort of implies that astrology cannot be proven scientific.

(B)   This option is **inconsistent** and **inconclusive.** The premise states that in the past, the intellect of people was good enough to analyze and understand the nuances of astrology from a scientific perspective, so this option does not add any value to the argument.

(C)   This option **supports** the conclusion rather than weakens it.

(D)   This is the **correct** answer. This option states that with the passage of time, beliefs may change in the light of newer proof and accepted scientific notions. It shows that the past people may have had scientific reasons to believe in astrology when they did.

(E)   Nonscientific basis aspect is outside the scope of the argument.

The correct answer is option D.

Question 4

Argument construction

Statistics show that children who are beaten usually grow up believing that it is appropriate to beat their children as well. The intermediate conclusion is that—*this cycle is just one instance of violence perpetuating violence.*

But a certain religious sect claims that beating children is a form of discipline, not violence, and that this discipline is necessary to develop certain good habits in children, because children are too emotional and not capable of responding to situations with reason and logic until they reach adolescence.

Conclusion: Beating is necessary to develop certain good habits in children until they reach adolescence.

Predict A Weakener

The justification provided by advocates of child beating in the argument is that children must be beaten because they are not able to make logical conclusions and are unable to respond appropriately to their surroundings. The correct option must directly contest that assertion, weakening the argument. We have to show that child beating is unnecessary and that children have the requisite amount of intelligence to grow up to be responsible adults.

Predictive Weakener: Children are capable of responding to situations with reason and logic.

Answer choices explanation

(A)   This option is **strengthener.** It supports the reasoning of the child beaters who say that children are too emotional.

(B)   This option is **irrelevant.** If anything, it shows that there is an effective way to beat children.

(C)   This is the **correct** answer. It is aligned with our predictive weakener. It shows that beating children is not the solution.

(D)   This option is **irrelevant.** This just finds different reasons for beating children but does not argues against beating children.

(E)   This option is **rephrase** of the argument. We already know this. It's not weakening the argument.

The correct answer is option C.

Question 5

Argument construction

UK has hiked tax on tobacco and alcohol, making it proportionally the world's leading collector of excise tax. UK has defended the tax rise as being the only effective deterrent against tobacco and alcohol abuse.

However, critics claim that such policies are flawed as the vast money gathered annually funds so many governmental activities and expenses. They state that if tobacco and alcohol consumers were really discouraged, the government would have collapsed.

Conclusion: Hiking tax on tobacco and alcohol to deter against tobacco and alcohol abuse is pretense and is meant to gather money.

Predict A Weakener

The justification provided by the critics is that the government runs most of its activities using the money collected as taxes. They claim that if the taxes had deterred the users of alcohol and tobacco, the government would have run out of money. We need to contest these assertions by proving that government does not have a selfish motive in raising and collecting higher taxes. We can do this by either providing a valid use for the collected money or by showing that the high taxes do act as a deterrent for the smokers and drinkers.

Predictive Weakener 1: Sum needed to treat tobacco and alcohol related ailments are rising high.

Predictive Weakener 2: World over, similar countries like the UK have effectively control tobacco and alcohol abuse by hiking tax on them.

Answer choices explanation

(A) This option is **inconclusive.** The statement is tricky. At first sight it seems to be aligned with predictive weakener 1, but reading the statement carefully, we find that the sum gathered is not used up for the medical care for tobacco and alcohol abusers instead it is used for all. Secondly, the sum is also used up for other services apart from medical services. This implies that the government does indeed need the tax money to run its various agencies and that it does not really want to hike taxes to reduce smoking and drinking. This would strengthen the critics' arguments.

(B) This option is **strengthener.**

(C) This option is **out of scope**. Other country aspect is not within the scope of argument.

(D) This is the **correct** answer. It says that consumption of tobacco and alcohol use is gradually decreasing, so the incremental tax rises will compensate for the diminished revenues. It clearly advocates that the vested motive behind tax hike is not to gather money from tobacco and alcohol abusers. It proves that the tax from smokers and drinkers will go down, implying that smoking and drinking will be controlled, and that the government won't collapse because it will find other sources of money.

(E) This option is **inconclusive**. "Some" a quantity word range 1 to 99%. We cannot conclude on the basis of some.

The correct answer is option D.

Question 6

Argument construction

The computer manufactures' share of the industry revenues has declined from 75 percent three years ago to 60 percent today. But for the same period the revenue share of companies selling computer parts increased from 15 percent to 25 percent, while that of service companies increased from 10 percent to 15 percent.

Conclusion: The claim that computer-industry's revenues are declining is overstated.

In other words, we can say that the conclusion means that the computer-industry revenues are not declining.

Predict A Weakener

Let us understand the question stem. It states that the data given in the argument does not provide any evidence to support the conclusion .

Why does the author state this? The total revenue for the computer industry is made up of revenues from manufactures, computer parts, and service companies. It is to be noted that all the data points given are in percentages. Let us list down the scenario for today and for three-years-ago.

Scenario	Today	Three-Year-Before
Computer Manufacturers	60	75
Computer parts companies	25	15
Service companies	15	10
Total Revenue (%)	**100%**	**100%**

From the table, we cannot infer the absolute values of revenue three-year-ago and today. We can only infer that the percentage revenue share of computer manufactures is declining, while that for computer parts and service companies is rising. Hence, for all we know, the computer industries revenues may have decline or may have gone up. Just percentage shares imply no absolute information.

Answer choices explanation

(A)   The question is concerned about whether data given provides evidence to support the conclusion. The explanation for why the revenue shares of three sectors of the industry changed is not relevant. We have to concern ourselves with whether the industry revenues are declining.

(B)   This option is **inconclusive.** There is no reason to doubt the veracity or the consistency of data. We have to concern ourselves with whether the industry revenues are declining.

(C)   This option is **inconclusive** and **irrelevant** because it does not deal with the industry revenues.

(D)   This is the **correct** answer. The argument lacks the information about computer industry's overall revenue today and three-years-ago. It only provides information on the percentage shares of the various industry companies.

(E)   This information is **irrelevant.**

The correct answer is option D.

Question 7

Argument construction

The wholesale price of mustard has increased substantially in the last six months, whereas that of groundnut has decreased.

Conclusion: The retail price of mustard oil at grocery shops will increase.

Predict A Weakener

Predictive Weakener: For mustard oil, the successive elements of costs of mustards and oil, after the wholesaler sells mustards till it reaches the grocery shops, decreased significantly.

We need to show that for some reason, the cost of mustard and oil will not increase.

Answer choices explanation

(A)   If the operating costs of the grocery shops have been constant for the last three quarters, it will strengthen the conclusion rather than weaken it.

(B)   This option is **not relevant.** It compares the wholesale prices of mustard and groundnut.

(C)   This is the **correct** answer. If the cost of processing of mustard oil has decreased during the last year, it is likely that the distributor may have offset the increase in price, making the grocery shop not pay more to the distributors. So, it is probable that the oil price will not increase.

(D)   This option is **irrelevant.** Harvesting of mustard is an activity prior to wholesale trading. We are concerned about the effect on the prices of mustard oil after the mustards were harvested.

(E)   The statement means that per capita consumption of mustard oil is almost constant. This information does not help weaken the conclusion.

The correct answer is option C.

Question 8

Argument construction

Allegation of workers of community X: The company is biased against them in the recruitment.

Counter-evidence by the company: 65% of the applicants belonging to the community X have been employed in the company against 55% of the applicants not belonging to community X. (Read: more are employed from community X)

Conclusion: The company is not biased against the community X.

Predict A Weakener

Your job is to argue against the counter-evidence. What could be the flaw in the counter-evidence: *65% of the applicants belonging to the community X have been employed in the company against 55% of the applicants not belonging to community X.*

There could be two predictable flaws; one, 65% figure must be significantly more, or/and second, 55% figure must be significantly less.

Predictive Weakener 1: Significantly more than 65% of the applicants belonging to the community X should have been employed in the company.

Predictive Weakener 2: Significantly less than 55% of the applicants not belonging to the community X should have been employed in the company.

Answer choices explanation

(A)   This is **out of scope.** The argument focusing on the community Y is beyond the scope of argument.

(B)   This is the **correct** answer. It is in line with predictive weakener 2.

(C)   This is **inconclusive.** Stating that there are a large number of workers employed in the company not belonging to community X does not mean that there are a few workers employed in the company belonging to community X.

(D)   This is **irrelevant.** It tries to distract you by alluding that maybe due outside consultant's fault, this situation persisted.

(E)   Large number of resumes of non-recruited applicants belonging to community X maybe not fit for the job. The company has every right to invites new applications from the workers from any community including the community not belonging to community X.

The correct answer is option B.

Chapter 11

Evaluate the Argument

11.1 Evaluate the Argument Question type

Evaluate the Argument question asks you to select a question, data, or piece of information from among five options that would best help to establish the validity of the argument. In other words, you have to choose the option that confirms whether the argument is valid.

Evaluate the argument questions also belong to assumption based family. There may a logical gap in the argument. We recognize this gap by posing a question which when answered either increases or decreases the validity of the argument. So, we can say that *Evaluate the Argument questions are a combination of a Strengthen the Argument and a Weaken the Argument.*

Look at the image below. There is dialogue taking place between two people. What do you could be an evaluating question here?

Following illustration depicts your job for evaluate the argument question type.

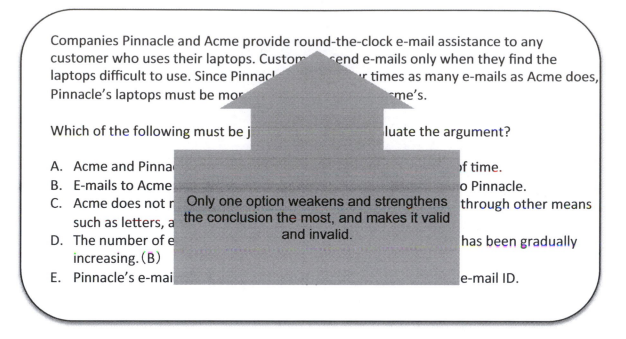

Companies Pinnacle and Acme provide round-the-clock e-mail assistance to any customer who uses their laptops. Custom... send e-mails only when they find the laptops difficult to use. Since Pinnac... ...r times as many e-mails as Acme does, Pinnacle's laptops must be mor... ...me's.

Which of the following must be j... ...luate the argument?

A. Acme and Pinna... ...f time.
B. E-mails to Acme... ...o Pinnacle.
C. Acme does not r... ...through other means such as letters, a... ...
D. The number of e... ...has been gradually increasing. (B)
E. Pinnacle's e-mai... ...e-mail ID.

Only one option weakens and strengthens the conclusion the most, and makes it valid and invalid.

Question Stem

Evaluate the argument question stem: Most evaluate question stems will contain one of the following:

"evaluate"; "determine"; "investigate"; "judge"; "assess"; "whether..."; Asking what would be "useful to know" or "necessary to establish" or "important to know" to determine the validity of the conclusion.

Evaluate the argument question stems may look like following.

· Which of the following must be judged in order to evaluate the argument?

· Which of the following would it be most important to know in establishing whether laptops of Pinnacle are difficult to use than Acme's?

· The answer to which of the following questions would help most to assess the argument?

Evaluate the argument question may use different phrases/words from the above, but the objective will be same—what is significant to study or assess or understand or validate the argument?

11.2   Process Of Solving Evaluate The Argument Questions

The 4-step approach is same as mentioned in Find the Assumption chapter.

The 4-step approach

(1) Recognize the question type

(2) Understand the argument construction

(3) Predict the qualifier

(4) Eliminate incorrect options

We have seen the 4–step approach to solve an ASP question. It is applicable to "Evaluate the Argument" type also. There is some additional work to be done at step 3.

Predict the qualifier

As we do in assumption questions, the third step is still to predict assumption(s), but in the next step you have to predict the evaluator(s) too in question form. Basically, we have to answer what additional information would help us establish the validity of assumption.

Let us see 'Pinnacle and Acme' argument. Say, the question stem is—"Which of the following must be judged in order to evaluate the argument?"

> Companies Pinnacle and Acme provide round-the-clock e-mail assistance to any customer who uses their laptops. Customers send e-mails only when they find the laptop difficult to use. Since Pinnacle receives four times as many e-mails as Acme receives, Pinnacle's laptops must be more difficult to use than Acme's.

11.2.1   Predicting Evaluator

We will predict few evaluators to validate the argument. As per the 3rd step, we need to first predict assumption(s). Well, we have done this exercise in ASP concepts chapter, so, we simply reproduce the same.

Predictive Assumption 1: Acme does not receive more complaints than Pinnacle does through other means such as letters or phones. An evaluating question framed from this assumption will be as follows:

Predictive Evaluator 1: Does Acme receive more complaints than Pinnacle through other means such as letters or phones?

If above question is answered correctly, it will validate the argument. Let us see how.

If Acme receives more complaints than Pinnacle receives through other means such as letters, and phones, then the conclusion that Pinnacle's laptops are difficult to use is <u>invalidated</u>.

Conversely, if Acme does not receive more complaints than Pinnacle does through other means such as letters, or phones, the conclusion that Pinnacle's laptops are difficult to use is <u>validated</u>.

This establishes that the above question is the correct question to raise to check the validity of the conclusion/argument.

One assumption may lead to multiple evaluating answer choices.

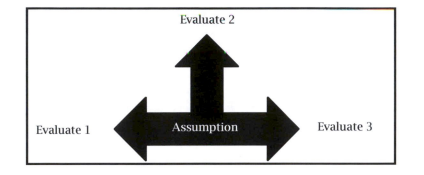

Let us see how.

Predictive Assumption 2: Acme does not sell significantly fewer laptops than Pinnacle.

Predictive Evaluator 2.1: Does Acme sell significantly fewer laptops than Pinnacle?

If Acme sells significantly fewer laptops than Pinnacle, it is logical that Acme will receive fewer e-mails than Pinnacle, and then the conclusion that Pinnacle's laptops are difficult to use will be <u>invalidated</u>, since the comparison is illogical and size-biased.

Conversely, if Acme does not sell significantly fewer laptops than Pinnacle, it is logical that the number of laptops sold by Acme are comparable to the number sold by Pinnacle, and then the conclusion that Pinnacle's laptops are difficult to use is <u>validated</u>.

This establishes that the above question is the correct question to raise to check the validity of the conclusion/argument.

Predictive Evaluator 2.2: Does Pinnacle sell significantly more laptops to newbies than Acme?

Predictive Evaluator 2.3: Does Pinnacle sell significantly more high-end configured laptops than Acme?

By now you must have gone through "Pinnacle and Acme" argument few times. Try answering above questions once with a "yes" and then with a "no". You will notice that the above questions are the correct questions to raise to check the validity of the conclusion/argument because one answer will strengthen the conclusion and the other one will weaken the conclusion.

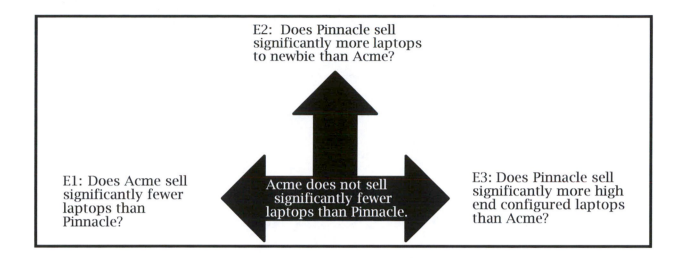

11.2.2   The Evaluation Test

You may come across couple of close contenders for the correct answer in a particular question. To pick one of those two apply the evaluation test.

We have so far understood that the correct option is a question which when answered will validate the argument.

As per the evaluation test, you have to answer the close contenders once with **yes** and then with **no**. The correct option's answers will strengthen and weaken the conclusion. For example, if the answer "yes" weakens the conclusion, the answer "no" will strengthen the conclusion. This can work vice versa too. However, in wrong options, both answers will either weaken or strengthen or do nothing. The wrong options can also be irrelevant to the conclusion. Only the correct answer choice will reflect its **bi-polar** behavior. Let us see this in action!

We take two close contenders from 'Pinnacle and Acme' argument – options A and B.

Option A: *Does Acme receive more complaints than Pinnacle through other means such as letters or phones?*

Answer with yes: Yes, Acme receives more complaints than Pinnacle receives through other means such as letters, and phones.

Since Acme receives more complaints through letters, and phones, while Pinnacle receives through e-mails, the conclusion that the laptops of Pinnacle are difficult to use is **weakened** or **invalidated.**

Answer with no: No, Acme does not receive more complaints than Pinnacle receives through other means such as letters, and phones.

Since Acme does not receive more complaints through letters or phones, while Pinnacle receives more complaints through e-mails, the conclusion that laptops of Pinnacle are difficult to use is **strengthened or validated.**

Option A reflects its **bi-polar** behavior, hence the correct answer.

Option B: Is the length of e-mails to Acme, on average, more than that to Pinnacle?

Answer with yes: Yes, the length of e-mails to Acme, on average, is more than that to Pinnacle.

Does this strengthen or weaken the conclusion?

No. The conclusion is based on the number of e-mails rather than the length of e-mails.

Answer with no: No, the length of e-mails to Acme, on average, is not more than that to Pinnacle.

Does the 'answer with no' strengthen or weaken the conclusion? No; hence this cannot be the correct answer option.

Example

Questions

11.3 Examples

Example 1

McDougals and Deep Fry are two fast food chains locked in a bitter contest to dominate the minimal pay yet labor intensive, fast food business in the north east states. Both chains are eager to expand but McDougals lacks capital because it spends almost forty percent of its gross profits on wage bills. To raise funds to finance expansion, McDougals plans to cut the wages of newly hired staff by 12% and the wages of experienced staff by 10%.

The answer to which of the following is the most important to know in order to raise fund as per the proposed plan?

(A) Are the areas in which MacDougals intends to expand already served by a successful fast food chain?

(B) Is wage rate a crucial factor in attracting fast food business staff?

(C) Has McDougals acquired a reputation for good service and food quality?

(D) Has Deep Fry planned to open two branches for every one opened by McDougals?

(E) Has the Union of Restaurant Workers protested the proposed wage cut?

Argument construction

The argument is easy to understand.

Conclusion: By cutting the wages of newly hired staff by 12% and of experienced staff by 10%, McDougals can save funds to finance its expansion.

Predict an Evaluator

The question specifically asks us to evaluate only the fundraising plan and its chances of success with the given plan. So, we have to find an option that will reveal whether McD's fundraising is likely to work. Let's put ourselves into McDougal's place and figure out the reasoning and assumptions behind the proposed wage cuts for raising funds. McD is assuming that the employees would go along with the wage cuts and not quit. McD is also assuming that the given amount of wage cuts would be sufficient for its expansion plans.

Predictive Assumption 1: Despite cutting the wages, McDougals can hire new staff, and retain experienced staff.

Predictive Evaluator 1: Can McDougals hire new staff, and retain experienced staff despite cutting the staff's wages?

Predictive Assumption 2: By cutting the wages of newly hired staff by 12% and the wages of experienced staff by 10%, McDougals can sufficiently save the funds to finance expansion.

Predictive Evaluator 2: Is the sum accrued out of wage cut sufficient enough to finance expansion?

Answer choices explanation

(A) This option is **irrelevant**. It does not answer to the question whether McDougals must cut wages to raise funds. This deals with another scenario.

(B) This is the **correct** answer. This is aligned with predictive evaluator 1. If wage is a crucial factor in fast food business, it follows that attrition of competent workforce may severely affect McDougals' operations. If we answer "yes" to this option, the conclusion is weakened, while "no" strengthens the conclusion.

(C) This option is **irrelevant** to determine whether McDougals wage cutting will work to fund its expansion.

(D) This option is **irrelevant** to determine whether McDougals wage cutting will work to fund its expansion.

(E) This option is a tricky one, but is **inconclusive.** Even if the Union of Restaurant Workers protests the proposed wage cut, it does not necessarily mean that the Union has **rejected** the wage cut. Option B is the more important to know to determine whether McDougals wage cutting will work to fund its expansion. This option will become operative once the plan is deemed feasible.

The correct answer is option B.

Example 2

The music industry has demanded that the government pass legislation preventing internet-based companies from playing music over the net. Such services invite consumers to illegally download music to CD recorders and there by damage sales of legally marketed CDs. This, they claim, takes as much as 25% of their potential profits and harms artists struggling to launch their careers.

Which of the following need to be evaluated to validate the conclusion?

(A) Are the internet companies willing to pay for the rights of music they play on the net?

(B) Has the reduction in sales of recorded music CDs led to reduced tax bills for music companies?

(C) Is the quality of pirated CDs more or less equal to that of conventionally recorded CDs?

(D) Does piracy mainly target world famous groups, singers and musicians?

(E) Is the price of pirated CDs fractionally low compared to conventional CDs?

Argument construction

The music industry wants that the government must prevent internet-based companies from playing music over the net. Since the consumers illegally download music to CD recorders, this eats up the sales of legally marketed CDs. The music industry claims that it eats up as much as 25% of their potential profits and thereby harms artists struggling to launch their careers.

Conclusion: The government must prevent internet-based companies from playing music over the net because it reduces profits and harms struggling artists.

Predict an Evaluator

Based on our understanding of the argument, we can draw some predictive assumptions and its associated evaluators.

Predictive Assumption 1: Most music piracy is taking place from internet-based companies.

Predictive Evaluator 1: Is most music piracy is taking place from internet-based companies?

Predictive Assumption 2: Most people do not wish to spend money on buying conventional CDs.

Predictive Evaluator 2: Do most people avoid spending money on buying conventional CDs, yet enjoy the music freely available over the internet?

Predictive Assumption 3: There is no way using technology that the internet companies can continue airing the music while preventing the illegal downloading.

Predictive Evaluator 3: Is there is any way using technology that the internet companies can continue airing the music while preventing the illegal downloading?

Answer choices explanation

(A) This is the **correct** answer. Answering "yes" to the question will weaken the conclusion implying that there is no need to prevent the internet companies from playing music over the net because the music companies can earn from them; answering "no" will strengthen the conclusion implying that internet companies will continue to play the pirated music over the net harming the sales of CDs.

(B) If the reduction in sales of recorded music CDs led to reduced tax bills for music companies, we cannot conclusively infer that the reduction in sales of recorded music CDs is due to internet piracy. There may be a number of reasons why the sales plummeted. This option does not qualify to be evaluated because "yes" or "no" will be irrelevant to the conclusion.

(C) If the quality of the pirate CDs is more or less equal to that of conventionally recorded CDs, people will be motivated to illegally download the music; it validates the conclusion. Conversely, even if the quality is bearable, not as good as the convention CDs, people may still choose to download from the net. The conclusion is not invalidated. This option does not reflect the requisite bi-polar behavior.

(D) Whether piracy mainly targets only the world famous groups, singers and musicians or the newcomers, in either case it will eat up the profits of music companies. This option does not qualify to be evaluated because "yes" or "no" will be irrelevant to the conclusion.

(E) If the price of pirated CDs is significantly lower than that of conventional CDs, people will be motivated to illegally download the music; it validates the conclusion. Conversely, even if the price is relatively low, though not fractionally low, than that of the convention CDs, people may still choose to download from the net. The conclusion is not invalidated. This option does not reflect the requisite bi-polar behavior.

The correct answer is option A.

Example 3

Residents of Delta City want to have a cleaner environment in their city and a better quality of life. This means construction of more parks and greenways in the city center. If they build more parks and designate certain areas as greenways, however, housing prices will go up in the long term as less land will remain available for habitation. The rise in housing prices will then have a negative impact on their quality of life as they will have to pay more for the same amount of space.

The answer to which of the following questions would be LEAST relevant to evaluating whether the residents indeed face the choice the author says they do?

(A) Could park and greenway developments be carried out under an alternative plan without increasing the cost of living?

(B) Would development of parks and greenways benefit the residents of other cities?

(C) Would the jobs created to develop the parks and greenways be filled by the residents of Delta City?

(D) Do residents of Delta City support or oppose development of these parks and greenways?

(E) Will the cost of housing remain at current prices without development of parks and greenways?

Argument construction

The argument is easy to understand. The citizens want better life and environment. However, doing so will raise the real estate prices.

Conclusion: Allocating land for parks will negatively affect residents' lives.

Predict an Evaluator

This question is to find the least relevant option that helps to evaluate. Unlike in standard 'Evaluate the Argument' type of questions, in this question you will find 4 options that qualify as evaluators. The option that is not an evaluator is the answer.

Predictive Assumption 1: The benefit derived out of building parks is less than the negative impact of the rise in housing prices.

Predictive Evaluator 1: Is the benefit derived out of building parks less than the negative impact of the rise in housing prices?

Predictive Assumption 2: Housing prices are either not rising or rising at a slower rate.

Predictive Evaluator 2: Are housing prices either not rising or rising at a slower rate?

Basically, the author says that building parks would mean less benefit to the resident than we think it is. Hence, his conclusion is that the parks will have a negative impact. A good evaluator in this question will be anything that shows that parks can have positive impact too (or negative) as long as it shows both strengthen and weaken. Anything that shows that parks may actually not benefit the residents at all will only strengthen the conclusion but not weaken it. Thus, there's nothing "bipolar" about it. We must orient our thinking towards the option that does not show any benefits for the residents. That option would be the correct answer.

Answer choices explanation

(A)   This option qualifies to be **evaluated**. It talks about reduction in cost—a matter of interest to the residents and the "yes/no" answer to this would strengthen and weaken the conclusion.

(B)   This is the **correct** answer. This option does not qualify to be evaluated. It talks about benefit to other city—a matter of no interest to the residents.

(C)   This option qualifies to be **evaluated**. It talks about job creation—a matter of interest to the residents and the "yes/no" answer to this would strengthen and weaken the conclusion.

(D)   This option qualifies to be **evaluated**. It talks about apprehensions of residents-a matter of concern to the residents and the "yes/no" answer to this would strengthen and weaken the conclusion.

(E)   This option qualifies to be **evaluated**. It talks about rise in house prices—a matter of interest to the residents and the "yes/no" answer to this would strengthen and weaken the conclusion.

The correct answer is option B.

Example 4

Privatization of the utilities has led to higher prices despite promises that it would lower prices. The streamlining and paring down of workforces may well have reduced costs but these savings have been used to pay the dividends of shareholders instead of being passed on to customers. The amount of capital investment made has also been acquired, particularly in relation to water supplies. Consumer associations claim that water companies are overcharging consumers. In answer to such accusations, the companies claim that the higher charges are due to the constant need for repairs and maintenance.

Which of the following must be studied in order to validate the conclusion put forth by the water company?

(A) Are companies legally obliged to supply water regardless of cost?

(B) Have unusual weather conditions resulted in a severe water shortage in many states?

(C) Does the number of paying customers far outnumber the number of non-paying customers?

(D) Was service prior to privatization worse than the service currently provided?

(E) Is 'Repairs and Maintenance cost' a secondary cost in water supply and management cost?

Argument construction

Privatization of the utilities was done so that the bills would go down, but on the contrary, it went up. The restructuring of workforces in the companies may have reduced the costs, but the savings out of this were used to pay the dividends of shareholders and not passed on to the customers. Capital investment has also been attained back, especially in the case of water companies. Consumer associations claim that water companies are overcharging consumers. The companies refute the claim by stating that the higher charges are due to the constant need for repairs and maintenance.

Conclusion: The higher water bills charged to consumers are due to the constant need for repairs and maintenance.

Predict an Evaluator

We must validate the conclusion that the higher bills charged are due to the constant need for repairs and maintenance. What would justify the frequent need for repairs and maintenance? It may be that machineries and pipelines are old; maybe previous company did poorly on maintenance.

Predictive Assumption 1: Water supply machineries and pipelines have aged.

Predictive Evaluator 1: Have the water supply machineries and pipelines aged?

Predictive Assumption 2: Previous company that supplied the water maintained water supply machineries and pipelines poorly.

Predictive Evaluator 2: Did the previous company that supplied the water maintain water supply machineries and pipelines poorly?

Answer choices explanation

(A)   This option is **inconclusive**. We have to judge the conclusion that states that the reason for overcharging is excessive repairs. This option does not relate to the reason for over-charging of the companies. This option poses a moral question. If we answer **yes,** that the companies are **obliged** to supply water regardless of the cost, the conclusion remains that they are overcharging because of repairs. If we answer no, that the companies are **not obliged** to supply water regardless of the cost, the conclusion remains that they are overcharging because of repairs. This option's range does not affect the conclusion at all.

(B)   This option is tricky. 'Unusual weather conditions' may be inferred to wear and tear to the equipment and water pipes. However, the option states that the weather causes water shortage. Our conclusion does not deal with complaint about water shortage but about overcharging in the current water scenario. If we say yes, the weather causes shortage, the conclusion that there is a lot of repair work is unharmed. If we say no , that the weather does not cause water shortage, the conclusion about extra costs of repairs still remains intact. Hence, this option is not the right answer.

(C)   This option is **irrelevant.** It has no relevance to the claim. We are discussing the company's charging being valid or invalid and not the customers paying those bills or not.

(D)   This option is the **correct** answer. If we answer **"yes",** that before privatization, the government too provided bad service, the conclusion that there is a lot of repair work to be done can be justified **(strengthened)**. If we say **"no",** that before privatization, the government did not provide bad service; the conclusion that there is a lot of repair work to be done is invalid **(weakened)**. Hence, determining the answer to this option will help us judge the validity of the conclusion.

(E)   This option is also tricky one, but is **inconclusive**.

Let us apply the evaluation test.

Yes, 'Repairs and Maintenance' cost is a secondary cost in water supply and management cost. The conclusion that excessive charges are due to repairs remains intact.

No, 'Repairs and Maintenance' cost is not a secondary cost in water supply and man-agement cost. It does not mean that it is primary cost; it may be tertiary cost too. The conclusion that excessive charges are due to repairs remains intact.

The correct answer is option D.

Practice

Questions

11.4 Practice Questions

11.4.1 Questions

Question 1

Many small children have problems with nightmares. Recent studies made by psychologists show that these nightmares can be reduced by letting the children fall asleep with the lights on. Two groups of children took part in one of these studies. The group that fell asleep with the lights off indicated that they had more nightmares than the group that fell asleep with the lights on.

Which of the following questions would be most useful for evaluating the conclusion?

(A) Are nightmares more prevalent among children than among adults?

(B) Did teenagers who fall asleep with the lights on had the same number of nightmares as before?

(C) Are children who play violent computer games more likely to have nightmares?

(D) Did children who previously had problems with nightmares show a markedly decreased incidence of nightmares after five months of falling asleep with the lights on?

(E) Do children with a high level of self-esteem have fewer problems with nightmares than children with average levels of self-esteem do?

Question 2

You have seen the following question previously. We present to you its 'evaluate the argument' version.

Recent research into obesity suggests that although certain amphetamines are capable of quelling physical hunger pangs, they also have a mood altering affect that frequently leads to food binging. Of the 63 patients that took part in tests carried by Hopkins Institute scientists, 43 admitted to periodically binging to assuage depression and at the conclusion of the eight week trial were found to have gained weight. From these results, scientists have concluded that appetite quelling amphetamines are often counter-productive and should be prescribed to patients only in controlled environments.

Which of the following would help best to assess the argument?

(A) Whether all amphetamines cause depression.

(B) Whether the patients in controlled environments have been known to binge secretly.

(C) Whether the degree of weight gain varied according to the individual patient.

(D) Whether some of the patients who gained weight were given higher doses of amphetamines than those who lost weight.

(E) Whether the other patients were also reported as suffering from depression.

Question 3

The recent increase in the value of the dollar is worrying US exporters who see themselves as being undercut by foreign competition. The rise was triggered by an upward interest rate modification declared by the Federal Reserve but the rise would not have occurred had there not been simultaneously announced cutbacks in this year's defense spending budget.

Which of the following should most qualify to be evaluated to test the conclusion?

(A) Whether past increases in defense spending, were frequently followed by simultaneous rise in interest and decreased value of the dollar.

(B) Whether the recent decline in export sales is more because US goods are not able to manage very price sensitive foreign marketplace.

(C) Whether defense cutbacks are often the result of economic declines coupled with budget deficits.

(D) Whether a rise in the percentage of export trade captured by foreign competitors often results in increased defense spending to emphasize US military superiority.

(E) Whether an over-valued dollar is sometimes accompanied by a rise in US exports of IT goods.

11.4.2 Answer-Key

(1) D | (2) B | (3) A

Solutions

11.4.3   Solutions

Question 1

Argument construction

The argument is easy to understand.

Conclusion: Children sleeping with the lights on will have significantly fewer nightmares that those sleeping with the lights off.

Predict An Evaluator

Predictive Assumption 1: Both groups studied to have nearly the same number of nightmares before the experiment.

Predictive Evaluator 1: Did both groups have nearly the same number of nightmares before the experiment?

This question is necessary to evaluate because if the group that slept with lights on already had significantly fewer nightmares before the experiment, the conclusion is invalidated.

Predictive Assumption 2: Repeating the experiment by switching the groups will yield the same result.

Predictive Evaluator 2: Will repeating the experiment by switching the groups yield the same result?

Predictive Assumption 3: Repeating the experiment at later dates will yield the same result.

Predictive Evaluator 3: Will repeating the experiment at later dates yield the same result?

Answer choices explanation

(A)   This option is **out of scope.** Adults are beyond the scope of the argument.

(B)   This option is tricky. If teenagers who fall asleep with the lights on had the same number of nightmares as before, the conclusion is invalidated. Conversely, if teenagers who fall asleep with the lights on did not have the same number of nightmares as before, then we cannot conclude whether they had fewer nightmares now than before. So, the option only weakens the conclusion but does not strengthen it.

Similarly, note that the argument compares the number of nightmares between two groups—those who slept with lights on vs. those who slept with lights off, but option B compares the number of nightmares before and after within the group that slept with lights on.

Also, this option is ruled out on the basis of its focus on 'teenagers' only, which is a sub-set of the group "children". 'Teenagers' cannot be representative of the entire group.

(C)   This option is **out of scope**. Video games are beyond the scope of the argument.

(D)   This is the **correct** answer. If children who previously had problems with nightmares showed a markedly decreased incidence of nightmares after five months of falling asleep with the lights on, the conclusion is **validated**. Conversely, if teenagers who previously had problems with nightmares did not show a markedly decreased incidence of nightmares after five months of falling asleep with the lights on, then conclusion is **invalidated**. It shows the bi-polar nature of the option. It strengthens and weakens the conclusion in its two possibilities.

Also, it is aligned with predictive evaluator 3.

(E)   This option is **out of scope.** The argument deals solely with the effect of lights on reduction of nightmares in children and not with self-esteem.

The correct answer is option D.

Question 2

Argument construction

A research into obesity suggests that although certain amphetamines are capable of suppressing physical hunger pains, they also have a mood altering affect that frequently leads to food binging. Of the 63 patients that took part in tests carried by Hopkins Institute scientists, 43 admitted to periodically binging to soften depression and at the conclusion of the eight week trial were found to have gained weight.

Conclusion: Appetite quelling amphetamines are often counter-productive and should be prescribed to patients only in controlled environments.

Predict An Evaluator

Concluding that amphetamines should be prescribed to patients only in controlled environments implies that there is an underlying assumption here—food binging will not be allowed in controlled environments.

Predictive Assumption: Patients will not be allowed food binging in controlled environments.

Predictive Evaluator: Whether the patients will be allowed to binge secretly in controlled environments.

Answer choices explanation

(A)   This option is **irrelevant.** It is not related to food binging. The conclusion remains intact whether you answer "yes" or "no", because the argument specified certain amphetamines.

(B)   This is the **correct** answer. It is aligned with the predictive evaluator. Answering "yes" will weaken the conclusion, while "no" will strengthen it.

(C)   This option is **out of scope.** Degree of weight is beyond the scope of argument. The conclusion remains intact because whether you answer "yes" or "no".

(D) This option is **out of scope.** Degree of doses of amphetamines is beyond the scope of argument. The conclusion remains intact because whether you answer "yes" or "no". Note that when you answer "yes", the answer is not that **all** patients who gained weights were given a higher dose of amphetamines, but the answer is that yes, **some** patients who gained weight were given more amphetamines. The "yes" answer does not impact the conclusion because only some of those who gained weight were given more amphetamines.

(E) This option is **irrelevant.** The conclusion remains intact because whether you answer "yes" or "no". The answer "yes" does not change the fact that 43 gained weight and neither does the answer "no".

The correct answer is option B.

Question 3

Argument construction

US exporters are worried about the recent increase in the value of the dollar. They claim that because of high price of dollar they lose business to foreign competition.

The rise in dollar was triggered by simultaneous occurrence of an upward interest rate modification declared by the Federal Reserve, and cutbacks in this year's defense spending budget.

Conclusion: The rise in dollar was triggered by the simultaneous occurrence of an upward interest rate and cutbacks in this year's defense spending budget.

Predict An Evaluator

From the argument, we can infer that the effect—rise in dollar was triggered by *cause— upward interest rate modification + simultaneously announced cutbacks in defense spending budget.*

Predictive Assumption 1: Upward interest rate modification with cutbacks in defense spending budget mostly trigger a rise in dollar.

Predictive Evaluator 1: Whether upward interest rate modification with cutbacks in defense spending budget mostly trigger a rise in dollar.

Predictive Assumption 2: The rise in dollar is not due to other reasons.

Predictive Evaluator 2: Whether the rise in dollar is not due to other reasons.

Answer choices explanation

(A) This is the **correct** answer. This option is the inverse of our predictive evaluator 1. The answer to this question will prove whether a cause and effect relationship of the type mentioned in the conclusion of the argument exists. If we answer "yes" to this, the conclusion is strengthened, and "no" will weaken the conclusion because 'no' will prove that the argument is making a flimsy connection for the three events (rise in price of dollar, upward interest rate modification and cutbacks in defense spending).

(B)   This option is a **rephrase.** We already know this from premise: *The recent increase in the value of the dollar is worrying US exporters who are seeing themselves undercut by foreign competition.* Thus we need not determine this information to evaluate the validity of the conclusion.

(C)   This option is **tricky but incorrect.** It sounds like this option is also discussing the three events that are mentioned in cause and effect relationship in the argument's conclusion but this option is incorrect because it does not specifically discuss those three events. It discusses generally the three events, and requires us to make a lot of assumptions, not sanctioned by the argument, before we can accept it as correct. To say economic decline is linked to dollar price, we will need to assume that economic decline always affects dollar price. Similar assumptions need to be made about budget cuts and upward interest rate modification. Hence, this option is incorrect because by itself it proves nothing. If we say "yes" or "no", the conclusion remains intact.

(D)   This option is **irrelevant** too. It suffers from the same flaws as option C.

(E)   This option is **irrelevant** too. It establishes the relationship between dollar and exports of IT goods alone and it out of scope.

The correct answer is option A.

Chapter 12

Resolve the Paradox Argument

12.1   Resolve the Paradox Argument Question type

 Resolve the Paradox or Explain the Discrepancy questions consist only of premises, mostly factual statements, and sometimes claims. Since arguments contain only premises, the conclusion is missing from the arguments. The two premises presented will be contradictory in some way, and will seem almost mutually exclusive, creating confusion. Resolve the Paradox questions belong to evidence based family.

Frequently, the argument will employ phrases or words denoting contradiction, such as "surprisingly", "yet", "however", "although", "paradoxically", and "but".

Your job is to select one of the five true premises given as the options that will act as a third premise, and resolve the paradox. The option you choose should address both the facts without denying either fact and justify why the contradiction is happening. If you read the argument along with the correct premise, the argument will make complete sense.

Look at dialogue between two people in the image. What could be a resolution here?

The following illustration depicts your job for Resolve the Paradox question type.

In 1999, America Mart, which previously sold merchandise only through retail outlets, began selling on the intern███le keeping its retail stores open. Although total sales increased in 1999████████s than the profits in 1998.

Which of the following, if tru███████to explaining why America Mart's profits were more in 1998 th███

A. There was a███████████████████at consumers had to pay on all re█████
B. A greater nu██████████████████ere made available to previous cus████████████████ped at America Mart before.
C. In 1999, Am██████████████████ased by a smaller amount than███████████████et site.
D. Customers who had never purchased products from America Mart purchased, on average, fewer products in 1999 than previous customers did.
E. The increase in costs due to setting up the web site in 1999 was greater than the increase in revenue from sales in 1999.

Only one option will resolve the paradox.

Question Stem

Most discrepancy question stems will include some form of the words "explain" or "resolve" and the vast majority will also contain the words "if true." This means that you have to attempt the question keeping in mind that the information given in the options is unquestionable and is to be taken as fact.

A typical 'resolve the paradox' question stem looks like the following.

· Which of the following, if true, most helps to resolve the paradox described above?

- Which of the following, if true, most helps to explain the discrepancy described in the argument?

- Which of the following, if true, best reconciles the apparent discrepancy described above?

- Which of the following hypotheses best justifies the contradiction occurred above?

12.2   Process Of Solving Resolve The Paradox Questions

The 4-step approach is same as in Find the Assumption chapter.

The 4-step approach

   (1) Recognize the question type

   (2) Understand the argument construction

   (3) Predict the qualifier

   (4) Eliminate incorrect options

First 2 steps are same for resolve the paradox questions. Let us jump directly to predict the qualifier step.

Predict the qualifier

We already are familiar with this step. Let us see how to predict a "resolution" in an argument.

> In 1999, America Mart, which previously sold merchandise only through retail outlets, began selling on the internet while keeping its retail stores open. Although total sales increased in 1999, profits were less than the profits in 1998.
>
> Which of the following, if true, contributes most to explaining why America Mart's profits were more in 1998 than in 1999?

Understand the argument: The argument is easy to understand. It says that in the year 1999, America Mart (AM), began selling merchandise over the internet while keeping its retail stores open. Despite the total sales having increased in the year 1999, profits were less than the profits in the year 1998.

The paradox: Sales in the 1999 is higher than the sales in the 1998. The common knowledge plays a role here. It is implied that, when sales increase, profits increase proportionately. However, the argument states that the profits decreased.

To resolve the paradox, we must predict possible factor(s) that reduced the profits despite good sales. This phenomenon is not new in the modern world. The possible reasons could be that AM sold merchandise at relatively low sales price to promote the website, or that the investment (startup costs) to establish the internet portal was substantially high affecting profits.

Predictive Resolutor 1: AM sold merchandise at significantly low sales price.

Predictive Resolutor 2: Profit accrued from the increased sale could not offset the investment made to establish internet portal.

Let us see the 5 options to this question.

(A) There was a two percent increase in sales tax in 1999 that consumers had to pay on all retail purchases.

(B) A greater number of promotions for their internet sites were made available to previous customers than to people who had never shopped at America Mart before.

(C) In 1999, America Mart's wholesale purchase costs increased by a smaller amount than did the selling price of goods on their internet site.

(D) Customers who had never purchased products from America Mart purchased, on average, fewer products in 1999 than previous customers did.

(E) The increase in costs due to setting up the web site in 1999 was greater than the increase in revenue from sales in 1999.

Let us understand each option.

(A) Increased tax was absorbed by the customers, and not by AM, implying no extra cost for AM per product. From AM's perspective, the revenue per product did not decrease. This option does not help explain the paradox.

(B) This is not relevant. Who purchased more out of the promotions is not relevant as long as the increased sales happened. Also, greater number of promotions on internet site is not sufficient enough to conclude that AM spent huge sums on the promotions, causing lower profits.

(C) This option is an opposite answer. All it means is that in 1999, input costs increased by a smaller amount, but the selling price of the goods on their internet site increased by a relatively larger amount. This further strengthens that profits in 1999 should be more than those in 1998. It increases the discrepancy rather than resolves.

(D) This option is also an opposite answer. This option implies that in 1999, first-time customers of AM purchased fewer products than did old-timers. This fact is irrelevant as the sale from first-time customers to AM is still additional revenue. This further strengthens that profits in 1999 should have been more than those in 1998. It increases the discrepancy rather than resolves it.

(E) This is the **correct** answer. It is aligned with our predictive resolutor 2. The increase in costs could not be offset by the increase in revenue leading to relatively lower profits in the year 1999. It explains the paradox.

Example

Questions

12.3 Examples

Example 1

In the years of 2000, nine percent of the refrigerators built by WhirlBlue required major compressor and condenser coil repairs. However, the corresponding figure for the refrigerators that WhirlBlue built in the 90s was only four percent.

Which of the following, if true, most helps to explain the discrepancy?

(A) Government regulation of white goods usually requires all refrigerators, whether old or new, to be inspected for carbon monoxide emission levels prior to sales.

(B) Owners of new refrigerators service their refrigerators more regularly than do the owners of old refrigerators.

(C) The older a refrigerator is, the more likely it is to be discarded for scrap rather than repaired when major compressor and condenser coil work is needed to keep the refrigerator in operation.

(D) The refrigerators that WhirlBlue built in the years 2000s incorporated simplified compressor and condenser coil designs that made the compressor and condenser coils less complicated than those of earlier models.

(E) Many of the repairs that were performed on the refrigerators that WhirlBlue built in the 90s could have been avoided if periodic routine maintenance had been performed.

Argument Construction

Major compressor and condenser coil repairs were performed on 9 % of the refrigerators built by WhirlBlue in the years of 2000. However, the corresponding figure for the refrigerators that WhirlBlue had built in the 90s was only 4 %.

Predictive Resolutor

The paradox: Usually, it is logical to infer that if any electronic products, say, refrigerators, are in use for a relatively longer duration of time, those products will require more repairs and service than those in use for shorter duration of time. But the facts presented in the argument contradict the typical situation.

When comparing two things, groups, individual or in this case a product, a reliable issue to check is whether the two things being compared are similar and comparable.

What if the refrigerators produced in the 90s were superior in technology, and manufacturing techniques compared to its counterparts, produced in the years of 2000, it is logical that the ones produced lately will invite more repairs and services than the earlier ones. This resolves the paradox.

Predictive Resolutor: The refrigerators produced in the 90s were superior in quality compared to the ones produced in the years of 2000.

Answer choices explanation

(A)   The stated regulation is applicable to both old and new refrigerator. This information does not help to resolve the discrepancy.

(B)   This option is an opposite answer. If owners of new refrigerators service their refrigerators more often than do the owners of old refrigerators, it is likely that new refrigerators would perform better. Instead of resolving the discrepancy, the information further worsens the discrepancy.

(C)   This is the **correct** answer. The gap of 5 percentage points (9%-4%) could be because many old refrigerators must have been discarded for scrap rather than put up for repairs when major compressor and condenser coil work is needed to keep them in operation. Although this option is not aligned with our predictive resolutor, it rightly differentiates the comparable products in their characteristics implying that had the figures of discarded refrigerator been taken into account, the percentage figures of 1999, and 2000 were comparable. It helps to explain the discrepancy by providing a reason there seems to be more of the latest refrigerators for repairs.

(D)   This option is an opposite answer. If the refrigerators built in the 2000s had incorporated simplified compressor and condenser coil designs, it was likely that new refrigerators would have performed better. Instead of resolving the discrepancy, this information further worsens the discrepancy.

(E)   This option is an opposite answer. If many of the repairs on the refrigerators built in the years 1990s could have been avoided had periodic routine maintenance been performed, the 4% figure would have been further low making the argument unexplainable.

The correct answer is option C.

Example 2

Automobile manufacturers defend their substitution of steel frames in cars with cheaper plastic components by claiming that consumer demand for light cars with crumple zones rather than corporate profit motives led to the substitution. However, carbon reinforced tubing, which is lighter than steel but stronger, was not employed.

Which of the following, if true, best explains the exclusion of carbon tubing from the market while maintaining the manufacturers' claim?

(A) Most consumers prefer steel to plastic components because of their durability.

(B) Prototypes of vehicles with carbon tubing have not been shown at major auto shows.

(C) The manufacturing process for plastic frame components and carbon tubing is quite different from that of traditional steel frames.

(D) Automobile manufacturers have not yet resolved certain quality control problems in production of carbon tubing in high volumes.

(E) Carbon is more expensive than steel.

Argument Construction

Automobile manufacturers substituted steel frames in cars with cheaper plastic components. They claim that because of consumers' desire for light cars with crumple zones, they chose plastic and not because of profit motives. However, carbon reinforced tubing (CRT), which is lighter than steel but stronger, was not used instead of plastic.

This question is different from the typical resolve the paradox questions. We have to resolve the discrepancy, but we cannot attack the manufacturer's claim as the question asks us to preserve the claim.

Predictive Resolutor

The paradox: The paradox is that despite CRT being lighter yet stronger than steel was not used instead of plastic to substitute steel frames in cars, if, as the manufacturers claim, the consumers want lighter cars.

There are two underlying assumptions here—one, CRT *is stronger than plastic*. In both aspects—weight and strength, CRT scores well enough, yet not it was not used instead of plastic, which is not as strong as CRT. The manufacturers used plastic but not CRT and in defending plastic, they said that profits did **not** drive the decision.

So, in resolving the paradox, we have to defend the manufacturers for not using CRT without using higher costs or profits as the reason.

Our main task is to provide a non-financial reason for not using CRT. One such reason could be that the manufacturers do not have dependable supplier of CRT; the paradox will be resolved if we can find some production level problems in CRT.

Predictive Resolutor: The manufacturers do not have dependable supplier of CRT.

Answer choices explanation

(A) This option is **irrelevant.** The argument is about selection of CRT over plastic; but this option talks about steel.

(B) This option is tempting, but **inconclusive.** Lack of representation of prototype vehicles with CRT at major auto shows does not imply that CRT is not ready for the being used in cars. Participation in major auto shows is not a necessary quality certification. It does not explain why CRT isn't being used.

(C) This option is **inconclusive.** We cannot infer anything from this. Different manufacturing process to manufacture CRT does not necessarily mean that it is difficult. Different and difficult are not the same thing. This does not provide an adequate reason for not using CRT instead of plastic.

(D) This option is the **correct** answer. It says carbon tubing has quality control problems making it less safe, or less reliable than plastic. This resolves the discrepancy because it justifies why the manufacturers did not use CRT instead of plastic.

(E) This option is also correct, but we cannot go against the instruction given in the question stem, which explicitly asks us to preserve the manufacturers' claim that *plastic is not used because of profit motives,* implying that CRT is not employed because of reasons other than profitability.

The correct answer is option D.

Example 3

Teacher Unions are demanding a higher salary for their members. Their principal complaint is that despite the years of study, dedication and training necessary to obtain the qualifications, the teachers earn far less than a mechanic in real terms. These complaints have been rejected by the State Budgetary Commission who has produced figures compiled by an independent team of auditors proving that mechanics earn far less than teachers.

Which of the following does **NOT** at least partially explain the apparent paradox expressed in the passage above?

(A) The two months paid leave teachers enjoy annually is offset by the unpaid hours worked in lesson preparation.

(B) Mechanics have the possibility to take advantage of workplace facilities to carry out repairs on their own cars and bikes.

(C) Many teachers also earn through private tuitions.

(D) Some rich customers gift their old cars to their mechanics.

(E) Pension payments awarded to teachers upon retirement are higher than the pensions awarded to mechanics.

Argument Construction

We have to select an option that does NOT help in any way to resolve the paradox. Four options will at least partially explain the apparent paradox.

Teacher Union's complaint is that despite the years of study, dedication and training, the teachers earn far less than a mechanic in real terms. But these complaints have been rejected by the State Budgetary Commission (SBC) who has produced counter facts proving that mechanics earn far less than teachers.

Predictive Resolutor

The paradox: The paradox expressed in the passage is that the union claims that the teachers earn earn far less than a mechanic, however, the SBC says exactly the opposite.

While one group claims that the other enjoys more benefit that what their group does, the other group conclusively claims that it is other way round. It seems that each group finds the other earning more.

A possible resolution in these types of situations is that each group either does not count the benefits it receives or counts non-existent benefits for the other group.

Predictive Resolutor: A group either does not count the benefits it receives or counts non-existent benefits for the other group.

Answer choices explanation

(A) This option means that the pay the teachers get for the holiday is, in fact, a justified remuneration to them as they prepare lessons during the holidays. So such paid leave is not an undue advantage to the teachers. This option does not resolve the paradox. This option seems to be the **correct** answer.

(B) This option offers a partial resolution. This option provides one reason the teachers may be justified in saying that their income is less than that of the mechanics in real terms. The mechanics can boost their income by getting free repairs done on their own cars and bikes. One group gets uncounted benefit but the other does not.

(C) This option too offers a partial resolution. This option provides one reason the SBC may be justified in saying that mechanics' income is less than that of the teachers in real terms. If many teachers can earn through private tuitions, extra income, one group gets some uncounted benefit but the other does not.

(D) This option too offers a partial resolution. This option provides one reason the teachers may be justified in saying that their income is less than that of the mechanics in real terms. Getting old cars free is a benefit to some mechanics implying one group gets uncounted benefit but the other does not.

(E) This option too offers a partial resolution. This option provides one reason the SBC may be justified in saying that mechanics' income is less than that of the teachers in real terms. Post-retirement benefits weights more for teachers than mechanics implying one group gets uncounted benefit but the other does not.

The correct answer is option A.

Example 4

There is statistical evidence that the number of AIDS patients in the US has increased by approximately 8% over the last five years. Surprisingly, those involved in AIDS treatment in San Francisco have reported a sharp decline in the number of patients visiting free clinics over the last five years.

Which of the following, if true, could by itself best explain the difference expressed in the above passages?

(A) The statistics refer to the US as a whole.

(B) Many people from cities like San Francisco, Boston and Philadelphia are not more likely to attend private clinics than free clinics.

(C) Many people from San Francisco attend only private clinics.

(D) Globally, there has been an 18% rise in the number of AIDS patients.

(E) AIDS awareness among US cities is vastly different.

Argument Construction

The number of AIDS patients in the US has increased by 8% over the last five years. However, San Francisco reported a sharp decline in the number of AIDS patients visiting free clinics over the same period. Note that the figures don't state that the number of people visiting clinics is not mentioned.

Predictive Resolutor

The paradox: The paradox is that if the number of AIDS sufferers in the US has increased by 8% over the last five years, why a similar figure is not reflected in San Francisco, a popular city of the US.; on the contrary, the city reported a sharp decline in the number of AIDS patients visiting free clinics over the same 5-year period.

The argument has sufficient scope to be resolved with various possibilities. One possibility is that SF is not representative of the US, and differs vastly in the health care aspect. Another possibility is that while 8% figure represents the whole country, the average does not mean that the figures for every region must be around 8%. Every region has different demographic, geographic, cultural, ethical, and health characteristics that may drastically vary from each other.

Predictive Resolutor 1: SF differs widely from the US in aspects that relate to AIDS.

The second premise states that *SF has reported a sharp decline in the number of patients visiting free clinics.* SF figures showed a decline in the number of AIDS patients visiting free clinic. However, no data has been given about the number of patients visiting private clinics.

If the figures for private clinic for similar 5-year period showed drastic increase in the number of patients visiting them, the discrepancy is resolved.

Predictive Resolutor 2: The figures for private clinic showed a drastic increase in the number of AIDS patients visiting them.

Answer choices explanation

(A)   We already know that in the US, number of AIDS patients increased by 8%. This statement is just a rephrased version. It does not resolve the contradiction.

(B)   This option is the opposite of what we need. Considering SF only, the option statement means that almost equal number of patients visits free and private clinics. This further strengthens that number of AIDS patients in SF declined, and does not help to explain the paradox.

(C)   Although this option is not truly aligned with our predictive resolutor 2, it is in line with it. The difference in the figures expressed in the argument is the fact that although the number of AIDs sufferers nationally has increased, the number of AIDs sufferers in San Francisco has declined. This option is a proper justification as it helps to explain the discrepancy why, though the number of patients visiting free clinics declined, the figure for patients vising private clinics is high.

(D)   This option is out of scope. The statistics of the passage relate to only the US.

(E)   This option is tempting, but inconclusive. In the real world, we may be swayed by this information, and infer that the difference in the figures between the US and SF has something to do with awareness; but in the GMAT, we can only infer what must be true. We cannot conclude anything on the basis of variation of awareness. Moreover the scope of the argument is limited to AIDS patients, and not AIDS awareness and there's no necessary link between patient visits and awareness.

The correct answer is option C.

Practice

Questions

12.4 Practice Questions

12.4.1   Questions

Question 1

Recently many people in a certain county have stopped buying new apartments primarily because high taxes have been introduced by the county tax office, and because the rate of unemployment in the county is high. However, the average price of a new apartment has almost doubled in the county.

Which of the following, if true, best explains the increase in the average price of a new apartment?

(A)   The price of used apartments has climbed steadily over the past five years.

(B)   There will be a tax reduction later in the year which is expected to aid moderate and low income families.

(C)   The market for new apartments has been unaffected by current economic conditions.

(D)   Economic conditions are expected to get significantly worse before the end of the year.

(E)   In anticipation of low demand for new apartments there has been a large decrease in construction.

Question 2

The results of an endurance test, comprising three tests, of micro-automobiles showed that models from Japan, France and Italy were on average 18% more efficient fuel burners than models from the US and England, apart from possessing 14.5% better braking also. It was also found that models from the US and Germany were 12% less efficient in the tests relating to engine wear and tear. The final results of the test series announced last week showed the US models to be the clear winners.

Which of the following could best possibly explain why US models are the clear winners?

(A)   The climatic conditions under which the tests were held favored the Japanese models.

(B)   The judges of the test were drawn from representatives of all the participating automobile producers.

(C)   Only four US models were allowed to participate in the tests.

(D) All the participating US models were standard and unmodified vehicles.

(E) The test series was composed of 12 different tests carried out on each vehicle after the completion of 5000 miles.

Question 3

Having urged the government to sign the United Nations Human Rights Charter, the intellectuals of a Balkan country now have a government sponsored petition appealing against a UN decision that imposes sanctions on their country for human rights violations. Although morally and ethically opposed to the use of torture and imprisonment without trial, those intellectuals nevertheless feel obliged to support the authorities in their crack down on insurgents and they are fully aware that such violations are taking place.

Which of the following, if true, would best explain the apparent paradox expressed in the passage above?

(A) The country is on the verge of being overrun by insurgents.

(B) The intellectuals are related to the insurgents.

(C) The intellectuals support the stand of the insurgents.

(D) The intellectuals are not being pressured by the authorities.

(E) The human rights abuses referred to are of an extreme nature.

12.4.2 Answer-Key

(1) E	(2) E	(3) A

12.4.3 Solutions

Question 1

Argument construction

Recently many people in a county have stopped buying new apartments. This has happened because of two reasons, one, high taxes levied on buying apartments, and two, the high rate of unemployment in the county. Surprisingly, the average price of a new apartment has almost doubled in the county.

Predictive Resolutor

The paradox: The paradox is that despite many people not purchasing apartments (low demand), the average price of new apartments has almost doubled.

There is a paradox because prices reflect the relationship between supply and demand. Low demand should mean low prices and vice versa. Higher unemployment and taxes may decrease demand. A decrease in demand should have decreased the price, but on the contrary, the prices have increased.

Predictive Resolutor: We need a factor that explains why the prices have gone up, despite the low demand. Any option that explains what made the prices go up is the right answer.

Answer choices explanation

(A)   This option is **irrelevant** since it talks about used apartments. The argument is concerned about only new apartments.

(B)   This option is **irrelevant.** It talks about the future scenario which does not impact the paradox right now. It does not justify why the prices have gone up despite low demand. At best, this should form the basis for steady prices but certainly not increased prices.

(C)   The information that the market for new apartments has been unaffected by current economic conditions, does not answer why the new apartment prices doubled. It does not resolve the discrepancy.

(D)   This option is an opposite answer. The inference of the information that the economic conditions are expected to get significantly worse before the end of the year will make people very cautious while making investment. It may be another reason people stopped buying new apartments, but this option does not resolve the discrepancy.

(E)   This option is the **correct** answer. In anticipation of low demand for new apartments there has been a large decrease in construction. It means that low demand caused significantly lower supply. Consequently, the lower supply meant that the apartments in the market are priced high because the supply has gone lower than the low demand. It is possible that because of a large decrease in construction, the buyers, however few, had to compete for the fewer apartments, leading to doubling of its prices.

The correct answer is option E.

Question 2

Argument construction

The argument is fully loaded with data. After reading the question stem, we know that the question is "Resolve the Paradox" type. We have to resolve the discrepancy why the US models are clear winners. This suggests that the argument will provide data that would not seemingly favor the victory of US models. So, let's focus on the US data only.

The endurance test:

Test (Efficiency of fuel burners)—Toppers—Models of Japan, France and Italy - 18% more efficient fuel burners than the US models; US models were not the winners.

Test 2 (Efficiency of braking)—Toppers—Models of Japan, France and Italy - 14.5% better braking than the US models; US models were not the winners.

Test 3 (Engine wear and tear)—Toppers—Do not know - but US models were not the winners. Despite losing 3 tests, the final results of the test series announced last week showed that the US models are the clear winners.

Predictive Resolutor

The paradox: The paradox is that despite not being the winners in any of the three mentioned endurance tests, the US models are declared the winners.

This question demands attention while reading the argument. The argument talks about the data of endurance test, but the conclusion is derived for the test series. This implies that there must be more tests, other than the endurance tests, in the test series, and in a majority of them the US won. Such a situation would resolve the discrepancy.

Predictive Resolutor: US models topped in most of the other tests in the test series.

Answer choices explanation

(A) This option is **irrelevant.** It focuses on Japan; we are concerned with the US. A condition favoring Japan further worsens the discrepancy.

(B) This option does nothing in terms of resolving the discrepancy. If the judges of the test were drawn from representatives of all the participating automobile producers, there is more justification to believe that the testing is fair and impartial.

(C) Like option A, this option too does nothing in terms of resolving the discrepancy. Even if only four US models were allowed to participate in the tests, the discrepancy stands as to why the 4 US models win, despite losing the three endurance tests.

(D) Like option A and B, this option too does nothing in terms of resolving the discrepancy. Even if the participating models from other countries were not standard and modified vehicles, the puzzle is unresolved why the US models won despite losing the endurance tests.

(E) This option is the **correct** answer. It explains how the US models won by stating that there were 9 other categories tested, in which the US models must have won. It is aligned with our predictive resolution. So, despite losing in 3 endurance categories, the US models, by winning in most of the other ones, won the series.

The correct answer is option E.

Question 3

Argument construction

The argument is written from the position of intellectuals of Balkan country. Previously they had insisted the Balkan government to sign the United Nations Human Rights Charter (UNHRC) pledging that the government would not carry out crack down on the insurgents implying no human rights violations. But now they along with the government have appealed against the UNHRC, which impose sanctions for not carrying out crack down on insurgents. Although the intellectuals realise that from moral and ethical perspective, the use of torture and imprisonment without trial is wrong, but they nevertheless feel obliged to support the government's crackdown on insurgents.

Predictive Resolutor

The paradox: Previously, the intellectuals were against human rights violations, but they apparently seemed to have changed their position now to support the government in carrying out activities against the insurgents, activities that imply human rights violations. The paradox is that intellectuals are supporting human rights violation even though they initially were strictly opposed to it.

The argument deals with moving from one position to another, seemingly contradictory position over a period of time. One reason could be that the circumstances now are vastly different.

Predictive Resolutor: Circumstances prevalent now in Balkan made the intellectuals change their stance regarding human rights violation.

Answer choices explanation

(A) This option is the **correct** answer. It is aligned with our predictive resolutor. While the intellectuals may be strictly against human rights violation, they may have an even-stricter position about insurgency and subverting the government. The intellectuals may have found the insurgents harming the country to such an extent that they may see certain violations as a necessary evil required to get rid of the insurgents. So, earlier, when the situation was not as grave as it is now, they had supported UNHRC. In dire situations principles are sometimes sacrificed.

(B) This option explains why the intellectual are on the side of the insurgents, but does not explain why the intellectuals are allowing the government to carry out human rights violation against the insurgents..

(C) Like option B, this option too explains why the intellectual are on the side of the insurgents, but does not resolve the paradox.

(D) This option is an opposite answer. *The intellectuals are not being pressured by the authorities* implies that the intellectuals have changed their stance on their own and were not influenced by the government. This worsens rather than resolve the discrepancy.

(E) Like option B and C, this option too explains why the intellectual are on the side of the insurgents, but does not resolve the paradox why they are allowing human rights violations against the insurgents.

The correct answer is option A.

Chapter 13

Inference Argument

13.1 Inference Argument Question type

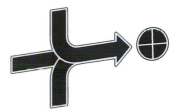 Like Resolve the Paradox or Explain the Discrepancy arguments, inference arguments consist only of premises, mostly factual statements, and sometimes claims. Since the arguments contain only premises, the conclusion is missing from the arguments. Inference questions also belong to evidence based family.

Inference questions are not as frequent as assumption, strengthen or weaken questions; however, you will see at least a couple of questions in your GRE.

Inference questions ask us to select an option that must be true as per the information in the argument. Mostly, the correct option may be inferred using only some of the information in the argument; however you are free to use all.

Look at dialogue between two people in the image. What could be inferred here?

The following illustration depicts your job for Inference question type.

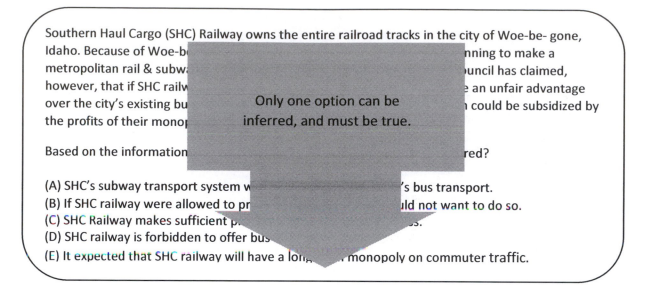

Southern Haul Cargo (SHC) Railway owns the entire railroad tracks in the city of Woe-be- gone, Idaho. Because of Woe-b[...] [...]nning to make a metropolitan rail & subw[...] [...]uncil has claimed, however, that if SHC rail[...] [...]e an unfair advantage over the city's existing bu[...] [...] could be subsidized by the profits of their monop[...]

Based on the information[...] [...]red?

(A) SHC's subway transport system w[...] [...]'s bus transport.
(B) If SHC railway were allowed to pr[...] [...]ld not want to do so.
(C) SHC Railway makes sufficient p[...] [...]s.
(D) SHC railway is forbidden to offer bus[...]
(E) It expected that SHC railway will have a lo[...] [...] monopoly on commuter traffic.

Only one option can be inferred, and must be true.

Question Stem

Most inference question stems will include some form of the words "conclude" or "support" or "infer".

A typical 'inference' question stem looks like the following.

· Which of the following can be "logically concluded" based on the information in the argument?

· The information above most strongly supports which of the following conclusions?

· Which of the following can be "properly inferred" based on the information in the argument?

· The information above "best supports" which of the following claims?

· Which of the following "must be true" based on the information in the argument?

13.2   Difference Between Strengthen And Inference Question Types

Like strengthen questions, inference question stems too may contain the phrase "most strongly support", so it is important to make sure that you do not get confused between the two question types. Following table highlights the difference between the two.

	Inference question type	Strengthen question type
Who supports whom?	The argument supports the correct option.	The correct option supports the argument.
Presence of conclusion	There is no conclusion in the argument.	The conclusion is always present in the argument.
Role of assumption	Since there is no conclusion in the argument, there is no role of assumption.	Since the conclusion is present in the argument, the assumption has its role.
Truthfulness of options	Only the correct option is true. Incorrect options are either "not necessarily true" or "could be false."	All the options are true, and unquestionable.
Question stem	The argument above most strongly supports which of the following?	Which of the following most strongly supports the argument above?

13.3   Process Of Solving Inference Questions

The 4-step approach is same as in Find the Assumption chapter.

The 4-step approach

   (1) Recognize the question type

   (2) Understand the argument construction

   (3) Predict the qualifier

   (4) Eliminate incorrect options

First 2 steps are same for the inference questions. Let us jump directly to the "predict the qualifier" step.

Predict the qualifier

We already are familiar with this step. Inference questions test how you treat what is within scope and what "must be true" and not what "could be true". Your inclination to reasonably assume or infer something is cleverly tested by the test maker with a trap of classic wordplay; the key is to think skeptically.

The test maker will tempt you into inferring something beyond the scope of the argument; the incorrect inference will seem true when you supplement the argument with the real-world information. However, you must not bring in outside information into the argument.

Let us see following argument.

Moderate consumption of carbonated soft drinks may keep your sugar level at check. Excess sugar is one of the primary reasons of obesity.

Let us see one of the seemingly correct options.

Option: Excess consumption of colas causes obesity related diseases.

If we supplement the argument with real-world information, then the option seems correct. However, we need not do so. You can make a "must be true" inference–*Excess consumption of colas may cause obesity.* The above one is wrong because we cannot assume that the excess consumption of colas will surely cause obesity related diseases. Diseases are out of scope. Also, the second premise states that excess sugar is one of the reasons, though primary, of obesity, but that does not mean that the excess consumption of colas raise the sugar level higher causing obesity related diseases.

Another common trap is a "cause and effect" mix up. If the argument says that X causes Y, we cannot necessarily conclude that Y causes X too; however, the test maker will sell such a tempting option in a way that seems correct.

Let us see following example.

If the Barcelona's star Messi scores a hat-trick, Barcelona will win the match.

It is simple cause and effect example, where X, the cause is 'Messi scoring a hat-trick', and Y, the effect is 'Barcelona winning the match'.

Correct inference: If in a match, Messi scored three or more goals, we can infer that Barcelona must have won the match.

Incorrect inference: If Barcelona won the match, we cannot necessarily infer that Messi must have scored three or more goals. There is a possibility that Barcelona could have won because of superlative performances by other players'.

So, $X \Rightarrow Y \neq Y \Rightarrow X$

"Taking the inference to the extreme" is also one of the common trap answer.

Let us see following example.

Lack of practice affects your marks significantly.

Correct inference: Scoring below the expected level could be due to insufficient practice.

Incorrect inference: One may fail in the exam because of falling short of practice.

The argument does not necessarily mean that due to lack of practice, the marks will be affected to such an extent that one might fail. In the real-world, it is reasonable to infer to this extent, but in a GRE argument, you must avoid inferring something to the extreme until there is a reason to do so.

Let us see how to predict an "inference" from a GRE-like argument.

> Major corporations have condemned the doubling of the annual license fee demanded by Microsoft for the use of specialized software as surrender to the organized piracy that continues in a number of S.E. Asian countries. Microsoft has conceded that piracy continues to eat into profits but claims that the price hike is due to increased research and development costs.

Understand the argument:

The argument is easy to understand. It says that Microsoft has doubled the annual license fee for the specialized software used by major corporations. The major corporations oppose this move. Their viewpoint is that Microsoft is soft on the organized piracy taking place in a number of S.E. Asian countries, resulting into lowered profits and raised costs. Microsoft does acknowledge that the piracy eats into profits; however, it claims that the price hike is required because of the need for more funds for increased research and development.

While understanding the argument, and predicting the inferences, you must pay attention to key words in the argument. These key words will dictate the scope of the argument. For example, the argument is limited to "specialized software" only, any inference regarding non-specialized, generic and popular software, like Windows, is out of scope. Similarly, it's only the major corporations that have condemned the move. If an option talks about ethically upright corporations, then it falls in the category of "could be true" and not in "must be true". Another extreme case could be to include all the Asian countries. Remember that the scope is limited to South East Asian countries.

Let us predict few inferences.

Predictive Inference 1: Both Microsoft and the major corporations acknowledge that the piracy of specialized software could not be fully checked.

Predictive Inference 2: Major corporations strongly feel that mechanism of controlling software piracy by Microsoft is ineffective.

Predictive Inference 3: Major corporations purchase specialized software through legitimate sources.

Above inference is a "must be true" inference as the major corporations will oppose the move from Microsoft only if they are affected by the price to be paid to the legitimate software seller.

Let us see some of the options to this argument.

(A)   The previous license cost was dictated by major companies.

(B)   There is no evidence in the argument to infer that the previous license cost was dictated by major companies. On the contrary, this may fall in the category of "could be false" as despite condemnation by major corporations, Microsoft doubled the license fee.

(C)   Microsoft is lenient towards the piracy of their software. This option is incorrect because the argument states that the major corporations feel that Microsoft is lenient towards the piracy of their software, but we cannot infer that Microsoft is necessarily lenient towards the piracy of their software. Such an inference would imply that feelings always reflect only reality.

(D)   Acquisition of software by major companies is through legitimate channels. This is the correct "must be true" inference. It is aligned with our predictive inference 3.

(E)   Research and development costs incurred by Microsoft have increased beyond anticipated levels. This is a case of extreme inference. This "could be true", but not "must be true". Justifying the price hike due to R & D outlay does not necessarily mean that R & D cost has increased beyond anticipated levels.

(F)   Major corporations fear the competition posed by those organizing the software piracy.

This option is an example of clever wordplay. It looks promising, but not correct. While the corporations may fear the competition by those using the pirated software, clearly those organizing the piracy are not their direct competitors. In any case, we cannot say that this is absolutely true. It may or may not be true.

Example

Questions

13.4 Examples

Example 1

According to a recent report on higher education in the United States, the 15 universities with the highest annual tuition fees also gave out the largest financial aid awards to incoming students with outstanding achievements. Because of a belief in equal opportunity, these universities are able to redistribute resources from those who can afford to give to those students who deserve aid by virtue of merit.

Which of the following can be correctly inferred from the statement above?

(A) Following a belief in equal opportunity is a good way to mask charging higher tuition fees.

(B) It is possible for a university that believes in equal opportunity to put different financial demands on different students.

(C) A university that offers large financial aid awards must do so because it believes in equal opportunity.

(D) Universities that have high tuition fees tend to give out little financial aid.

(E) Universities that have large endowments tend to give out lots of financial aid.

Argument Construction

The 15 US universities who charge the highest annual tuition fees among all the universities also gave out the largest financial aid to their incoming students who secured outstanding achievements. These universities believe in equal opportunity, and are able to charge more fees from those who can afford to pay, and charge less from those who cannot afford the fees.

Predict An Inference

The language used in the argument is extreme. The 15 universities charge the highest fees, and gave out the largest aid. Since the aid is based on the virtue of merit and achievement, total cost for students varies. If some paid full $100, some may have paid $80 or $60 or $40.

Predictive Inference 1: Annual tuition fee for students taking the courses in the universities vary.

We have established that the universities charge full fee from some and less fee from some others, but still, they must be able to collect an ample sum to run the university courses.

Predictive Inference 2: Despite charging less from some incoming students, the universities can accrue sufficient funds to run the courses.

Answer choices explanation

(A)   We cannot infer that following a belief in equal opportunity is being carried out to dis-
       guise charging higher tuition fees. This option is too judgmental and does not go with
       the tone of the argument.

(B)   Yes, it is possible for a university that believes in equal opportunity to put different
       financial demands (different fee structures) on different students based on their merit
       and needs. This is the **correct** answer. It is aligned with our predictive inference 1.

(C)   It may seem like a rephrased statement from the argument, but is not. The argument
       states that a university that offers large financial aid awards must would do so because
       it believes in equal opportunity. However, the language in the option statement uses the
       verb "must do", implying compulsion. We cannot infer this necessarily.

(D)   We cannot infer that all the universities that have high tuition fees tend to give out little
       financial aid. The scope of the argument is limited to the universities that have the
       highest fees and that believe in equal opportunities.

(E)   We cannot infer that all the universities that have large endowments tend to give out lots
       of financial aid. Like option D, the scope of the argument is limited to the universities
       that have the highest fees and that believe in equal opportunities.

The correct answer is option B.

Example 2

Badly hit by the recession, an automobile company decided to split its production into two
categories, a division to make private vehicles and a division to make commercial vehicles. It
proved to be a wise decision. Over the following four years, the private division, primarily due
to increased sales of luxury limousines to the United Nations, accounted for approximately
40% of dollar sales and 20% of the overall profit. The commercial division was responsible for
the entire balance.

Which of the following can be inferred concerning the performance of the company over the
last four years?

(A)   Expensive luxury cars were more profitable products than the commercial vehicles.

(B)   The private division has realized lower profits per dollar than the commercial division
       achieved.

(C)   The commercial division had to face stiffer competition than the private division.

(D)   The range of luxury limousines accounted for a higher percentage of profits than any
       products sold by the commercial division.

(E)   The company's program failed to improve overall profits.

Argument Construction

The private division, primarily due to increased sales of luxury limousines, accounted for approximately 40% of dollar sales and 20% of the overall profit of the company. The commercial division was responsible for the rest.

Predict An Inference

According to the passage, the private division accounted for 40% of dollar sales and 20% of the overall profit, so the commercial division would have accounted for 60% of dollar sales and 80% of the overall profit.

We can deduce that the private division accounted for 20%/40% = 0.50 profit per dollar sales, and the commercial division accounted for 80%/60% = 1.33 profit per dollar sales.

Predictive Inference: Profits per dollar sales for the commercial division is more than double that for the private division.

Answer choices explanation

(A)   We cannot infer that the expensive luxury cars were more profitable products than the commercial vehicles. We can only conclude that the commercial division was more profitable than the private division.

(B)   This is the **correct** answer. It is aligned with our predictive inference. The private division has realized lower profits per dollar (0.50) than the commercial division achieved (1.33).

(C)   We cannot infer that the commercial division had to face stiffer competition than the private division. This is out of scope of the argument.

(D)   We can infer that the luxury limousines accounted for the highest percentage of profits than any products sold by the private division, but we cannot compare the same with any product in the commercial division.

(E)   This is "must be false" option as the argument states that it (i.e. splitting program) proved a wise decision.

The correct answer is option B.

Example 3

Lately many people in a certain post-communist country have decided to emigrate for economic reasons. The people who want to leave the county in search of a job or a better life are either those who have no money or those who know multiple foreign languages.

Of the following persons, who is LEAST likely to emigrate?

(A)   A person who knows two foreign languages, but doesn't have any money.

(B)   A person who knows two foreign languages, but is afraid to travel.

(C)   A person who has no money to travel and knows a second language at an elementary level.

(D)   A person who knows no foreign language, but has money to travel.

(E)   A person who has no money to leave the country, and is dejected with his/her present situation.

Argument Construction

The people will leave the county either of a job or a better life; these people either do not have money, or know multiple foreign languages.

Predict An Inference

Read the question stem clearly—Of the following people, who is LEAST likely to emigrate? We have to find the person who is NOT eligible to emigrate. What is the qualifying criterion to emigrate? The criterion is either people do not have money or they know multiple foreign languages.

Predictive Inference (LEAST likely to leave): Person with sufficient money and no knowledge of any foreign language.

Answer choices explanation

(A)   This person is certain to emigrate. He fulfills both the criteria—knowing two foreign languages, and having no money.

(B)   This person is likely to emigrate too. He fulfills one criterion—knowing two foreign languages. Remember that afraid to travel is not a criterion in the argument. It is real-world knowledge trap laid by the test maker. They want you to assume that a person won't travel when he is afraid of traveling. However, the argument clearly mentions that a likely emigrant is one who knows foreign languages. By that criterion, this person is highly likely to emigrate.

(C)   This person is likely to emigrate too. He fulfills at least one criterion—no money. No money to travel is a trap for you to bring in the real-world wisdom. We must not use our brain on the details of the travel without money. It is beyond the scope of argument. Knowing the second language is inconclusive, because we don't know whether it is foreign language. However, answer to this does not impact the decision as the person fulfills one criterion—no money. Thus, according to the argument, this person is very likely to emigrate.

(D)   This is the **correct** answer. This person is LEAST likely to emigrate. He does not fulfill any criterion. This person does not know any foreign language, and has money, and so no reason to emigrate

(E) This person is likely to emigrate. He fulfills one criterion—no money. Like option C, no money to leave, and dejected with his/her present situation are the traps for you to bring in the real-world wisdom. Moreover, dejected with his/her present situation is not a criterion as per the argument. However, the argument clearly mentions that a likely emigrant is one who doesn't have money. By that criterion, this person is highly likely to emigrate.

The correct answer is option D.

Example 4

The cost of electricity is high because there is no effective competition among those who produce this vital source of energy. The utility companies have blamed the price of electricity on the need to invest in new plants to serve the ever-growing market in the region. This offers little consolation to the consumer who could be compared to a tourist with diarrhea stranded in a strange city where all the public washrooms cost as high as $100 to use.

The analogy above serves to make which of the following points?

(A) The use of public washrooms has become a luxury and should be free of charge.

(B) The cost of electricity is being kept high by the producers to encourage consumers to use less.

(C) Without electricity, society would be unable to sustain its infrastructure and public services.

(D) The essential products like electricity should be supplied free of cost.

(E) Price fixing can keep charges for an essential product artificially high.

Argument Construction

The cost of electricity is high because there is no competition among its producers. The companies blame the high price on the need to invest in new plants to serve the ever-growing need of electricity. The argument provides an analogy to ridicule the high price by quoting that this scenario is similar to a situation in which a tourist with diarrhea is stuck in a strange city where all the public washrooms cost as high as $100 to use.

Predict An Inference

The key to this question is to understand the question stem. The question stem is unlike a typical question stem used for an inference question. It means that which of the following can be inferred based on the analogy used in the argument.

Let us understand what the purpose of analogy is, and what we can infer from it. The tourist with diarrhea stuck in a strange city has no choice but to use the washroom even if unwilling to pay exorbitantly high price for the services. We can infer that this example is quoted to draw a parallel for the high cost of electricity. So, we can conclude that the analogy serves to mean that due to the monopoly of utility companies, consumers have no choice, but to pay high price for the electricity.

Predictive Inference: Due to the monopoly, consumers have no choice, but to pay high price for the essential commodities.

Answer choices explanation

(A)   This is a classic real-world trap, but is an incorrect option. The question stem wants us to infer from the public washrooms example and not about the example. The argument is not about why availing the service of washroom is a city should be free; instead it is about the high price of electricity.

(B)   We cannot infer that the cost of electricity is being kept high by the producers to encourage consumers to use less. The motive behind producers' actions is not discussed.

(C)   This is again a classic real-world trap, but is an incorrect option. It is true that without electricity, society would be unable to sustain its infrastructure and public services, but this aspect is not mentioned in the argument. So, this option is out of scope.

(D)   This option is tricky and tempting, but too extreme to be the right answer. From the analogy, we cannot infer that the argument is about offering the services of essential products free; rather it is concerned about unjustifiably high prices.

(E)   This is the **correct** answer. For both the essential products—electricity, and washroom services, price fixation can be unjustifiably or artificially high.

The correct answer is option E.

Practice

Questions

13.5 Practice Questions

13.5.1 Questions

Question 1

A private bus company wanted to increase profits. For 20 years it worked to make its buses more economical and faster by reducing the number of bus stops. Although the company was in some measure successful, the economy grew worse, and the industry almost went bankrupt. Assumptions and realities were vastly different. The real problem came not from passengers who wanted faster transport but from the number of passengers who stopped using the bus service because of the limited number of bus stops.

Which of the actions below would most likely lead to a solution to the problem faced by the bus company, as it is analyzed above?

(A) Providing buses with engines that run on a cheaper type of fuel than that traditionally used.

(B) Providing double-decker buses that will stop at more bus stops.

(C) Providing buses that have more seating rooms than any other existing buses.

(D) Implementing a system to ensure that buses are loaded to capacity.

(E) Implementing a market plan that focuses on routes that are known to be less used by other bus companies.

Question 2

Southern Haul Cargo (SHC) Railway owns the entire railroad tracks in the city of Woe-be-gone, Idaho. Because of Woe-be-gone's sudden population explosion, SHC is planning to make a metropolitan rail & subway system using its pre-existing tracks. The city council has claimed, however, that if SHC railway were to offer subway transport, it would have an unfair advantage over the city's existing bus routes, because SHC's subway transport system could be subsidized by the profits of their monopoly on cargo transport.

Based on the information given above, which of the following can be inferred?

(A) SHC's subway transport system would be as efficient as city's bus transport.

(B) If SHC railway were allowed to provide bus transport, it would not want to do so.

(C) SHC Railway makes sufficient profit in cargo transport business.

(D) SHC railway is forbidden to offer bus transport.

(E) It expected that SHC railway will have a long-term monopoly on commuter traffic.

Question 3

An electric piano designed to have perfect frequency for each note would sound different from the best Baldwin or Steinbach Grand Piano currently available.

To professional pianists, a piano that sounds different from the best Grand Pianos sounds less like a piano and therefore worse than the best-sounding existing pianos.

Professional pianists are the only acceptable judges of the quality of pianos.

Which of the following would be best supported by these statements?

(A) Only amateur pianists should be asked to judge the sound of electric pianos.

(B) Professional pianists assist in designing electric pianos.

(C) The best sounding grand pianos have been around for more than 100 years.

(D) It is currently impossible to create an electric piano that accepted judges will evaluate as being an improvement on the existing grand pianos.

(E) It is possible to create an electric piano that sounds better to everyone except a professional pianist.

Question 4

The level of financial aid given by the rich nations to poorer nations in order to raise the poorer nations' industrial capacity is directly influenced by the extent to which the donors fear competition and the threat of diminished exports. The amount of aid recommended by Congress is invariably reduced and redistributed by Presidential decree according to the findings of a select committee judging aid packages purely from an American business perspective. As a consequence, many poorer nations have to find areas of industrial activities that pose no threat to the industrial global order.

If the above statements are true, which one of the following must also be true?

(A) The most needy countries are those with the smallest industrial output.

(B) The amount of aid for industrial projects received by poorer nations is in ratio to the extent to which they develop new industrial bases that pose no threat to rich nations.

(C) The poorer nations depend on foreign aid to advance industrial economy.

(D) The wealth of the richer nations has expanded thanks to a policy of withholding foreign aid.

(E) The amount of foreign aid given by the richer industrialized nations to poorer nations has been reduced to safeguard existing export markets.

13.5.2 Answer-Key

(1) B | (2) C | (3) D | (4) B

Solutions

13.5.3   Solutions

Question 1

Argument construction

The argument is simple to understand. A private bus company wanted to increase profits. Over the years, it worked to make its buses more economical and faster by reducing the number of bus stops. The real problem came from passengers who stopped using their bus service because they wanted more number of bus stops.

Predict A Solution

The question stem of this question may stump you. Which category does this question belong to? The question stem asks for the solution. The solution will come out from the information given in the argument. This is what we do in an inference question.

What is the problem with the bus company's logic? They kept cutting out bus stops to decrease transit time until they had virtually no customer base left. The only way to have a bus route that makes money is to have it pick up plenty of people from different stops to make a profit. If you have too few stops, how do you correct this? By adding more stops.

Predictive Solution: Make the buses stop at optimum number of places.

Answer choices explanation

(A)   Providing buses with engines that run on a cheaper type of fuel than that traditionally used will certainly reduce the operational cost, but they would still lack the customer base. The solution should address customers' convenience in catching the buses. This option does not address it.

(B)   This is the **correct** answer. By providing double-decker buses, the company can cut cost, whereas by making the buses stop at more bus stops will ensure that the increased capacity of the buses is availed by more customers who use the buses because of more bus stops.

(C)   Providing buses that have more seating rooms than any other existing buses will certainly increase the revenue, but they would still lack the customer base. The solution should address customers' convenience in catching the buses. This option does not address it.

(D)   Like option C, this option too does not address the core issue of customers' convenience in catching the buses.

(E)   On the same lines as option C and D, this option too does not address the real problem.

The correct answer is option B.

Question 2

Argument construction

Southern Haul Cargo (SHC) Railway owns the entire railroad tracks in the city. SHC is planning to make a Metropolitan Rail & Subway system using its pre-existing tracks. The city council is skeptical about this plan; it fears that if SHC railway were to offer subway transport, it would affect the city's existing bus routes, and transport; because SHC has the capacity to reduce the commuting cost substantially. The council claims that SHC would subsidize subway transport system with the profits they accrued through cargo transport business over the years.

Predict An Inference

Since SHC Railway owns the entire railroad tracks in the city, we can infer that no other company offers subway transport services and so the city council claims that the bus routes will be affected by SHC. We can infer that only SHC can offer the subway services because the city council seems concerned about SHC's impact on the bus routes if SHC provides a subway system.

Predictive Inference 1: No other railway company offers metropolitan rail & subway transport services in the city.

Predictive Inference 2: The network of SHC's railroad tracks is widely-spread enough to affect many major bus routes.

Answer choices explanation

(A) The argument did not talk about the efficiency of any transport system. We cannot infer that SHC's subway transport system would be as efficient as city's bus transport. We don't even know that the bus transport is efficient to begin with.

(B) From the information in the argument, we cannot infer that SHC railway would not provide bus transport if it were allowed to do so. SHC's position on providing bus transport is not given in the argument.

(C) This is the **correct** answer. SHC's expansion plan and the council's claim that SHC may subsidize its proposed subway service imply that SHC Railway has been making sufficient profit in cargo transport business.

(D) No legal aspect is discussed in the argument. We cannot infer that SHC railway is forbidden from offering bus transport.

(E) This option is based on future projections that haven't been made in the argument.

The correct answer is option C.

Question 3

Argument construction

An electric piano is designed to have perfect frequency for each note, and sounds different from (but not necessarily better than) the best Baldwin or Steinbach Grand Piano currently available. Professional pianists, who are the only acceptable judges of the quality of pianos, find that when the sound of the electric piano (or any piano) is different from the best grand pianos, the sound is worse than that from best-sounding existing pianos. Their measure of a good-sounding piano is based on the best grand pianos and any piano that does not sound like the best grand pianos cannot be deemed acceptable by those pianists.

Predict An Inference

It is currently impossible to create an electric piano that the acceptable judges will evaluate as being an improvement on existing grand pianos. The argument clearly states that professionals consider a piano that sounds different from the best grand pianos like a piano and therefore worse than the best-sounding existing pianos. So, it is not possible for an electric piano to sound better than a grand piano because an electric piano is currently made such that it will sound different from a grand piano. Nothing is said about technical improvements etc. to prove this false. Also, the argument does not state that the electric piano is *better* than the grand pianos, just that it is different.

Predictive Inference: It is impossible for an electric piano to sound better than a grand piano.

Answer choices explanation

(A)   This option is directly opposing the premise stating that it is not the amateur pianists but the professional pianists, and, who are the only acceptable judges of the quality of pianos.

(B)   There is nothing mentioned about professional pianists designing these pianos; the argument only talks about judging the quality of pianos. Thus, this option cannot be inferred.

(C)   Nothing in the argument tells us anything about the age of these pianos. This is out of scope of the argument.

(D)   This is the **correct** answer. It is aligned with our predictive inference that it is impossible to create an electric piano that sounds better than a grand piano.

(E)   We are not told about how people other than the professional pianists might perceive perfect "frequencies". Note that we cannot necessarily infer that the electric piano, just because it has "perfect frequencies" will sound **better** than the grand piano. The argument mentions only that the electric piano will necessarily sound different from the grand piano. Hence, we cannot infer that people prefer perfect frequencies and will like the electric piano.

The correct answer is option D.

Question 4

Argument construction

How much financial aid should be given by the rich nations to poorer nations to raise their industrial capacity depends on the extent to which the rich nations fear competition from would-be-competent poorer nations and the consequent threat of reduced exports. The amount of aid recommended by the US is invariably reduced and redistributed by a select committee judging aid packages purely from an American business perspective. As a consequence, many poorer nations have to find areas of industrial activities that pose no threat to the industrial activities of rich nations if they want to receive donations from the rich nations.

Predict An Inference

The passage states that the proportion of US aid relates to the extent that the industries being aided compete with US industries. The more the poorer nations compete, the less the aid given by US is.

Predictive Inference: The amount of financial aid to poorer nations would be proportionately less if the industrial activities of the receiving nations affect America's business interest, or else the aid would be optimum.

Answer choices explanation

(A)   We cannot conclude that the neediest countries are those with the smallest industrial output. The argument does not imply this. A nation can be rich even if industrial output isn't high, and the economy is based on agriculture or export of abundant natural resources.

(B)   This is the **correct** answer. It is almost a restatement of the provided facts. It is aligned with our predictive inference.

(C)   We cannot conclude that poorer nations depend on rich nations for developing their industrial economy as a whole. The argument implies that the poorer nations get restrained financial aid to develop their industrial base in areas other than the ones US deals in.

(D)   We cannot conclude that the wealth of the richer nations has expanded because of a policy of withholding foreign aid. The argument does not imply this. This is too judgmental.

(E)   The argument does not say that the aid is reduced as a rule. The aid is reduced and redistributed by judging aid packages purely from an American business perspective. We can infer that if American business is unaffected because of the aid, the aid would not be reduced.

The correct answer is option B.

Chapter 14

Complete the Argument

14.1 Complete the Argument Question type

Argu___.

Recently and gradually the importance of "Complete the Argument (CA)" questions is increasing. CA questions cannot be categorized into any one family of questions. These question types are not followed by any question stem after the argument. The argument ends with a "blank-line" asking to be completed with one of the options.

The "fill-in-the blank" statement could be a conclusion, a premise either strengthening or weakening the argument, or even an inference or a reconciling statement. Mostly, however, most CA arguments are similar to assumption or strengthen questions; most CA questions will ask us to select an option that makes a claim or conclusion true or more likely to be true. The correct option may even be restatement of the argument.

Look at the dialogue between two people in the image. What can complete the argument?

Brian, you think you crack the GRE in Two weeks because_____.

Yes! I can crack the GRE in two weeks because I've cracked many aptitude tests with flying colors.

Complete the argument

The following illustration depicts your job for 'complete the argument' questions.

Which of the following best completes the argument below?

In an internet _____ o cheating
on their wives _____ nate the
proportion of _____
because_____

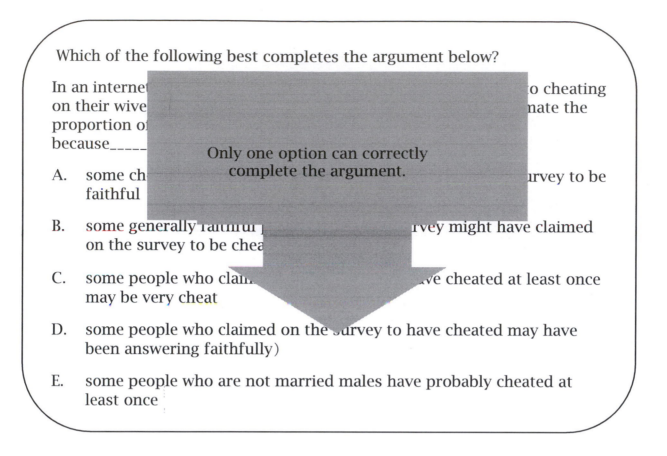

Only one option can correctly
complete the argument.

A.   some ch_____ rvey to be
     faithful

B.   some generally faithful _____ rvey might have claimed
     on the survey to be chea_____

C.   some people who clai_____ ve cheated at least once
     may be very cheat

D.   some people who claimed on the survey to have cheated may have
     been answering faithfully)

E.   some people who are not married males have probably cheated at
     least once

Question Stem

CA question do not contain any question stem, hence it becomes important to understand
what the question intends to ask. The key is to read the preceding word before the "blank-
line", which may start with "therefore", "since", "because", and other words or phrases. Read
the following table and you will understand the type of question.

Preceding word	Option statement	Question type
Since, Because, As etc........	Premise	Assumption, Strengthen, Weaken, or Resolve
Therefore, Thus, Hence, As a result etc.........	Conclusion	Inference
Above situation is similar to........	Parallel analogy	Parallel argument or mimic the argument

14.2   Process Of Solving Complete The Argument Questions

The 4-step approach is same as in Find the Assumption chapter.

The 4-step approach

   (1) Recognize the question type

   (2) Understand the argument construction

   (3) Predict the qualifier

   (4) Eliminate incorrect options

First 2 steps are the same for CA questions. Let us jump directly to the "predict the qualifier" step.

Predict the qualifier

Since the CA questions can be of any type of ASP questions, we must first see which category the question belongs to, and accordingly, we must apply the approach we have learnt for each of those question types. Say the question type is strengthen the argument, we must predict a strengthener best supporting the conclusion; similarly, if it belongs to weaken the argument type, we must predict a weakener shattering the conclusion; likewise for inference, or other question types.

Let us see an example to better understand the approach.

> Which of the following best completes the argument?
>
> Since an experienced, top-rated race-car driver is now constantly losing races he had always won before he acquired a certain race car, he plans to junk the race car he is currently using and replace it with a better model. The improved new race car model is more likely to improve the race-car driver's performance than will any other factor because..

Reading the preceding word before the "blank-line", we understand that the question asks for a premise, but we are still not sure whether it asks for an assumption, strengthener, or weakener.

Understand the argument:

An experienced, top-rated race-car driver is constantly losing a race he had always won. He blames the loss on the model of car he is using. He intends to raise his performance by replacing the car with an improved new race-car model.

Conclusion: The improved new race-car model is more likely to improve the race-car driver's performance than will any other factor.

The word "because" following the conclusion indicates that we must plug in a strengthener to support the claim that the improved new race-car model is more likely to boost the race-car driver's performance than will any other factor. So, this is a "strengthen the argument" question.

Let us predict a couple of strengtheners.

Predictive strengthener 1: Over the years, top racers observed that the quality of car constitutes 80% of the factors in winning races.

Predictive strengthener 2: Some advanced systems used in the new model keep it in control even at very high speeds.

Let us see some of the options to this argument.

(A) the driver may have new personal problems that have nothing to do with his car's performance

This cannot be answer as the option lays the onus of losing the race on the driver rather than the car. The importance of car is diluted and the argument is weakened rather than strengthened.

(B) races tend to judge more the quality of the car than the quality of the driver

This is the **correct** answer. It is aligned with our predictive qualifier. This is a strengthener. It emphasizes the importance of quality of the car in winning the races and strengthens the argument.

(C) decisions to switch race-cars should be based on that particular model's success rate

This option focuses on the selection of any particular model of car for racing, whereas the argument is concerned about whether the quality of car itself is the most important factor in the races.

(D) the driver may not necessarily have been able to overcome other obstacles during recent races

Like option A, this cannot be answer as the option lays the onus of losing the race on the driver rather than the car. Again, the importance of car is diluted and the argument is weakened rather than strengthened.

(E) improved race-cars are very expensive and difficult for many teams to afford

This option focuses on the price aspect of car for racing, whereas the argument is concerned about whether the quality of car itself is the most important factor in the races.

Example

Questions

14.3   Examples

Example 1

Many airlines have been pushing the federal government for assurances of greater security in case of terrorists attack onboard flights. One of these airlines expects the improved security to help increase revenue by $20 million a year, mostly from people who ....

Which of the following most logically completes the argument above?

(A)   are afraid of traveling by plane because of terrorist attacks

(B)   travel by luxury trains

(C)   spend more money on traveling

(D)   travel by plane because of status symbol

(E)   travel by plane when they are pressed for time

Argument Construction

Airlines have been pushing the government for greater security to be prepared for terrorists attack onboard flights. One of these airlines expects improved security to increase the revenue by $20 million a year. The increased revenue will mostly come from the class of people who ....

Predict An Inference

With the understanding of the argument, we can infer that is a question on inference. If it is true that the improved security will increase the revenue by $20 million a year, what type of people will bring in the increased revenue?

Certainly, the people who were scared of insufficient security onboard flights will feel confident now and start taking flights more often.

Predictive Inference: <who> were scared of insufficient onboard flight security.

Answer choices explanation

This is an easy question. As discussed, the answer is A. It is aligned with our predictive inference.

The correct answer is option A.

Example 2

Which of the following best completes the argument below?

The main disadvantage of the new promotion scheme is that it places more emphasis on seniority than capability. While not wishing to degrade the work record of certain executives, who have faithfully served the company for a good many years, ...

(A)   other more qualified personnel have been promoted before them

(B)   they clearly should be in positions of more responsibility

(C)   perhaps it's time to let them go

(D)   one has to ask oneself whether they deserve automatic promotion

(E)   they might well consider such an appointment as a demotion

Argument Construction

The author criticizes the new promotion scheme. He reasons that it places more emphasis on the seniority of the employees in the workplace than on their capability. **Although** he acknowledges the work record of certain senior employees, ...

Predict An Inference

With the understanding of the argument, we can infer that while the author is against the new promotion scheme for basing its decisions on seniority rather than on merit, he does not refute the contribution of ALL the senior employees, and even acknowledges the contribution of some of the senior employees.

Understand the tone and the intent of the author. The word "while" shows that he does not back down from acknowledging the value of some senior employees, but also that he wants to take cognizance of "capability" in the promotion process. He, therefore, implies that not all senior employees deserve promotion juts because they are senior. The correct option would be the one against senior employees or one that emphasizes capability as a basis for promotion.

Predictive Inference 1: capability should also have its say while considering the promotion.

Predictive Inference 2: many competent employees are juniors to non-as-competent seniors.

Answer choices explanation

(A)   "other more qualified personnel have been promoted before them" is a factual statement. It does not support capability over seniority. The correct option must be author's opinion. This is incorrect.

(B)   "they clearly should be in positions of more responsibility" is clearly in favor of the seniors. We want something against the seniors. This is incorrect.

(C)   "perhaps it's time to let them go" is certainly against the seniors, but is an extreme statement. The author does not refute the contribution of ALL the senior employees; he even acknowledges the contribution of some senior employees. This is incorrect.

(D) This is the **correct** answer. "one has to ask oneself whether they deserve automatic promotion." is against the seniors, and is justified inferable opinion of the author.

(E) "they might well consider such an appointment as a demotion" is out of scope. The author cannot conclude the argument with seniors considering such promotions as demotions. There's no hint for such a deduction.

The correct answer is option D.

Example 3

Which of the following best completes the argument below?

The price of computers is dictated more by the price of computer chips than by any other computer component. Due to this fact, the fortunes of computer chip manufacturers have risen dramatically as the computers now have become an indispensable element of modern life. When the prices of computer chips rise in any given year over the prices of the previous year, the prices of computers rise accordingly. This has a knock on effect with sales of new computers falling when purchase costs increase. In 1999 sales of home computers went up by 29%, therefore, it can be concluded that ....

(A) the cost of computer chips in 1998 was at least as high as it was in 1999

(B) the cost of chips rose by at least 29% in 1999

(C) the prices of all models of computers in 1998 were 29% lower than the prices in 1999

(D) sales by computer chip manufacturers rose by 29% in 1999

(E) total sales by computer manufacturers rose by 29% in 1999

Argument Construction

The crux of the argument is that whenever the prices of computer chips rise in any given year, the prices of computers rise accordingly. This in turn causes the sales of new computers to go down. In 1999 sales of home computers went up by 29%, therefore, it can be concluded that ....

Predict A Conclusion

As stated that the crux of the argument is that whenever the prices of computer chips rise in any given year, the prices of computers rise accordingly. We need to draw a conclusion from the argument.

The meaning of *the prices of computers rise accordingly* is that if chip price drops, then the computer price must go down, and vice-versa. The data given for 1999 states that the sales of home computers went up by 29%, therefore, it can be concluded that the price of home computers must not be higher in 1999 than that in 1998. This further concludes that the price of chip must not be higher in 1999 than that in 1998.

Predictive conclusion: the price of chips must not be higher in 1999 than it was in 1998.

Answer choices explanation

(A) The meaning of the option statement is that the cost of computer chips in 1998 was almost equal to what it was in 1999. So, if the sales of home computers went up by 29%, the price of home computers, and chips could not have risen. So, option A is the only valid conclusion.

(B) This is an opposite answer. It is inconsistent with the fact that *when the prices of computer chips rise in any given year over the price of the previous year, the prices of computers rise accordingly.*

(C) We cannot conclude this. The data given in the argument is regarding home computers only, and not for all the computer models.

(D) Like option C, we cannot conclude that sales by all computer chip manufacturers rose by 29% in 1999 as the data given in the argument is regarding home computers only.

(E) Similarly, like option C, and D, we cannot conclude that sales by all computer manufacturers rose by 29% in 1999 as the data given in the argument is regarding home computers only.

The correct answer is option A.

Example 4

Which of the following best completes the argument below?

Chrysler has been undergoing some dramatic changes. Gone is the image of a company focused solely upon the US. Now, both the products and the work force have begun to reflect the global nature of the company. The new works team is composed of engineers from all over the world. All of the mechanical engineers are the product of an in-house training program although, as yet, none of the engineers specializing in hydraulics has won the prestigious Order of Merit bestowed by the Mechanical Engineers Union. So far, only engineers winning the Order of Merit have gone on to become department heads. Therefore ....

(A) all of the department heads have received the Order of Merit

(B) all of the winners of the Order of Merit have received in-house training

(C) none of the department heads who have specialized in hydraulics are the product of an in-house training program

(D) none of the department heads are from the US

(E) none of the non-US mechanical engineers who are the products of in-house training have the Order of Merit

Argument Construction

The argument is long in size but easy to understand. The crux of the argument is that the new works team in Chrysler is composed of engineers from all over the world. All of the mechanical engineers are the product of an in-house training program, but no engineer specializing in hydraulics has won the Order of Merit award. Till now, only engineers winning the award have become department heads (HoDs). Therefore ....

Predict An Inference

We can further simply the facts for better understanding.

- All the mechanical engineers received training program

- No engineer specializing in hydraulics (a branch of mechanical engineering) won the award

- Only award-winning engineers became department heads(HoDs)

Let us see what we can conclude out of this information. Since only engineers who won the award have become the (HoDs), and none from hydraulics could win it so far, we can infer that the HoD for hydraulics department would be not an in-house mechanical engineer specializing in hydraulics.

Predictive inference: HoD for hydraulics department is not an in-house mechanical engineer specializing in hydraulics.

Answer choices explanation

(A)   This option can be eliminated as the argument merely states that of the engineers promoted to department head, all had won the Order of Merit but maybe non-engineers had been made department heads. HoD for hydraulics department may be a non-award-winning non-engineer person or an outside recruit who's not been promoted internally.

(B)   This option can be discarded as the argument only states that all the mechanical engineers are the product of in-house training schemes.

(C)   This is the **correct** answer. It is just a restatement of the facts provided by the argument. It is aligned with our predictive inference.

(D)   This can easily be eliminated as the argument does not differentiate between the US and the non-US works team.

(E)   With the same reason as for option D, option E is incorrect.

The correct answer is option C.

Practice

Questions

14.4 Practice Questions

14.4.1 Questions

Question 1

Which of the following best completes the argument below?

In an internet-survey of married males, 23.78 percent admitted to cheating on their wives at least once. However, the survey may underestimate the proportion of married males who are cheats, because..

(A)   some cheats taking the survey might have claimed on the survey to be faithful

(B)   some generally faithful people taking the survey might have claimed on the survey to be cheat

(C)   some people who claimed on the survey to have cheated at least once may be very cheat

(D)   some people who claimed on the survey to have cheated may have been answering faithfully

(E)   some people who are not married males have probably cheated at least once

Question 2

Which of the following best completes the argument below?

The prospects for the future of the seal are far from rosy. Poaching and abuse of quotas have become endemic throughout the sealing regions of Canada and Russia. Seal hide dealers, motivated by the high profits to be made selling hides to the fashion industry, are ignoring the distinctive markings on the skins which show that hides come from illegally culled animals. An internationally supported initiative to police the trade was launched last year..

(A)   and has been very successful

(B)   but has proved highly effective

(C)   which goes some way to explain the current situation

(D)   although much has been achieved

(E)   but has had little practical effect

Question 3

Which of the following best completes the argument below?

Each time X grocery store raises the price of goods by 10 percent, sales drop by 20 percent. However, when the price of apples increased, the quantity of apples sold was the same as before the price increase. This is because ....

(A) whenever there is an increase in price, the amount of a certain product sold must drop.

(B) shop assistants should take care to try to interest clients in other fruits besides apples.

(C) the drop in sales is consistent with quarterly trends forecast by the grocery store.

(D) apples are, on average, are more expensive than other fruit in the grocery store.

(E) the sale of apples is dependent not only on their price, but on other factors.

Question 4

Which of the following best completes the argument below?

Recent research by the Tropical Disease Division of the Army Medical Corps suggests that the malaria parasite's incubation period is accepted to be a maximum 90 days.

Surprisingly, the studies of more than 80 male and female service personnel who were infected have revealed that, although the 90 days limit remains generally true, 18 of the patients had succumbed to the parasite more than 90 days after returning to the US from a zone containing malaria bearing mosquitoes, the longest being a pilot who had developed malaria 133 days after returning to the US from a spell of duty in Africa. This exception is understandable because ....

(A) insecticide resistant mosquito swarms have become a common phenomenon in the US

(B) pilots have frequently complained of mosquitoes getting trapped aboard planes

(C) the malaria parasite's incubation period is accepted to be a maximum 90 days barring the exception to the maximum of 1% of the cases

(D) the incubation period of the malaria parasite varies according to the species of mosquito as host

(E) anti-malaria immunization has become less effective over the last 20 years

14.4.2 Answer-Key

(1) A | (2) E | (3) E | (4) B

Solutions

14.4.3   Solutions

Question 1

Argument construction

The argument is simple to understand. In an internet-survey of married males, 23.78% admitted to cheating on their wives at least once. However, the author is skeptical about the survey results. He is of the opinion that the figure may be higher, because...............................

Conclusion: The survey may underestimate the proportion of married males who are cheats.

Predict A Stregthener

The conclusion states that the figure 23.78% may be even higher. We must think how survey respondents can make this figure skewed. It is possible that some cheats incorrectly claimed on the survey that they are faithful. Such a situation will show how the survey can underestimate the number of cheats.

Predictive strengthener: Some cheats claimed on the survey that they are faithful.

Answer choices explanation

(A)   This is the **correct** answer. It is aligned to our predictive strengthener.

(B)   If some generally faithful people taking the survey claimed on the survey to be cheats, the survey will overestimate rather than underestimate the proportion of married males who are cheats.

(C)   This option is irrelevant. It talks about the degree of cheating.

(D)   This information will neither underestimate nor overestimate the proportion of married males who are cheats.

(E)   Cheating by non-married males is outside the scope of the argument.

The correct answer is option A.

Question 2

Argument construction

The author laments the prospects of the seals' existence and the likelihood of its survival. Poaching and the abuse of quotas are to blame. Seal hide dealers sell hides to the fashion industry, and ignore the distinctive markings on the skins of seals which show that the seals come to them illegally. An internationally supported initiative to regulate the trade was launched last year...............................

Conclusion: The prospects for the future of the seal are far from rosy.

Predict A Stregthener

The clue is the negative idea suggested in the first sentence—the conclusion: the prospects of the seal livelihood are in danger. The author lists the threats to the seal and concludes with one inadequate positive step. It can be inferred that the concluding statement would be in a negative tone supporting the conclusion that seals are in danger despite the measures taken to ensure the survival of their species. Hence this is a strengthen question.

Predictive strengthener: however, a little could be reaped out of it.

Answer choices explanation

Options A, B, and D are positive in meaning, while option C is neutral. The only option that is aligned with our predictive strengthener is option E.

The correct answer is option E.

Question 3

Argument construction

The argument is simple to understand. Each time the grocery store raises the price of goods by 10 percent, sales drop by 20 percent. However, behavior of the price of apples did not follow the rule. This is because ....

Predict A Resolutor

This question can be treated as "Resolve the paradox" type.

The paradox: Despite the increase in the price of apples, the quantity of apples sold did not decrease.

Predictive resolutor: the price of apples was lower than normal; the increase in the price did not make any difference to the customers.

Answer choices explanation

(A) This option is merely a mandate which states the rule. It does not help to explain the paradox.

(B) This option is irrelevant. Whether shop assistants should take care to try to interest clients in other fruit besides apples does not relate to the paradox.

(C) Consistency in dropping in sales with quarterly trends forecast does not to explain the paradox.

(D) Comparing the price of apples with other fruit does not help to resolve the paradox.

(E) This is the **correct** answer. If the sale of apples is dependent not only on price, but also on other factors, the increase in price will not significantly impact the quantity sold.

The correct answer is option E.

Question 4

Argument construction

Recent research suggests that the malaria parasite's incubation period is a maximum 90 days. Surprisingly, the studies of more than 80 male and female service personnel who were infected have revealed that 18 of the patients had succumbed to the parasite more than 90 days after returning to the US from a zone containing malaria bearing mosquitoes, the longest being a pilot who had developed malaria 133 days after returning to the US. This exception is understandable because ....

Predict A Resolutor

This is a question on "resolve the paradox".

The paradox: The malaria parasite's incubation period is a maximum 90 days, but 18 out of 80 patients found infected with malaria well after the 90 days period.

We have to resolve the discrepancy while maintaining that the malaria parasite's incubation period is a maximum 90 days, but 18 out of 80 patients got malaria infection 90 days after returning to US from zone containing malaria bearing mosquito.

It is possible that malaria bearing mosquitoes bit those 18 patients after they returned to the US.

Predictive resolutor 1: Malaria bearing mosquitoes bit those 18 patients after they returned to the US.

It is possible that the apex medical research body refuted the findings presented by Tropical Disease Division of the Army Medical Corps by suggesting that the malaria parasite's incubation period may go well over 90 days.

Predictive resolutor 2: The apex medical research body suggested that the malaria parasite's incubation period may go well over 90 days.

Answer choices explanation

(A) This option states that swarms of mosquitoes will take over the US but the puzzle is over the incubation period of the parasite, not the mosquito. Also, this option discussed malaria infections occurring in the US, but the argument talks about 18 patients infected returning to US (thus getting infected outside US).

(B) This is the **correct** answer. The mosquitoes getting trapped aboard planes may have made their abode in the workplace of the patients in the US and bit them there.

(C) 1% of 80 patients is approximately 1 patient. So as per this option, there can be an exception of 1 patient, but the data suggests that there are as many as 18 infected patients. This information does not resolve the discrepancy.

(D) This option can be eliminated because the argument states that the maximum incubation period is 90 days so any variations according to species must be below this limit.

(E) The argument is concerned about the incubation period of the parasite, not the about the effectiveness of anti-malaria immunization.

The correct answer is option B.

Chapter 15

Bold Face Argument

15.1   Bold Face Argument Question type

Bold Face or Role Play question types are not as common as Strengthen or Weaken question types, but not as rare as Parallel Reasoning question types.   You are may face a Bold Face question in the test.

Boldface questions also belong to structure based family. Usually, in the argument of a typical Bold Face question, two specific portions are written in boldface font. This type of question is easy to recognize because unlike the arguments of other GRE question types, it has portions in bold. Very rarely, you may encounter an argument with only one boldfaced portion; however, your task, approach and strategy to answer remains the same as for two portions in bold.

The question stems asks you to identify the roles the boldfaced portions play in the structure of the argument or in relation to each other.

What is the meaning of "Role Play"? Simply put, the role is the purpose the boldfaced portions serve in the argument. A typical argument may have a premise, a counter-premise, an intermediate conclusion, or background information. The intermediate conclusion could also be a counter-conclusion. Counter-conclusion is a conclusion against which the author makes his main conclusion.

Look at the following dialogue to get a broader understanding.

By now you must have gone through earlier chapters, and understood various elements of the arguments. It may seem that if Bold Face questions are limited to identifying a premise, a counter-premise, an intermediate conclusion, or background information, they can be easily tamed. However, the scope is not limited to this extent. The arguments of Bold Face questions are usually complex and lengthy, and use abstract diction and convoluted verbiage. Moreover, identifying the relationship of one boldfaced portion with other boldfaced portion or the other not-boldfaced portions compounded with the usage of abstract non-definitive terms make things complicated.

However, there's an approach to deal with these questions.

The following illustration depicts your job for the boldface question type.

CEO: Some of the board members claim that the company's current market undervaluation has been caused by my policies, and that I am responsible for the undervaluation. Although I admit that **the company has encountered market undervaluation during my tenure**, I do not agree that I am at fault for this problem. The busi   urrent undervaluation, an   **my administration, th   en even worse.**

In the CEO's argu   f the following roles?

A) The first is a pre   the second supports the board members.

B) The first is a statement ac   second is a consequence of the board members' claims.

C) The first is a fact that   radict his conclusion; the second offers support in con   sion.

D) The first is evidence of unethi   e CEO; the second is evidence offered by the CEO to explain that ac

E) The first is evidence that undermines the CEO's position; the second is a statement that follows from that position.

Only one option will rightly describe the roles both the boldfaced portions play.

Question Stem

Bold Face question type does not use many formats of question stems. As said earlier, this type of question is easy to recognize because unlike the arguments of other question types, the argument of this kind of questions has some portion of it boldfaced. Two most common question stems are:

· In the argument above, the two portions in boldface play which of the following roles?

· What function do the statements in boldface fulfill with respect to the argument presented above?

Diction

Usage of key terms and their inter-relationship in the context of the argument deserve a lot of attention. So far, we have seen the key terms like premise, counter-premise, intermediate conclusion, background information, evidence, fact, position, support, strengthen, weaken, and a couple of others; but there are many more to be studied by you.

The Bold Face questions, particularly in the options, may contain terms such as circumstance, finding, data, observation, judgment, stance, prediction, opinion, synopsis, allegation, consideration, explanation, justification, etc. Your job is to understand the nuances of these key terms. Below is a partial list of these terms classified into "Fact", "Claim", or "Fact or Claim".

The list is not exhaustive, and the categorization is suggestive; it may change according to the context of the argument.

Fact	Claim	Either—Fact or Claim
Premise	Conclusion	Consideration
Counter-Premise	Intermediate-Conclusion	Explanation
Evidence	Counter-Conclusion	Justification
Finding	Opinion	Support
Circumstance	Position	Reasoning
Data	Belief	Advocacy
Information	Prediction	
Observation	Judgement	
	Stance	
	Synopsis	
	Notion	
	Theory	
	Hypothesis	
	Phenomenon	

Verbiage

Many times, the verbiage of the options may cloud your thinking process and you may get caught in a trap laid by the test makers.

Let us see a couple of option statements; we will understand their meaning.

Option 1: The first is a prediction that is challenged by the argument; the second is a finding upon which the argument depends.

Meaning: Here "first" means the first boldfaced portion; "prediction" can be substituted with <u>claim</u> as suggested by the table above; "challenged by the argument" means that the author opposes the claim made in the first boldfaced portion; "second" means the second boldfaced portion; "finding" can be substituted with <u>fact</u> as suggested by the table above; "upon which the argument depends" means that the conclusion is drawn based on the fact presented by the second boldfaced portion.

In other words, we can rewrite the option as:

"The first boldfaced portion is a claim that the author opposes; the second boldfaced portion is a fact on which the conclusion is drawn."

The option becomes much more comprehensible than it was before.

Option 2: The first is an opinion put forth to support a conclusion that the argument rejects; the second is a consideration that is introduced to counter the force of conclusion.

Meaning: "Opinion" can be substituted with <u>claim</u> as suggested by the table above; "put forth to support a conclusion" means that the claim strengthens the conclusion drawn in the argument; "conclusion that the argument rejects" means that the author opposes the claim; "consideration" can be substituted with <u>claim</u> or <u>fact</u> depending upon the context of the argument; "consideration that is introduced to counter the force of conclusion" means that the consideration (fact or claim) works against the conclusion.

In other words, we can rewrite the option as:

"The first boldfaced portion is a claim that strengthens the conclusion; the second boldfaced portion is a fact or claim that works against the conclusion."

15.2   Process Of Solving Resolve Boldface Questions

The 4-step approach

(1) Recognize the question type

(2) Understand the argument construction

(3) Analyze each statement

(4) Eliminate incorrect options

First 2 steps are the same for Boldface questions. Let us jump directly to analyze each statement step.

Analyze each statement

Usually Boldface arguments are lengthy and comprise three to four statements. After understanding the argument, you should understand and analyze what role each statement, and not just the boldfaced portion, plays. This step can further be divided into 6 steps.

(1) Understand the conclusion; it may not necessarily be one of the boldfaced portions.

(2) Understand inter-mediate/counter-conclusion, if any.

(3) Categorize each statement as conclusion, intermediate/counter-conclusion, premise, counter-premise, fact, claim, or as either fact or claim.

(4) Understand what each statement and boldface portions mutually play in the argument.

(5) Understand whether both the boldfaced portions are on the same side or opposite side.

(6) Pre-phrase what role each boldface portion plays. It is likely that you will encounter different terms used to articulate the roles boldfaced portions play in the options; you should replace the synonymous key terms as suggested in the "Diction" heading above, and select the correct option.

Example

Questions

15.3   Examples

Example 1

While some people complain that the democratic system of governance is impotent and lack-luster, **the same people do not protest when a pseudo-dictator tries to swindle the system.** These people are missing out on a basic proposition: a system is always bigger than an individual. Taken this way, **democracy is de facto the best form of governance.**

The two boldface portions play which of the following roles?

(A)   The first is a generalization accepted by the author as true; the second is a consequence that follows from the truth of that generalization.

(B)   The first is evidence that supports one of two contradictory points of view; the second supports the point of view that first supports.

(C)   The first is a commonly held point of view; the second is the support for that point of view.

(D)   The first is one of two contradictory points of view; the second is the other point of view.

(E)   The first concedes a consideration that weighs against the viewpoint of the author; the second is that viewpoint.

Argument Analysis

Some people crib about the democratic system of governance. They see it as a powerless and a boring form of governance. The author changes the direction here; he blames the same people by arguing that they do not raise their voices when a powerful individual akin to a dictator exploits the system. The author further adds that the people ignore the fact that the system is always bigger than an individual or a dictator. The author concludes that democracy is by default the best form of governance.

Predictive Role Play

Let's dissect this argument.

The easiest part of the question is to find what role does second boldfaced portion play. While understanding the argument, we found that it is the conclusion of the author or argument.

Conclusion: (Bold Faced 2): Democracy is de facto best form of governance.

Statement 1: (There are.......lackluster.): This statement can be a fact or the author's opinion. The author rejects this fact. Hence, this is not supporting the author.

Statement 2:   (Bold Faced 1): This statement can be a fact or the author's opinion. The author accepts this fact but he accepts it as a fact that goes against the earlier sentence which states that democracy is bad. How is "Bold Faced 1"—BF1 related to "Bold Faced 2"— BF2: the conclusion? We can simply infer that both BF1 and BF2 are on the same side, and BF1 helps BF2—conclusion build its ground. BF1 is the evidence the author provides to prove his point (BF2) that democracy is the best form of government and to prove his opposition's point that democracy is bad wrong.

Statement 3: (Moreover........individual): This statement is also in line with statement 2. It also supports BF2—conclusion.

Statement 4: (Bold Faced 2): As discussed. It is author's conclusion.

Hence, we can predict that BF1 is the evidence that author uses to prove himself right and prove his opposition wrong and that BF2 is the author's position.

Answer choices explanation

(A) **BF1:** What does *generalization accepted by the author as true mean?* It can be inferred that generalization is a word used for opinion. However, we know that BF1 is a fact that the author uses to support his point and against the generalization given in the argument.

    BF2: What does a *consequence that follows from the truth of that generalization mean?* It means that BF2—conclusion—follows from the consequence of BF1. This is not correct. Let us phrase it—*It is true that some people do not raise their voices against the dictators when they exploit the system, but this does not follow that democracy is the best form of governance.*

(B) **BF1:** *points of view?* They are **point of view 1:** Democracy is bad; **point of view 2:** Democracy is good. The option statement states that BF1 supports one of the points of view. Yes, it is correct. It does support 2nd point of view. So far going well.

    BF2: This is also right. In our analysis, we concluded that BF1 and BF2 are on the same side, and this option says so. Hence, option B is the **correct** answer.

(C) **BF1:** This is incorrect. The BF1 is author's evidence against the commonly held point of view—Democracy is bad.

    BF2: This is wrong. The BF2 is a conclusion that opposes that point of view.

(D) **BF1:** This is incorrect. As discussed above, the BF1 is a fact that the author uses against his opposition and to support himself. This option calls BF1 a conclusion and one that opposes the author.

    BF2: This is correct. The BF2 is the other (opposing) point of view. This is the correct answer.

(E) **BF1:** The first part of the option statement means that BF1 provides a consideration that is against the viewpoint of the author. It is wrong. We concluded that BF1 and BF2 are on the same side, but this option says otherwise.

BF2: This is correct. BF2 is the viewpoint of author.

The correct answer is option B.

Example 2

Supermarkets frequently offer commodity brands with innovative and appealing mega-sale-discount schemes comparable to offers from competing peers and other stores. **Because mega-sale-discount schemes are quickly copied by competing peers and other stores,** many retail giants charge as less as possible for commodity brands to extract as much volume of sales as possible. However, sales generated by mega-sale-discount schemes give stronger incentives to competitors to copy the discount schemes. Therefore, **the best strategy to maximize overall sales from mega-sale-discount schemes is to charge more than the lowest possible price.**

The two boldface portions play which of the following roles?

(A)   The first is an assumption that supports a described course of action; the second provides a consideration to support a preferred course of action.

(B)   The first is a consideration that helps explain the appeal of a certain strategy; the second presents an alternative strategy endorsed by the argument.

(C)   The first is a phenomenon that justifies a specific strategy; the second is that strategy.

(D)   The first is a conclusion that demonstrates why a particular approach is flawed; the second describes a way to amend that approach.

(E)   The first is a factor used to rationalize a particular strategy; the second is a factor against that strategy.

Argument Analysis

The argument is easy to understand. We outline the crux.

Supermarkets frequently offer mega-sale-discount schemes. Since mega-sale-discount schemes are quickly copied by the competition, many retail giants charge as less as possible to sell more numbers. However, this strategy is copied quickly. Therefore, the best strategy to maximize overall sales from the discount schemes is to charge more than the lowest possible price.

Conclusion: The best strategy to maximize overall sales from mega-sale-discount schemes is to charge more than the lowest possible price.

Predictive Role Play

There are two strategies discussed here:

Strategy 1: Charge as less as possible
Strategy 2: Charge more than the lowest possible price

The easiest part of the question is to find what role does second boldfaced portion play. While understanding the argument, we found that it is the conclusion of the author or the argument.

Conclusion:(BF 2): The best strategy to maximize overall sales from mega-sale-discount schemes is to charge more than the lowest possible price. It is strategy 2.

Statement 1: (Supermarkets.......stores): It is either a fact or background information or simple premise.
Statement 2: (BF 1): It is fact or premise that supports strategy 1(many retail.......possible).
Statement 3: (However.......scheme): It is a counter-premise that goes against the strategy 1. It supports strategy2—BF2.

Answer choices explanation

(A) **BF1:** assumption is also a premise, but BF1 is a fact not an assumption.
     BF2: It is not a consideration to support a preferred course of action implying strategy. BF2 itself is a strategy or the main conclusion.

(B) **BF1:** This is correct. It is a consideration (fact) that helps to explain the appeal of strategy 1.
     BF2: This is correct. It is an alternative strategy (strategy 2) endorsed by the argument. It is the **correct** answer.

(C) **BF1:** This is correct. It can be called a phenomenon that justifies a specific strategy (strategy 1).
     BF2: This is wrong. BF2 is strategy 2 and not strategy 1.

(D) **BF1:** This is wrong. It is not the conclusion. BF2 is the conclusion.
     BF2: This is correct. BF2 does propose alternate strategy.

(E) **BF1:** This is correct. BF1 does rationalize strategy.
     BF2: It is not a factor used against strategy 1, but it is the strategy itself.

The correct answer is option B.

Example 3

A biologist Mark claimed that **microorganisms have a much larger impact on the complete ecosystem than scientists typically recognize.** Now a team of researchers has gathered and archived the results of hundreds of studies, on animal-bacterial interactions, and clearly shown that Mark is right. The combined analysis suggest that the evidence supporting his view has reached a critical point, demanding that scientists re-examine the basic characteristics of life through the lens of the complex, interwoven relationships among microorganisms and other very different organisms. **The results will deeply change the way the researchers continue with their own areas of interest.**

In the argument given, the two boldfaced portions play which of the following roles?

(A)   The first identifies the content of the conclusion of the argument; the second is the main claim of the argument.

(B)   The first provides support for the conclusion of the argument; the second identifies the content of that conclusion.

(C)   The first states the conclusion of the argument; the second calls that conclusion into question.

(D)   The first provides support for the conclusion of the argument; the second calls that conclusion into question.

(E)   Each provides support for the conclusion of the argument.

Argument Construction

A biologist claimed that microorganisms are more important that we believe them to be. Recent studies have proved this. This in turn will bring about a rewriting of fundamentals and change most areas of study.

Predictive Role Play

Statement 1 (BF 1)—(microorganisms....recognize) This is the claim by the biologist Mark. Hence, BF1 is a claim. The portion in boldface is the claim that is proven right in the argument and supports the argument's intermediate conclusion that Mark is right.

Statement 2—(Now a team.......Mark is right) This statement is clearly the evidence that the author uses to state that Mark is right. However, the part "Mark is right" is an **intermediate conclusion** of the author.

Statement 3—(The combined......very different life forms.) This sentence consists of additional facts that support Mark and the author's claim and it also contains predictions of what the claim will bring about.

Statement 4 (BF 2)—(The results.......of study) This statement is a claim that will happen because Mark is right. Thus, BF2 is the main conclusion of the author.

Answer choices explanation

(A)   This is the **correct** answer. BF1 is the claim part only of the argument. We can consider BF1 as "content of the conclusion"; BF2 is the main conclusion.

(B)   While BF1 can be taken as support for the argument, we cannot say that BF2 is the content of the main conclusion. We discussed above that BF1 is the claim, and BF2 is the main conclusion.

(C)   While BF1 is the claim, BF2 is not calling the conclusion into question.

(D) While BF1 can be thought of as supporting the conclusion, BF2 is not calling the conclusion into question.

(E) BF1 is not a fact. This option calls both BF supports, i.e. facts. We discussed above that BF2 is a conclusion.

The correct answer is option A.

Example 4

Many intellectuals feel that **strong copyright and patent laws are necessary to encourage and nurture creativity.** Many argue that the competitors are free to steal ideas, create knockoffs and drain profits from innovators, when such protections are not in place. Yet, these people fail to consider that a number of major industries such as fashion, cuisine, open-source software, finance, font design, stand-up comedy and more thrive, compete and innovate even without much legal protection for intellectual property. As a matter of fact, in most of these industries, copying and blatant imitation is widespread. In fact, this imitation sets trends and propels people and boosts the economy. **Fashion industry is the best representative of the idea that that imitation encourages innovation and creativity.**

In the author's argument, the two portions in boldface play which of the following roles?

(A) The first is a claim that has been used to support a conclusion that the argument accepts; the second is that conclusion.

(B) The first is evidence that has been used to support a conclusion for which the argument provides further evidence; the second is the main conclusion of the argument.

(C) The first is a finding whose implications are at issue in the argument; the second is a claim presented in order to argue against deriving certain implications from that finding.

(D) The first is a claim that the argument strongly disputes; the second is evidence put forth to establish the contradictory conclusion that the argument proposes.

(E) The first is a finding whose accuracy is evaluated in the argument; the second is evidence presented to establish that the finding is accurate.

Argument Construction

The above argument claims that while the traditional wisdom holds that copyright and patents increase creativity, the opposite is true. The argument states many examples in support of this.

Predictive Role Play

Statement 1 (BF 1)—(strong copyright....creativity) The first portion in boldface is the traditional belief that the argument strongly disputes.

Statement 2—(Many argue.....not in place) This is evidence that supports the conventional beliefs and claims.

Statement 3—(Yet these people fail.....widespread) Notice the use of contrast word "yet", which shows a distinctive change in direction. This statement is evidence, but it does not support the conventional beliefs. Thus, it supports the author's beliefs and the author holds beliefs that are contradictory to conventional beliefs.

Statement 4—(In fact,....economy) This seems to be the crux of the author's talk, i.e. his main conclusion.

Statement 5 (BF 2)—**(Fashion industry........creativity)** the second portion is an example cited as evidence for the main conclusion of the argument that copying sets the trend. This main conclusion is contradictory to the traditional belief.

Answer choices explanation

(A) While BF1 is a claim, the argument does not accept this claim. BF2 is not a conclusion, but a fact/example.

(B) BF1 is not evidence/fact that the argument accepts. BF2 is not the main conclusion of the argument, as discussed above.

(C) BF1 is not a finding even though it is at issue in the argument. BF1 is a claim. BF2 is not a claim/conclusion, even though it argues against BF1.

(D) This is the **correct** answer. BF1 is being strongly disputed in the argument and BF2 does provide evidence that supports a contradictory (main) conclusion.

(E) BF1 is not a finding even though its accuracy is being evaluated in the argument. BF2 argues against BF1 and does not prove BF1 right.

The correct answer is option D.

Practice

Questions

15.4 Practice Questions

15.4.1 Questions

Question 1

CEO: Some of the board members claim that the company's current market undervaluation has been caused by my policies, and that I am responsible for the undervaluation. Although I admit that **the company has encountered market undervaluation during my tenure,** I do not agree that I am at fault for this problem. The business policies of the prior CEO caused the current undervaluation, and **were it not for the business policies of my administration, the current undervaluation would have been even worse.**

In the CEO's argument, the two boldface portions play which of the following roles?

(A) The first is a premise that has been used against the CEO; the second supports the board members.

(B) The first is a statement accepted by the CEO; the second is a consequence of the board members' claims.

(C) The first is a fact that the CEO believes does not contradict his conclusion; the second offers support in consideration of that conclusion.

(D) The first is evidence of unethical activity by the CEO; the second is evidence offered by the CEO to explain that activity.

(E) The first is evidence that undermines the CEO's position; the second is a statement that follows from that position.

Question 2

There is not one good reason for allowing managers to work from home, while there are several good reasons to deny the same. For one, it would be an additional operational challenge to businesses. Businesses are already facing many challenges all over the world, and so adding additional impediment is not an option. If the manager behaves like a manager, he can manage the family as well. **If the manager doesn't behave like a manager, he will not be able to manage the family, regardless of whether he is at home or at work.**

In the argument given, the two portions in boldface play which of the following roles?

(A) The first is the primary conclusion of the argument and the second is a secondary conclusion.

(B) The first is the advocacy of the argument and the second raises doubts about this advocacy.

(C) The first provides evidence as to why a certain policy should not be adopted by businesses and the second further strengthens this evidence.

(D) The first is a conclusion that the argument disagrees with; the second provides the reasoning behind this disagreement.

(E) The first is the primary conclusion of the argument and the second provides reasoning supporting the primary conclusion.

Question 3

Using graphic simulations and conceptual frames scientists projected the effects of almost negligible (about a pinch of salt per person per day), steady annual cutback of sodium intake in the U.S. diet, cutting sodium consumption by 40 percent to about 2,200 mg/day over a decade. A gradual cutback in sodium intake by 40 percent to about 2,200 mg/day over a decade is projected to save between 280,000 and 500,000 lives. Even a better result is possible and **about 60 percent more deaths could be averted over this decade** if these same cutbacks could be achieved faster by upping the cutback amount (500,000 to 850,000 lives).

In the argument given above, the two boldface portions play which of the following roles?

(A) The first is a prediction that, if accurate, would provide support for the main conclusion of the argument; the second is that main conclusion.

(B) The first is a prediction that, if accurate, would provide support for the argument; the second is a conclusion drawn in order to support that main conclusion.

(C) The first is an objection that the argument rejects; the second is the main conclusion of the argument.

(D) The first is an objection that the argument rejects; the second presents a conclusion that could be drawn if that objection were allowed to stand.

(F.) The first is a claim that has been advanced in support of a position that the argument opposes; the second is a claim advanced in support of the main conclusion of the argument.

15.4.2   Answer-Key

(1) C | (2) E | (3) B

Solutions

15.4.3 Solutions

Question 1

Argument Analysis

Let us understand the argument.

Some board members think that CEO's business policy is the reason for company's undervaluation in the market. However, the CEO does not think so. His position is—I am not responsible for it. While he admits that the company's market position became undervalued during his tenure, he reasons that it is because of his predecessor's policies and not his. Further, he strengthens his position by stating that had his policies not been implemented, the situation would have been much worse than it is now.

Conclusion: I am at fault for this problem of current market undervaluation.

Predictive Role Play

By now you must have followed the detailed approach to attack the boldfaced questions. Let us attack this question with an alternate approach.

Let us dissect the argument and understand the positions of board and CEO.

Board Members: CEO's policies are at fault.

CEO: I am not at fault. I admit the problem occurred during my tenure, but my predecessor is at fault.

Bold Face 1: It is a fact based on which board members make CEO liable for the problem.

Bold Face 2: It is a possibility used by the CEO (counter-evidence) using which he strengthens his position and supports the conclusion (that he is not at fault).

Answer choices explanation

(A)   The first part of the option is correct; however, the second bold face does not support the board members, it in fact contradicts them.

(B)   The first part of the option is correct. CEO admits that the problem exists. The second bold face, however, is not a consequence of the board members' claims. It is CEO's counter-evidence to strengthen his position.

(C)   This is the **correct** answer. The first bold face is a fact which cites a problem, but the CEO believes that this fact does not contradict his conclusion. The second bold face supports CEO's conclusion.

(D) This option is irrelevant. There is no discussion of unethical activity committed by the CEO.

(E) While the first part of the statement is correct, the second bold face does not follow from CEO's position or the conclusion —*I am not at fault.* In fact, the reverse is true—CEO's position follows from the second bold face because the second boldface is the evidence CEO uses for his position.

The correct answer is option C.

Question 2

Argument Analysis

The first statement is against the policy of allowing managers to work-from-home. This statement can easily be understood as the main position of the argument and the author. The argument cites a reason that allowing such a thing would be an additional operational challenge to businesses and that working-from-home will pose more challenges. The argument also ventures a judgment why work-from-home policy should not be implemented. It says that if the manager behaved like a manager, he could also manage the family well and conversely, if he doesn't behave like a manager; he will not be able to manage the family as well, regardless of whether he works from home or the office.

Predictive Role Play

Let us solve this question with the alternate approach.

Let us dissect the argument and understand the role of boldfaced portions.

Conclusion: There is not one good reason for allowing managers to work from home.

Bold Face 1: It is the conclusion.

Bold Face 2: It is the judgment of the author that supports the main conclusion.

Answer choices explanation

(A) The first bold face is certainly the primary or main conclusion, but the second bold face is not a secondary conclusion, it is a judgment advanced in support of the main conclusion.

(B) The first bold face is not is the advocacy or the reasoning of the argument. It is the conclusion. The second bold face is the advocacy of the argument, but it does not raise doubts, it rather reasons why the conclusion is justified.

(C) The first bold face is not evidence, it is the main conclusion. The second bold face does strengthen the first bold face, but it is not evidence, it is a judgment.

(D)   The first bold face is certainly a conclusion, but the argument agrees rather than disagrees with it. The second bold face does provide the reasoning behind this agreement rather than disagreement.

(E)   This matches our argument analysis, and so this is the **correct** answer.

The correct answer is option E.

Question 3

Argument construction

The argument discusses the projected effects of sodium intake cutback on the lives and longevity. It provides various figures with different expectancy rates based on the amount of sodium cutback. The first part shows current projections and plans but the second part shows some further predictions and figures. The author's main reason in furnishing this extra data is to state that "a better result is possible". Thus, "even a better result is possible" is the main conclusion of the argument.

Predictive Role Play

Statement 1 (BF 1)—(Using computer.....the U.S. diet) The first portion in boldface states the study of tests that might save lives.

Statement 2—(A gradual cutback.....500, 000) This statement is another prediction that forms the basis of the claim that lives can be saved by this whole exercise.

Statement 3 (BF 2)—(Even a better.....(500,000 to 850,000 lives)) This sentence contains the main conclusion "even a better result is possible". However the main conclusion part is not bold. BF2 is further predictions (or inter-mediate conclusions) that will prove the main conclusion right.

Main conclusion - Even a better result is possible.

Thus BF1 is a prediction supporting the argument and BF2 is part of the conclusion that supports and contains the main conclusion of the argument.

Answer choices explanation

(A)   While BF1 part of this option is correct, BF2 is not the main conclusion, as discussed above.

(B)   This is the **correct** answer. BF1 is a prediction that, if accurate, supports the argument and BF2 is a conclusion that helps the main conclusion.

(C)   The argument does not reject BF1 and BF2 is not the main conclusion, as discussed above.

(D)   The argument does not reject BF1 and BF2 is not standing in opposition to BF1.

(E) BF1 is a claim but the argument does not go against this claim. BF2 is a claim that supports the main conclusion of the argument.

The correct answer is option B.

Chapter 16

Parallel Reasoning Argument

16.1   Parallel Reasoning Argument Question type

Parallel Reasoning or Mimic the Argument questions are super rare in GRE-ASP. These kinds of questions will seldom appear in your GRE. Learning this chapter would be fruitful from understanding "application-based" reading comprehension questions.

Parallel Reasoning questions belong to structure based family. The Parallel Reasoning questions ask you to select an argument from the given five option arguments that is similar in structure and reasoning to the question argument. In a nutshell, you have to analyze 1+5 = 6 arguments, and select one argument that is similar to the question argument. Some test-prep companies also name it Mirror the Argument question type.

The topic of the arguments may or may not be the same. In fact, they would mostly be different. Say, the topic of the question argument is "concern over the fall in the production", the topics for option arguments may vary from "school education" to "anthropology" to "economy" to "astrology". So, it is important that you don't pay attention to the similarity or the diversity of topic as one of the factors in selecting the correct option, instead you focus only on the structural and the reasoning aspects of the arguments, and deduce the parallelism in the argument.

Question Stem

Here are several question stem examples:

- Which one of the following is most closely parallel in its reasoning to the reasoning in the argument above?

- Which of the following presents a pattern of thinking that is most closely analogous to the preceding situation?

- In terms of its logical features, the argument above most closely resembles which one of the following?

· Which one of the following arguments is most similar in its pattern of reasoning to the argument above?

· Which of the following is logically the most similar in the argument above?

The following illustration depicts your job for the Parallel Reasoning question type.

The demand for large, family-sized vehicles will slump dramatically over the next ten years; major automobile companies are cutting orders for steel plating usually placed five years i̶n̶ ̶a̶d̶v̶a̶n̶c̶e̶ ̶o̶f̶ ̶d̶e̶l̶i̶v̶e̶r̶y̶ ̶t̶o̶ ̶o̶p̶t̶i̶m̶u̶m̶ ̶p̶r̶i̶c̶e̶ ̶r̶e̶d̶u̶ction.

Which of the follow_____st closely
analogous to the p_____

Only one option will rightly
describes the method used by
the author to form the argument.

(A) A newspaper p_____per due to reduced circulation.
(B) A State Govern_____cause of fall in crime rate.
(C) A major political party incre_____dget because of decreasing support among the elector_____
(D) Because of a predicted low_____ing, building companies cease buying up vacant development plot____
(E) Because of the cyclical nature of a certain strain in flu that appears every five years, pharmacies are stocking up on anti-flu remedies.

16.2   Process Of Solving Parallel Reasoning Argument Questions

Unlike other question types, Parallel Reasoning question involves a 5-step approach.

The 5-step approach

    (1) Recognize the question type

    (2) Understand the argument construction

    (3) Run through the options

    (4) Develop the argument's approach

    (5) Eliminate incorrect options

First 2 steps are the same for Parallel Reasoning questions. Let us jump directly to "Run through the options" step.

Run through the options

After identifying that the question belongs to Parallel Reasoning question type, we run through the options quickly. A quick rundown on the options helps to develop the approach to attack the question.

Remember that the topics of the arguments are not important, but the structure and the reasoning are. Do not invest more than necessary time on each option at this stage; only fair idea is sufficient to develop the approach.

Develop the argument's approach

There are many kinds of arguments, and each argument can be mimicked. We have discussed four questions in this chapter that will help you understand the approach aspect. You need to figure out the elements used in the argument to derive the conclusion. The most important aspect in Parallel Reasoning question type is that you must not look for the sequential ordering of the premises, the counter-premises and the conclusion. However, you need to match the essential elements of the question argument to the essential elements of the option arguments.

Look at the following arguments, and deduce which of the two given arguments' argument 1 or argument 2 is parallel to the question argument.

Question Argument: "John is an intelligent boy. However, he did not study well for the exam. Therefore, he will not score well in the exam."

Argument 1: "It is clear that all-terrain vehicle "Potent3250" will breakdown after 200,000 miles. Chassis tempering is surprisingly ignored, although chassis itself is super strong."

Argument 2: "Suzy is an ardent dancer. She did not study well for the exam due to dance practice. Therefore, she will not score well in the exam."

Let us understand each argument.

Question Argument:

Premise: John is an intelligent boy; **Counter-Premise:** He did not study well for the exam; **Conclusion:** Therefore, he will not score well in the exam.

The arrangement of the argument is—**Premise—Counter-Premise—Conclusion**

Meaning: Despite being intelligent, John will not score well in the exam, since he did not study well for the exam.

Argument 1:

Conclusion: It is clear that all-terrain vehicle "Potent3250" will breakdown after 200,000 miles. **Premise:** Chassis tempering is surprisingly ignored; **Counter-Premise:** Although chassis itself is super strong;

The arrangement of the argument is—**Conclusion—Premise—Counter-Premise**

Meaning: Despite having super strong chassis, the vehicle will breakdown, since the tempering aspect of the chassis is ignored.

Although the arrangement of the argument is not identical to the question argument, the structure, and reasoning aspects are parallel. Therefore, Argument 1 is parallel to the question argument.

Argument 2:

Premise: Suzy is an ardent dancer; **Additional-Premise:** She did not study well for the exam due to dance practice; **Conclusion:** Therefore, she will not score well in the exam.

The arrangement of the argument is—**Premise—Additional-Premise—Conclusion**

Meaning: Since Suzy did not study well for the exam due to dance practice, she will not score well in the exam.

Note that the conclusion can be derived sans the premise. Thus, the premise is not an essential element of the argument. Only the additional-premise is sufficient to conclude, hence the argument is not parallel to the question argument in the structure and the reasoning aspects. It is insignificant that the arrangement of premise, counter-premise, and the conclusion of the argument is identical to the question argument.

However, since argument 1 contains exactly similar elements as the question argument, i.e. premise, counter-premise and conclusion, argument 1 contains reasoning parallel to that of the question argument.

Another important feature of Parallel Reasoning argument is that the arguments may or may not contain the conclusion. The argument may have only two premises or a premise and a counter-premise or merely one premise. Whichever be the case, you need an approach to solve the question.

Example

Questions

16.3 Examples

Example 1

The recent winding up of Amco Chemicals proves that board of directors who are out-of-touch foster lack of trust, resulting into decreased morale and, eventually falling production.

In terms of its logical features, the argument above most closely resembles which one of the following?

(A) When managers stop believing that elephants can dance, cost escalates and revenues fall.

(B) When a kitten and a mouse mutually exchange vibes of hatred, the trust is lost and they start hating each other.

(C) When people go to watch a movie with the anticipation that it will be bad, they notice its bad points more than its good points.

(D) When consumers begin to doubt the purity of a city's drinking water, complaints to the authorities soar and water supply administration overheads increase.

(E) When a car acquires a reputation for having design faults, generally it does suffer many breakdowns.

Argument construction

After identifying that this is a question on 'parallel reasoning', we run through the options quickly. We notice that all the five options are on different topics, and each option has a factor leading to other factor(s). Unlike other question types, a quick rundown on the options helps develop the approach to attack the question.

Let us understand the meaning of the argument and analyze its components.

A phenomenon was observed in Amco Chemicals. BoD who was out-of-touch, (factor 1) fostered lack of trust between them and employees. This led to low morale of employees (factor 2) and that resulted into drop in production (factor 3).

In a nut shell, we observe that there are three negative factors—one leads to the other—a series of three factors. The option with this pattern of reasoning and structure will be the correct answer.

Answer choices explanation

(A) "When managers stop believing that elephants can dance, cost escalates and revenues fall."—This proverb-style statement has two flaws; One is that the meaning of 'elephant' is not clear. It could refer to a large organization lacking agility; but we cannot infer such a meaning here. The second flaw is that "cost escalates and revenues fall" are two complementary effects of one factor. So, this statement consists of two factors only. This option does not mimic the question argument.

(B) "When a kitten and a mouse mutually exchange vibes of hatred, the trust is lost and they start hating each other". This statement is written in such a way that you seem to identify three factors. Factor 1— exchange vibes of hatred; factor 2—the trust is lost; factor 3—start hating. But it is not the most appropriate parallel reasoning argument vis-a-vis the question argument, because the factor 1 and 3 are in fact the same. Factor 1 talks about the "hatred" and so do the factor 3. It is a case of circular reasoning rather than parallel reasoning.

(C) "When people go to watch a movie with the anticipation that it will be bad, they notice its bad points more than its good points." It has only two factors. Factor 1—with the anticipation that it will be bad; factor 2—notice its bad points more than its good points. This option does not mimic the question argument.

(D) This is the **correct** answer. "When consumers begin to doubt the purity of a city's drinking water, complaints to the authorities soar and water supply administration overheads increase". It has three negative factors in order—one leading to other. Factor 1—begin to doubt the purity of a city's drinking water; factor 2—complaints to the authorities soar; factor 3—water supply administration overheads increase. It is to be noted that factors 2 and 3 are negative in meaning as the meanings of 'soar' in the phrase—complaints to the authorities soar', and 'increase' in the phrase—water supply administration overheads increase' are negative.

(E) "When a car acquires a reputation for having design faults, generally it does suffer many breakdowns".—It has only two factors. Factor 1—acquires a reputation for having design faults 2—suffer many breakdowns. This option does not mimic the question argument's structure of a phenomenon happening because of three factors.

The correct answer is option D.

Example 2

An important consequence of a hot summer is increased incidence of skin cancer. However, the last three summers have not been hot, so there has not been a high incidence of skin cancer.

Which of the following is logically the most similar in the argument above?

(A) When the police are hailed as the guardians of society's values, they infiltrate and arrest gangs of traffickers, seizing large amounts of narcotics. Recently, no traffickers have been arrested so society has no values.

(B) When they infiltrate and arrest gangs of traffickers, seizing large amounts of narcotics, the police are hailed as the guardians of society's values. Recently, no traffickers have been arrested so society has no values.

(C) When they infiltrate and arrest gangs of traffickers, seizing large amounts of narcotics, the police are hailed as the guardians of society's values. Recently, many traffickers have been arrested so society has many values.

(D) When they infiltrate and arrest gangs of traffickers, seizing large amounts of narcotics, the police are hailed as the guardians of society's values. Recently, no traffickers have been arrested so the police are not hailed as the guardians of society's values.

(E) When the police are not hailed as the guardians of society's values, they don't infiltrate and arrest gangs of traffickers, seizing large amounts of narcotics. Recently, many traffickers have been arrested so society has many values.

Argument construction

After identifying that this is a question on 'parallel reasoning', we rundown the options quickly. We notice that all the five options are on same topic, and have identifiable four parts. This question is a typical cause & effect argument.

Let us understand the argument and analyze its components. We name the cause as X and the effect as Y.

X: the hotter the summer; Y: greater the incidence of skin cancer. We can its draw generic version as

Premise: If X then Y.
Conclusion: Therefore, when no X, no Y.

No X: no hot summer; So, no Y: no incidence of skin cancer

Basically, the argument structure is that If "X happens, Y happens" and therefore, conversely, when "no X happens, so no Y can happen". The option parallel to this reasoning and structure is the **correct** answer.

Answer choices explanation

Let us name the cause as X and the effect as Y.

(A) X: police are hailed as the guardians of society's values; Y: Police arrest traffickers
Logically, 'No X and No Y' should be
No X: police are not hailed as the guardians of society's values; No Y: Police do not arrest traffickers

However, the converse 'No X' and 'No Y' parts as per the option statement are
No X: no traffickers have been arrested; No Y: society has no values.

Neither 'No X' nor 'No Y' matches. This option does not mimic the question argument.

(B) X: Police arrest traffickers; Y: police are hailed as the guardians of society's values
Logically, 'No X' and 'No Y' should be
No X: police do not traffickers; No Y: police are not hailed as the guardians of society's values

However, the converse 'No X' and 'No Y' parts as per the option statement are
No X: no traffickers have been arrested; No Y: society has no values.

While 'No X' is parallel to the argument as infiltration and trafficking are used interchangeably used in the argument, 'No Y' is not parallel. This option does not mimic the question argument.

(C)   X: Police arrest traffickers; Y: police are hailed as the guardians of society's values
Logically, the converse 'No X' and 'No Y' parts should be
No X: police do not arrest traffickers; No Y: police are not hailed as the guardians of society's values

However, the converse 'No X' and 'No Y' parts as per the option statement are
No X: traffickers have been arrested; No Y: society has value Neither 'No X' nor 'No Y' matches. This option does not mimic the question argument.

This is the **correct** answer.

(D)   X: Police arrest traffickers Y: police are hailed as the guardians of society's values
Logically, 'No X' and 'No Y' should be
No X: police do not arrest traffickers; No Y: police are not hailed as the guardians of society's values

'No X' and 'No Y' as per the option statement are
No X: police do not arrest traffickers; No Y: police are not hailed as the guardians of society's values

Both 'No X' and 'No Y' match rightly parallel.

(E)   X: police are not hailed as the guardians of society's values; Y: Police do not arrest traffickers
Logically, 'No X' and 'No Y' should be
No X: police are hailed as the guardians of society's values; No Y: Police arrest traffickers.

However, the converse 'No X' and 'No Y' parts as per the option statement are

No X: Police arrest traffickers; No Y: society has many values

Neither 'No X' nor 'No Y' matches. This option does not mimic the question argument.

The correct answer is option D.

Practice

Questions

16.4 Practice Questions

16.4.1 Questions

Question 1

The demand for large, family-sized vehicles will slump dramatically over the next ten years; major automobile companies are cutting orders for steel plating usually placed five years in advance of delivery to obtain maximum price reduction.

Which of the following presents a pattern of thinking that is most closely analogous to the preceding situation?

(A) A newspaper publisher cuts back on orders for printing paper due to reduced circulation.

(B) A State Governor reduces the number of police stations because of fall in crime rate.

(C) A major political party increases its publicity budget because of decreasing support among the electorate.

(D) Because of a predicted low demand for housing, building companies cease buying up vacant development plots.

(E) Because of the cyclical nature of a certain strain in flu that appears every five years, pharmacies are stocking up on anti-flu remedies.

Question 2

Discovered during construction work of a new civic library, the now excavated Roman brothel of Salonika has proved such a lucrative tourist attraction that the city council has decided to abandon the civic library project and preserve the brothel as a permanent museum.

In terms of its logical features, the situation above most closely resembles which of the following?

(A) The site chosen for the John Dillinger Museum, dedicated to the famous gangster, is in one of the Chicago banks he had robbed.

(B) The donation of valuable books by a once notorious Hollywood Madam to a local library.

(C) The transforming of an infamous Japanese prison camp in Malaysia into a 5 star tourist hotel and recreation center.

(D) The old city building planned as city church had numerous interesting books that people started coming to it for reading, and eventually, it was converted to library.

(E) The preservation of the London Millennium Dome as a permanent exhibition instead of a temporary one as originally planned.

16.4.2 Answer-Key

(1) D | (2) D

Solutions

16.4.3   Solutions

Question 1

Argument construction

We notice that all the five options are on different topics. This question is a typical cause & effect argument.

Let us understand the argument and analyze its components. The argument can be simplifies as

It is found that, in the next decade demand for a certain type of car will go down. Companies generally order their steel plating 5 years in advance to get maximum discount. It follows that the companies would have ordered steel plating for this car type years in advance when the cars were popular. Now, after they learn that the demand will go down, they want to cancel the orders for steel plating they made for cars they would have made in the future but now won't because of decreasing demand.

A generic version can be derived out of it as

Due to an expected future slump, a activity planned for the future ceases The option that matches this pattern of reasoning would be the correct answer.

Answer choices explanation

(A)   This option is not mimicking the argument as the newspaper publisher cuts back on orders for printing paper due to the current (slump) reduction in the circulation. It is unlike the scenario in the question argument in which the activity planned for the future is stopped to guard against an expected future slump.

(B)   Like option A, this option also has the same problem. The State Governor reduces the number of police stations due to the current (slump) fall in the crime rate.

(C)   In this option both parts don't mimic the argument. One, the party increases its budget rather than decreases as opposed to the question argument (in which activities planned for the future are cut down); two, a current (slump) decrease in support among the electorate, whereas in the argument current status is profitable but future slump is expected.

(D)   This is the **correct** answer. "Predicted low demand" is parallel to "an expected slump in demand", "building companies cease buying up vacant development plots" is parallel to "activity planned for the future is stopped". It is to be noted that the 'vacant development plots' would have been bought in advance to eventually develop into buildings (just as steel plating would be bought in advance to use for cars to be made).

(E)   This option implies that because of periodical reoccurrence of an event, pre-orders are executed to obtain leverage on it. It is the opposite of the question argument.

The correct answer is option D.

Question 2

Argument construction

We notice that all the five options are on different topics. Let us understand the argument and analyze its components.

The argument: During the construction work of a new civic library, the city council discovered an ancient Roman brothel of Salonika. This discovery started attracting many tourists and generating good money for the city council. The council, therefore, decided to abandon the civic library project and reserved the brothel as a permanent museum.

The argument can be simplified in a generic version as follows:

An activity was started with a goal in mind, however, due to accidental gain, the planned goal and the activity were cancelled and the gains from the accidental activity were continued.

We need to find an option that matches this pattern of reasoning.

Answer choices explanation

(A)   This option is irrelevant. It says that that the location of the museum dedicated to the famous gangster John Dillinger is in one of the Chicago banks he had robbed. It does not repeat the idea of planning something initially, but discarding those plans to follow through on some accidental but profitable discovery.

(B)   This option is irrelevant. It is a plain statement with no attributes of the question argument. It does not contain any plans that are later discarded.

(C)   This option means that an infamous Japanese prison camp in Malaysia was transformed into a 5 star tourist hotel and recreation center. However, it does not present the idea of planning something initially, and discarding those plans to follow through on some accidental but profitable discovery.

(D)   This is the **correct** answer. This option repeats the idea of planning something initially, and then changing those plans because something different but profitable was accidentally discovered.

(E)   Only this option can be close to the correct option D. However, 'the preservation as a permanent instead of temporary' does not mirror 'original project was shelved and another project was started'. The preservation of the London Millennium Dome (Original project) was still executed.

The correct answer is option D.

Chapter 17

Summary

Approaches for different ASP question types in a nutshell

Question family	Question type	Area of focus	Option	Approach
Assumption Based	Find the As-sumption	Conclusion	Premise	Identify the **unstated assumption derived from the argument filling the logical gap in the argument** and making the conclusion believable.
	Strengthen the argument	Conclusion	Premise	Make the conclusion more believable with the help of **additional information.**
	Weaken the argument	Conclusion	Premise	Identify the logical gap in the conclusion, and make the conclusion less believable with the help of additional information.
	Evaluate the argument	Conclusion	Premise in question form	Raise a question, which when an-swered "yes" and "no" will **strengthen and weaken** the argument.

Structure Based	Boldface/ Role Play	Structure of the argument; role of each statement	Describing the role reach each boldface portion plays.	Understand the structure of the argument, and the role of each statement. Paraphrase the **predictive role play** answer, and look for the correct option.
	Parallel Reasoning/Mimic the argument	Structure of the argument, and reasoning	Similar argument with premise(s) and conclusion	**Understand the structure and reasoning of the argument.** Ignore the subject matter. Understand each option one by one and select the one that is similar to the question argument.
Evidence Based	Resolve the paradox/ Explain the discrepancy	Contradiction of two premises (facts)	Premise	Select the premise that resolves the contradiction in the argument. The correct option will make the two contradictory premises sensible not paradoxical.
	Inference	Premises (Mostly facts/claims)	Conclusion	Select the option that **"must be true"** based on the information given in the argument. Beware of "could be true" and true based on the "real-world information".
No family	Complete the Argument	This is a question type which is not independent. The area of focus depends on the category of question.	Conclusion or premises	The approach depends on the category of question.

Chapter 18

Talk to Us

Have a Question?

Email your questions to info@manhattanreview.com. We will be happy to answer you. Your questions can be related to a concept, an application of a concept, an explanation of a question, a suggestion for an alternate approach, or anything else you wish to ask regarding the GRE.

Please do mention the page number when quoting from the book.

GRE - Resources from ETS

· *Official Guide*: It is one of the best resource to prepare for the GRE revised General test. It is a complete GRE book with everything you need to do your best on the test — and move toward your graduate or business school degree. It includes a couple of full-length practice test and two simulated, computer-based GRE practice tests., which help you measure your capability beforehand. The book also includes a *POWERPREP II* CD.

· *GRE Big Book*: It is a big fat book and includes 27 previously administered full-length tests. There are over 5000 actual ETS questions and answers. The strategies and tips to crack the computerized GRE is worth reading.

Best of luck!

Dr. Joern Meissner and Manhattan Review team